GERMANS AGAINST GERMANS

OLAMOT SERIES IN HUMANITIES AND SOCIAL SCIENCES
Irit Dekel, Jason Mokhtarian, and Noam Zadoff

GERMANS AGAINST GERMANS

The Fate of the Jews, 1938–1945

—⚏—

MOSHE ZIMMERMANN

TRANSLATED BY
NAFTALI GREENWOOD

INDIANA UNIVERSITY PRESS

© Aufbau Verlag GmbH & Co. KG, Berlin 2008
Copyright © 2008 Moshe Zimmermann

This book is a publication of

Indiana University Press
Office of Scholarly Publishing
Herman B Wells Library 350
1320 East 10th Street
Bloomington, Indiana 47405 USA

iupress.org

© 2022 by Olamot Center

Manufactured in the United States of America

First printing 2022

Library of Congress Cataloging-in-Publication Data

Names: Zimmermann, Mosche, author. | Greenwood, Naftali, translator.
Title: Germans against Germans : the fate of the Jews, 1938-1945 / Moshe
  Zimmermann ; translated by Naftali Greenwood.
Other titles: Deutsche gegen Deutsche. English | Fate of the Jews,
  1938-1945
Description: Bloomington, Indiana : Indiana University Press, [2022] |
  Series: Olamot series in humanities and social sciences | Translation
  of: Deutsche gegen Deutsche : Das Schicksal der Juden, 1938-1945. |
  Includes bibliographical references and indexes.
Identifiers: LCCN 2022002877 (print) | LCCN 2022002878 (ebook) | ISBN
  9780253062291 (hardback) | ISBN 9780253062307 (paperback) | ISBN
  9780253062314 (ebook)
Subjects: LCSH: Jews—Germany—History—1933-1945. | Holocaust, Jewish
  (1939-1945)—Germany. | Germany—Ethnic relations—History—20th
  century.
Classification: LCC DS134.255 .Z5613 2022 (print) | LCC DS134.255 (ebook)
  | DDC 940.53/18—dc23/eng/20220429
LC record available at https://lccn.loc.gov/2022002877
LC ebook record available at https://lccn.loc.gov/2022002878

To my parents,
Johanna (Hannah) née Heckscher and Karl (Akiva) Zimmermann,
who by being forced to leave Germany in 1937 and 1938, respectively,
avoided the fate of the Jews who stayed behind.

CONTENTS

LIST OF ABBREVIATIONS

JSS—Jewish Social Studies
LBYB—Leo Baeck Yearbook
VfZ—Vierteljahreshefte für Zeitgeschichte
ZfG—Zeitschrift für Geschichtswissenschaft

GERMANS AGAINST GERMANS

THE DECLINE OF GERMAN JEWRY

THE DECLINE OF GERMAN JEWRY drew attention in various contexts even before the National Socialists acceded to power. As early as 1911, Felix Theilhaber published a scholarly work titled exactly that, discussing the demise of the Jews of Germany from demographic and sociological points of view.[1] Theilhaber, an Orthodox Jew and a Zionist, traced the onset of German Jewry's decay back to the nineteenth century in the belief that the assimilation of this population group into its non-Jewish German surroundings had become unstoppable by then. Antisemites, in contrast, totally disagreeing about the sunset of German Jewry, spoke of "Judaism's victory over Germanness."[2]

From 1933 onward, the word "decline" was unquestionably valid in describing the history of German Jewry, although from a diametrically opposite direction—in other words, the days of assimilation and equality had passed. From that time on, the war cry "Germany, awake! Jews to the stake!" was heard everywhere in the cities and villages of Germany and became a guiding principle in German authorities' operative policies. In a certain sense, the Middle Ages had reemerged in Germany, ushering the Jews of Germany into a process of disentitlement, discrimination, and ultimately deportation from the German lands. Accordingly, Gustav Krojanker, a Zionist who had emigrated to Palestine, titled his Hebrew-language booklet, published in 1937 in Palestine, *The Rise and Fall of German Jewry*.[3] Although Krojanker saw 1933 as the tipping point in the decline, its economic and cultural portents had appeared long before. After World War II, historians carried this trend of thought further and regularly stopped their accounts of the history of German Jewry in 1933. When the liberal rabbi and historian Ismar Elbogen published his *History of the Jews in Germany* in 1935, three years before he left for America, one could understand and accept his specification of 1933 as the end year of his historical account and his "uncertainty about the future." When the popular historian Amos Elon chose to wind up the historical description in his book *German Requiem: Jews in Germany before Hitler* in 1933 and titled his book accordingly, his decision was one not of technical discretion but, beyond all doubt, of principle. This approach makes it seem as though anything that happened afterward was not a new chapter but in fact the end or something after the end. Andreas Reineke, in his *History of the Jews in Germany 1781–1933* (2007), follows the same trend of thought. An even more radical approach is taken by Albert Bruer in *Rise and Fall: A History of the Jews in Germany 1750–1918*,[4] in which 1918 is seen as the year of demise. For Bruer, the Weimar Republic already belongs to the postemancipation era. Even the Leo Baeck Institute, devoted to research on German Jewry and its culture, long invested scanty attention to the fate of German Jewry after 1933. In this state of affairs, one is almost tempted to say that the National Socialist policies sank roots in historiography as well: from the historians' standpoint, it was in 1933 that German Jewry crossed its finish line.

And if, all these postulates notwithstanding, the history of German Jewry under National Socialist rule after 1933 is described, this period is examined, by and large, separately and out of context with everything that preceded it, as though the National Socialist authorities not only introduced a new policy toward the Jews but also created a new German Jewry. Even if in no way intended to document the continuation, and least of all the end, of German Jewish history, this firmly demarcated investigation of post-1933 developments, in disregard of everything that happened before, has to some extent become a prequel to the history of the Holocaust in its broad sense.[5] It usually spans the 1933–1938 period, up to the event—the pogrom of November 9—known as Kristallnacht. What happened to the German Jews *after* 1938 is assimilated into and embedded in the story of the Holocaust, since when they deal with World War II, historians and their readers obviously train their gaze on the history of European Jewry at large.

Thus, the fate of German Jewry in its final decline, from 1938 to 1945—between the November pogrom and the end of World War II—is poorly represented in the historiographic literature and emerges either as a negligible part of the history of the Holocaust or as a small appendix to German Jewish or general history. Namely, it is marginalized or, in the best case, set within a context that transcends the history of German Jewry. As a rule, even Götz Aly's approach to the Final Solution since 1995, and his take on the dispossession of the Jews by the Nazi regime in his 2005 book,[6] leaves no room for focused or specific attention to German Jewry, for understandable reasons. On methodological grounds, Saul Friedländer, in volume 2 of his monumental work, chose to subsume the history of German Jewry into the general history of relations between the Third Reich and the Jews of Europe. In Wolfgang Benz's *Die Juden in Deutschland 1933–1945*, the last chapter, devoted to the 1938–1945 period, evolves into an appendix. The same may be said about the four-volume *Modern German-Jewish History*,[7] published by the Leo Baeck Institute, and *History of the Holocaust: Germany*, a collection of articles published in two voluminous tomes under the editorship of Abraham Margaliot and Yehoyakim Cochavi. Only about one-fourth of the content of these works is devoted to the 1938–1945 period; the remainder takes up the 1933–1938 years. The authors of *Jews under the Swastika*, published in 1973 in the German Democratic Republic (East Germany), also fail, for both historiographic and ideological reasons, to pay close and consistent attention to the 1939–1945 interval, even though in their subtitle they promise to discuss "the Persecution and Extermination of the German Jews 1933–1945."

This chapter in the history of German Jewry, however, deserves more than an encyclopedia entry, such as that in *Pinkas Hakehillot: Encyclopedia of Jewish Communities*, published by Yad Vashem, and is owed a description that exceeds that of an appendix. It deserves its own synthesis, sedulous investigation, a monograph, and close photography, not only because no such things have yet been published but also, and mainly, because the specifics of German Jewish history in this context should be clearly sketched within the framework of the general history of the Holocaust, the Third Reich, and World War II, and the continuities and discontinuities of this community's history should be given emphasis.

Unlike European Jews outside of Germany, who could clearly differentiate between "the Germans" and "the Nazis" and the collective that they perceived as "us," for German Jews the enemies—the criminals and their supporters—also in fact belonged to "us," irrespective of how they were understood. The singularity and tragicality of this nexus of criminals and victims germinates not only in the lengthier duration of the Holocaust in Germany, starting in 1933 and not only when the war began in 1939, but also in the disposition of the struggle and the war, the deportations and the murders, as *Germans against Germans*—at least from the standpoint of the victims, the Jews of Germany.

The road to correcting the status of this interval in history is already being paved, and important strides down it have been taken since this book first appeared in 2008 in German. The past two decades have seen a perceptible upturn in historiographic interest in German Jewish history of 1938–1945. Several important aspects of the topic have been thoroughly researched and analyzed. Much new information and knowledge have been amassed, most involving the use of new methodological approaches. The works of Beate Meyer, Wolf Gruner, Frank Bajohr, Avraham Barkai, Alexandra Przyrembel, Rivka Elkin, Konrad Kwiet, and Doris Tausendfreund are impressive examples. Archive research continues relentlessly. The Bundesarchiv (the German Federal Archive), for example, launched a documentary project on the deportation and murder of European Jewry, and volumes 2, 3, 6, and 11 concerning the Jews of the Reich from "Kristallnacht" to the end of the war have already appeared.[8] In addition, survivors steadily continue to publish memoirs. Despite all these efforts, however, no historical synthesis has yet been created devoted solely to this chapter in history on the basis of study of the monographs that have been published on the topic in the meantime. By "synthesis," I mean the history of a group of people in the course of one period, in the sense of a self-standing chapter grounded in existing documents and secondary literature dealing with secondary aspects. This is the rationale behind the study that follows. My purpose is to describe and explain a phenomenon, a multifaceted connection of things, without drowning in innumerable unnecessary details. As in all historiography, this work of course presents only an interim reckoning that will surely expand and improve as research progresses. As evidence, the twelve-year period between the publication of the book in German (2008) and its translation into English has seen the appearance of a respectable list of new books and articles on the topic.

One who deals with the history of German Jewry in 1938–1945 should broaden the perspective to an area that transcends the technical geographic borders of the Third Reich. This is because many who lived outside these borders at that time—both in the German-occupied territories and in sundry diasporas beyond the German authorities' reach—considered themselves German Jews. Furthermore, paradoxically, German Jews who relocated to new milieus represented, in their own eyes and among those who viewed them, not only German Jewry but also, simply, "the Germans"—equally in Minsk, New York, and Tel Aviv.

Neither should it be forgotten that after 1933, and after 1938 as well, only from antisemites' point of view in reference to German Jews were Germans and Jews embroiled in confrontation; for everyone else, it was an intra-German tussle. In fact, the events of that time are but a chapter in German history because, when all is said and done, the array of forces was comprised of Germans against Germans, non-Jewish Germans against Jewish Germans, who in no way intended to harm other Germans. In this context, people largely overlook the question of who sought to dispose of whom. Even German Zionists or Orthodox German Jews did not aspire to repudiate Germany, Europe, or Germanness.

It was non-Jewish Germans who invented the separation and then translated it into the language of political action. The Third Reich earned its peculiarity by thrusting the wheel of history into reverse, revoking and obliterating the emancipation that the Jewish population had already attained. It declared the Jews non-Germans, enemies of the people and the state; thus, by legal means the Jews lost all their civil rights and, by the time it ended, their human rights as well. The SS pithily summarized the authorities' judicial, political, and social stance toward the Jews of Germany. In "Instructional Manual 4: Know the Enemy: What Does the 'Friend of the Jews' Say?" published on August 15, 1937, the following catechistic statements appear:

8. The Jew speaks German and therefore is German. We reply: Accordingly, a black who speaks German would also become German. . . . However, one cannot learn to be German; one can only experience it, provided German blood makes one fit to have such an experience.
9. . . . But at least the veteran Jews have assimilated among the Germans to the point of having sunk roots throughout Germany. . . . We reply: . . . Even lengthy residence in Germany cannot surmount the foreignness of blood inside. At the crucial moment, the mask will fall off the faces of the assimilated. . . . Where were the Jewish defenders of Germanness?[9]

The presentation of Jews as "non-Germans," aliens, rivals, and enemies legitimized the "struggle" against them. Every anti-Jewish act was shown as a response to a Jewish provocation and was received accordingly.

An additional factor in German Jewish history in 1938–1945 places historians in an exceptional predicament. The ordinary or average observer of events is of course aware of the bitter denouement of German Jewry. In greater part, however, she or he also senses that this demise was predestined, at the latest after the nighttime pogrom in 1938—either predestined by the German Jews' failure to grasp the post-Enlightenment reality or predetermined by the perennially eliminationist nature of German antisemitism or of the Nazis' anti-Jewish policies. This knowledge, however, does not flow from a probing analysis; it is but a corollary of the random advantage of those who know the final outcome of a process that could have played out differently. It resembles stock trading: one cannot tell whether bear markets have already bottomed out and which response—staying in or cashing out—is riskier. No one could have known ab initio that the post-1933 years and the post-1938 period would see humankind's most extreme act of ruination.

When even historians who step forward to clarify our topic use the same post factum knowledge, they unknowingly and unintentionally promote an ex post confirmation of the prejudices of National Socialist or other antisemitic societies: the Jews should have realized that *they had to leave Germany*, not only because they could have known that the Nazis were scheming to exterminate them but also because they truly were strangers in German society. Even today, it is not uncommon to find such a stance among wise-after-the-fact Zionists and "good Germans." Ultimately, it leads to the conclusion that, at day's end, the parties at fault for the events were not the criminals and the many accomplices who facilitated and even profited from the terrifying deeds but the victims themselves, who must not have wanted to escape from the menace, may have lacked the requisite civil courage, and, in any event, did not realize that they were not German in Hitler's Gestapo state. In our inquiry, we will pay consistent and strict attention to this difference. Namely, we know not only the criminals' identity but also the magnitude of the crime. Thus, responsibility for the final outcome cannot in any way be foisted on the victims—least of all after the night of the pogrom, the eruption of the war, and the ban on Jewish emigration from Germany.

By 1940, Charlie Chaplin in his film *The Great Dictator* addressed himself to the fate of German Jewry and elucidated its intrinsic *problematique*. Between the lines of this impressive artistic achievement, the film also discusses the accusation already then being leveled at the Jews concerning their failure to resist their disentitlement. In one of the key scenes, set in a "Jewish ghetto" somewhere in Tomainia (none other than Germany), the erstwhile "stormtrooper commander Schultz," now an opponent of the regime, scours the Jewish population of the ghetto in search of someone who might assassinate the dictator. The Jewish heroine of the film, the lover of the Jewish barber played by Chaplin, answers correctly: the Jews have no interest in spearheading resistance to the regime because they're in such danger to begin with!

What Chaplin saw clearly back in 1940 should be even clearer to today's historians. It does not seem that way, however, despite all the results of modern historical research. The title of John Dippel's 1996 book, which translates from the German into *The Great Delusion: Why the Jews of Germany Refused to Leave Their Homeland*,[10] accuses the Jews of Germany of blindness, passivity, or both. The famous historian Peter Gay (formerly Peter Fröhlich), who with his parents emigrated from Germany to the United States, summarized the retrospective questions that he faced because his father had waited until 1938 to leave Germany. In his memoirs, he lists queries that always upset him: "Why didn't you leave then and there? . . . Was your father paralyzed (and I am not

inventing those snide inquiries) by fear that he might make less money abroad?"
Gay answered thus: "I have already raised the key response with two questions
of my own: Who would have us, or in time? How could my father, with no foreign language and no marketable skills, live abroad at all?"[11] Victor Klemperer,
keenly aware of the social isolation that descended on him and his wife and of
the loss of all traces of freedom of action, explained in his real-time letters that
he saw emigration as the sole path to rescue but even then with grave vacillations. He was willing to head for any destination, including Palestine despite
his staunch opposition to Zionism, on one condition: that he could make a
living in his new place of settlement and not become a burden to his relatives.
This was his explicit stance on the matter immediately after Kristallnacht, and
so it remained in January 1941. To appreciate this, one must understand how
the extreme uncertainty of the time impaired the capacity for judicious thinking: Klemperer continually oscillated between fearing "to go too early [or] to
stay too late."[12]

Jochen Köhler, who in 1979 anthologized his studies and interviews of the
perpetrators' generation and then turned his attention to Helmuth von Moltke,
the hero of the anti-Hitler resistance, haughtily and anachronistically inter-
rogates Ilse Rewald (b. 1918), who in 1943 "submerged" (went underground)
in Berlin and thus survived: "What role did the Jewish community play . . . ?
Did it participate in decisions relating to their own self-extermination? Did
this organization motivate its members in any manner, however minimal, to
resist the menace of extermination? The first deportations took place in 1941!
The question is why they did not prepare some form, any form, of resistance."
Rewald replies tellingly, "You see this in retrospect as our failure, even though
plainly the entire [German] people should be faulted for a much greater failure." The interviewer, however, does not desist: "Who's supposed to start the
resistance, if those suffering [the Jews] do not sound off in protest against their
suffering?"[13] It is a hair-raising allegation not only because the Jews had been
dispossessed of all tools with which to express protest since the Nazi accession
(and Jews who did resist paid a heavy price) and not only because the duty of
resistance belonged to that part of society that took part in discriminating
against the Jews but mainly because it was written by a member of the successor
generation, which should have learned, if only slightly, the lessons of the previous generation and should have understood the difference between a minority's
ability to respond in a democracy and what it can do under dictatorship. I call
the accusation hair-raising because it attests to the tendency in Germany, to
this day, to commend those who hold the victims, the Jews, responsible for
their extermination. Thus Beate Meyer, a scholar of the history of the German

8

GERMANS AGAINST GERMANS

Jewish leadership after "Kristallnacht," tellingly describes the absurdity of this commendatory tendency, which she seeks to thwart resolutely. To do this, she adds a crushing rejoinder: unlike what happened in wartime Eastern Europe, there was no large-scale German resistance to the regime that the Jews could join. Partisans who were willing to accept Jews did not fight in the forests of Germany.[14] The allegation of nonresistance is all the more ghastly because we have become aware since then of courageous attempts at resistance and protest by Jews as individuals, even though most ended in death and destruction.[15]

The study that follows defies the anachronistic conventional wisdom, foremost in telling the history of the Jews after the night of the pogrom. To do this, the debate will focus, as it must, on the expectations and desires of the contemporaries themselves as an underlying premise and a perspective—without invoking the advantage rooted in our always being smarter after the fact.

A problem in itself is the question of the terminology to use in a project such as this. Although generations have passed since the end of World War II, we are still too much hostages of the National Socialist lexicon, what Victor Klemperer called LTI—*lingua tertii imperii*. A few lines above, I wrote "since the end of World War II." Would it not, however, be more appropriate to say "since the demise of the Third Reich"? And should the term "Third Reich" be invoked with no further thought? What, too, about terms such as "Mischlinge" (offspring of miscegenation), "intermarriage," "Aryanization," "racial defilement," "transport," "preventive arrest," and many others? Should the National Socialists' brace of euphemisms be replaced with the real thing? Or might it suffice to bracket dubious expressions in "scare quotes" in order to express distance and caution? Profuse use of quotation marks might interfere with the narrative presentation. Therefore, in this study the terms harvested from the National Socialist vocabulary usually appear in quotation marks but without making the text, for consistency's sake, into a caricature in which the sheer quantity of quotation marks drives everything into absurdity.

The so-important terms "Jew" and "Jewish," too, should not be used without forethought, particularly in our context. That is, the National Socialists' racist definition of a "Jew" should be rejected, if only on scientific and ethical grounds, but we have no single valid alternative. What is the decisive criterion for a person's Jewishness? Affiliation with a Jewish community? Biological descent? Or observance of the Jewish religious commandments, which, of course, are also subject to interpretation? The answer is hybrid: the definition should be based on the collective's self-definition along with the personal decision of the individual in question. That is, a person who sees and presents himself or herself as Jewish belongs to the group that calls itself Jewish.

If, however, one views Jewishness as a religion, then the definition of a Jewish person should be framed solely by the religious commandments. And if one grasps Jewishness as a nation or a partnership of fate and a cultural community—as Zionists do—then the imperatives of Orthodoxy are in no way an absolute frame for the definition of the concept of "Jewish." Furthermore, the National Socialist legislation and its implementation were racially based and applied to individuals who neither saw nor defined themselves as Jews; such people were regarded as Jews and were even sent to their death as Jews. Thus, we must ask ourselves: Should we base the definition on something different that would exclude these people from the history of the persecution of Jews? Christians or nonreligious individuals of Jewish origin, as well as so-called half-Jews or quarter-Jews, unwillingly belonged to the group that the National Socialist authorities targeted for discrimination, persecution, and murder on account of their Jewishness. They, too, should be included in the frame of study of the history of German Jewry. After all, if Jewishness is construed as a partnership in fate, it follows that these people belonged, albeit involuntarily, to the community of people who shared this fate and thus take part in our topic of study. The infamous January 1942 Wannsee Conference, where much time was invested in redefining the concept of "Jew" in Germany according to National Socialist rules, is a salient and horrifying example in this sense.

The term "German Jew" also raises questions. Obviously I totally reject the National Socialist authorities' decision to replace, on racist grounds, the expression "German Jews" with "Jews in Germany." Even objective treatment of the term "German Jew," however, presents formal and cultural problems. Is it limited to German citizens? To those born in Germany? Are "Ostjuden" (East European Jews) who lived in Germany considered German Jews? Did the Jews of Austria and Bohemia become German Jews once these areas were "repatriated" to the Reich in 1938–1939? And what about Jews in regions that had belonged to Imperial Germany until 1918 and became Polish, Danish, or French under the terms of the Versailles treaty? As this study proceeds, all Jews who lived in the "Altreich"—that is, within the borders of the German Reich until 1937—will be identified as German Jews. When I take up cultural matters associated mainly with language, I will have to expand this term in certain cases, whereas in other contexts I will need to distinguish between German Jews and Jews of the German Reich. Be that as it may, Jews who were deported from Germany or emigrated from Germany will continue to be called German Jews below.

Since the history of German Jewry focuses too often on the most conspicuous representatives of the high culture, one is encouraged to infer that all

German Jews were Nobel Prize laureates, academics, and writers. Ostensibly, this depiction makes the crime against the Jews of Germany, or of Europe, all the more monstrous or at least more bewildering. Such an approach crowds "normal," "simple" Jews, and even representatives of popular culture, out of the collective memory and the historical narrative. Julius Hirsch, a member of the German national soccer team before World War I, was also sent to Auschwitz. Exemplars of popular culture had to emigrate, too, be they the film actresses Elisabeth Bergner and Elise Bassermann; members of the Comedian Harmonists ensemble Harry Frommermann, Roman Cycowski, and Erich Collin; the footballer Gottfried Fuchs, who scored ten goals in one game for the German team; or the German high-jump champion Gretel Bergmann, who was excluded from the German team in the 1936 Olympic Games.

The expression "for example" in historical literature is usually used thoughtlessly. What may serve as an example of a given phenomenon, process, trend, and so on, and accordingly may represent it, and what in contrast may serve as an "exception to the rule," can be determined systematically only on the basis of statistical data. Absent appropriate statistics, the anecdotes, stories, and quotations that are cited as representative examples are but outcomes of a historian's intuitive work or an illustration of her or his interpretation of events. The question of how representative the examples quoted here and elsewhere are is debatable. I try in this book not to confuse anecdotes with examples.[16] This is especially important because when one asks about the extent of Germans' knowledge about the persecution of the Jews, the behavior of the majority, the already-discussed accusation of unresponsiveness on the Jewish side, and other aspects as well, the matter is not put to rest merely by elucidating the facts; instead and ultimately, it also pertains to moral judgment of the society being investigated. Thus, below I treat the concept of "example" very warily.

In the chapters that follow, I first discuss historical developments up to the deportation and murder of the Jews of Germany and track them on the basis of chronological order. Even after Germany was declared *Judenrein* in 1943, however, the history of German Jewry continued in exile; accordingly, I describe it within this frame. It is a history in which obvious binaries of perpetrators and victims but also gradual transitions in complex shades and nuances find expression. The sources left behind by the perpetrators and those bequeathed by the victims—documents created and preserved in very different ways—are taken into account in this discussion. The entire exposition, however, is distinguished by the troubling question: What did people surmise—and at what point in time—about the fate that was meted out to, or intended for, the erstwhile Jewish citizens?

NOTES

1. Felix Theilhaber, *Der Untergang der deutschen Juden Eine volkswirtschaftliche Studie* (Berlin: Reinhardt, 1911).

2. Wilhelm Marr, *Der Sieg des Judenthums über das Germanenthum* (Berlin: Rudolph Costenoble, 1879).

3. Gustav Krojanker, *The Rise and Fall of German Jewry* (Hebrew) (Tel Aviv: Hitachduth Olej Germania, 1937).

4. Albert Bruer, *Aufstieg und Untergang Eine Geschichte der Juden in Deutschland 1750–1918* (Köln, Weimar, Vienna: Böhlau, 2006).

5. For an example of a different approach to this history, consult Doron Niederland, *The Jews of Germany: Emigrants or Refugees?—A Study on the Patterns of Interwar Emigration* (Hebrew) (Jerusalem: Magnes, 1996), based on idem, PhD diss., 1988.

6. Götz Aly, *Hitler's Beneficiaries: Plunder, Racial War, and the Nazi Welfare State* (New York: Henry Holt and Company, 2005).

7. Michael A. Meyer, ed., *Deutsch-jüdische Geschichte in der Neuzeit*, vol. 4 (Munich: C. H. Beck, 1996).

8. *Die Verfolgung und Ermordung der europäischen Juden durch das nationalsozialistische Deutschland*, vol. 2: Deutsches Reich 1938–Aug. 1939 (Munich: 2009); vol. 3: Deutsches Reich und Protektorat Sept. 1939–Sept. 1941 (Munich: 2012); vol. 6: Deutsches Reich und Protektorat Böhmen und Mähren Oktober 1941–März 1943 (Berlin: 2019); vol. 11: Deutsches Reich und Protektorat Böhmen und Mähren April 1943–1945 (Berlin: 2020).

9. SS Leitheft 4, August 15, 1937, in Jürgen Matthäus et al., eds., *Ausbildungsziel Judenmord? "Weltanschauliche Erziehung" von SS, Polizei und Waffen-SS im Rahmen der "Endlösung"* (Frankfurt: Fischer, 2003), 182ff.

10. John Van Houten Dippel, *Die große Illusion: Warum deutsche Juden ihre Heimat nicht verlassen wollten* (Munich: Propyläen Econ Ullstein, 2001). The title of the English edition sounds less accusatory: *Bound upon a Wheel of Fire: Why So Many German Jews Made the Tragic Decision to Remain in Nazi Germany* (New York: Basic Books, 1996). William D. Rubenstein, *The Myth of Rescue* (London: Routledge, 1997), uses the same argument to substantiate his thesis about "why the democracies could not have saved more Jews from the Nazis." He held the "blindness" of the German Jews responsible for their remaining in Germany at least until the November 1938 pogrom. For a totally different approach, see Jochen Thies, *Evian 1938. Als die Welt die Juden verriet* (Essen: Klartext, 2017).

11. Peter Gay, *My German Question: Growing Up in Nazi Berlin* (New Haven and London: Yale University Press, 1998), 123–24.

12. Victor Klemperer, *I Will Bear Witness: A Diary of the Nazi Years, 1933–1941* (New York: Random House, 1998), 276.

13. Jochen Köhler, *Klettern in der Großstadt. Geschichten vom Überleben zwischen 1933–1945* (Berlin: Das Arsenal, 1981), 78–80.

14. Beate Meyer, *A Fatal Balancing Act: The Dilemma of the Reich Association of Jews in Germany, 1939–1945*, trans. William Templer (New York: Berghahn, 2013), 3–4; and idem,

Paul Eppstein—Eine tödliche Gratwanderung (Mannheim: Mannheimer Abendakademie und Volkshochschule GmbH, 2014), 36.

15. Wolf Gruner, "Expel Hitler," *Yad Vashem Studies* 39, no. 2 (2011): 13–54; idem, "Indifference? Participation and Protest as Individual Responses to the Persecution of the Jews as Revealed in Berlin Police Logs and Trial Records 1933–1945," in S. Schrafstetter and A. Steinweis, eds., *The Germans and the Holocaust* (New York and Oxford: Berghahn Books, 2016), 59–84.

16. David Bankier also gives repeated attention to this methodological question. See Bankier, *The Germans and the Final Solution: Public Opinion under Nazism* (Oxford: Blackwell, 1992).

TWO

—ᴍᴍ—

THE TABULA RASA POLICY

THE POGROM THAT TOOK PLACE all over Germany on November 9–10, 1938, known as "Kristallnacht," is usually considered the final word in the epilogue to the history of German Jewry. By November 1938, the shock was already profound—and not only in Germany. From then on, when the National Socialist authorities' persecution of the Jews is studied, both contemporaries and historians turn away from the events in Germany itself and focus instead on the distress of the Jewish population outside the "Altreich." However, the history of German Jewry did not end with that nighttime pogrom in November 1938; in the year between that event and the eruption of the war, the status of the Jews of Germany continued to deteriorate at an accelerating pace. From today's perspective, the interval between November 1938 and September 1939 is the preface to the history of German Jewry in World War II, an interval that historiography has largely overlooked. It is this period of time on which the discussion and analysis in this chapter centers.

Just as the November 9, 1938, pogrom did not mark the end of the epilogue to the history of the Jews of Germany, so the meeting called for November 12, 1938, at the offices of Hermann Goering's Ministry of Aviation (today the seat of the German Ministry of Finance), with roughly fifty participants convening to deal with the "Jewish question," in no way signified the mere onset of the exclusion of German Jewry. That process had begun on January 30, 1933, when Adolf Hitler was named Chancellor of the Reich, and it accelerated in September 1935 with the promulgation of the racial statutes known as the Nuremberg Laws. The meeting at the Ministry of Aviation did, however, topple the false front and ended the delusion, which endured after 1937 as well, that "even in Nazi Germany one can live safely."[1] The encounter, for the first time, translated the idea

13

of a "comprehensive solution" for German Jewry into an official platform with clear performative contours. The situation was tellingly summarized in the final report for 1938 of the Berlin office of the Security Police (SD): the Jewish question has entered its final phase.[2] Implementation, however, did not come about in one go. The death throes of German Jewry continued for another four years at least. The meeting called by Göring in his capacity as superintendent of the Four-Year Plan, however, established, even more than did the pogroms and riots of the preceding days, that the Jews of Germany were outlaws—de facto and de jure—and hostages in the political game of the Third Reich. On the participants' agenda was the continuation of the pogrom by other means: a "public degradation ritual" of the Jews.[3]

The minutes of the meeting have been preserved in greater part and are immensely detailed. They show that the participants leapfrog each other in their proposals for escalating the abuse of the Jews of the Reich. In particular, politicians from the leadership ranks—the Reich Commissioner of Aviation and Plenipotentiary for the Four-Year Plan, Hermann Göring; the Minister of Propaganda, Joseph Goebbels; the Minister of the Interior, Wilhelm Frick; the Minister of Finance, Johann Ludwig "Lutz" Graf Schwerin von Krosigk; the Minister for Economic Affairs, Walther Funk; and the Minister of Justice, Franz Gürtner—competed with each other and with the SD of Reinhard Heydrich, who was in attendance, on how to foist the financial damage caused by the pogrom on the Jewish population most efficiently and, concurrently, how to organize the Jews' isolation and expulsion in the most radical way. Those at this encounter ranked much higher than did the participants in the so-called Wannsee Conference, which took place more than three years later. "Bold struggles for the solution," Goebbels wrote in his diary. "I represent the most radical point of view. Funk is somewhat soft. . . . In any event, we are creating a tabula rasa now. . . . The radical view has triumphed."[4]

In his opening remarks at the meeting, Göring said that Adolf Hitler, in telephone conversations and letters, had authorized him "to give the Jewish question comprehensive and uniform treatment" and "solve it one way or another" and in so doing "to focus the decisive measures centrally." Declaring the anti-Jewish steps taken since 1933 insufficient, he repeatedly proclaimed the watchword, "Now something has to happen!" Continuing, he elaborated: "Laws have to be passed that will show the nation clearly that something is being done about this matter." This was a typical turn of phrase in the Third Reich among those who wished to prove that everyone who had dealt with something or other before them had been insufficiently effective and that only they could implement the Führer's wishes and the national goals. It was also a clear jab at

Goebbels, who was responsible for the savageries of Kristallnacht and, accordingly, for the economic damage that they had caused—something that Göring, in his capacity as Chief Plenipotentiary for Economics, regretted. In crude and vulgar phrasing, Göring said that it should be seen to "that Judaism will take one bashing after another this week."[5] What he meant, mainly, was "Aryanization," the across-the-board and irrevocable ouster of the Jews from the German economy, coupled with their dispossession. However, particularly for Goebbels and Heydrich, more than economic wishes and questions of property were at stake. Goebbels, the master orchestrator of the November pogrom with Hitler's approval, now proposed to enjoin the Jews against visiting "German" theaters and cinema houses, circuses and places of entertainment, public swimming pools, beaches, "German" forests and public parks, and other recreation venues. He wished to convert the land occupied by the torched synagogues into parking lots without delay. Goebbels's and Goering's detailed discussion about separate compartments for Jews in railroad sleeping cars, or in rail travel generally, sounds after the fact like a bad parody. However, it is representative of the vulgarity of the whole debate, not to speak of the inhumanity of the proposals bruited for discussion.

Examination of the role of Goebbels, the Reichsminister for Public Education and Propaganda, in this context clearly reveals the grotesqueness of the meeting and of the November 9 "Judenaktion." For Goebbels, who in the preceding months had organized several "Judenaktionen" in conjunction with the Chief of Police in Berlin, Count Wolf-Heinrich von Helldorff, the November pogrom was an opportunity to prove that his policy was paying off and to present himself as the Führer's confidant. The anti-Jewish measures served him, in a certain sense, as a lightning rod "at the most difficult time" in his life, brought on by a marital crisis: his love affair with the movie actress Lida Baarova had driven him to the brink of divorce, forcing Hitler himself to intervene in order to put the farce to an end. As though possessed by a demon, Goebbels made it his goal to bar Jews from theaters and cinema houses—he wrote about this in his diary day after day—even if the whole "Jewish thing" was not his foremost concern but was instead relegated to some place between the birthday of his wife, Magda, invitations to the annual conference of the Reichskulturkammer (the Reich cultural chamber), reviewing films with Hans Moser and Joseph "Joe" Stöckel, and working on a new book. "And then, tired, to bed. A hard day's work was this day, even though it's Saturday."[6] The reflection in Goebbels's diary of November 12, 1938, a day that marked the end of the world for the Jews of Germany, is a paragon of the negligibility of German Jewry's fate in the eyes of the perpetrators.

Heydrich, representing the SD and the SS and their policy toward the Jews, expressed a simple demand at the meeting: "The Jews must leave Germany." The Minister of Finance, "Lutz" Graf Schwerin von Krosigk, an ostensibly apolitical personality whose grip on the portfolio predated Hitler's accession, affirmed this goal and expressed it succinctly: "*Raus* [out!] Whomever can be removed!" Heydrich mentioned the Zentralstelle für jüdische Auswanderung (Central Office for Jewish Emigration) in Vienna, established by Adolf Eichmann after the annexation ("Anschluss") of Austria to the Third Reich in March 1938, and noted, "After all is said and done, we have managed to remove 50,000 Jews from Austria by its means."[7] By the end of 1938, this bureau had arranged the emigration of some seventy-nine thousand Jews from the region now called "Ostmark." The discussants now mulled the possibility of establishing a corresponding central bureau for all of Germany. Heydrich's junior aide, Adolf Eichmann, was also there to explain how things would be done; Heydrich, having prepared well, also expounded on whether Jews should be marked and ghettoized. He proposed that Jews be made to wear a special identifying mark; Göring argued in favor of uniforms and ghettos. The reason for Heydrich's objection to the literal ghettoization of the Jews was typical of a policeman: it would spell the loss of control of his police, or of "the watchful eye of the population at large," over the vestiges of Jewish society.

The Nazi authorities then leveled a one billion Reichsmark ransom ("contribution") on the Jews on account of the pogrom, as if to atone for it in cold cash. Thus they presented the Jews, and not the rioters, as those responsible for the damage. In a regulation concerning restoration of the appearance of streets, the following was stated: Jewish owners or Jewish businesses must defray at once the cost of all damage caused on November 8, 9, and 10, 1938, to Jewish businesses and dwellings on account of popular rage at world Jewry's incitement against National Socialist Germany. This law, "the first enactment concerning the expulsion of the Jews from Germany's economic life," ordering the closure of all Jewish-owned retail establishments and workshops by January 1, 1939, was not the only absurdity that emerged from that meeting.[8] Organized looting went into high gear. Less than a month after the pogrom, on December 3, 1938, an instruction "for the depositing of Jewish property" was issued. Jews were to sell "within a fixed period of time" businesses, real estate, securities, jewelry, valuables, and works of art or to deposit them with a trustee who would "close the deal." The principal looter, the state, would have to wrestle over the booty with the small looters, various party members, until February 1939. It was then that a new regulation ordered the stiff taxation of "unjustified profits [by party members] from the de-Judaization process." "I saw shocking things in the past in this context," Göring said at the November 12 meeting. "Gauleiters' little chauffeurs growing rich to the extent of half a million in wealth."

The goal was to disengage the Jews from the German economy by the middle of 1939, *before* the war. From then on, Jews would be allowed to function economically among themselves only.[9] The Reichsvereinigung der Juden in Deutschland (Reich Association of Jews in Germany) would become the principal employer of German Jews.

Goering's speech at the beginning of the meeting left the impression, as stated, that the anti-Jewish measures up to 1938 had been inadequate. Here the Plenipotentiary for the Four-Year Plan evidently invoked a rhetorical device to criticize, indirectly, the government ministries that the other conferees represented. I say this because the "Aryanization" process and other anti-Jewish measures had already speeded up immensely since the Verordnung über die Anmeldung jüdischen Vermögens (Regulation Regarding the Registration of Jewish Assets) went into effect on April 26, 1938. The number of "lone-wolf" actions, too, including arson against Jewish institutions, spurted powerfully that year.

The international conference at Evian in July 1938 did practically nothing to solve the Jewish refugee problem because none of the thirty-two participating countries offered the refugees unconditional asylum. The decision to create an Intergovernmental Committee for Refugees looked like an alibi only. The high and mighty in Germany correctly interpreted this, ahead of the pogrom, as carte blanche to radicalize their anti-Jewish measures. The first to experience this outcome in their flesh were the fifty thousand or so Jews who held Polish citizenship or were stateless and living in Germany. Some one-third of them were brutally deported in October. As the reader will recall, Herschel Grynszpan, the offspring of one such family, which had been evicted to the no-man's land between Germany and Poland, gave "Kristallnacht" its pretext by assassinating a junior diplomat at the German embassy in Paris, apparently in revenge for what had befallen his parents.

The Executive Order on the Law on the Alteration of Family and Personal Names (August 17, 1938), requiring Jews to add "Sarah" or "Israel" to their given names and the invalidation of Jewish passports (October 5, 1938) by the imprinting of a red "J" on them, applied to the entire Jewish population in the Reich, of course. These and other humiliating measures were imposed *before* the pogrom.

The minutes of the November 12 meeting make it clear that those using the expression "the Jewish question" at that time meant only the "question" of

German Jewry. The "question" of European Jewry or of "world Jewry," in the sense of this term in the Nazi jargon, was not a topic of discussion. Accordingly, Göring quipped as the meeting wound down, "I would not like to be a Jew in Germany."

Addressing an audience of Gauleiters on December 6, 1938, Göring stressed that the objective of all these measures was "the removal of the Jews to other countries with all possible celerity and efficiency, stepping up the pace of emigration with all possible pressure." As he had on November 12, here, too, Göring crudely joked about Germany's Jewish policy: "I've got no doubt that no Jew will come back here once he's 'gone,' especially after the recent events."[10] Ten days later, Interior Minister Frick presented his scheme to expedite emigration. Since emigration from one country cannot but entail immigration to another, the Foreign Ministry had to get involved. In a circular dated January 25, 1939, to all German foreign missions, the Foreign Ministry's Jewish affairs expert, Emil Schumburg, elaborated on "the Jewish question as a factor in foreign policy in 1938." In this document, Schumburg again emphasized the ultimate goal of German policy toward the Jews: "emigration of all Jews who reside within the boundaries of the Reich."[11] Shortly after the Sudetenland crisis but before the pogrom, the SS newspaper, *Das Schwarze Korps*, warned that in the event of war, "the Jews who are among us . . . will be treated exactly as enemy nationals in wartime are customarily treated." The opportunity that the SS was waiting for arrived about a month later, on November 7, when Herschel Grynszpan assassinated the diplomat Ernst vom Rath in Paris. The same newspaper, in its infamous editorial "Jews—What's Next?" on November 24—after the pogrom—presented the total impoverishment of German Jewry and, with it, the upturn in crime that should be expected after the November 12 meeting, as reason to obliterate "the Jewish underworld in fire and sword." "The result will be the practical and final demise and the total annihilation of Judaism in Germany."[12] In its annual report for 1938, a department at the Düsseldorf police used similar phrasing: the total (*restlos*) solution of the Jewish question in Germany has taken a step forward.[13] Even if the policy was taking an increasingly radical turn, its principal addressee was the Jews of Germany.

Given the logic of antisemitism, however, ultimately it proved impossible to have only the Jews of Germany in mind where the "Jewish question" was concerned. The Foreign Ministry's Jewish affairs expert knew after the Evian conference that the "problem" was international and that even the final deportation of German Jews would not answer the "Jewish question" once and for all. He stated in so many words that it was his ministry's duty to diffuse antisemitism around the world so that other countries would know how to solve their Jewish problem in a manner amenable to Germany. One who reads this circular, which every German embassy in the world received, realized that an even more comprehensive solution to the "Jewish problem" would soon have to be found, in one of two ways: concentrating the Jews in a "reservation" somewhere or, if no "somewhere" were located, eradicating them.[14] Even Hitler's infamous "prophecy" in his January 30, 1939, speech, delivered five days after the Foreign Ministry gave its report—that in the event of war the result would be "the annihilation of the Jewish race in Europe" and not only in Germany—was not a new tune in foreign diplomats' ears. That the actualization of war would bring a new situation about, in which "Germany would rid itself of its Jews either by emigration or, if necessary, by starvation or killing, because in the event of war [Germany] must not endanger itself with the presence of a hostile minority in its land," had already been announced by Franz von Pfeffer, a member of Rudolf Hess's bureau staff, in a conversation with a British diplomat on November 21, 1938. In this context, von Pfeffer added that something similar would happen to the Jews of Poland, Hungary, and Ukraine if the German Reich were to occupy those areas.[15] On the agenda on November 12, 1938, however, was the connection between war and radicalization in "solving the Jewish problem" and not the nexus of a German "solution" and an international one. Göring did allude to Hitler's upcoming January 30, 1939, "prophecy" in the course of the meeting, but only in reference to Germany: "If the German Reich finds itself in some external conflict in the foreseeable future, then obviously in Germany, too, we shall think first about doing a fundamental reckoning with the Jews."

Was it the intention to carry out this reckoning only in Germany within its November 1938 confines or to do it farther afield as well, as indicated in the German Foreign Ministry position paper? This question was left unanswered.[16] After all, the goal implied by the unflinching wording of Goering's threat was, mainly, to prompt the Jews of Germany to emigrate at once, not to induce an adverse international reaction. Thus, around two months later and a week before Hitler's January 30, 1939, speech, Alfred Rosenberg explained to the foreign press that, from his standpoint, the Jewish question would be solved "when the last Jew leaves the territory of the Third Reich."[17] Had Hitler's warning toward the Jews, expressed in a speech marking the anniversary of his accession, suggested a genuine policy watershed, then Goebbels, one of the radicals among the Jew-haters, would have discussed it in his diary entry that related to the speech. Instead, he restricted his entry to anti-American polemics, the question of colonialism, the matter of the Church, and the alliance with Italy. In fact, a year would pass before he would rediscuss this segment of Hitler's speech.[18]

Roughly half a year after the annexation of "Ostmark" and shortly after the establishment of the Central Bureau for Jewish Emigration in August 1938 under Adolf Eichmann, it was decided, as Heydrich had proposed on November 12, to give prime importance to the enforcement of emigration—that is, ensuring the expulsion of the Jews from the entire "Altreich." By order of Himmler on November 14, some thirty thousand relatively affluent Jews who had been sent to concentration camps in the course of the November pogrom would be released only "when emigration papers are in their possession."[19] Liberated first, however, were prisoners who had served on the front (November 28, 1938), followed by men over age fifty (December 12, 1938), youth under age eighteen (January 21, 1939), and, finally and gradually, the rest. From the authorities' perspective, the concentration camps—until 1941—served in a sense as sluices for the regulation of Jewish emigration. In the course of 1938 and 1939, and particularly between "Kristallnacht" and the beginning of the war, the German Jewish population of the "Altreich" declined rather quickly from around 300,000 to some 185,000 (around 60 percent of them women).[20] The same tendency emerged not only in the lands annexed to the Reich—Austria (with 195,000 Jews) and the Sudetenland, Bohemia, and Moravia (259,000 Jews) prior to their annexation—but also in Danzig, which only after the war started would "come home to the Reich." On November 14, 1938, a pogrom took place there, and after the Nuremberg Laws went into effect there on November 23, 9,700 Jews were counted in the city among the 12,000 or so whom the most recent census had identified.

All the demographic data and all definitions of a "Jew," however, are problematic in this context. From the authorities' standpoint, the operative definition was based not only on self-designation or religious affiliation but mainly on racial theory. The official statistics from the May 1939 population census counted—apart from 330,892 "full Jews" (including some 97,000 in "Ostmark" and the Sudetenland), 72,378 "Mischlinge of the first degree" and 42,811 "Mischlinge of the second degree." These numbers not only modify the statistical base; they also broaden the frame of our discussion. The fate of these people, whom legislation, the police, and the public regarded as Jews according to the descriptions in effect, is germane to our topic even if those so addressed may have preferred to consider themselves otherwise. The National Socialist policy was also applied to the nineteen thousand or so married couples that were "mixed" or "*priviligiert* [privileged]-mixed"—a concept that Göring unveiled on December 28, 1938, as a decision of the Führer and that would be enshrined in the April 1, 1939, Law on the Renting Situation of Jews. The fate of spouses in "miscegenational marriages" would become a story unto itself, particularly during the war.[21]

The Kindertransport to Britain and other countries, as well as immigration to Mandate Palestine under Youth Aliyah—in which some twelve thousand children and adolescents participated in 1938–1939—increasingly shifted the age pyramid of German Jewry toward the demographic of an aging population. In 1933, only 48 percent of the Jewish population was over forty; shortly after the war began, 75 percent were that old, and two-thirds were more than sixty years of age.

Many of those who were being pursued by police and wished to save their property by circumventing the laws attempted to flee the country illegally. Although it was of supreme importance to the Gestapo to "distance" Jews from the Reich, police stations were instructed on December 23, 1938, "to prevent all illegal emigration of Jews by all measures" and to send those arrested to concentration camps. The eagerness to harass the Jews and the general wish to dispossess them outweighed the slogan *Juden raus*. The story of Richard Willstätter, Nobel laureate in chemistry, may serve as a case in point. Back in 1924 in Munich, Willstätter renounced his professoriate in protest against antisemitism, but, as a German patriot, he remained in the city even after 1933. On the night of the pogrom, he was able to evade arrest and dispatch to the Dachau concentration camp and decided to emigrate once and for all. Only after five long months of unrelenting patience, much good luck, and multiple humiliations despite his international reputation, however, was Willstätter able to leave for Switzerland.[22]

After the November pogrom, another attempt was made to use international support for the emigration of Jews as a way to enrich the Reich. The President of the Reichsbank, Hjalmar Schacht, and George Rublee, Chairman of the Intergovernmental Committee for Refugees that had been established in Evian, conducted in late 1938 and early 1939, in Berlin and London, negotiations over a scheme to finance the mass emigration of four hundred thousand Jews within three years. The talks among Schacht (who after his retirement was succeeded by Helmut Wohlthat of Goering's ministry), Rublee, and others were nothing but a farce, an attempt to extort resources from world Jewry and rob the Jews of Germany of their own. The negotiations, which continued until April, were doomed from the start and can be assessed only as a trial balloon. Public opinion in the largest potential immigration country—the United

States of America—was almost unanimously critical in its response to the pogrom; some of it was horrified. Roughly 60 percent of Americans, however, held the Jews partly or even solely at fault for it. This stance in no way encouraged the authorities to admit terrified German Jews to the United States.[23] Instead, it inspired Hitler's dastardly reprimand in his infamous speech on January 30, 1939:

> If the rest of the world cries out with a hypocritical mien against this barbaric expulsion from Germany of such an irreplaceable and culturally eminently valuable element, we can only be astonished at the conclusions they draw from this situation. For how thankful they must be that we are releasing these precious apostles of culture, and placing them at the disposal of the rest of the world. In accordance with their own declarations they cannot find a single reason to excuse themselves for refusing to receive this most valuable race in their own countries.

The November 9, 1938, pogrom opened a new chapter in the history of German Jewry in the concentration camps on Reich territory.[24] Since the March 1938 annexation of Austria, the number of Jews being sent to concentration camps had been much on the rise. About two thousand people were taken first to Dachau and then to Buchenwald. Until then, such punishment was administered for socialist or communist activity, the crime of "racial defilement," "antisocial behavior," or an incorrigible wish to reimmigrate. Now, it was imposed solely because the Jews had become the main objects for "cleansing." In the organized reaction to Grynszpan's assassination of vom Rath on November 7, 1938, the number of Jews sent to concentration camps—Buchenwald, Dachau, and Sachsenhausen—increased dramatically, to at least twenty-seven thousand from all parts of the Reich. This was by no means a "Nacht und Nebel" (night and fog) operation. Many local communities showered the Jews with invective, stones, and even, sometimes, expressions of sympathy. Thus, some 10 percent of the remaining Jews in the Reich reached concentration camps in the Reich between November 1938 and September 1939. Almost no Jewish family was left unscathed.

To describe the indescribable—the mass experiencing of concentration camps—just the same, a German Jew resorted to the following words: "Imagine a Prussian noncommissioned officer and the most terrible overseer magnified ten times over." The path of torments continued in a "typical German" way: "For the prisoners in Buchenwald, the shortage of water was the main torture. We had to eat without a spoon, with hands that had not been washed in weeks. After the barracks were locked, you could not visit the latrine even when a large portion of the prisoners suddenly fell ill with diarrhea. Many had to live within their own feces."

The next morning, hundreds stood around the latrines and tried to clean their clothing. "Doctors, lawyers, scholars, the cream of the intellectual crop—were treated like beasts."[25] Some one thousand people among those arrested in the course of the pogrom died in the concentration camps. The cruel living conditions drove many others insane.

The purpose and intention of this confinement was, as noted, plain and unequivocal: to humiliate the Jews and thus force them to emigrate. Accordingly, 8,311 inmates from Buchenwald and 10,415 from Dachau, for whom emigration papers and Aryanization of their property could be arranged, were released from "preventive detention."[26] The concentration camps' administration seized the opportunity to rob these Jews, of course. The authorities' twin aspirations—deporting the Jews and dispossessing them—carried the risk of being mutually exclusive. The poorer a Jew was who applied to emigrate, the less likely it was that he or she would be admitted to another country or raise the sum needed for the voyage and the entry visa. In addition, the temptation of sundry party members and bureaucrats to loot the Jews in the most effective and intensive way, to line either their own pockets or the state's, often overwhelmed the wish to be rid of them. Officials at tax offices, the SS, the Gestapo, municipal authorities, and customs all tried "to rob the Jews' property by means of painstaking implementation of directives and regulations and sometimes even by means of an 'innovative' interpretation on their part," even if the price at that point in time—that is, before the "alternative" of murdering the Jews existed—was the nullification or at the very least the delay of their emigration, which was in fact the authorities' express goal.[27]

Men in preventive detention were treated differently from women because women's concentration camps had hardly any room for Jewish inmates at this time. A Jewish woman from Grünstadt who resisted the looting of her villa attempted suicide after being placed in the court's confinement cell for "preventive detention."[28] Moringen and Lichterburg served as concentration camps also for women, before it was decided in November 1938 to establish a special concentration camp for women in Ravensbrück. Jewish women at this time were interned mainly as "political prisoners" or as prostitutes convicted of "racial defilement"—that is, they were not confined in order to expedite their emigration. One of the best-known women political prisoners, Olga Benário Prestes—a communist activist from Munich whom the Brazilian authorities extradited to Germany, or better said, to the Gestapo, in 1936—was taken in the first transport from the Lichtenburg concentration camp to Ravensbrück in the spring of 1939.[29]

Brimming with the bourgeois hypocrisy of National Socialist society, the authorities consistently imposed gender separation in the concentration camps; accordingly, internment in the camps pertained mainly to males at first. From November 1938 onward, however, Jewish women joined Jewish men as victims of this terror. Indeed, 40 percent of Jews murdered in the pogrom were women. In the language of the rapportage, the following, for example, was said: "The Jewess Fraulein Julie Hirschfeld, born on September 29, 1856, in the city of Horn . . . is nearsighted and fell down the stairs for this reason."[30]

In the aftermath of the pogrom, the police assigned "free" Jewish women a new task: promoting emigration. Recha Freier, who continued to arrange the emigration of youth to Palestine, was one of the best-known personalities in this context. Additional women activists, such as the sociologist Cora Berliner; Hedwig Eppstein, wife of Paul Eppstein; and Hannah Karminski helped to keep Jews' daily lives viable by distributing food, handing out ration cards, and taking on similar duties as leading members of the Reichsvereinigung (the Association of Jews in Germany). Thousands of wives, daughters, and mothers who yearned to have their husbands released from concentration camps and had to feed their families took over a new role in Jewish society.[31] Marion Kaplan, in her book *Der Mut zum Überleben* (The courage to survive), emphasizes that after the pogrom the task of teaching in Jewish schools was entrusted largely to women and a few elderly male teachers. That women often rescued or supported their husbands is indubitable. It was their duty, for example, to bribe corrupt bureaucrats in order to save lives or property. Kaplan allows Martha Wertheimer to speak for all these women who remained in Germany instead of emigrating: "But even to be an officer on the deck of the sinking ship 'Jewry' and to survive heroically and fill the vessels that remained—that's valuable, too."[32]

As early as 1938, relations in the concentration camps between Jews from the "Altreich" and "other" inmates—that is, those from Austria—were perceptibly tense. The two hundred Jewish prisoners from "Ostmark" who had been sent to Dachau from March 1938 onward considered the Jewish inmates from the "Altreich" excessively arrogant and loyal to Germany. One Jewish detainee from the "Altreich" described the situation as follows: "It is from them that I first heard at the Dachau concentration camp . . . the slur *Piefke* [stuffed shirt], used in Austria as a slur for Germans from the Reich [Prussians], invoked specifically against fellow Jews from the Altreich. . . . We were angry at the Austrians [because they failed to keep up the pace in order drills] and they, in turn, raged at us because they thought we were acting like Prussian militarists."[33]

What still seemed a marginal problem then would become meaningful in the long term. As victims, deportees, or prisoners, German Jews considered themselves a breed apart and so were seen by others, as would become manifest throughout Europe as the Reich areas expanded, notwithstanding the claim of uniformity in "solving the Jewish problem."

The proposals raised at the November 12, 1938, meeting were swiftly translated into laws, regulations, and actions. Now, as at the meeting itself, every politician, government office, and public institution took measures independently. Heydrich and Himmler, Göring and Goebbels strove after November 9 to seize the helm in dealing with the "Jewish question." Goebbels, for example, made sure to implement "his" proposals in respect to culture, a field in which he had been long competing with Göring. This rivalry would lead to absurdity: Goebbels insisted that the Jüdischer Kulturbund (Jewish Cultural Association), being in his purview, remain in operation—at least for the time being—whereas all other Jewish institutions should not. Many other politicians came out with their own initiatives. Interior Minister Frick called a meeting at his office on December 16, 1938, to coordinate Jewish policy across the entire Reich. Even earlier, on November 15, Bernhard Rust, Minister of Education and Science, ordered the expulsion of Jewish children from German schools: "Jews must not attend German schools. They may attend Jewish schools only."[34] To surmount the shortage of teachers in the Jewish schools, which now had to accommodate all Jewish children who had not attended them until then, Paula Fürst, head of the education department at the Reichsvereinigung der Juden in Deutschland, approached the Gestapo and asked it, in this exceptional case, not to condition the release of teachers who had been interned in concentration camps on their receiving emigration permits. Only in February 1939, shortly before the war, was the education system placed in the care of the Reichsvereinigung.[35]

On November 19, 1938, the Ministers of the Interior and Finance, joined by the Minister of Labor, Franz Seldte, promulgated the "Regulation Concerning Public Relief for Jews." This enactment excluded Jews from the public welfare system and stated that support and public assistance in their broad sense would henceforth be funded by Jews from Jewish sources. Jewish pensioners and Jewish casualties of physical defects, war, disability, and frailty were the victims of this measure, which was manifested in additional regulations.[36] This was yet another act of state robbery in broad daylight, since the social insurance provisions that Jews had been making all along remained in the Reich exchequer.

Many regulations had no purpose other than to assail the Jews' self-respect and -image. On November 16, 1938, Jews were enjoined against wearing uniforms. The police regulations of November 28 and December 28 narrowed Jews' appearance in public to certain hours or locations. The Berlin Chief of Police determined where the "Jew ban" would apply: all theaters, movie houses, museums, playgrounds and sports pitches, swimming pools, and main streets where, for example, many "party members" regularly circulated. On December 3, "National Solidarity Day," Jews were placed under curfew. After losing their drivers' licenses and their right to own private vehicles (under a regulation enacted on December 3), Jews were required on December 14, with logical consistency, to sell their private cars. The *Völkische Beobachter* justified this measure in its December 4, 1938, issue: "Jews no longer have what to search for in Germany behind the wheel!" If they rode the train, they were forbidden by the Ministry of Transport to use sleeping and restaurant cars (March 2, 1939).

The public was expected to accept and even justify these and other strictures, as they were during the "Judenaktion," the November 9 pogrom, on the basis of the assumption that all such measures would be construed as responses to the menace that the Jews posed to the German people. Namely, the strictures were meant to render the Jews "harmless." The blame was always put on the Jews; anti-Jewish measures were presented as retaliation only. This evidently also explains the enactment of absurd regulations that forbade Jews to buy and possess weapons, ammunition, explosives, and carrier pigeons (November 11, 25, and 29). Beyond all this, however, the plain intent of the enactments was "to extinguish [the Jews'] appetite to remain in the Reich." "Accordingly, the legal measures that target Judaism were received with full understanding," remarked the author of one of the many official reports that followed the meeting.[37] The regulations and, of course, the state of general exclusion inspired Jews to express their reluctance to continue living as Jews in the Reich in a more emphatic way: suicide. To remain in Germany idle, defamed, depatriated, and dispossessed had by now become unbearably difficult even in unexceptional cases.[38]

Here, however, I must point out a disparity that may do much to further our understanding of the nature of the persecution of Jews in its general sense. At the time of the pogrom and in subsequent anti-Jewish public events, manifestations of consent in principle by the Volksgemeinschaft (the "national community") and staunch support from sworn National Socialists and antisemites were accompanied by qualms about, and at times even criticism of, the ostentatious measures. SD reports concerning the public's state of mind, corroborated by the reportage of Jewish eyewitnesses, show that enthusiasm for the "Judenaktion" was not particularly keen overall: "The nature of the activity aimed against Jews' businesses . . . was generally not understood," one SD rapporteur noted. Another commented, "When they began to deport those

THE TABULA RASA POLICY

wretched-looking figures, the population did not demonstrate . . . sympathy for this action." Not only were "clear signs here and there of pity" observed but also, in the city of Freden, protest demonstrations against "the operation against the Jews."[39] The expressions of sympathy for the victims trace to the brutality, disorder, and chaos of the affair. People raised as good burghers regularly surmount inhibitions and pangs of conscience by abstractionalizing and depersonifying. Once confronted by the palpable brutality and bestiality of an operation that they consider legitimate in principle, however—say, the humiliation of someone whom they know personally—their consent diminishes considerably. To take the comparison further: even in a war against insects, a person who received a "good" bourgeois upbringing would flinch from witnessing personally the prosecution of a war that he or she considers just if not crucial in theory. Thus, the criticism of the treatment of the Jews, where such was expressed, flowed not necessarily from an argument of moral principle but from inhibitions originating in having been raised not to look life's ugliness in the eye.

The reactions varied from town to town and region to region, of course. Religiosity and level of schooling also appear to have played a role. For example, the gendarmerie in a small town complained sarcastically about "the dirge [of the townspeople] for those decent and consummately honest Jews."[40] As long as the treatment of the "Jewish question" did not take place in plain view and was not accompanied by dramatic riots as in November 1938, and as long as the anti-Jewish actions "were undertaken within the framework of the law," either they did not really notice them—after all, they affected less than 1 percent of the population—or they essentially got used to them.[41] As evidence, complaints about some two thousand cases of "racial defilement" were recorded in 1938, a 50 percent increase over the previous year even though the Jewish population in Germany had fallen—further evidence that much of the Volksgemeinschaft took part actively, individually, and concretely in hounding the Jews.

After the pogrom, the propaganda machine ramped up its engagement in the "Jewish question" in order to encourage indifferent or disapproving Germans to assent to the radical measures. "I have now instructed the press, the radio, and the assembly to prepare a large antisemitic campaign," Goebbels informed his diary on November 18, 1938. Indeed, "the daily explanation of the Jewish question before the radio news is proving itself as an excellent educational device," the president of one of the district governments reported in January 1939. Prime-time propaganda conduced to the ex post favorable public acceptance of the "operation against the Jews": "We should have begun it sooner."[42]

The attitude of non-Jews toward German Jews in the Third Reich continually reflected the gap between the abstract and the concrete: signs of empathy for actual Jews as opposed to consent to, or at least acquiescence in, the regime's treatment of the Jewish population at large. The lengthy historiographic debate about whether the non-Jews' apathy sealed the Jews' fate has not resolved itself unequivocally. Victor Klemperer summarized matters on New Year's Eve 1939 thus: "I believe the pogroms of November '38 made less impression on the nation than cutting the bar of chocolate [= removing it from the Christmas ration]."[43]

This aside, explicit criticism of the pogrom measures was often prompted not by compassion and empathy toward the victims but by concern for totally different values: "What was not understood [was] the destruction of national property [because] it was inconsistent with the aims of the Four-Year Plan"—the master plan by which Germany was to be readied for war—or because the property at issue "would have passed into Aryan hands anyway, sooner or later." Some also feared that "now that the synagogues have been burned down, it will come the turn of the churches." This argument was not groundless. In the district capital of Wunsiedel, for example, a mob taking part in the "Judenaktion" on November 9, 1938, detained three Evangelical clerics at the police station. Also encountered was a stance typical of order-craving citizens: "Along with damage to the reputation and authority of the police . . . it is possible to discern an undeniable brutalization among youth and certain other elements."[44] That is, children should not see adults throwing stones, setting fires, or looting, even if the grown-ups were impelled to do this by "popular rage" against the Jews. Moreover, as I show below, thought should be given to differences in the non-Jewish German population's attitude toward "their" German Jews as against its take on "other" Jews, particularly in the east.[45]

The day of the "Judenaktion" marked the absolute end of the Jewish organizations in Germany. The political entities—the CV (Centralverein deutscher Staatsbürger jüdischen Glaubens, Central Association of German Citizens of the Mosaic Faith), the Zionist Organization, the German Reich Union of Jewish Front Soldiers, and so on—and, of course, the organs of the various religions streams—were dismantled. The Jewish sports clubs, bastions of Jewish self-confidence in the National Socialist era, were shuttered, as were the Jewish publishing houses. To preserve the institutional functions of these federations and foundations just the same, it was decided to amalgamate them under the to-be-formed Reichsvereinigung Der Juden in Deutschland (Reich Association of Jews in Germany). This was done not due to concern for the Jews in Germany but to preserve an organizational setting through which the Third Reich could subject the Jews' affairs to centralized management and efficient supervision so as to bring the solution to the "Jewish question" to fruition.

As noted above, the Jüdischer Kulturbund was allowed to continue operating. As the emigration of Jewish artists and consumers of the arts accelerated, however, it became necessary, for example, to merge the two orchestras in Berlin; the Jewish opera closed its doors even before the war began. Since Jews were barred from "German" movie theaters, a film department was established under the Kulturbund to acquire films for distribution in Jewish cinema houses. Thus, for Jews more than for others, going to the movies was a crucial way to gain some distraction from daily life but also to finance the activities of the now centralized (*gleichgeschaltet*) Kulturbund.[46]

The only legal Jewish newspaper that outlasted the pogrom, the *Jüdische Nachrichtenblatt*, announced on February 17, 1939, the establishment of the Reichsvereinigung der Juden in Deutschland (National Association of the Jews in Germany). In a circular dated February 20, 1939, the Düsseldorf police advised, "The national representation of the Jews in Germany . . . has been tasked with ensuring that all Jewish organizations that have existed thus far disappear." Only when Amendment 10 to the Citizenship Law (i.e., the "Nuremberg Laws") was promulgated on July 4, 1939, was the Reichsvereinigung officially established.[47] The State Secretary at the Interior Ministry, Dr. Wilhelm Stuckart, marked the occasion by saying, "With this, the legislation on the Jewish question is culminated in a certain sense. . . . It means that it has come to the home stretch on the way to a final internal-state solution of the Jewish problem." One repeatedly encounters this and similar allusions to "finality." Although the "Nuremberg Laws" were already considered a "final solution," again and again some new and even more "final" solution appeared. The establishment of the Institut zur Erforschung der Judenfrage (Institute for Research on the Jewish Question) under Dr. Wilhelm Grau on April 15, 1939, proved that the regime was already well along in its quest for a "solution," even though the festive inauguration of the institute would wait until March 1941.

Long before the pogrom, the German Jewish leadership asked for permission to start preparing for the establishment of a Reichsvereinigung. On purely legal grounds, the status of the main Jewish organizations and the various Jewish communities had to be revised because on March 28, 1938, they had ceased to be public entities and, accordingly, became tax-liable. From the standpoint of the German Jewish leadership, the original purpose of the new Reichsvereinigung was "to concentrate the Jews in the German Reich by dint of their nature as Jews and to promote their religious, cultural, social, and other needs by massing all forces." "Our strength is about to run out," the *Jüdische Rundschau* wrote on July 29, 1938, long before the pogrom.[48] As the "Judenaktion" shook the ground, however, the initiative behind the establishment of the Reichsvereinigung came from "above." Thus, after many discussions in February–July 1939, the Reichsvereinigung was created as an instrument of the authorities, foremost the police.

The SD in particular prodded the authorities to act expeditiously to set up an organization for central oversight and emigration of the Jewish minority. On December 16, 1938, at a meeting at his ministry that concerned itself with the "Jewish question," the Minister of the Interior, Frick, already announced the establishment of the Reichsvereinigung and explained its purpose in a manner that leaves no room for misunderstanding: "The sole purpose of the organization . . . is to prepare for the emigration of the Jews. Therefore, we will not abandon the principle that states that the preparations for the Jews' emigration should be handed over in considerable part to the Jews themselves."[49]

Even after the pogrom, however, no "miracle" (i.e., swift deportation of the Jews) was foreseen. Therefore, like it or not, additional functions for the new central organization had to be weighed. Concentrating all activities of the Jewish minority—emigration, welfare, education, and so on—under one roof was in any case well suited to the conventional thinking in the Third Reich about unifying things (Gleichschaltung). Furthermore, from the standpoint of the SD and also that of the threatened Jews, the organization had already existed de facto three months after Kristallnacht; the official go-ahead, handed down only in July 1939 as mentioned above, was just a legal formality. Practically speaking, it meant placing an unprecedentedly large budget, purposed mainly for welfare and emigration, in the hands of a central organization of Jews in Germany, funded specifically from the proceeds of the emigration tax paid by Jews who had left Germany and from the founding capital of the dismantled associations and unions. One of the contradictions that found expression at this time, however, was that even under these terrifying circumstances, it seemed that a central organization of Jews could be useful to the Jewish population and might even ensure some autonomy, however limited.

Heydrich's Central Bureau for Jewish Emigration, the office set up at Goering's initiative on January 24, 1939, went into action on February 11, as did the Reichsvereinigung. Although its purpose was to bring together all aspects of the emigration process, until the war began it had enough leeway for local and other initiatives, such as those of Jewish organizations abroad. Accordingly, it also caused confusion and disorientation. The Berlin office of the bureau was much less "successful" than its counterpart in Vienna. Since the Central Bureau was supposed to cooperate with the Reichsvereinigung, it could be effective only after the Reichsvereinigung's organizational and legal affairs were put in order. By the time this happened, in July 1939, war was at the gates and, with it, the structural overhaul of the police system—that is, the establishment of the Reich Security Main Office. This by necessity caused priorities to change.

Slave labor, too, did not begin only with the eruption of the war. As noted above, as far back as the Sudetenland crisis, the SS had planned to intern German Jews in labor camps in the event of war. However, it was not the war, which thanks to the Munich agreement had again been put off for a while, but rather the pogrom that ultimately caused this scheme to be implemented, albeit with some modifications. Thus, on December 20, 1938, the labor exchanges were instructed to arrange work for unemployed Jews immediately in order to keep them off the dole. This directive was given the additional rationale of its ability to deal with "a growing shortage of German manpower." Thus, the placement of Jews in slave labor in the middle of 1939—before the war began—was in "full momentum," and the instructions of December 20, 1938, and May 19, 1939, gave Jews' unpaid servitude an ostensibly legal basis until the deportations began in October 1941. At first, more Jews from "Ostmark" than from the aging Jewish community of the "Altreich" were put to this duty. However, when the SD found that the National Socialist outlooks had made hardly any inroads in Catholic areas,[50] it was decided, in accordance with the racial policy, that Jews would be posted to "closed labor brigades" (i.e., "separated from the community"). When they were sent out to build roads, construct dams, dig trenches, or remove waste, Jewish slave laborers could be concentrated in separate camps with no problem whatsoever. However, it was not always possible to prevent contact between Jewish workers and others. Even before the war, some thirty camps were under the supervision of the national employment organization. In sum, alongside exploitation by means of "Aryanization," some twenty thousand Jews were subjected to merciless exploitation as slave laborers. Once the war began, their situation would worsen.[51]

After the November pogrom, the Jewish leadership, cowed to begin with, came under mounting pressure. The only leader not sent to a concentration camp in the "Judenaktion" was the President of the Reichsvertretung, Rabbi Leo Baeck. Otto Hirsch, Administrative Chairman of the Reichsvertretung, and Julius Seligsohn, manager of the organization's Emigration Department and ex officio liaison with the communities, had to spend several days in detention before they were released to help expedite the Jews' departure. At the local level, too, public officials and rabbis received no special respect. Two rabbis from Munich, Drs. Baerwald and Ehrentreu, for example, reached a concentration camp after "Kristallnacht" and underwent severe abuse.

The Zionist movement leaders in Germany, who after the emigration of Kurt Blumenfeld in 1933 were considered "second rank"—Siegfried Moses, Benno Cohen, and Franz Meyer—now also emigrated, as did Ernst Herzfeld, the last chairman of the CV. Accordingly, the establishment of the Reichsvereinigung also represented a structural change in the leadership of the rump Jewish society. Leo Baeck, who had served as rabbi in Berlin since 1912 and turned sixty-five at the time the Reichsvereinigung was established, continued to chair the organization. Seventy-year-old Heinrich Stahl, chair of the Jewish community in Berlin—the largest in Germany—was appointed to Baeck's clerical post. Otto Hirsch, fifty-three years old, was named chair of the board of directors. Another member of the board was Paul Eppstein, thirty-seven years of age, who until then had directed the association of Jewish youth organizations and from now on would serve as a liaison to the Gestapo. Moritz Henschel, who replaced Stahl in 1940 as chair of the community in Berlin; Philip Kotzover, aged forty-four; and Julius Seligsohn, forty-eight, also represented the "young" generation on the board. These personalities aside, Cora Berliner, forty-eight; Hannah Karminski, forty-one; and Paula Fürst, forty-five, in charge of education and welfare affairs, also belonged to the leadership echelon of German Jewry. Their shoulders sagged under the decline of their population group. With the exception of Leo Baeck, Holocaust historiography has treated them marginally; the scientific biography of Otto Hirsch is merely the exception that proves the rule. Only in very recent years has a perceptible change of trend occurred.[52]

Another figure who deserves mention at this early juncture is Walter Lustig, a physician and a member of the board of the National Association of Organizations of East European Jews in Germany, who took part in 1938 in the negotiations over the Polish Jews who had been deported from Germany. After the aforementioned representatives of the Jewish leadership were deported or murdered, he would serve as the director of the remnants of the community.

An invisible ghetto took shape long before the war began. Under the National Socialist regime, German Jewry, or "the Jewish presence in Germany," was crowded out of economic, public, and cultural life. For the Volksgemeinschaft, however, this was not enough. The next step was "to separate non-Jewish tenants from Jews in the most complete manner that the law allows." Albert Speer's department demanded and, at the early going of September 14, 1938, received an enlarged supply of housing by evicting Jewish rental tenants. Speer even exploited the pogrom night to seek the evacuation of 10,000–12,000 Jewish-owned apartments. Indeed, by the outbreak of the war, 3,400 such apartments would be vacated in Berlin alone.[53] The cumulative result of dispossession, impoverishment, and the authorities' intervention in Jewish renters' rights was the establishment of "Jew-houses," into which thousands of Jews were compressed. It was all done lawfully, of course. The law concerning letting apartments to Jews, promulgated on April 30, 1939, stated, "Jews have no legal rental entitlements as against a non-Jew. . . . Jews are entitled to sign subletting contracts with Jews only." To keep homeless people from marring the aesthetics of the street, "Jew-houses"—not specially marked at first—became increasingly common. According to the underlying principle of this institution, as long as the Volksgemeinschaft countenanced the expulsion of the Jews, they should not be allowed to become a burden to the Volksgemeinschaft. "However, care should be taken," a regulation based on the law cautioned, "that the designation of these houses not lead to undesirable ghettoization." Heydrich had explained the reason for this at the meeting on November 12, 1938. If so, once again not only individuals took part in the ouster of the Jews; so did a large number of ambitious "Volksgenossen" (members of the Volksgemeinschaft), not to speak of the many who derived utility from these measures. The principal partakers, apart from Heydrich and his staff, were bureaucrats from the Ministry of Labor and the Ministry of the Interior and municipal councilors.

Anyone who wished to cling to illusions could still do so at this time. Jewish movie theaters were still allowed to show German and American films, and Jews who managed to obtain medical referrals could still visit therapeutic springs and use convalescent homes.[54] This remaining wiggle room made it possible to step up the pressure and restrict and harass the Jews of Germany even more. The latter also realized that they still had something to lose. The regime knew the rule: only those who had nothing left to lose would pose a menace.

The notion that "things could still be worse" explains, beyond the existence of the terror mechanism of the SS, the Gestapo, and the concentration camps, the Jewish organizations' willingness to collaborate in the implementation of these decrees. Ever since Raul Hilberg dealt with this *problematique*, it has been tumultuously debated in the research literature. Hannah Arendt and H. G. Adler also devoted much attention to the question of the Reichsvereinigung as a Judenrat. Hilberg never ceased to insist that the Reichsvereinigung was the prototype of the Judenrat: "Because these men were not puppets, they retained their status and identity in the Jewish community throughout their participation in the process of destruction, and because they did not lessen their diligence, they contributed the same ability that they had once marshalled for Jewish well-being to assist their German supervisors in operations that had become lethal."[55]

Arendt outdid Hilberg, alleging that more Jews could have been saved had the Jewish leadership not collaborated with the German authorities.[56] Adler emphasized that once a person agreed, or felt compelled, to collaborate with the Gestapo, he or she no longer had the leeway and the freedom to make decisions.[57] These views, however—the products of ex post insights about the Holocaust—wrongfully accuse the Reichsvereinigung of having, so to speak, followed a path on which the annihilation and murder of European Jewry was preordained. Beate Meyer takes a totally different approach in her recent book about the Reichsvereinigung. She defines the operating space of the German Jewish leadership as wedged between hope, necessity, steadfastness, and collaboration, and she explicitly avoids fault-finding and sweeping after-the-fact indictments.[58] Thus, to test the validity of the criticism of this leadership's activity, we need to ask ourselves an analytical hypothetical, contrafactual question: In what manner would the point of view about the leadership's actions in 1938 and 1939 have changed had the attempted assassination of Hitler on November 9, 1939, succeeded? Would the Reichsvereinigung's calculus— save what can be saved and buy time—not have appeared correct at the time?

On the question of the "Jew-houses," a German historian wrote bluntly in 1987: "From today's point of view, it is hard to understand and explain why the leaderships of the Jewish communities . . . the *responsables* of the Reichsvertretung der Juden and its successor, the Reichsvereinigung, agreed unresistingly to collaborate with the implementation of anti-Jewish measures and passed on the Gestapo's orders without protest."[59]

In these matters, as with other players who represent the "contemporaneous point of view" (see chap. 1) and fail to differentiate between regimes that respect human rights and those that disdain them, the intensity of the terror aimed at the Jews is overlooked. What would have happened had resistance been mounted? This is not even a hypothetical question. In cases of even the slightest suspicion of resistance, Jewish community leaders were sent to concentration camps. Hirsch, Seligsohn, Eppstein, Berliner, and others were murdered there! One should also take account of the psychology behind the persecution mechanism. The Jewish functionaries thought that by obeying they could salvage something or, at least, impede something. The historian quoted above undervalues her own insight about this collaboration—that is, that the Jewish leaders hoped to find a way out of their communities' desperate situation by obeying and not standing out.[60] Dan Diner adroitly describes the paradox: they had stumbled into an unprecedented predicament in which they tried to think rationally, think as Nazis would, and buy time as long as the system carried on in a counter-rational (*gegenrational*) way.[61] Ultimately, the accusing finger is pointed at the wrong culprit; the main malefactor was the non-Jewish population. The media concurred and collaborated in the anti-Jewish terror without having to be coerced. The population—apart from a few exceptions—participated actively, observed from the sidelines, or turned a blind eye. How could Jews in Germany have effectively opposed this constellation?

As an example of the hopelessness of dramatic resistance, consider the labors of the only Jewish newspaper still being published at that time, the *Jüdische Nachrichtenblatt*. Its publisher was Erich Liepmann, who until November 1938 had put out the Zionist paper *Jüdische Rundschau*. In April 1939, he was able to emigrate and was succeeded by Hanna Marcus. She reports having been summoned each day to the Ministry of Propaganda. She also describes the abuse dished out to Dr. Martin Brasch, Director of the Jüdischer Kulturbund, who was also regularly ordered to report to the Ministry of Propaganda until he was sent to Sachsenhausen concentration camp for "disobeying orders." (He died after being released, the day before Nazi Germany attacked Soviet Russia.) Even in Hebrew one could not drop antiregime hints because Dr. Gerhard Lock, a bureaucrat at Goebbels's Reich Ministry of Propaganda, to whom the daily report had to be presented, was fluent in this language.[62] What kind of resistance could one even imagine under such conditions? Or might the article "Emigration as a Final Solution," published in the *Jüdische Nachrichtenblatt*, have been written as a conspiracy?[63]

The after-the-fact charge of nonresistance on the part of the leaders of German Jewry is even more ridiculous if we recall that, at the end of the day, it was the Great Powers that acquiesced in the German policy toward the Jews and even submitted to it. The negotiations after the Evian conference (the aforementioned Rublee–Schacht talks), like other engagements of that type, did not take place under the self-evident assumption, "from the contemporaneous point of view," that any policy of persecuting and deporting a group of people by a European country deserves furious condemnation and is so illegitimate as to warrant boycotting the country that adopts it. On the contrary: the Powers attempted to meet Germany's demands, treated the regime's attitude toward the Jews—and even that of regimes in Eastern Europe—understandingly, and quibbled over numbers: how many Jews would be received, at what price, and under what conditions. Here, too, the consideration that vengeance or resistance might touch off the next pogrom was served up as an argument or an excuse. One could see by early 1939 that the international negotiations had failed. Thus, where the mightiest of the Powers had stumbled, the Jews within the confines of the "Third Reich," of all people, could not pin their hopes on resistance; they could only fend off the evil decree and hope that the world would revisit its attitude toward the antisemitic policy and toward Hitler. The exertions of Wilfried Israel, the Berlin department store owner, to arrange emigration visas mainly to Britain fall into the category of operations that could rescue Jews who were already in concentration camps; they surely delivered more utility than showy feats of hopeless resistance.

Instead of contemplating resistance to orders from high places, the community leaders tried to find circumventions that would make life in Germany a little more tolerable and a little more secure (e.g., paying protection money to Gestapo men or removing obstacles to emigration and thereby outwitting the Third Reich). Thus, thousands of Jews emigrated on tourist visas or purchased foreign passports or bogus documents attesting that they were farmworkers or landowners in South America, thus qualifying for entrance visas to all kinds of countries. Some bought certificates of baptism with which they could emigrate to Brazil or Ecuador. Many other examples can be presented in this context.[64] Nevertheless, it seemed that the number of Jews emigrating did not satisfy the Central Bureau for Jewish Emigration (i.e., the SD). Therefore, in the middle of May 1939, Heydrich sent two members of the Reichsvereinigung board, Wilfried Israel and Paul Eppstein, to London in order to prod "world Jewry" and the countries participating in the Evian conference to step up their "cooperation." In Berlin, Eppstein and Israel were given a threat: if they returned without results, "the police would be unable to prevent a new wave of persecutions."[65] At what point were these Jewish functionaries supposed to launch their resistance? The Zionist leader Benno Cohen does describe a scene at a meeting of Jewish leaders with Adolf Eichmann in March 1939: Paul Eppstein, after Eichmann cursed him, stressed that those present represented the Jews of Germany, and, as such, they expected to be heard and treated with respect, even if they could be sent to a concentration camp straight away.[66]

In their eagerness to be rid of the Jews, the German authorities often allowed refugee ships to sail from German ports even though some passengers lacked valid entry visas to the destination countries. The fault for the murder of these refugees belongs as much to the countries that barred them as it does to the Third Reich. Thus, in February and March 1939, sixty-two refugees aboard three different vessels lacked the requisite visas. Twenty-five of them were aboard the SS *Cap Arcona*, which steamed to South America and then back to Hamburg with these passengers; as the war wound down, it foundered while carrying more than four thousand prisoners from a concentration camp. The best-known case in this context, however, is the MS *St. Louis*. On May 27, 1939, shortly after Eppstein's and Israel's mission, the ship docked at Havana, Cuba, with 936 refugees from Germany aboard. Only twenty-nine of them were allowed to debark; the others had to sail back to Europe after the United States turned them away. Among them, 288 found refuge in Britain. The rest were admitted to continental countries, where many fell prey to the German occupation.[67]

The connection between war and the escalation of anti-Jewish measures was also discussed on November 12, 1938, as mentioned above. Jews speculated about what was in store, which was even passed on to Britain along diplomatic channels. This is known because, on November 21, 1938, Ashton Gwatkin of the British Foreign Office was advised that "the reason that Germany wishes to rid themselves of its Jews is simple: in the case of war, they do not want to feed 500,000 useless persons and potential traitors; accordingly, they should be thrown out or exterminated."[68]

The Jews of Germany feared the outbreak of war even, and especially, if Germany were to lose.[69] The hostages—the Jews of Germany—did not overlook Hitler's speech on January 30, 1939. It was also under this threat that the Jewish leadership had to operate.

On September 1, 1939, it came time to carry out the threats. Again German Jewry tumbled into what Dan Diner calls the "counter-rational": for the first two years of the war, the Jews in the prewar Reich faced "only" the sword of the decrees that the regime continued to flash—that is, a step-by-step tactic as opposed to an abrupt turning point, such as that experienced by the Jewish population in the European lands that were occupied from September 1939 onward in the course of the war.

NOTES

1. Jacob Toury, "Ein Auftakt zur Endlösung," in Ursula Büttner et al., eds., *Das Unrechtsregime*, However, vol. 2 (Hamburg: Hans Christians Verlag, 1986), 164–88.

2. Otto Dov Kulka and Eberhard Jäckel, eds., *The Jews in the Secret Nazi Reports on Popular Opinion in Germany, 1933–1945* (New Haven, CT: Yale University Press, 2010).

3. Peter Loewenberg, "The Kristallnacht as a Public Degradation Ritual," *LBYB* 32 (1987): 309–23.

4. Joseph Goebbels, *Tagebücher 1923–1945*, ed. Elke Fröhlich (Munich: Institut für Zeitgeschicht, 1993–2007), entry of November 12, 1938.

5. "Protokoll der Sitzung im Reichsluftfahrtministerium," *International Military Tribunal*, 1946, vol. 28, 499–541.

6. Joseph Goebbels, *Tagebücher*, entries August 18 and 31, and November 12 and 13, 1938.

7. "Protokoll der Sitzung im Reichsluftfahrtministerium," *International Military Tribunal*, 1946, vol. 28, 534.

8. Avraham Barkai, *Vom Boykott zur "Entjudung." Der wirtschaftliche Existenzkampf der Juden im Dritten Reich 1933–1943* (Frankfurt: Fischer, 1988); cf. Joseph Walk et al., eds., *Das Sonderrecht für die Juden im NS-Staat Eine Sammlung der gesetzlichen Maßnahmen und Richtlinien—Inhalt und Bedeutung*, 2nd ed. (Heidelberg: C. F. Müller, 1996), "Verordnung vom 12 November 1938," 254.

9. Avraham Barkai, "The Struggle for Economic Existence in 1933–43," in Abraham Margaliot and Yehoyakim Cochavi, eds., *History of the Holocaust: Germany* (Hebrew) (Jerusalem: Yad Vashem, 1998), 567–72.

10. Susanne Heim and Götz Aly, "Staatliche Ordnung und 'Organische Lösung,' Die Rede Hermann Goerings 'Über die Judenfrage' vom 6 Dezember 1938," in Wolfgang Benz, ed., *Jahrbuch für Antisemitismusforschung* 2 (Frankfurt: Campus Verlag, 1993), 385.

11. ADAP, D V, Nr.664, Runderlass des Auswärtigen Amtes 25.1.1939; Magnus Brechtken, "Madagaskar für die Juden," *Antisemitische Idee und politische Praxis* (Munich: Oldenbourg Verlag, 1997), 210.

12. *Das Schwarze Korps*, November 3 and November 24, 1938.

13. Kulka and Jäckel, *The Jews in the Secret Nazi Reports*.

14. Eckart Conze et al., *Das Amt und die Vergangenheit. Deutsche Diplomaten im Dritten Reich und in der Bundesrepublik* (Munich: Blessing Verlag, 2010), 173–74.

15. Brechtken, "Madagaskar für die Juden," 198.

16. "Protokoll der Sitzung im Reichsluftfahrtministerium," *International Military Tribunal*, 1946, vol. 28.

17. Quoted in Brechtken, *"Madagaskar für die Juden,"* 74.

18. Cf. Joseph Goebbels, *Tagebücher 1923–1945*, entry of January 31, 1939.

19. Walk, *Das Sonderrecht für die Juden*, 256.

20. According to statistics kept by the Reichsvereinigung der Juden in Deutschland (Reich Association of Jews in Germany), 78,227 Jews emigrated from the Altreich between January 1, 1939, shortly after the pogrom, and June 3, 1940.

21. Cf. Beate Meyer, *"Jüdische Mischlinge": Rassenpolitik und Verfolgungserfahrung 1933–1945* (Hamburg: Dölling and Galitz, 1999), 162ff.

22. John Van Houten Dippel, *Bound upon a Wheel of Fire: Why So Many German Jews Made the Tragic Decision to Remain in Nazi Germany* (New York: Basic Books, 1996), 6, 249–52, 257–58.

23. Cf. Fritz Kieffer, *Judenverfolgung in Deutschland—eine innere Angelegenheit? Internationale Reaktionen auf die Flüchtlingsproblematik 1933–1945* (Stuttgart: Steiner, 2002), 347, 357–73.

24. Cf. Leni Yahil, "Jews in the Concentration Camps in Germany before World War II," in Yisrael Gutman and Rachel Manber, eds., *The Nazi Concentration Camps: Structure and Intentions, the Image of the Prisoner, Jews in the Camps* (Hebrew) (Jerusalem: Yad Vashem, 1984), 55–80.

25. Hans Berger in Monika Richarz, ed., *Jüdisches Leben in Deutschland*, vol. 3: *Selbstzeugnisse zur Sozialgeschichte 1918–1945* (Stuttgart: Deutsche Verlags-Anstalt, 1982), 323–35; Peter Gay, *Meine deutsche Frage Jugend in Berlin 1933–1939* (Munich: C. H. Beck, 1999), 159f.

26. Cf. Ulrich Herbert, ed., *Nationalsozialistische Vernichtungspolitik 1939–1945: Neue Forschungen und Kontroversen* (Frankfurt: Fischer Taschenbuch Verlag, 1998), 222; Fritz Kieffer, *Judenverfolgung in Deutschland—eine innere Angelegenheit? Internationale Reaktionen auf die Flüchtlingsproblematik 1933–1945* (Stuttgart: Steiner, 2002), 353.

27. Cf. Katharina Stengel, ed., *Vor der Vernichtung Die staatliche Enteignung der Juden im Nationalsozialismus* (Frankfurt: Campus Verlag, 2007), 38.

28. Kulka and Jäckel, *The Jews in the Secret Nazi Reports*, 340, report pertaining to November 10, 1938.

29. Cf. Rochelle G. Saidel, *The Jewish Women of Ravensbrück Concentration Camp* (Madison: University of Wisconsin Press, 2004).

30. Kulka and Jäckel, *The Jews in the Secret Nazi Reports*, 358, Bielefeld police headquarters.

31. Cf. Marion Kaplan, *Der Mut zum Überleben: Jüdische Frauen und ihre Familien in Nazideutschland* (Berlin: Aufbau Verlag, 2001), 182–87; Rita Thalmann, "Jüdische Frauen nach dem Pogrom 1938," in Arnold Paucker et al., eds., *Die Juden im nationalsozialistischen Deutschland/Jews in Nazi Germany 1933–1943* (Tübingen: Mohr, 1986), 296.

32. Kaplan, *Der Mut zum Überleben*, 202.

33. Alfred Schwerin in Monika Richarz, *Jüdisches Leben in Deutschland*, 346.

34. Walk, *Das Sonderrecht für die Juden*, 254.

35. Joseph Walk, "Jewish Edcuation in Nazi Germany," in Abraham Margaliot and Yehoyakim Cochavi, eds., *History of the Holocaust: Germany* (Hebrew) (Jerusalem: Yad Vashem, 1998), 667ff; Otto D. Kulka, ed., *Deutsches Judentum unter dem Nationalsozialismus* (Tübingen: Mohr, 1997), 441ff.

36. Cf. Wolf Gruner, *Öffentliche Wohlfahrt und Judenverfolgung Wechselwirkung lokaler und zentraler Politik im NS-Staat 1933–1942* (Munich: Oldenbourg, 2002), 167ff.

37. Monthly report from Governor of Lower Bavaria, December 8, 1938, quoted in Martin Broszat et al., eds., *Bayern in der NS-Zeit Soziale Lage und politisches Verhalten der Bevölkerung im Spiegel vertraulicher Berichte* (Munich: Oldenbourg, 1977), 473.

38. Christian Goeschel, "Suicides of German Jews in the Third Reich," *German History* 1 (2007): 1, 29.

39. Kulka and Jäckel, *The Jews in the Secret Nazi Reports* 352–63, 385.

40. Ibid., 387.

41. In this matter, cf. Ian Kershaw, "Reactions to the Persecution of the Jews," *Popular Opinion and Political Dissent in the Third Reich Bavaria, 1933–1945* (New York: Clarendon Press, Oxford University Press, 1983), 257ff.

42. Kulka and Jäckel, *The Jews in the Secret Nazi Reports*, 375, 385.

43. Klemperer, *I Will Bear Witness*, 324, entry of December 31, 1939.

44. Kulka and Jäckel, *The Jews in the Secret Nazi Reports*, 352.

45. In this matter, cf. Ian Kershaw, "Die öffentliche Meinung in Deutschland und die Judenfrage 1939–1943: Weitere Betrachtungen," in Arnold Paucker et al., eds., *Die Juden im nationalsozialistischen Deutschland/Jews in Nazi Germany 1933–1943* (Tübingen: Mohr, 1986), 365–86.

46. Cf. Margaliot and Cochavi, *History of the Holocaust: Germany*, 782; Jörg Osterloh, *"Ausschaltung der Juden und des jüdischen Geistes"* (Frankfurt: Campus, 2020), 497.

47. On the formation of the Reichsvereinigung, see Dov Kulka, "The National Association of the Jews in Germany," in Yisrael Gutman, ed., *The Image of the Jewish Leadership in the Nazi-Controlled Lands 1933–1945* (Hebrew) (Jerusalem: Yad Vashem, 1980), 37–48; Esriel Hildesheimer, *Jüdische Selbstverwaltung unter dem NS-Regime* (Tübingen: Mohr, 1994); Beate Meyer, *A Fatal Balancing Act: The Dilemma of the Reich Association of Jews in Germany, 1939–1945*, trans. William Templer (New York: Berghahn, 2013), 15–30.

48. Cf. July 1938 statutes in Otto D. Kulka, ed., *Deutsches Judentum unter dem Nationalsozialismus* (Tübingen: Mohr, 1997), 418, 425.

49. Hildesheimer, *Jüdische Selbstverwaltung*, 85.

50. Kulka and Jäckel, *The Jews in the Secret Nazi Reports*, 430.

51. Wolf Gruner, *Jewish Forced Labor under the Nazis: Economic Needs and Racial Aims, 1938–1944* (New York: Cambridge University Press, 2006), 3–8.

52. See, for example, biography of Paul Eppstein in Wolfgang Benz, ed., *Juden im 20sten Jahrhundert: Eine Geschichte in Porträts* (Munich: Beck, 2011); and Beate Meyer, *Paul Eppstein, Eine tödliche Gratwanderung* (Mannheim: Mannheimer Abendakademie und Volkshochschule, 2014).

53. Marlis Buchholz, *Die hannoverschen Judenhäuser Zur Situation der Juden in der Zeit der Ghettoisierung und Verfolgung 1941–1945* (Hildesheim: A. Lax, 1987), 14; Susanne Willems, *Der entsiedelte Jude: Albert Speers Wohnungspolitik* (Berlin: Henrtrich, 2002), 83.

54. Kulka and Jäckel, *The Jews in the Secret Nazi Reports*, 458ff, RSHA, Berlin, July 8, 1939.

55. Raul Hilberg, *The Destruction of European Jewry* (London: Holmes & Meier, 1985), 213.

56. Cf. Hannah Arendt, *Eichmann in Jerusalem: A Report on the Banality of Evil* (New York: Viking Press, 1963).

57. Cf. H. G. Adler, *Der verwaltete Mensch Studien zur Deportation der Juden aus Deutschland* (Tübingen: Mohr, 1974), 355.

58. Meyer, *A Fatal Balancing Act*, Introduction and chapter 2; Kaplan, *Der Mut zum Überleben*, 224; cf. Marc Roseman, *A Past in Hiding: Memory and Survival in Nazi Germany* (Los Angeles, CA: Reed Business Information, 2000).

59. Marlis Buchholz, *Die Hannoverschen Judenhäuser* (Hildesheim: August Lax, 1987), 18.

60. Ibid., 16.

61. Dan Diner, *Beyond the Conceivable: Studies on Germany, Nazism, and the Holocaust* (Berkeley: University of California Press, 2000), 130–37.

62. Fabius Schach, "Auswanderung als Endlösung," *Jüdisches Nachrichtenblatt*, February 2, 1939; Herbert Freeden, *Die jüdische Presse im Dritten Reich* (Frankfurt: Athenäum, 1987), 169–78.

63. Ibid., 175.

64. Fritz Kieffer, *Judenverfolgung in Deutschland* (Stuttgart: Franz Steiner, 2002), 436.

65. Ibid., 456.

66. Quoted in Margaliot and Cochavi, *History of the Holocaust: Germany*, 296; see also Meyer, *A Fatal Balancing Act*, 61ff.

67. Sarah A. Ogilvie and Scott Miller, *Refuge Denied: The St. Louis Passengers and the Holocaust* (Madison: University of Wisconsin Press, 2010).

68. Fritz Kieffer, *Judenverfolgung in Deutschland* (Stuttgart: Steiner, 2002), 332.

69. Marvin Lowenthal, *The Jews of Germany: A Story of Sixteen Centuries* (London: Lindsay Drummond, 1939).

THREE

—ᛞᛞ—

"DAYS OF GRACE" IN A MOUSETRAP

IN NOVEMBER 1939, THE AMERICAN Jewish historian Marvin Lowenthal published his *The Jews of Germany: A Story of Sixteen Centuries*. In the last chapter, which concerns itself with 1936–1939, he predicts that this "new Egyptian bondage will terminate—with gruelling labor, taskmasters' blows, and collapse through exhaustion—the present generation of German Jews. . . . What the Jews must now endure," he says, "is slavery at the hands of a master who has already promised them death." Lowenthal then adds, with hyperbole, that "a war of extermination upon all Jews everywhere is a conscious and avowed aim of the German government."[1] His prime interest in the book, however, is with the Jews of Germany; therefore, his prognosis centers on them. Victor Klemperer, a German who qualified as a Jew by the National Socialist definition, answered the question "What is going to be?," which came up repeatedly at the beginning of the war, as follows: "And the two of us [Klemperer and his non-Jewish wife] right in the middle, helpless and probably lost in either case—whether Germany would win the war or lose it." Less than a year after the war began, Klemperer quoted a German Jew as having told him that "the Jews in Berlin were praying for Hitler to win [the campaign against Britain]," in fear of what would become of them if he were to lose it.[2]

Even those who frowned on taking the most extreme anti-Jewish slogans at face value knew before the German offensive against Poland on September 1, 1939, that from the standpoint of National Socialist policy, the Jews were Germany's archenemies and that any of them remaining in the "Altreich" would automatically be considered a fifth column in the event of war. As the Wehrmacht advanced, however, a paradoxical situation came about: notwithstanding the rhetorical drumbeat about "international Jewry," the National Socialist regime

41

was unable, if only on legal grounds, to introduce and implement a standard policy toward the Jewish population in all areas of its by-now-expanded "Third Reich." Not only were the fate and legal status of the Jews of Germany, including those in the "Ostmark" and the "Protectorate of Bohemia and Moravia," distinct from those of the Jewish population in the areas of Europe that were occupied in the first year of the war—first all of Poland and then Norway, Denmark, France, the Netherlands, and Belgium—but one also gets the impression that the "purge at home," radical measures to "remove" the Jews of Germany to the non-German sphere, was not taking place after all and did not enjoy top priority to say the least. This, of course, was not due to compassion, mercy, or human sentiment. Nor had the Nazis suddenly lost interest in a Judenfrei Reich. Even the delays that came about due to "technical" or legal problems were secondary in this context. In truth, the Jews of Germany had ceased to occupy center stage for the time being because the highest priority had shifted to a new mission: introducing a comprehensive population policy in the occupied Polish territories and later in the west. This being a greater challenge, it led to clashing plans. In other words, in the eyes of the non-Jews of Germany, the German "Jewish question" had been more or less solved, or at least had lost its priority, by September 1939. The events that followed the November pogrom seemed to confirm the social death of German Jewry once and for all.

The continuation and radicalization of the prewar Jewish policy in the "Altreich" sufficed to make the "marginality" of the remaining Jews even more marginal. The decision makers would hold what they considered a "Final Solution" in abeyance until the end of the war. The phrase "after the war" recurred over and over in declarations by Hitler, Himmler, Goebbels, and other functionaries. No one knew what we know today about how long the war—especially the campaign against Britain—would last and how the conditions for a "total" or "final" solution of the Jewish problem would manifest afterward. This must be kept in mind if we wish to understand, above all, the discussions that followed the invasion of the Soviet Union. After the victory over Bolshevism (i.e., the defeat of the USSR), the "solution" was supposed to be found and applied not only in reference to the Jews of Germany but also, and equally, to all of European Jewry. If we fail to take a historical view of future expectations that were entertained in the past and adopt what actually happened as our point of departure, as though the way things played out was the only way they could have, then our understanding of the historical process will be deficient. This rule holds not only in the case at hand.

Several months before the war began, no more than 331,000 Jews remained in the German Reich territories, including post-Anschluss Austria, the annexed

Sudetenland, and the "Protectorate of Bohemia and Moravia." This is according to the official records, which from May 1939 onward counted so-called racial Jews. Of the total, around 185,000 lived in the "Altreich" territories. Some 60 percent of the latter were women. Relative to the enormous Jewish population that would be sucked into the sphere of control of the "Third Reich" during the war, this was a small group. Thus, it is no wonder that not only contemporary decision makers but also subsequent historians neglect and marginalize it. As I emphasized in the introduction to this book, however, the Shoah of German Jewry deserves special attention from today's perspective not only because such a discussion has been marginalised thus far and the German Jews certainly deserve their day in the historical sun but also, and mainly, because the singularity of this history, in view of that of all Jews in the "Third Reich," brings the complexion of the National Socialist system of control, on the one hand, and the Jews' modes of comportment, on the other, into sharper and brighter view.

In the first few weeks of the war—by which I mean September and October 1939—about half of the Jewish population of Poland found itself under "Third Reich" rule, after which a "Jewish policy" both terrifying and muddled was instituted in the occupied areas. For the Jews in the "Altreich," in contrast, these weeks were devoid of dramatic developments such as mass escape, license to commit mass murder, and ghettoization. Also in contrast to Jews in the Generalgouvernement and Warthegau areas, these Jews were not required to wear the yellow patch or an armband. Even their fear of an additional pogrom, festering since November 1938, appears to have waned when the war broke out: "Jew-baiting appears to be suspended for the moment," wrote Victor Klemperer.[3] With the whole country under military dictatorship, he remarked, "We probably do not need to fear a pogrom."[4] From the German Jews' standpoint, nothing happened at first "except" further radicalization of disentitlement, isolation, and abjection. For a while, too, it seemed, when contemplated on a spot basis, that things were even "improving." The Jüdischer Kulturbund, for example, which was supposed to deactivate on September 1, 1939, received on September 24, 1939, authorization to carry on for another two years. Until the United States entered the war in December 1941, the Third Reich rulers considered the German Jews political hostages of sorts, with whose assistance they could blackmail Washington. And one does not kill hostages prematurely, as everyone knows.

The optics of relatively endurable conditions of life for the Jews in the Reich are misleading, of course. It is true that the fear of being thrown into a concentration camp or slaughtered proved to be exaggerated at first, but the process of radicalization did not stop.[5] In fact, it is in terms of further escalation that the history of the Jews in Germany up to the June 1941 invasion of the Soviet Union should be depicted. The Reich persisted in its efforts to dispossess and banish "its" Jews in various ways, including expulsion, as described below. By September 1939, the German Jews had amassed six and a half years of experience in National Socialist rule. The presence of a rump German Jewish population in Germany after the war began may have given the Volksgemeinschaft sadistic satisfaction and, certainly, continual proof of the triumph of "German-ness" over Jewishness. Beyond humiliating the Jews, the authorities had two goals in mind. First, they wished to make it clear to the German public that the Jews of Germany still posed a threat, one that would steadily escalate during the war. The construction of an "enemy within" is one of the most effective devices in war propaganda because it enhances the cohesion of the majority society. Accordingly, the German media reported on the "Jewish matter" and published the regulations that pertained to it. Second, the authorities wished to take advantage of the state of war in order to continue tightening their restrictions on the Jews and exploiting them in more and more extreme ways while expanding their segregation from the Volksgemeinschaft.

The measures taken against Jews' freedom of movement belong to the first category of decrees—those against the "enemy within." Immediately after the war broke out, various mayors imposed curfews or ordered the confiscation of radio sets and the like from Jewish homes. The SD nullified such directives swiftly, on September 7, because they did not emanate from a central authority (i.e., the chief of the SD) and because they might be exploited for the exigencies of anti-German propaganda abroad. Two weeks later, however, the Reichssicherheitshauptamt (Reich Main Security Office—RSHA) reinstated the very same regulations. Now Jews were officially enjoined against possessing radio sets on the argument that they were tuning into foreign stations and disseminating "atrocity propaganda." The RSHA deliberately chose Yom Kippur as the deadline by which Jews had to surrender their radios. Afterward, homes were searched to make sure the rule was being obeyed. Possession of weapons had been forbidden to Jews for about a year by then, but from now on Jews were liable to a three-week stay in a concentration camp for possessing a foil, a piece of fencing equipment.[6] Jews were not allowed to address members of the Wehrmacht nor to leave their dwellings between 8:00 p.m. and 6:00 a.m. (in the summer, from 9:00 p.m. to 5:00 a.m.). The press justified this curfew, imposed on all Jews in Germany, on the grounds that the Jews might exploit the dark of night to waylay Aryan women.[7] Since a state of war tends to turn heads toward more radical reactions in general, it is no wonder that, at the early going of September 6, 1939, an SD contact person in Münster reported public disgruntlement against the Jews: "People are already talking about ... putting [the Jews] up against the wall to be shot, 10 Jews for every German killed in combat." Alternatively, the NSDAP District Direction in Kitzingen could detect on September 11, 1939, "substantial spying activity on the part of the Jews."[8]

To save the strained food supplies for the sole consumption of the Volksgemeinschaft, rations for the Jewish population were repeatedly slashed. Jews received less meat, vegetables, and butter than did others and were allotted no chocolate, real coffee, or new clothing at all ("Chocolate confiscated," Victor Klemperer wrote on September 25, 1939). Eventually, they lost their share of tomatoes and canned food as well. One may expand the list to one's heart's content. Parenthetically, the Minister of Propaganda, true to form, was the living spirit behind the decision to annul the chocolate ration: on November 17, 1939, Goebbels launched a propaganda war that ultimately prompted the Reich Minister of Food and Agriculture, Richard Walther Darré, to forbid, on December 2, 1939, the sale of chocolate to Jews. This is an impressive example of the way the authorities used gratuitous abuse to embitter the lives of Jews in Germany.[9]

Since Jews no longer received clothing rations, the Reichsvereinigung had to provide them with used attire. Thus Klemperer writes, "Even before a corpse is cold the Jewish Community is already asking for the things."[10] In July 1940, a regulation was enacted to deprive Jews of telephone use; the instruments were disconnected on September 30. Since the Jews continued to be listed in the telephone books, however, the police could arrest, after the fact, anyone who had "neglected" to report the first names that Jews had been forced to adopt.[11] After being banned from public libraries, now they were denied lending-library services altogether. Next, their typewriters were confiscated. Thus, it was a protracted process of constriction. Due to fear of criticism and propaganda from abroad, however, the police issued public warnings not to riot against the Jews. The authorities had no interest whatsoever in letting the hostility culminate in a new "Kristallnacht." Their idea was that the pejorative image of the Jew should help to legitimize the National Socialist policy toward Jews and, in fact, National Socialist policies at large.

Included in the second category of decrees, those of exclusion and dispossession, was the instruction to the Jewish communities, promulgated by the national Chief of Police on the very first day of the war, to set up air-raid shelters for the Jewish population at the communities' expense. In the directive, it was stated explicitly that the "German Volksgemeinschaft" could in this manner spare itself the expense of protecting Jews' lives. A year later, however, on October 7, 1940, the Reich Minister of Aviation had to admit that Jews could not be denied the use of the regular shelters. Accordingly, they were assigned special rooms or places behind barriers in general-use rooms. Segregation spread. Jews were allotted special grocery stores; the word *"Jude"* was imprinted in large red letters on their ration cards to emphasize their total disjuncture from the population at large and to control their shopping. Instructions to order Jews in each city to use only one post office and to declare city squares or quarters "no-go zones" had the same intent. To stress the Jews' ostensibly harmful and exploitive nature, a search of homes to detect "hoarding" was announced on September 12, 1939.

The edicts and enactments that served the second goal—using the war as a pretext for intensified dispossession—were not always forwarded to the general German media; neither were they fully advertised in the *Jüdische Nachrichtenblatt*. Just the same, the Jewish newspaper noted on September 5, 1939, on its front page, "In the current situation, it is self-evident that every Jew and Jewess in the German Reich is duty-bound to obey exactingly the regulations that the authorities have established and the instructions of the government authorities and ministries. . . . Unpleasant results will await those who lack the necessary willingness."[12] The threatening tenor, the sharing of responsibility, and the faux legalism were more powerfully manifested now that wartime had arrived.

The disjuncture and isolation had the additional result of forcing Jews increasingly to be concurrently victims and executors of the National Socialist policy toward them. About a month after the war broke out, not only the few Jewish unions that still existed, such as the youth associations, which until then had huddled under the umbrella of a national Reich committee, or the Jews' sports association in Bamberg but also the Jewish winter aid project and the central welfare bureau were merged into the Reichsvereinigung.[13] On January 1, 1941, the Jewish community in Berlin, destined in any case to play a central role because it was the largest Jewish collectivity, represented the Reichsvereinigung as the sole bearer of responsibility for helping the Jewish needy. As these organizational and structural changes progressed, the state and the authorities, and of course municipal councils, dismantled their special Jewish affairs departments if they had not done so before. The Jewish affairs desks at the various government offices were not deactivated; instead, all their expenses and disbursements were foisted on the Reichsvereinigung with absolute cynicism in this organization's capacity as the umbrella association for all Jewish activities and the sole liaison with the RSHA. This was particularly the case in respect to welfare. Step by step, the Reichsvereinigung and the various Jewish communities were made to fund the subsistence of Jewish poor and other relief activities from their own resources. Since 28 percent of German Jews were dependent on such welfare by the beginning of the war, the regulation that established the new purview created an enormous organizational task and caused additional expenses. The state treasury and the municipal chests, in contrast, where the Jews' savings had been kept, profited from this act of looting, of course. That is, the 9,000 Jews who still received welfare benefits from state resources in September 1939 dwindled to only 1,200 in June 1941—and to a mere 250 in all of Germany some three months later![14] On the shoulders of Hannah Karminski, who continued to oversee relief and welfare for the Reichsvereinigung, a mammoth task fell: stretching the steadily contracting Jewish resources to fund the overcrowded seniors' homes, orphanages, and children's homes; support soup kitchens for more than 2,700 needy in Berlin; and provide care and medicines for the many who had fallen ill.[15]

The disconnection and isolation harmed anyone whom the law defined as Jewish. The decrees, however, were particularly harsh for children. Apart from being expelled from German schools and admitted to the Reichsvereinigung education system after "Kristallnacht," their leisure hours were segregated once the war began. Here, too, the rules tightened as time passed. From 1941 onward, Jewish children and youth could not go on outings in the forest during summer vacation, engage in sports publicly, or use public playgrounds. Ultimately, their only potential places to play were graveyards. "In Germany, the cemeteries are not only the elders' final resting places but also the only playgrounds for Jewish children."[16]

In the literature on the lives of German Jews at this time, it is customary to note the major difference between Berlin and the other cities. Roughly half of the Jews in Germany now lived in the capital. Here, despite all the hardships, Jews enjoyed relative albeit limited safety. In November 1940, an acquaintance of Victor Klemperer's said, "1,000 Jews from Dresden are easier to evacuate than 120,000 from Berlin. . . . The whole world, that is the Jewish world, wants to move there. . . . They say there you're 'freer' there."[17] The historian Hermann Simon notes disapprovingly that the literature often reports experiences in provincial towns as having happened in Berlin.[18]

The instruction from the Reich Ministry of Economic Affairs to complete the "Aryanization" process and the liquidation of Jews' businesses by the end of 1940 was impossible to conceal.[19] After all, not only party members and small and large businesses participated in "Aryanization"; so did banks, pawn shops, and no few "little people." Many amassed profits, took a cut, and thus partook in the dispossession of the Jewish population through the intermediation of banks. In February 1940, for example, Dresdner Bank received "a commission in the sum of 50,000 Reichsmarks for its share in cleansing [the Simons and

Prowein company] of Jews."[20] Auctions of Jewish property were advertised in newspapers and grew in number as the onset of the deportations approached. Thus the soccer player Fritz Szepan, the most famous member of the Schalke 04 club and the national team in the 1930s, managed pursuant to the "Aryanization" of the Jewish-owned textile firm Rode and Co. "to profit handsomely from the Jewish owners' distress and use [the earnings] as a springboard to the economic advancement" of the Nazi state's soccer universe, which was kept amateur for ideological reasons (i.e., officially the players were unpaid); thus a way was found to remunerate outstanding players.[21]

It was common knowledge that Jews were allowed to hold closed bank accounts only—that is, they could not access even their personal accounts. Murky and irregular instructions on the topic, however, persisted, such as the one that urged the Mayor of Frankfurt not to pay Jews for property transferred to "Aryan" hands; after all, Jews should be considered enemies. The Mayor, like many others, did not wait for guidelines from the ministry, failing to realize that even in plundering the Jews the foundation of civil order must be maintained.[22] When someone wanted to steal rare or first edition books from Jewish citizens' private libraries, he would issue a search warrant for "the confiscation of cultural assets" in the proper bourgeois manner.

It was in this state of affairs that the few surviving Jewish organizations and communities, foremost the Reichsvereinigung, tried to secure the minimum leeway to alleviate the general distress of the Jewish population or create a buffer zone between the National Socialist authorities and the victims. Accordingly, several years after the war, a person who had not managed to emigrate from Germany in time but had survived Auschwitz could lodge the following accusation:[23] "People took too much of an interest—the efforts of the Jewish organizations also had this as their aim—in lending content and meaning to life under Nazi rule and making it as pleasant as possible, instead of forcing people—perhaps with the Nazis' help—to emigrate."[24]

As I show below, the charge is overstated. Against the backdrop of the aforementioned anti-Jewish measures, a policy that might add a little meaning to life is not incomprehensible. Another psychological mechanism explains the victims' ostensible pessimism: "Again and again I would encounter irrational people such like these, who would fool themselves into thinking that if the next two or three months would pass without any particular anti-Jewish actions, it's a sign that no further deterioration would occur and therefore the current situation should be seen as a base on which one could now slowly build one's future existence." This, in any event, is how a Jew who had managed to reach Switzerland illegally in 1940 described the situation.[25]

To clarify the situation, a counterfactual view of the problem is definitely helpful. We need to ask ourselves what would have happened had the individual and institutional adjustment described above not taken place. Would the radicalization have been arrested or the opposite—worsened? Ex post faulting of the Reichsvereinigung's tactic, similarly adopted by the Jewish leadership, certainly would have given the true criminals of the time, those who were not Jewish, further satisfaction. Such charges have the effect, somewhat, of making people trapped like mice into the scoundrels' collaborators.

Furthermore, the intensive official and public propaganda and judicial use of the topic of "the Jews," even when the presence of live Jews was hardly perceptible, appears to have been deliberately sustained and energized. In any case, the enemy, while less visible than before, was recognized as "threatening." By decision of the Reich Ministry of Science, Education, and Culture on October 20, 1939—shortly after the end of the military campaign in Poland—doctoral students were allowed to cite Jewish authors whom they still encountered in the literature but who were no longer at the university "only when it is unavoidable and for scientific reasons." In bibliographies, Jewish authors had to be listed separately. Since matters no longer pertained to "full Jews" only—that distinction was long gone—universities had to stop admitting "Mischlinge." Even though no official regulation made this necessary at first, university heads often simply did not want to draw fire as "friends of the Jews."[26] Until December 11, 1939, athletic and sports clubs affiliated with the national gymnastics union were allowed to issue more stringent requirements "in the matter of the purity of German blood" than those set forth in the "Nuremberg Laws." Anti-Jewish sensitivities had always been particularly acute in the domains of science and sports. Here and in other fields, exceptional cases or theoretical occupation with the topic now replaced having to deal with real live Jews.

When World War I erupted in the summer of 1914, German Jewry spared no effort to demonstrate its patriotic state of mind. At the end of the war, the Jews were indeed immensely proud of the hundred thousand of their number who had fought for Germany and the twelve thousand who had died for her. In September 1939, of course, Jews were not allowed to head into the battlefield as soldiers. Furthermore, not only was enthusiasm over Germany's triumphs affectively and practically problematic for them; it was even forbidden to them. From 1935 onward, Jews were enjoined against flying the German flag from their homes. The sense of being not only shunned but also considered a fifth column or a population of evaders in wartime was especially bitter for the Jews of Germany. Even the right to donate blood was denied to them by the Minister of the Interior on racist grounds.[27] To spare the Volksgemeinschaft from cognitive dissonance, the Jewish soldiers from World War I were expunged from the collective memory. Thus, when the jubilee of the establishment of the Eintracht Frankfurt soccer club was celebrated in 1939, the three Jewish players who had fallen in World War I were left off the lists of fatalities.[28]

Since Jews were not allowed to serve in the army, it seemed legitimate to mobilize them for "labor activity." Bearing in mind that they would soon be "rid" of the Jews, however, the decision makers did not impose slave labor on all Jews when the guns of World War II first opened fire. Only on February 18, 1941, did Göring issue a secret order for the general mobilization of Jews for collective labor. Two weeks later, the Reich Ministry of Labor instructed that Jews be housed in separate camps to minimize their contact with the non-Jewish population. At this time, 24,500 Jewish men and 16,500 Jewish women in the "Altreich" and "Ostmark" were in "closed labor battalions."[29]

Jews were first put to harvesting, roadbuilding, and other public construction jobs as well as garbage removal and grueling and largely unskilled "dirty work." Afterward, they replaced manufacturing workers who had been sent to the front. They were deprived of ostensibly universal entitlements such as holiday pay, holiday grants, and child benefits, of course. In the first year of the war, steadily growing numbers of Jewish men aged eighteen to fifty-five and Jewish women eighteen to fifty were drafted for slave labor in manufacturing. In November 1940, it was decided to leave only married women homemakers and, of course, Jewish men and women in "mixed marriages" off-limits. The Jewish work week was set at sixty hours. From 1941 onward, Jews paid a special social insurance levy at the rate of 15 percent of their dismayingly skimpy wages. Women were put to men's labor. Jews were barred from showering facilities and canteens. Finally, the conditions that existed de facto became official. Practically speaking, German Jews no longer engaged in licit "labor relations." Even if sundry government offices failed to reach a consensus on an official arrangement backed by regulations before the invasion of the Soviet Union, Jews were lowered to the status of disentitled slaves. From 1941 onward, Jewish forced labor was overseen jointly by the Ministry of Labor and the RSHA.

Even the *hakhsharot*, originally meant to train young Jews in agriculture and crafts, were integrated into the slave-labor system. They had started out as pioneering ventures long before the Nazis seized power, mainly with the participation of Zionists, in order to prepare young Jews for productive labor and, in fact, for emigration to Palestine. After 1933, they did become important instruments of emigration but not only for Zionists. In 1939, the Reichsvereinigung undertook to supervise them, too. To keep this institution alive and spare its agricultural enterprises and its camps from "Aryanization," those attending them were employed as unpaid laborers, mostly in agriculture. Thus, it turns out, the *hakhsharot*, on the one hand, became "useful" as providers of harvest labor and, on the other, secured their continued existence in the institutional sense. The historian Wolf Gruner calls these farming projects and camps at this stage "Reichsvereinigung camps," thereby giving the impression, which ignores the negligible maneuvering room of the Jewish leadership, that the Reichsvereinigung collaborated with the RSHA in exploiting Jewish slave labor.[30] Recha Freier, the living spirit of Youth Aliyah, which organized the emigration of Jewish adolescents from Germany to Palestine, already admitted in 1953 that by 1939 the *hakhsharot* had effectively become labor camps that eventually evolved into slave-labor camps where young Jews wore a red "J" on their backs.[31] In this case, too, the Reichsvereinigung's tactic was plain to see: it wished to save the *hakhsharot* and buy time even if it had to collaborate with the police or other authorities to do so. The fact that the *hakhsharot* ultimately became places of concentration for Jews ahead of their transport to the east is but the outcome of manipulation of the Jewish leadership by state authorities, a common occurrence in the Third Reich. Between March and August 1941, the *hakhsharot* were shut down, as were other Jewish vocational retraining projects. Some two thousand youth and retrainees were now sent to slave labor under even harsher conditions.[32] The Reichsvereinigung managed to stave this off for a while.

Shortly after Operation Barbarossa began, up to fifty-three thousand Jews—roughly one-third of the Jewish population, including women, men, and some under age eighteen and over sixty-five—toiled in "closed labor battalions." By then, four camps for Jewish slave laborers had been established on German soil. The goal was not just to exploit them in rational maximum utilization, so to speak, of a "free" labor force at a time of shortages and distress but also to humiliate the Jewish population and exact "vengeance" against a group that the antisemitic propaganda regularly and traditionally tarred as "indolent." The true intent behind this measure was to recast the respected Jewish lawyer as a dirt laborer.

Amazingly, Jewish emigration from Germany continued even after the war began, although it was downscaled by the state of war, which, of course, ruled out direct and overt departure to "enemy countries." On February 29, 1940, Himmler divulged to the Gauleiters his program for that year: "Emigration of Jews ... to the greatest numerical extent possible ... some six thousand to seven thousand per month . . . to Palestine, South America, and North America." He called this measure "normal emigration."[33] The RSHA, in its instructions concerning the emigration of Jews of April 24, 1940—eight months into the war—recommended "stepping up" emigration from the Reich;[34] the *Jüdische*

Nachrichtenblatt, on March 1, 1940, also described "expedited emigration" as "the task and the goal." The Central Office for Jewish Emigration, headed by Eichmann—who succeeded Kurt Lischka in Berlin in October 1939—even demanded that the Reichsvereinigung furnish him with fifty names of prospective emigrants each day (some 18,000 per year). In actuality, around 25,500 Jews from the Reich (including "Ostmark" and the "Protectorate") emigrated in the first two years of the war. Of them, 16,789 did so with support from the "Relief Organization" (Hilfsverein der Juden in Deutschland), 2,321 left with the help of the Palestine Office, and around 4,000 escaped to Palestine "illegally." Parsed by years, the breakdown is 6,000 in 1939, 13,361 in 1940, and 6,135 in 1941. From the beginning of the war onward, the Jews of Germany plainly knew they were trapped. Panic about forced transfer to Poland, specifically to Lublin, rocked the Jewish population even before the Stettin experiment in February 1940, which I shall discuss below. This fear gave the Jews additional motivation to emigrate, as the RSHA knew well.

At this time, a way was found to intensify the plunder of Jews who were willing to emigrate. In late 1939, the Reichsvereinigung was ordered to turn over a larger emigration levy for 1940 and cancel receipts that had already been issued on account of the collection of this "tax." The levy was charged retroactively to those who had already left the country. By means of "Aryanization," blockage of bank accounts, taxes, and levees, emigration proceeded without financial losses to any government office; it was all done at the expense of the Jewish community and with a clear gain for the Volksgemeinschaft.

The emigration target depended increasingly on the state of the war. On May 31, 1940, the *Jüdische Nachrichtenblatt* still asked itself, "Whither the wanderer?" and answered with a headline on the next page: "Shanghai Offers Opportunities." There, as many as fourteen thousand Jews from the Reich including "Ostmark" had found refuge; Eichmann insisted on this option because Shanghai could be entered without a visa. It was not the Japanese, Germany's ally that since 1937 had been at war with China, but the British of all powers, as well as Jewish relief agencies and the Baghdad Jewish community in Shanghai, who kept this opportunity from being utilized to the limit. Between November 1940 and November 1941—after the emigration embargo that had been imposed in October 1941—5,945 Jews from Germany reached Portugal and 3,930 (including 3,114 from the "Altreich") made their way to Spain (i.e., to neutral countries). By August 1940, 1,457 individuals had emigrated to Palestine, where the British Mandate authorities considered them "illegal immigrants."[35] Behind the "illegal immigration" to Palestine, however, also stood the Gestapo, which found it plainly legal and even welcome. Victor Klemperer, who only at the beginning of the war aligned himself with the Jewish community and who loathed Zionism as much as he despised the National Socialists, sarcastically summarized his impression of the situation by writing that "the Jewish communities in Germany nowadays became strong adherents of Zionism."[36] This, he thought, was explicable in terms of the policy of persecution and was more related to self-respect than to emigration. "Special transports" to Palestine—called "special *hakhsharot*"—already existed in March 1939; in the course of the war, they continued until the middle of 1940.[37] Additional emigrants reached Palestine with assistance from the APALA travel company. To make this possible, representatives of Zionist organizations stayed in touch not only with the Reichsvereinigung but also with the Gestapo. In this situation, selection was inevitable. For the Seventh SH ("Special *Hakhshara*"), for example, organized by the Palestine Office and setting out on August 17, 1940, the Gestapo approved the emigration of five hundred people among the thirty thousand who signed up. Presumably, even more people would have tried to join these special transports had they not feared—for good reason—that the Gestapo would trick them and send them off "to the east." Certainty and confidence about the eventuation of the trip to Palestine did not exist. Given the bitter fate that greeted some of those who took the risk, the skepticism was apt indeed.

Even in this state of emergency, the Reichsvereinigung, under whose umbrella the Hilfsverein (relief organization) and the Palestine Office operated, managed with help from the American Jewish Joint Distribution Committee (the US entered the war against Nazi Germany only in December 1941) to arrange visas, special trains, and ships. The success of emigration, however limited and relatively marginal it was, should be credited to this organization above all. Nevertheless, already by then and a fortiori afterward, the Reichsvereinigung faced grave accusations. On the one hand, as mentioned above, some thought it did not invest enough energy in emigration. On the other hand, it was accused of favoring a discriminatory selection procedure. The most famous denunciation of the Reichsvereinigung and the Palästinaamt (the Jewish Agency's Palestine Office) and, particularly, Paul Eppstein and Leo Baeck, was voiced by Recha Freier. None of them, in Freier's view, had done enough to enable the Polish Jews who had been arrested in Germany at the beginning of the war to emigrate. Freier described the protests of these Jews' wives in synagogues, in the community, and at the Reichsvereinigung as well as the cold shoulder given by Eppstein and Baeck. Only Heinrich Stahl, who had chaired the Berlin community since 1933 and served as acting chair of the Reichsvereinigung from 1939 onward, exerted himself on behalf of the Polish Jews—on account of which, Recha Freier charged, he had been dismissed from his position at the behest of Leo Baeck.[38] Paul Eppstein, however, believed that Freier's attempt to smuggle Jews out of Germany in illegal ways and with forged papers was highly dangerous because it might invite the RSHA to take heavily punitive measures. Instead of freeing these Polish-citizen Jews from detention, Eppstein argued, the police might arrest German Jews in order to enforce the issuance of "certificates" (immigration permits to British Mandate Palestine) or other visas for them. He evidently based this claim on his experience since "Kristallnacht." The result, Recha Freier charged, was that the detained Polish Jews were no longer being released.

Whichever side one believes, the Nazi campaign was steadily backing the Jewish leadership into a cul-de-sac in which no decision within the Jews' ostensible maneuvering room could be free of moral blemish anymore. The question of the alternative arises, especially where the period after the war began is concerned. How could something else, something more just, something more efficient have been done? How could alternative action have been taken, especially in view of the German Jewish tradition in which "German virtues" such as discipline, order, and precision figured so importantly? Klemperer, too, despite his somewhat jaundiced attitude toward the Jewish community, briefly reflected after the beginning of the war that, among the Jewish community staff, "each one of them has certainly already been inside, and each one is hourly in danger of rearrest. Brave people."[39]

Beate Meyer captured the plight of the leadership concisely: overall, she wrote, most representatives and staff of the Reichsvereinigung in Germany stayed behind due to a sense of responsibility and the belief that they were crucial for the institutions they served. They did so even though they had many opportunities to emigrate until February 1941, when the German Security Police forbade it.[40]

The Zionists in Germany had to develop selection strategies. Zionists, adolescents, and craftspeople received preferential treatment even after the war began, particularly in the distribution of "certificates." In such an emergency, one might grant such a strategy moral extenuation on the grounds that, otherwise, emigration to Palestine could not take place at all. The attitude of the Zionist movement toward the situation in Germany at large, however, was problematic, as was the movement's prioritization of Zionist interests over the objective of rescuing German Jews per se. Shortly after the night of the pogrom, at a Jewish Agency meeting in Palestine, Werner Senator, a German Jew, pleaded for action that would allow all German Jews to emigrate. Nahum Goldmann, however—he, too, an émigré from Germany—opposed this vehemently. Such a measure, he said, would inspire additional countries to rid themselves of their Jewish populations by means of anti-Jewish terror.

The Jewish Agency people were aware of the severity of the crisis, of course. Shortly before the war, Eliyahu Dobkin, head of the agency's Immigration Department, proposed to "put the problem of the Jews in the Reich into order" by arranging their total emigration within a year. When the war began, however, the question was how to use the 2,900 certificates that had already been issued to German Jews. Thus, German Jewry was effectively stricken from the roster of prospective immigrants. The proposals for alternative use of these certificates ranged from giving them to Polish Jews to shutting down the Palestine Office in Germany, as would happen in the end. By 1940, Moshe Shertok (Sharett), the future Foreign Minister of Israel, noted with acrid criticism that the German Jews were being dealt out of the immigration picture. Lacking in influence as he was, however, he could do nothing about it. When the refugee vessel *Pacific* dropped anchor off the coast of Palestine in November 1940, it was apparent that the organizations and institutions of the *Yishuv* (the organized Jewish community in Palestine) did not see the rescue of refugees as their highest priority; their interests were always more attuned to the success of the Zionist project in Palestine. Thus, it was rumored by elements in the Yishuv that the immigrants aboard the *Pacific* were a German fifth column.[41] Be that as it may, the RSHA did not prevent emigration to Palestine until the end of April 1941. Only afterward was an instruction issued to close down the Palestine Office and hand responsibility for emigration affairs to the Reichsvereinigung. By the autumn of 1941, when emigration was effectively prohibited, only 165,000 Jews, most of them elderly, remained in the "Altreich." Together with thousands of German Jews who had fled to sundry European countries before and during the war only to be sucked back into National Socialist Germany's sphere of control, they fell prey to the "Final Solution."

Today, every historian knows that the preferred practice of both the police and the authorities, planned for the long run at the very outset of the war, was not the orderly emigration but the deportation, displacement, and "evacuation" of German Jewry.[42] Even before the war, systematic emigration was not fast enough to render Germany *Judenrein*. Once the war began, dashing the possibility of emigration to "enemy countries," this was true a fortiori. Even though the RSHA continued to invest efforts in the emigration of German Jews, on August 15, 1940, nearly a year into the war, it summed up the situation as follows: "In view of the difficulties that are appearing everywhere, it will be complicated in the foreseeable future to bring the Jewish problem to an end by means of emigration, even from the confines of the Reich."[43] Since the temporal and geographic span of the war was unknown and kept changing with the passage of time, the designers of the deportation policy prepared all sorts of alternative scenarios, some based on the experience that had been amassed since the war began in September 1939, to create an emigration that was tantamount to deportation, not only for the Jews of Germany.

The general thrust of the policy was already determined in Heydrich's September 21, 1939, Schnellbrief: deporting the Jews, including those of Germany, eastward into Polish territory.[44] Accordingly, the SD, while stepping up the pace of emigration from the old and new German lands, plunged into concrete planning. In a memorandum of October 11, 1939, one already reads about "the beginning of a comprehensive operation, intended in the first stage for 300,000 indigent Jews from the territories of the great German Reich to Poland"—an action that was to end by the middle of 1940.[45] Brigadeführer Bruno Streckenbach, the chargé for central planning of population policy in the Generalgouvernement, sought an even faster course of action. On November 8, 1939, he ruled that the Jews from the Altreich and the new districts of the Reich must be evacuated and replaced by Volksdeutsche (ethnic Germans) from the "Generalgouvernement," the Baltic countries, Ukraine, and elsewhere. The evacuation from the new "districts" (Gaue) was to wind up before the end of February 1940.[46] This was also the gist of the "Final Solution to the Jewish problem in Germany" in the worldview of the Jewish affairs department of the SD police, as expressed on December 19, 1939.[47] Just the same, it would be an overstatement to present the deportation of all German Jews to the east in the very first year of the war as a "done deal." As usually happens in states of war, there were many detailed contingency plans, some short term and others long term. Since the decision ultimately had to come from the highest echelon and also depended on the course of the war, however, all the schemes were provisional alternatives. What would actually happen depended, as in other matters in the "Third Reich," on proximity to Hitler, the circumstances at any given moment, and personal and institutional rivalries in the ecosystem of the National Socialist state.

In fact, by the time the war began, some five thousand Jews had already been deported from Reich territory to the Nisko area, in the eastern part of occupied Poland, where the conditions they experienced foretold the future of Jewish deportees from Germany. In early November, however, Himmler suspended deportations from the Reich and on December 21, 1939, actually forbade them because, for military reasons and as part of the population resettlement program, a different set of priorities was needed, one topped for the time being not by the Jews of Germany but by the Volksdeutsche.[48] Even in late January 1940, when Heydrich repealed the prohibition on deporting German Jews, this did not lead to immediate and total deportation to the east but only to the expulsion of some 1,100 persons from Stettin and Pomerania to Lublin on February 12, 1940. On February 19, Göring ordered a moratorium on further deportations. The subsequent banishing of 165 Jews from Schneidemühl, on the Polish border, was an exceptional and relatively marginal event amid the partial restoration of the status quo ante. Heydrich refused to admit that a "retreat" had been made from the policy that he had dictated in his Schnellbrief five months earlier: on March 15, 1940, he explained that the deportations had been halted only due to the need to undertake a comprehensive "future examination" of the project of resettling the Jews in the east.[49] Further evidence of the backstage forces that affected the fate of German Jewry was the temporary ban, imposed by Göring on March 24, 1940, on deportations from the Reich to occupied Poland. Göring did this mainly in response to protests from Hans Frank, governor of the Generalgouvernement, who wished to thwart the formation of a Jewish reservation in his fiefdom.

Like the occupation of Poland, the occupation of France in June 1940 led to spot attempts to deport German Jews and to the drafting of much more comprehensive programs. At the initiative of the Ministry of Foreign Affairs, planning began for the "resettlement" of European Jewry in Madagascar within the frame of peace negotiations with newly defeated France. On June 3, 1940, Franz Rademacher, the thirty-four-year-old head of the Foreign Ministry's "Jewish Affairs Department," placed on the minister's table a scheme for the eviction of the Jews of Germany and Western Europe to that African island. A month later, on July 2, 1940, he presented his boss with "a plan for the solution to the Jewish question," in which Madagascar would become a "vast ghetto" for all the deported Jews of Europe. The RSHA, unwilling to leave such an initiative and such responsibility to another office, leaped into action at once. Directly approaching the Minister of Foreign Affairs, Ribbentrop, Heydrich explained that solving the Jewish predicament at large belonged to his purview and that Ribbentrop would have to settle for being co-opted into decisions on the final solution to this problem. In other words, it was none of the business of any Foreign Ministry bureaucrat to initiate and promote such a demarche.

The RSHA moved swiftly. On July 3, 1940, Eichmann explained to representatives of the Reichsvereinigung, Paul Eppstein among them, that a "total solution" was approaching "with the end of the war." France had been trounced, and Britain's defeat seemed to be but a matter of time. True to its way, the RSHA left the Jewish leadership in the dark as to the location of the "colonial preserve" that the Jews would be reaching. Therefore, for lack of choice, the

Reichsvereinigung prepared to cooperate with the authorities in carrying out the deportation plan. However, Leo Baeck, Otto Hirsch, and Paul Eppstein did not settle for obeying the directive; instead, they exploited the rumors about the Madagascar scheme to appeal to the pope through indirect channels. The idea of deporting Jews to Madagascar appears to have been no secret by then, despite attempts by Heydrich and Eichmann to smother it in fog. Even Victor Klemperer, who had no official entrée in matters of Jewish policy, mentioned on July 7, 1940, the possibility of his being sent to Madagascar. The Reichsvereinigung executives, assuming that the regime had ceased to see Lublin as the deportees' destination, feared that the African climate would place European Jews in an "intolerable situation." Accordingly, they sought an alternative. Therefore, in July 1940, Leo Baeck and the Reichsvereinigung officials around him made peace with their inability to oppose the idea of deportation in principle and to do anything practical to thwart it. All that remained for them was to find out how it would take place and where. Reading the relevant minutes of the Reichsvereinigung, one gets the impression that, at this point in time, they still believed they could influence the direction of immigration or deportation and that a silver lining might yet be found in the ominous cloud by channeling the mass emigration to Palestine.[50] Thus, the RSHA carried on, continuing to cultivate among the Reichsvereinigung leadership the delusion of its being able to influence, however slightly, the fate of its flock. By so doing, it repeatedly helped to foster the Reichsvereinigung's willingness to cooperate. Thus, the Madagascar interlude merely emphasizes the need to be cautious in ex post references to the question of Jewish collaboration in the "Final Solution."

By August 1940, it was clear to everyone involved—particularly Hitler himself—that the Madagascar plan could be implemented only "after the war" (i.e., after the surrender of Britain), if ever. France, however, was already occupied, and those who assigned top priority to the deportation of German Jewry realized that the new order in Alsace-Lorraine offered them a way to move forward. Thus, on October 22–23, 1940, some 7,500 Jews were deported from Baden, the Palatinate, and the Saar to the Vichy-ruled south of France. The pressure for this move came from the bottom. The Gauleiter of Saarland-Pfalz, Josef Bürkel, and his counterpart in Baden, Robert Wagner, who were in charge of Germanizing Alsace-Lorraine in any case, decided to take advantage of the "liberation" of the occupied provinces from the Jews to "cleanse" their original governates in the "Altreich." Hitler assented to this in his typical way: Really, why not? Thus, with nameplates around their necks and fifty kilograms of luggage each, the Jews were led out before a crowd of curious onlookers—as the photographed documentation shows—to a staging point ahead of delivery to the Gurs detention camp in southern France. The Reichsvereinigung, which had not received advance notice about the operation, attempted, as it had in February in the case of the Jewish population in Stettin, to persuade the decision makers to amend the order. Since Eppstein was in a concentration camp just then, Otto Hirsch complained vigorously but politely to Walter Jagusch, his Gestapo overseer. The Reichsvereinigung also protested in its own way, by declaring a day of fasting on October 31. Julius Seligsohn, the living spirit behind this pronouncement, was arrested afterward and shipped to the Sachsenhausen concentration camp, where he was murdered in February 1941. Otto Hirsch was sent to Mauthausen in February 1941, where he perished on June 19. Their fate refutes the argument about excessive eagerness on the part of the German Jewish leadership to collaborate and unwillingness to resist.

Here as before, it was not Jewish protest that ultimately terminated the deportation experiment but complaints from the destination—the Vichy regime—and, in turn, the pan-European perspective on the population policy and the prospects of a "total solution to the Jewish question." Again the German Jews allegedly won a reprieve: their stay within the original borders of the Reich would last until shortly after the onset of the second stage of the war, that of Operation Barbarossa in June 1941.

The vacuous slogan "after the war," referenced at the beginning of this chapter, is particularly relevant in this context. One could only speculate about when the war would end. Until then, there existed only intentions, plans—both "short term" and "long term"—and competing speculations. After the victories in the west and the futile operations against Britain, even Goebbels began to take an initiative of his own, although he did not manage to carry it out. What inspired him to resume the attempt to evict the Jews of Berlin was the presence of "this rabble," the Jews, in the crowd that had turned out to cheer the soldiers who had returned flush with victory from France and marched down the Kurfürstendamm. So said Goebbels, the Gauleiter of Berlin, at his daily staff briefing on July 19, 1940. He took that occasion to promise "to transfer to Poland" the Jews of Berlin but only "after the war," a period that would begin eight weeks on at the most. At this opportunity, Hans Hinkel, the Jewish affairs officer at Goebbels's Ministry of Propaganda, reported eviction plans that had been coordinated with the police. This discussion, however, took place more than two weeks after the RSHA had plotted the course to Madagascar—another matter that would have to ensue "after the war" because it entailed Hitler's consent, if not his command, and, no less, help from the RSHA. Therefore, it comes as no surprise that exactly a week later, on July 26, 1940, Goebbels told his diary about Madagascar as the new destination for all of European Jewry.

Just a month and a half after this, at a meeting on September 6, Hinkel repeated the plan to banish the Jews to "the east" after the war and noted that until then five hundred Jews per month would be sent away via southeastern Europe— the same route for which the Zionists of Germany were forced to cooperate with the Gestapo in order to make emigration possible.[51] Here, it seems, is yet another case of German polycracy in its nakedness. The intention of banishing German Jewry sought various unsynchronized avenues of fulfillment, and one institution or ministry could draw up more than one program and speak in more than one language. Leo Baeck and the other Jewish community leaders could know nothing more than what various and contrasting sources in government circles sent in their direction.

Heydrich ostensibly continued to cling to the Madagascar solution and, on October 30, 1940, still spoke in one of his circulars about "future evacuation to [a destination] overseas." After the occupation of Western Europe, however, he was even more perturbed by another question: the danger of a reverse flow of Jews holding German citizenship to Germany's sphere of control.[52] The possibility troubled him because he considered it important to attain the goal of a "Judenrein Germany" and because he assumed that, in the event of a "total solution," it would be easier to lay hands on German Jews abroad than it would be in Germany. Heydrich evidently believed that local populations abroad would make less trouble in the eradication process than would the non-Jewish population in Germany itself.

In December 1940—when the Madagascar scheme still seemed on the table for "after the war"—Hitler was presented with another bottom-up initiative, this time by Baldur von Schirach, Gauleiter of Vienna. Hitler, overlooking the planned "total solution" in Madagascar in his response, promised von Schirach that the Jews of Vienna would be deported to the Generalgouvernement "even while the war is running." Indeed, some five thousand Jews were deported from Vienna between January and March 11, 1941. Examining the implementation of Hitler's promise, or wish, we see clearly that most German Jews, unlike those in occupied Poland, ultimately stayed in waiting mode as long as it remained unclear how the war would evolve, how the "total solution" was supposed to look, and where the Jewish population was supposed to be moved to. Therefore, paradoxically, one may construe the first two years of the war after the fact as a "grace" period for the Jews of Germany. The fear of deportation, however, beset them continually, settling in from the second year of the war onward at the very latest, especially those who did not enjoy the anonymity of the large community of Berlin.[53] Indeed, these "days of grace" for the Jews of Germany apparently ended for good when plans for the offensive against the

Soviet Union brought a new concept of the war, total war, into being. From then on, the throwaway line "after the war" had to relate to a more distant future, after the successful culmination of the war against both Britain and the USSR.

Amid the preparations for that totally new era, the question of German Jewry was of secondary importance from the perpetrators' perspective. A day after the RSHA ordered the Reichsvereinigung to make payment for a possible mass deportation, and three months before the invasion of the USSR, Hitler assured Hans Frank (who by then had managed to slow the deportation of German Jews to the "Generalgouvernement" considerably) that, as part of the campaign against the USSR, "his" territory and not the "Altreich" would be the first to become Judenfrei.[54] At a time like that, with general pressure emanating from every direction and the Reich's political officials making rash decisions, only a historian could put forward a long-term forecast. Thus Wilhelm Grau, head of the Institute for the Study of the Jewish Problem, said upon the inauguration of his institute in Frankfurt on March 26, 1941, "The twentieth century . . . will not see Israel at all at its end [!] because the Jews will have disappeared from Europe by then." In a German city that still had a rump Jewish community of ten thousand souls, the historian, in his lecture on "historical solutions of the Jewish problem," described the alternative of "resettlement" as something other than the last word in the historical process.[55] This solution was consistent with the ideas of his boss, the party ideologue Alfred Rosenberg, who said at the same event, "The Jewish problem in Europe will be solved only when the last of the Jews leaves the European continent."[56] Where the Jews were supposed to go outside of Europe and who would send them there—even Rosenberg, the future Reich Minister for the Eastern Occupied Territories, did not know in March 1941.

Not only the matter of planning was fraught with complications; the topic of publicity was complicated, too. As long as Germany was not in a state of war with the United States, even after the beginning of Operation Barbarossa, foreign-policy considerations played a role in the planning and discussion of the deportation policy. For this very reason, it was forbidden to make public mention of goings-on in February 1940. When the foreign press reported on the transports from Stettin to the "Generalgouvernement," Goebbels instructed the German press to suppress the information.[57] The National Socialist leadership was concerned mainly with how the United States would respond, but in the case of the Jews of Baden it fretted about Vichy's reaction. Indeed, experience shows that it was very hard to keep information from leaking out of the country. Accurate reports about previous deportations appeared abroad in real time. By January 1940, the American Yiddish-language newspaper *Forverts* reported the deportation to the Lublin area, and the *New York Times* covered the deportation of the Jews of Stettin on February 14, 1940, four days after that operation began. On November 22, 1940, the World Jewish Congress in Geneva published a report on conditions in the Gurs camp, where the deportees from Baden had been interned since October.[58] It is no surprise that even after Germany declared war against the United States in December 1941, foreign-policy calculus influenced conduct in the Jewish matter and, above all, the dissemination of information about the Jews' fate.

The question of information about German Jewry had two facets—what Germany wished to report in order to promote its interests and what the American public and American politics were interested in hearing. One should bear in mind that even after the war began in September 1939 and even after the western countries were toppled in June 1940, American journalists and news agencies remained in the Reich and knew and reported—within the restrictions of censorship—what was happening there, including to the Jews. They did so until December 1941, when Germany declared war against the United States. The best-known journalist of them all, the CBS correspondent William Shirer, managed until December 1940 to keep a "Berlin Diary," which was published in America two days before the German invasion of the USSR. In this document, he already testified at the end of the war against Poland in November 1939, on the basis of testimony of an American friend, that "several thousand Jews from the Reich have also been sent to eastern Poland to die."[59] He also knew from a firsthand source about the discrimination against Jews in Berlin in the air-raid shelters. John M. Raleigh, who wrote for the *Saturday Evening Post*, published his book *Behind the Nazi Front* in London in July 1941, in which he reported eyewitness testimony about Warsaw after it was occupied, the mass murders in Bromberg, and the "disappearance" of the Jews of Łódź, which had been annexed to the Reich at the beginning of the war. In addition, even before the onset of transports from Germany in October 1941, Raleigh noted, "The practice of removing Jews from towns throughout Germany and shipping them away to Poland at a few hours' notice has become widespread in the Reich."[60] His account, which includes the loading of deportees onto freight trains, can only be a reference to the deportations to Lublin and the expulsions from Baden and Stettin. The CBS journalist Howard K. Smith, in his book *Last Train from Berlin*, devoted an entire chapter to the Jewish problem and described in minute detail what he had learned about it before the war and, until he finished his stint there, during it. He had also personally witnessed the beginning of the transport of Jews from the autumn of 1941 onward, as I discuss below.[61] Shirer's successor, Harry Flannery, reported on the definitive turning point in the fate of German Jewry that was crossed in the autumn of 1941—the Judenstern (yellow star) stricture and the deportations. Flannery reported a detail that Goebbels wanted him to mention—that the advent of the Judenstern revealed the "surprising and large" number of Jews who remained in Germany. He also gave detailed reportage about the transporting of Jews to the east, including Łódź.[62] The paradox is that Nazi Germany, which used the Jews of the country as hostages in order to influence American policy toward Berlin, probably wished to disseminate this kind of information about German Jewry via American correspondents so that it would reach the American public and help to keep Washington out of the war. If so, the Third Reich was very successful: despite the German atrocities, the United States did stay out of the war for more than two years, intervening even then only after Germany declared war on it (December 11, 1941).

The attempts in Munich, Köln, Hanover, Breslau, and other cities not only to concentrate Jews in "Jew-houses" but to establish Jew-barracks or Jew-camps for them show that the lower political echelons adjusted in the first two years of the war to the idea of deportation and accommodated it more and more. Even before Operation Barbarossa, the Jewish population of Köln and Hanover was given short notice to vacate not only "Aryan" apartments but also "Jewish" ones on the pretext of having to make room for townspeople whose homes had been bombarded by the RAF. By massing them in "Jew-houses"—which Victor Klemperer called "improved ghettos" and which were in effect prisons because even Jewish neighbors were not allowed to visit them in the evenings—the authorities placed them under stronger stigma and control. Large Jewish-owned buildings were particularly prized targets for Nazi looters. Thus, in December 1940, the Governor of Saxony, Martin Mutschmann, gave the Jewish hospital in Leipzig several hours to evacuate. This expropriation was connected with another stigmatizing measure: at the hospital's new premises—a clinic outside of Leipzig—management felt that it had to distinguish Jewish patients and staff from non-Jewish ones by introducing a visual signifier. Now—nine months before the yellow star was introduced throughout Germany—Jewish patients and staff had to wear a white armband embossed with a blue Star of David.[63] One gets the impression that mayors, Gauleiters, and small fry competed with each other over who could first make his purview Judenrein and signaled their intentions up the hierarchy. In the next stage, starting in June 1941, this would prove to be important.

Even under these conditions, however, Jews in the "mousetrap" made fitful attempts to buy a respite. The historian Marion Kaplan reports about teenagers in one of the "Jew-houses" who would occasionally dance to the tunes of records played on an "Aryan" friend's phonograph. Such attempts to distract themselves, however, did not truly counter the continual supervision and harassment of the police and the authorities.[64]

Since the beginning of the war, there had also been talk in German Jewish institutions about the attitude to take toward the "Ostjuden." This was, first of all, due to the goal of arranging the release from concentration camps of Jews who held Polish citizenship; since April 1940, these inmates had not been allowed to emigrate by order of Heydrich. Recha Freier invested efforts on behalf of this group and, as mentioned above, accused the Reichsvereinigung of heartless and typically "anti-Ostjuden" comportment.[65] Second, the occupation of Poland had brought many "Ostjuden" into Reich territory. However, the German Jews hardly made any real contact with the East European Jewish population that had stumbled into the abyss of Third Reich control during the war. Only one group was exceptional in this respect: the German Jews who were deported to Polish territories that had been occupied before the invasion of the Soviet Union.

No matter how often I call the two years from the beginning of the war to the onset of systematic transports to the east a relative "grace period" for German Jewry, it is worth bearing in mind that even then German Jews continued to be murdered in concentration camps or in the few "resettlement" operations mentioned above—although, unlike the new Reich territories and the Generalgouvernement, the "Altreich" saw neither pogroms nor mass murders of Jews. One group in the latter area, however, had already fallen victim to organized murder during this interval: Jewish patients in nursing homes, who were eradicated under Program T4 for the crime of leading "worthless" lives. As early as January 1940, German Jews were gassed to death in Grafeneck. From that summer onward, ill, disabled, and indigent Jews were concentrated in a small number of nursing institutions from which they were sent to three killing facilities: Grafeneck, Brandenburg, and Hadamar. Altogether, four thousand to five thousand Jews were murdered in this manner between January 1940 and February 1941. The "Aryan" welfare institutions at this time were virtually Judenrein. Here, too, murder was accompanied by looting: Jewish relatives and Jewish communities received—long after the ill were murdered—fictitious bills for treatments that the patients had ostensibly received in the "Generalgouvernement." The wards of the only Jewish institution that still existed after December 1939, Bendorf-Sayn, were deported and murdered only in 1942—no longer under Program T4 but in the Operation Reinhardt camps.[66]

The murder of Jewish women also deserves mention in this context. By the beginning of 1942, 1,060 women from Reich territory had reached the

Ravensbrück women's concentration camp. A transport from Ravensbrück set out in March 1941 for Bernburg, where hundreds of Jewish women were murdered in the gas chambers of the "euthanasia" facility, including the Jewish women "political" prisoners Olga Benário Prestes (April 23, 1941) and Käthe Leichter (March 17, 1942). Thus, the first mass murder of German Jews by gas was that of the women from Ravensbrück, on German soil.[67]

In all areas of the "Jewish policy", the question of "Mischlinge" and "miscegenation" ("mixed marriages") arose with greater intensity once the war was on. On the basis of a secret instruction from the Wehrmacht high command shortly before the fighting in the west began, "Mischlinge of the first degree" were discharged from military service and "Mischlinge of the second degree" were allowed to continue serving but not in command positions.[68] On April 8, 1940, some twenty-five thousand "Aryan" soldiers in "miscegenational" marriages were ousted. Among them, however, several dispensations were made: their Jewish wives were treated leniently in that, by order of the RSHA issued on July 1, 1940, they were exempted from curfew and compulsory slave labor in "closed labor battalions."[69] These were by no means the only exceptions. Notwithstanding an order from the Führer on April 20, 1940, "half-Jews" often continued to serve as soldiers; Hitler promised them equal status but obviously only after the final victory,[70] as Bryan Rigg describes in minute detail. Even if Rigg overstates the number of Jews who served in the Wehrmacht, he provides further evidence of the absurdity that the National Socialist racial policy had created by defining Jews as it did.[71] This is said not only about matters directly related to the war. For "Mischlinge of the first degree," the universities had also become a cul-de-sac, no longer allowed to admit them as of October 25, 1940.

The question of "mixed marriages" was especially acute and problematic in matters of housing. "Aryan" women who had "intermarried" had to move to "Jew-houses" along with their Jewish husbands, as in the case of Victor Klemperer and his wife in Dresden in May 1940. They also suffered by having to share their lives with recipients of "Jewish" food rations. This brings another typical plank in the National Socialist policy and the persecution of the Jews into clear focus: discrimination against women. That is, only Jewish women who had "Aryan" husbands enjoyed "protected mixed marriage" status. "Aryan" women with Jewish husbands did not unless they had offspring who were not being raised as Jews.

Wedged between forced emigration and deportation, the state of law ("justice within injustice," in the legal historian Michael Stolleis's coinage) needed new statutory definitions specially designed to neutralize the rights of German Jews. In December 1940, Wilhelm Stuckart, State Secretary at the Interior

Ministry, proposed that German Jews be lowered to the status of "protected subjects" of the German Reich and that this status be nullified upon their emigration, effectively meaning that they should be stripped of what remained of their citizenship. The process that began in this manner ended about a year later, on November 25, 1941, with the promulgation of the Eleventh Regulation to the Reich Citizenship Law. This regulation will be one of the important matters discussed in the next chapter.

A large proportion of Jews living in the areas that the Reich annexed after occupying Poland in 1939 could also be considered German Jews. There is no way of knowing the extent to which these Jews still perceived themselves that year as heirs to a German Jewish legacy, but they definitely had a special relationship with Germany from their own standpoint. Until the end of World War I in 1918–1919, Jews in Danzig and Western Prussia had been German Jews who held German citizenship, and in September 1939 they became, like it or not, "Jews in Germany." This is said in particular about the Jewish population in the new districts of Danzig-Western Prussia and the Warthegau. In an underground report about the deportation of the Jews of Posen and the vicinity (which had belonged to Germany until 1919) about two months after World War II began, it is explicitly noted that the deportation from this area included Jews who considered themselves German even after the annexation to Poland.[72] In accordance with Heydrich's plans, as sketched in his famous Schnellbrief of September 21, 1939, these districts, like the "Altreich," were to be "liberated from Jews . . . to the extent possible" at an early stage of a "final solution," unlike the so-called Generalgouvernement territories, where the Jews were to be concentrated for the purpose of "future measures."[73] In the view of the SD, this was a consistent policy that matched Hitler's intentions: first make the Reich Judenrein; then embark on a "comprehensive solution" to the Jewish problem beyond the old borders.

It was easier to cleanse the Reich by implementing the scheme first in the Polish areas that had been annexed in 1939. Therefore, on December 21, 1939, an action plan for imminent implementation was drafted by the commander of the SD in these territories: the deportation of some six hundred thousand Jews by April 1940 "from the new German areas in the east . . . but under no circumstances Jews from the Altreich."[74] They also set priorities within the limited framework of "cleansing" the Reich: "First, I must attempt to remove the Jews from the eastern provinces, Posen and Western Prussia, Eastern Upper Silesia, and Eastern South Prussia, from these four provinces," said Himmler on February 29, 1940, thereby approving the sequence of implementation that Brigadeführer Streckenbach had set forth at the meeting in Kraków on

November 8, 1939. "Then it will come the turn of the Altreich, and after it the Protectorate."[75] The sequence was determined not because the principals pitied the Jews of the "Altreich" or wished to treat them kindly in any way. The idea was to clear room quickly for more than 360,000 Volksdeutsche who, under Germany's agreements with the Soviet Union and Romania, were to evacuate the Baltic countries, Bessarabia, and Romania. If so, due to the state of war, the "Jew-cleansing" policy no longer centered primarily on the Jews of the "Altreich." For them, dispossession, humiliation, and torment would remain the operative aims. The purview of the Reichsvereinigung, as the central organization of German Jewry, was not extended to the new annexed districts in the east. There, German authorities could deport or plunder the Jewish population directly by using the Judenräte that they had activated.

Thus it is no wonder that the legal status of the Jews in the annexed provinces remained murky until these areas were "liberated of Jews." On October 7, 1939, Himmler was given the additional task of "fortifying the ethnic German character" (*Volkstum*) of the new territories. In a document titled "Thoughts about the Treatment of the Foreign Peoples in the East," dated May 23, 1940—after Goering's order of March 24, 1940, suspending deportations to the "Generalgouvernement"—he wrote on the assumption that the Jews would be migrating en masse to Africa or some other destination and thus would disappear not only from the Reich and Poland but also from all of Europe. Concurrently, however, competing schemes were concocted at the Interior Ministry. In an order from Himmler on September 12, 1940, to establish a "register of German peoples," the Jews in the new Reich provinces were excluded even from the group of "protected foreign subjects."[76] In other words, until 1941 no official and uniform decision was made about the legal status of this Jewish population, which in the Imperial era had definitely belonged, in part, to the collectivity of German Jews.

The deferral of the "solution" did not prevent the adoption of brutal measures in these provinces, sometimes to the point of murdering Jews and Poles. During the conquest of Poland and in the ensuing months, Einsatzgruppen, "self-defense" militias, and even Wehrmacht elements slaughtered thousands of Jews. An example is a German so-called reprisal Aktion on "Bloody Sunday" in Bromberg—a violent spree by Poles against "Volksdeutsche"—that was cynically exploited in Goebbels's propaganda. The 1,600 Jews who had been living in Danzig at the beginning of the war were among the first casualties of this German "reprisal."

Arthur Greiser, Gauleiter of the Wartheland, introduced in his fiefdom a harsh anti-Polish policy and an even harsher policy against the Jews. Jews in this area were required to wear the Judenstern front and back. What matters here is that the first Jews who qualified as Germans by the definition of this study and had to wear this artifact were those in the area that Germany had annexed. And more: the 385,000 Jews on the Warthegau faced sweeping dispossession, slave labor, a ban on cultural and religious activity, and, finally, multiple murders in the first few months of the occupation. By March 1941, some two hundred thousand of these Jews had been banished to the Generalgouvernement, and the rest were crowded into ghettos and labor camps until Operation Barbarossa.[77] It was at this stage that the horrific story of the Łódź ghetto began. Already then, the enclave more closely resembled a concentration camp than it did an urban quarter. The Gauleiter, as well as the police commanders in this area, plainly saw this arrangement as a provisional one ahead of the evacuation (*Aussiedlung*) of the Jews to somewhere else.[78]

Now the paradox of National Socialist rule recurred: the larger the German sphere of control became, the more Jews the German Reich had, countervailing the measures already taken to "distance" Jews from the "Altreich." This discordance was one of the most important stimuli for the quest for "final" or, at least, increasingly radical "solutions."

NOTES

1. Marvin Lowenthal, *The Jews of Germany* (London: Lindsay Drummond, 1939), 443.

2. Victor Klemperer, *I Will Bear Witness: A Diary of the Nazi Years, 1933–1941* (New York: Random House, 1998), 307, 346.

3. Klemperer, *I Will Bear Witness*, 311, entry of September 10, 1939.

4. Ibid.

5. Ibid., entry of December 10, 1940.

6. Ibid., 343, entry of May 31, 1940.

7. Joseph Walk, ed., *Das Sonderrecht für die Juden im NS-Staat. Eine Sammlung der gesetzlichen Maßnahmen und Richtlinien—Inhalt und Bedeutung* (Heidelberg: C. F. Müller Juristischer Verlag, 1981). September 15, 1939: "Secret! Guideline to the German press on justifying the curfew against the Jews," 305.

8. Kulka and Jäckel, *The Jews in the Secret Nazi Reports* (New Haven, CT: Yale University Press, 2010), 478, 476.

9. Cf. Uwe Dietrich Adam, *Judenpolitik im Dritten Reich* (Düsseldorf: Droste, 1972), 260.

10. Klemperer, *I Will Bear Witness*, 349, entry of July 18, 1940.

11. Gerhard Löwenthal, *Ich bin geblieben Erinnerungen* (Munich, Berlin: Herbig, 1987).

12. *Jüdisches Nachrichtenblatt*, September 5, 1939, quoted in Herbert Freeden, *Die jüdische Presse im Dritten Reich* (Frankfurt: Athenäum, 1987), 179.

13. Kulka and Jäckel, *The Jews in the Secret Nazi Reports*, Prime Minister of Upper Franconia and Central Franconia, Report for November 1939, December 7, 1939, 484.

14. Cf. Wolf Gruner, *Öffentliche Wohlfahrt und Judenverfolgung Wechselwirkung lokaler und zentraler Politik im NS-Staat 1933 bis 1942* (Munich: Oldenbourg, 2002), 245, 336.

15. Rivka Elkin, *The Heart Beats On: Continuity and Change in Social Work and Welfare Activities of German Jews under the Nazi Regime, 1933–1945* (Hebrew) (Jerusalem: Yad Vashem, 2004), 226–58.

16. Elisabeth Freund in Monika Richarz, ed., *Jüdisches Leben in Deutschland*, vol. 3: *Selbstzeugnisse zur Sozialgeschichte 1918–1945* (Stuttgart: Deutsche Verlags-Anstalt, 1982), 378; Klemperer, *I Will Bear Witness*, 361, entry of November 7, 1940; 363–64, entry of December 10, 1940.

17. Klemperer, *I Will Bear Witness*, entries of November 7, 1940, 361, and December 1, 1940.

18. Hermann Simon, "Die Berliner Juden unter dem Nationalsozialismus," in Arno Herzig and Ina Lorenz, eds., *Verdrängung und Vernichtung der Juden unter dem Nationalsozialismus* (Hamburg: Hans Christians, 1992), 249ff.

19. See Christoph Kreutzmüller, *Ausverkauf Die vernichtung der jüdischen gewerbetätigkeit in Berlin 1930–1945* (Berlin: Metropol, 2012); Benno Nietzel, "Die vernichtung der wirtschaftlichen Existeny der deutschen Juden 1930–1945—ein Literatur- und Forschungsbericht," *Archiv für Sozialgeschichte* (2009): 561–613.

20. Konrad U. Kwiet, "Nach dem Pogrom: Stufen der Ausgrenzung," in Wolfgang Benz, ed., *Die Juden in Deutschland 1933–1945 Leben unter nationalsozialistischer Herrschaft* (Munich: Beck, 1988), 560.

21. Nils Havemann, *Fußball unterm Hakenkreuz Der DFB zwischen Sport, Politik und Kommerz* (Frankfurt: Campus Verlag, 2005), 222.

22. Walk, *Das Sonderrecht für die Juden*, 305, instruction dated September 16, 1939.

23. In this matter, see Meyer, *A Fatal Balancing Act*.

24. Hans Winterfeldt in Richarz, *Jüdisches Leben in Deutschland*, Bd. 3, 340.

25. Memoirs of Alfred Schwerin, ibid., 356.

26. Klemperer, *I Will Bear Witness*, 352, entry of August 11, 1940.

27. Walk, *Das Sonderrecht für die Juden*, 318.

28. Matthias Thoma, *"Wir waren die Juddebube": Eintracht Frankfurt in der NS-Zeit* (Göttingen: Verlag die Werkstatt, 2007), 141.

29. See Wolf Gruner, *Der Geschlossene Arbeitseinsatz deutscher Juden Zur Zwangsarbeit als Element der Verfolgung 1938–1943* (Berlin: Metropol, 1997), 9–19.

30. Ibid., 48–57.

31. Recha Freier, *Let the Children Come: The Early History of Youth Aliyah* (London: Weidenfeld and Nicolson, 1961), 68.

32. Margaliot and Cochavi, *History of the Holocaust: Germany*, 298, 307.

33. Peter Longerich, *Politik der Vernichtung Eine Gesamtdarstellung der nationalsozialistischen Judenverfolgung* (Munich, Zürich: Piper, 1998), 268.

34. Walk, *Das Sonderrecht für die Juden*, 320.

35. Ruth Zariz, *Flight before the Holocaust: Jewish Emigration from Germany, 1938–1941* (Tel Aviv: Ghetto Fighters' House, 1990), 45.

36. Klemperer, *I Will Bear Witness*, 319, entry of November 21, 1939.

37. Heim et al., *Verfolgung und Ermordung*, 310ff.

38. Freier, *Let the Children Come*, 55–66.

39. Klemperer, *I Will Bear Witness*, 319, entry of November 21, 1939.

40. Meyer, *A Fatal Balancing Act*.

41. Zariz, *Escape before the Holocaust*, 74–88, 135; Kurt Jakob Ball-Kaduri, "The Illegal Alya from Nazi-Germany to Palestine," *Yalkut Moreshet* vol. 8, 1968 (Hebrew), 130–42.

42. Longerich, *Politik der Vernichtung*.

43. Brechtken, "Madagaskar für die Juden," 246.

44. Longerich, *Politik der Vernichtung*, 650.

45. Wolf Gruner, *Zwangsarbeit und Verfolgung Österreichische Juden im NS-Staat 1938–1945* (Innsbruck: Studien-Verlag, 2000), 137ff.

46. Peter Longerich and Dieter Pohl, eds., *Die Ermordung der europäischen Juden Eine umfassende Dokumentation des Holocaust 1941 bis 1945* (Munich: Piper, 1989), Document 7, 54.

47. Longerich, *Politik der Vernichtung*, 265.

48. Wolf Gruner, "Von der Kollektivausweisung zur Deportation der Juden aus Deutschland 1938–1945," in Birthe Kundrus and Beate Meyer, eds., *Die Deportation der Juden aus Deutschland. Pläne–Praxis–Reaktionen 1938–1945* (Göttingen: Wallstein, 2004), 31–35.

49. Ibid., 40.

50. Hildesheimer, *Jüdische Selbstverwaltung*, 191; Meyer, *A Fatal Balancing Act*, 93.

51. Christian T. Barth, *Goebbels und die Juden* (Munich, Vienna, Zurich: Verlag Ferdinand Schöningh, 2003), 179.

52. Longerich and Pohl, *Die Ermordung der europäischen Juden*, 56.

53. Klemperer, *I Will Bear Witness*, entry of November 7, 1940.

54. Götz Aly, *"Final Solution": Nazi Population Policy and the Murder of the European Jews*, trans. Belinda Cooper and Allison Brown (London: Arnold, 1999), 161.

55. Wilhelm Grau, *Die geschichtlichen Lösungsversuche der Judenfrage* (Munich: Heneichen, 1943), 7–15. The article already appeared in the journal *Weltkampf* in 1941.

56. Alfred Rosenberg, *Die Judenfrage als Weltproblem* (Munich: Zentralverlag der NSDAP, 1941), 17.

57. Walk, *Das Sonderrecht für die Juden*, 317, instruction dated February 15, 1940.

58. Alexandra Garbarini, *Jewish Responses to Persecution*, vol. 2, *1938–1940* (Lanham, MD: AltaMira Press in association with the United States Holocaust Memorial Museum, 2011), 319–33.

59. William L Shirer, *Berlin Diary 1934–1941* (New York: Knopf, 1941), 250.

60. John M. Raleigh, *Behind the Nazi Front* (London: Harrap, 1941), 236–37.

61. Howard K. Smith, *Last Train from Berlin* (London: Cresset, 1942), 129–51.

62. Harry W. Flannery, *Assignment to Berlin* (London: The Right Book Club, 1943), 296.

63. Manfred Unger, "Die Juden in Leipzig unter der Herrschaft des Nationalsozialismus" in: Arno Herzig & Ina Lorenz (eds.), Verdrängung und Vernichtung der Juden unter dem Nationalsozialismus (Hamburg: Hans Christians Verlag, 1992), 282.

64. Marion Kaplan, *Der Mut zum Überleben Jüdische Frauen und ihre Familien in Nazideutschland* (Berlin: Aufbau, 2001), 224; cf. Mark Roseman, *A Past in Hiding: Memory and Survival in Nazi Germany* (New York: Metropolitan Books, 2000).

65. Margaliot and Cochavi, *History of the Holocaust: Germany*, 326; cf. Freier, *Let the Children Come*.

66. Elkin, *The Heart Beats On*, 224. Cf. Henry Friedlander, *Der Weg zum NS-Genozid: Von der Euthanasie zur Endlösung* (Berlin: Berlin Verlag, 1997); G. Morsch and B. Perz, eds., *Neue Studien zu nationalsozialistischen Massentötungen durch Giftgas* (Berlin: Metropol, 2011).

67. Rochelle G. Saidel, *The Jewish Women of Ravensbrück Concentration Camp* (Madison: University of Wisconsin Press, 2004); Irith Dublon-Knebel, ed., *A Holocaust Crossroads: Jewish Women and Children in Ravensbrück* (London: Vallentine Mitchell, 2010); Judith Buber-Agassi, *The Jewish Women Prisoners of Ravensbrück: Who Were They?* (Oxford: Oneworld, 2007).

68. Walk, *Das Sonderrecht für die Juden*, 319, order dated April 8, 1940.

69. Meyer, *"Jüdische Mischlinge,"* 31.

70. Cornelia Essner, *Die "Nürnberger Gesetze" oder Die Verwaltung des Rassenwahns 1933–1945* (Paderborn: Schöning, 2002), 202.

71. Bryan Mark Rigg, *Hitler's Jewish Soldiers: The Untold Story of Nazi Racial Laws and Men of Jewish Descent in the German Military* (Lawrence: University Press of Kansas, 2002).

72. Susanne Heim, ed., *Die Verfolgung und Ermordung der Europäischen Juden*, vol. 4 (Poland) (Munich: Oldenbourg, 2011), 162.

73. Longerich, *Politik der Vernichtung*, 253.

74. Ibid., 190.

75. Ibid., 238.

76. Essner, *Die "Nürnberger Gesetze,"* 285–88.

77. For Greiser's Judenpolitik, see Catherine Epstein, *Model Nazi: Arthur Greiser and the Occupation of Western Poland* (Oxford: Oxford University Press, 2010), 180–90; Gerhard Wolf, "National-Socialist Germanization Policy in the Wartheland," *Journal of Genocide Research* 19, no. 2 (June 2017): 214–39.

78. Heim, *Verfolgung und Ermordung*, 337–40.

FOUR

—⚋—

FROM QUARANTINE
TO DEPATRIATION

AFTER A CHAT WITH HITLER on August 19, 1941, against the background of the decision to mark German Jews with the yellow star, Goebbels told his diary, "In the East, the Jews ought to pay the bill." One cannot know whether he was referring to Jews already living in the east or to those who should be shipped there. His next sentence, however, clearly evokes the Jews of Germany: "In Germany, they have already paid part of the bill and in the future will have to pay even more."[1] Even here, what Goebbels meant when he wrote "part" and "more" cannot be known for sure. More humiliation? More dispossession? More deportations? More murders? One thing has become apparent since then: SA methods, "Aktions of individuals," and pogroms were no longer considered legitimate ways of collecting on the bill. "The anti-Jewish incitement is enormous." Klemperer, reacting to the news that had been arriving from the east since Operation Barbarossa began, asked his diary on July 9, 1941, "Is there a pogrom in the offing?" However, the Nazi Party Chief of Staff, Martin Bormann, said explicitly that no Aktion such as that of November 9, 1938, would recur because "it is beneath the movement's dignity" for its members to harass individual Jews.[2] The Gestapo, too, warned on January 22, 1942, two days after the Wannsee Conference, that "according to a Secret Decree of the Reich interior minister, individual actions against Jews must categorically be halted, on order from the Führer." Anyone inciting to this "will be regarded and treated as provocateurs, rebels, and enemies of the state,"[3] no less! In other words, to attain the coveted goal, controlled and "dignified" methods that have already proved effective in ousting Jews from German society ought to be used. The expeditious murder of German Jews should take place somewhere outside

72

the Altreich and not in the form of a pogrom before the eyes of the German "Volksgemeinschaft."

Operation Barbarossa, like the eruption of the war on Poland, triggered a wave of regulations and measures against the 165,000 Jews who remained in the Reich. Beyond the familiar goals of humiliation and dispossession, the directives now centered on plastering the Jews with a mark of Cain, so to speak. First, some, foremost Joseph Goebbels, thought the Jews in Germany should be made to stand out; this would turn them into palpable and vulnerable objects for hatred of the archenemy, world Jewry. Second, the stereotyped image of the Ostjude should be plastered onto the Jews of Germany so that no one should consider "our" Jews to be different from the Ostjuden, whom newsreels and the media at large portray as repugnant bloodsuckers.

On June 22, 1941, it became clear that anti-Jewish regulations could be drafted and enacted in greater detail and with greater cruelty. On June 26, 1941, four days after the invasion of the USSR began, the party Chief of Staff ordered a halt to the distribution of soap and shaving-cream ration cards to Jews.[4] The idea was to force Jewish men to grow unkempt beards, thus conforming to the Ostjude stereotype, and to confirm the myth of the "dirty Jew" by severely compromising cleanliness and bodily hygiene. Ten months later, the effort to dirty the Jews took another step forward: on April 24, 1942, Jews were ordered to surrender electric shavers, unused combs, and hair scissors.[5]

The authorities' introduction of the yellow star was also meant to overcome the discordance between the repulsive Ostjude character and the common perception of the German Jew and make it clear to Germany's non-Jewish population that "its" Jews were in no way different from the Jews in the east, those whom in the first few weeks of the invasion of the USSR were depicted in the German media mainly as mass-murdering Bolshevists.

It had long been clear to Goebbels that "international Jewry" in the Anglo-Saxon countries should be blamed for the bombardment of the cities of Germany. Therefore, the Ministry of the Interior unhesitatingly issued the following order on July 20, 1941: "Jews shall receive no compensation under the Indemnification for War Damage Directive."[6] After all, it was "the Jew" who had bombarded the cities of Germany, and if his relatives' dwellings were struck in the raids, it was but an irony of justice for which, obviously, the German authorities should tender no compensation whatsoever.

Most of the aggressions now introduced are reminiscent of the medieval torture wheel. On July 9, 1941, Victor Klemperer reported "[the] latest Jewish decree: They are not allowed to use the popular Elbe steamers."[7] Effective

September 18, 1941, Jews were barred from certain means of transport even in their places of residence without presenting a special permit from the police when approached by an inspector.[8] In August, Jews were enjoined against smoking. "It seems," Klemperer wrote, "that the sign 'Jews prohibited' really is going to be hung on every shop door."[9] From September 1941 onward, Jews were not allowed to write checks or possess checkbooks. On November 13, 1941, it was ruled that typewriters and adding machines, mimeographs and cameras, bicycles, and binoculars should be confiscated from Jews' personal belongings. From December 12 onward, Jews were banned from public telephone booths; their private telephones had been seized long before. In Magdeburg, in addition to these injunctions, they were no longer allowed to go to the movies.[10]

However, the Jews of Germany were forced to partake in fundraising for soldiers on the eastern front and to contribute fur coats and woolen garments, among other things. Once they were deported to the east, this created the possibility of reencountering their clothing on the persons of their tormentors and murderers. On February 14, 1942, the party bureau decreed that bakeries and confectionaries must not sell cake to Jews and Poles. The next day, Jews were forbidden to have pets. Two days later, they could no longer buy newspapers. A month afterward, the Gestapo in Dresden bruited the idea of not allowing them to buy flowers. On May 15, 1942, Jews in Berlin who still had pets were ordered to surrender them so that they could be put down. Now not only "racially pure" Germans but also German flora and fauna had to steer clear of Jews.[11]

To prevent them from creating scandals by behaving provocatively in public, Jews were placed under curfew from December 24, 1941, to January 1, 1942, and were allowed out only for one hour of shopping on weekdays.[12] To keep this rule in effect in places where almost no "full Jews" remained to oppress, it was turned against "Mischlinge"—as in, for example, a regulation against "supplying foodstuffs to stateless Mischlinge," issued on March 4, 1942, and against "Judaism" in the abstract. Included in this war on Judaism were Hebrew and Aramaic studies at the universities. Community engagements in Jewish culture became unfeasible in September 1941, when the Gestapo dismantled the Jüdischer Kulturbund. Theater shows, which still took place after September 1939 in a small hall in Berlin and, sporadically, in Frankfurt and Hamburg, were terminated shortly after the war on Russia got underway; so were the activities of the only remaining Jewish publishing house.[13] Religious activity such as public worship persisted until October 1941 and even, in a few impromptu cases, until the autumn of 1942. The last Orthodox rabbi in Hamburg, the respected Joseph Carlebach, was deported to Riga on December 6, 1941. It was then at the latest that the underpinnings of Orthodox Jewish life in Germany were torn away.[14]

The imposition of regulations—the typical feature of the Jewish policy since September 1939—and their accompanying inspections and policing escalated in intensity from June 1941 onward. The historian Eric A. Johnson notes that the share of Jews in Gestapo files climbed from 20 percent before September 1939 to 35 percent afterward, even as the proportion of Jews in the population fell to less than 0.5 percent. At this time, the Gestapo and the other law-enforcement authorities abandoned their "reactive" approach, which had been based largely on denunciation and eavesdropping, in favor of active tactics that would make the Jewish people easier to exterminate, as Johnson expresses it. Thus, any breach of the general rules, for example, staying in a shelter meant for "Aryans" only, or—especially from September 1941 on—circulating without the yellow star, was severely punished. Concurrently, persecution of women was "normalized," rising to 40 percent of investigations as against fewer than 15 percent until then.[15]

Of all the instructions that typified the era following the invasion of the USSR, the Judenstern directive stood out. At the early going of July 7, 1941, Himmler decreed that the letter "J" must be emblazoned in red "not only on the first page of the passports of Jews of Germany but also on the first page of the passport cover."[16] Under pressure from Goebbels, who in April had sought to introduce an armband requirement for the Jews of Berlin, Himmler exploited the onset of Operation Barbarossa to place the matter on Martin Bormann's desk on July 3 and to take it up with Hitler on August 18. On August 26, Hitler assented to the introduction of the "Jewish star." Five days earlier, a media campaign primed by Goebbels sought to generate maximum public sympathy for the new measure by stressing the threat of Jewish subversion. On the second anniversary of the outbreak of the war, the "Police Regulation on Marking of Jews" was promulgated, effective September 15, 1941:

> Jews who have reached the age of six are forbidden to go out in public without wearing the Jewish Star.
> The Jewish Star is a six-pointed star, drawn in black lines, made of yellow fabric the size of the palm of one's hand and with the word "*Jude*" superimposed on it in black. It must be visibly displayed on the left side of the chest, firmly sewn to the piece of clothing.

In the same breath, the regulation enjoined the Jews of Germany against "wearing medals, decorations or other insignias."[17] The purpose was not only to warn "Volksgenossen" against "camouflaged Jews" but also to protect them from unpleasant facts such as the presence of an Iron Cross on a Jew's chest—attesting to his valor in World War I—something that might subvert the propagandized image of the Jew. Although some Jews reacted to the directive sarcastically, terming the yellow star "an additional medal," most found the Judenstern a blemish and a disgrace. Many attempted to conceal it as best they could by carrying a handbag, a briefcase, or some other suitable object[18]—as though it were the marked Jews and not the German "Volksgemeinschaft" that should have been embarrassed. As with other edicts, the authorities' intention here was to occupy the Jews endlessly with compliance. For example, they limited the number of yellow stars that each Jew was allotted but required each individual to wear one firmly sewn on his or her chest whenever stepping into the street. This put the Jews to interminable bother, especially since the inferior cloth that was used for the star frayed easily and posed a lengthy challenge to those who had to affix it to different pieces of clothing. What may seem trivial to the outside observer was a distressing chore for the victim of this stunt.[19]

What the Jews speculated about the underlying intention of the new rule may be adduced from an official notice on September 17, 1941, from the Jewish community council of Nuremburg, where Jews were supervised more stringently than in Berlin: "The introduction of an identifying insignia for Jews forces us all to behave much more modestly than before." Accordingly, the councilors recommended that Jews "go into the street as little as possible. . . . Do not stand in front of display windows to look. . . . Definitely refrain . . . from smoking in public! For your own good, wear the least conspicuous clothing possible! . . . In apartments and homes, maintain exemplary silence at any price!"

The concluding instruction in this litany—"Bear in mind that your behavior is now being tested in every detail however slight, even if you think you're not noticed!"[20]—indicates that totalitarianism prevailed in the "Third Reich," at least where the Jewish population was concerned.

"Upheaval and catastrophe for us . . . the worst blow so far, worse than the property assessment"—such was the judgment among Klemperer's circle of friends in Dresden (entries of September 8 and 15, 1941). Klemperer belonged to a group that felt especially aggrieved by the new regulation: Christians who were Jewish only under the National Socialist racial theory, Jews who had undergone baptism, and "three-fourths" or "half" Jews. The yellow star forced the Christian community to confront the question of whether an individual was Christian by faith or by the racial theory criteria. The latter condition would lead to the banishment of "Christian Jews" from the Church. Thus the racist system forced even the most tolerant of Christians to keep wearers of the star at arm's length. The "Aid Office for Christian Jews," established in Berlin by the theologian and pastor Heinrich Grüber and approved by the authorities, was shut down in December 1940 due to the internment of its founder in a concentration camp. Klemperer reports the fear of the Bekennende Kirche (Confessing Church), to which he belonged, "of being called a Jews' church" and facing "a complete prohibition by the Gestapo." It was even suggested to him there that he remit his church dues to the Jewish community.[21] After compelling the churches and the religious functionaries to explain where they stood, the regime settled the matter in its special way, by treating "Christian Jews" exactly as they did Jews by faith—that is, as targets for the "Final Solution."

The Ministry of the Interior not only dictated how and where to affix the Jewish star but also set penalties for transgressors. The Reichsvereinigung was brought into action only on September 8, when the RSHA summoned Drs. Paul Eppstein of Berlin and Josef Löwenherz of Vienna to discuss the distribution of yellow stars. On September 12, the *Jüdische Nachrichtenblatt* published a notice on the topic, and only five days later (but two days after the intended date of effect) were the stars handed out. The badges (nearly a million) were manufactured at the Geitel & Co. flag factory in Berlin, and the Reichsvereinigung paid three pfennig apiece for them, charging private Jews ten pfennig per patch in order to cover distribution expenses. From September 19 on, Jews were not allowed to appear in public without one. In addition to the personal identifying badge, the RSHA dictated the marking of Jews' apartments, decreeing on March 13, 1942, "To prevent camouflage, we instruct Jews to mark their dwellings with a black Jewish star on the entrance door."[22] By then, tens of thousands of Jews had been deported to the east.

In this case, as with any bureaucratic regulation, it was necessary to make room for exceptions. At one of the Security Police bureaus, complaints were expressed about "offending the nation's feelings" because, under Section 3 of the new regulation, "Jews married to Aryans are not required to wear this star." Conversely, the RSHA made a point of applying the regulation, "due to considerations of principle," also to "those connected with Jews." A Jew is a Jew. This aside, the police knew well that a special dispensation for informers would only generate mistrust toward them among their racial compatriots.[23] And a Jew being a Jew, even Jews in prisons had to wear the yellow star.

But since not all "Volksgenossen" vented wrath and hatred against the yellow-badged Jews, as I show in detail in chapter 7, the police felt it their duty to aim sundry instructions at the Volksgemeinschaft. Thus, the following was promulgated about a month after the yellow-star rule went into effect: "Persons of German blood who display a friendly regard for Jews shall be sent for educational reasons to preventive detention and, in grave cases, to a Class I concentration camp for a term of up to three months."[24] An incident in the town of Grenzhof may serve as evidence of the implications of this decision for the Jewish side. A retired jailer was called out for having exchanged words with a sixty-year-old Jew. The "Aryan" was held in detention for eight days; his Jewish interlocutor was deported to Lublin seven weeks after the conversation.[25]

The greatest challenge to the attempt to hermetically quarantine Jews from their non-Jewish surroundings was so-called racial defilement. Even though emigration had seriously depleted German Jewry and reduced potential "racial defilement" commensurably, the police and the judicial system hounded "race defilers" with greater and greater aggression. The opening of some fifteen thousand investigation files on the grounds of "racial defilement" from 1935 onward shows that this was no marginal phenomenon and that "Volksgenossens" knew how to put their denunciative qualities to creative use. Jewish men prosecuted for "racial defilement" were very severely punished. "German" men, too, were penalized "to the full extent of the law" for having shared their beds with the enemy at the time of Germany's existential struggle. The best known "racial defilement" trial, made famous due to the American film *Judgment at Nuremberg*, highlights the sexist aspect of the persecution of Jews and the gravity of the statutory punishment. Leo Katzenberger, a sixty-eight-year-old Jew from Nuremberg, was arrested on March 18, 1941, for "defiling the race" with thirty-one-year-old Irene Seiler. In September of that year, precisely as the yellow star was being introduced, the extremist judge Dr. Oswald Rothaug placed the case on his docket. By now, the crime included transgression of the September 4, 1939, *Volksschädlinge* regulation: "One who violates the law with prior intent while exploiting the irregular circumstances that the state of war has brought ... shall be executed if the healthy sense of the people so demands on account of the especially ignoble crime."

Thus, Rothaug sentenced Katzenberger to death because, according to the indictment, the latter had exploited the blackout for his assignations with Mrs. Seiler. ("The court is convinced with certainty that a sexual factor accounts for the fondling between the two defendants.") This persuasion was based on the neighbors' testimony, to the effect that Katzenberger, a "full Jew," had exploited the distress of his subtenant, "a woman of German blood," to have intimate relations with her. The sentence was handed down on March 13, 1942. This was not the only case of its kind in 1942.[26]

Given the new nature of the war in the east—a war of annihilation—new rules of the game for behavior in the rear, in the German Reich, were decreed, fueling an exceedingly radical "solution" to the "Jewish problem." This is neither disputed, as the measures described above demonstrate, nor astonishing. Another reason for radicalization was the very fact that the campaign in the

Soviet Union had not been progressing with the stirring success that Germany had foreseen, meaning that the trite expression "after the war" now sent a negative message of delay. It was precisely this, however, that many German Jews apparently failed to understand. On August 7, 1941, as the war in the east ground into a temporary impasse, Klemperer reported that "among Jewry there is the greatest optimism everywhere"—as though a German defeat could somehow save the Jews. However, now of all times—between great victories and unexpected downfalls—the regime saw an opportunity to step up its measures, particularly against the Jews of Germany, even beyond the yellow star and up to total deportation.

Historians still debate whether and when Hitler decided to exterminate European Jewry, even though more and more documentation about the circumstances of the accelerating transition from persecution to extermination is coming to light. For our purposes, it is important to examine the key role of German Jewry in this transition and explain why the decision to ship all the Jews of Germany to the east and to death was made in September–October 1941 and not earlier. This question, in my opinion, should be explored within the context of the military situation and the state of morale in Germany after the onset of Operation Barbarossa—an oscillation between euphoria and dysphoria, a manic-depressive state of sorts that influenced both the decision makers at various echelons and the public at large. The war, which had been supposed to end six or seven weeks after it started (i.e., in the first half of August), continued longer than expected, claiming vast numbers of German casualties (more than two hundred thousand dead in the first six weeks of the operation) and, consequently, sweeping away all traditional civilizing inhibitions. If Hitler's War Directive 32a of July 14 still reflects confidence that the army could still be planned for the postwar situation, by July 30, in Directive 34, this assumption is set aside and a dispute over prioritizing the fronts in Russia comes into sight. On July 16, at Hitler's meeting with Rosenberg (who in the meantime had been named Reich Minister for the Occupied Eastern Territories), Keitel, and Göring, the policy for action in the occupied eastern territories was laid down: "control, administer, exploit, annihilate." The excuse was ready-made: as Rosenberg expressed it in his diary (September 1, 1941),[27] Soviet Russia had "shed [its] European [civilized] veneer." From then on, anything was permissible.

By August 4, however, the public's sense that the war was not only unprecedentedly brutal but also unexpectedly lengthy found expression in an SD report titled "Meldungen aus dem Reich." On July 20, Rosenberg advised his diary of something that Hitler himself had told him as the two had taken a stroll in the forest: the Soviet arms buildup had been much better and larger than had been initially assessed. In early August, Foreign Minister Ribbentrop reported in a circular to the German embassies that it would take six to eight more weeks—toward the end of autumn—to wind up the war in Russia. This "new and improved" forecast spread optimism. Turning to his diary on August 19, Goebbels admitted that he and his associates had misapprehended the might of the Soviet Union. And then, in early September, it was conceded in an SD report that a sense of "discontent" had permeated the people and that the ghastly losses were making a stronger impression than were the various announcements about victories and Russian prisoners. The future was increasingly clouded, a scapegoat had to be found, and plans for "after the war" must not be shelved, least of all those concerning the expulsion of the Jews of Germany.

As previously pointed out, preparations for the deportation of German Jewry had begun before June 1941. Jews in all kinds of cities had been ordered to congregate in "Jew-houses" or barracks in the second year of the war. In Köln and Hanover, the process had begun in March 1941. On July 25, 1941, the Chief of Police in Breslau launched a "Jew housing Aktion"—that is, the eviction of the Jews from their homes. Some Jews in Breslau, however, had already been forced to vacate their dwellings in May and June. On September 3–4, 1941, some one thousand Jews in Hanover were given twenty-four to forty-eight hours to move out and congregate in "Jew-houses" as part of "Operation Lauterbacher," named for its prime mover, Gauleiter Hartmann Lauterbacher. The *Washington Post* reported this on September 9, 1941, under the headline "Nazis Round Up Hanover Jews for Eviction" (this was before the United States went to war with Germany) and noted the Gauleiter's excuse for this: an anti-German book titled *Germany Must Perish*, by the American Jew Theodor Kaufman (to be discussed in chapter 7). From the "Jew-houses," the Jews of Hanover were deported to Riga on December 15.

In October 1941, coinciding with Himmler's order to seal the German border against the emigration of German Jews, an administrative directive to vacate Jewish dwellings throughout Germany was issued. In retrospect, the rationale behind this decision seems clear: to deport the Jews from Germany, they had to be concentrated and their homes expropriated. The roundup, however, took place not only at different times and paces in each locality but also for different motives. From April 30, 1939, onward—even before the war—the law concerning the letting of apartments to Jews had caused Jewish residence to become concentrated, as municipal data prove. The party members' avarice was drawn more surely and crudely to Jews' property. What is more, urban planning programs could be implemented at the Jews' expense; the Berlin affair, in which, on the orders of chief architect Albert Speer, owners of land and houses received compensation payments from Jews' resources as part of the redesign of the Reich capital, is an early and especially significant example. In August 1941, even before the decision to deport the German Jews had been made, Speer's office had begun to vacate five thousand Jewish-inhabited apartments on the assumption that the occupants would be sent to the east.[28] As German cities increasingly came under bombardment, alternative dwellings for "Volksgenossen" had to be arranged. Here is an example of how it sounded in the Nazi bureaucratic jargon: "In the course of the war, the [Jew-]house shall be used to accommodate families that lost their shelter due to damage caused by the bombers."[29] In the vernacular, however, the connection was more extreme: in Lübeck, on November 10, 1941, shortly after the deportation of the Jews began, the following was heard: "The housing shortage in [the war areas is] ... catastrophic ... while a number of the Jews still resident here continue to occupy quite good apartments. Thought should be given to [deporting] these unpleasant fellows to the East."[30]

From October 1941 onward, after the Jews had been ordered to mark their homes and the decision to deport them had been made, it seemed a natural corollary to evict them from their dwellings and mass them in "Jew-houses" or designated buildings and barracks. This measure was useful to the Gestapo; it placed the Jews under more efficient control until they could be "gathered," and, all the more, it would streamline the gathering operation itself.

In a sense, concentrating the Jews in "Jew-houses" and marking them with the yellow star alluded to what the Jewish population would face upon reaching the ghettos in the East. The Gestapo raided homes almost every night, inspecting the inhabitants and subjecting them to abuse, humiliation, beatings, and harassment. "There was no reason for these floggings," one of the victims testified after the war.[31] In view of the arbitrary nature of these practices, the frequent use of another method of mistreatment comes as no surprise. At the early going of September 1939, a thirty-year-old man from Duisburg introduced himself to a Jewish girl as a police detective, forced her to accompany him to his apartment, and raped her there. In December 1941, a party member told a girl wearing a yellow star that he was a Gestapo operative, followed her home, and then compelled her to undress in front of him. It is true that both men were prosecuted and sentenced to prison,[32] but the method illustrates the possibilities of harassing Jews that became available at this time. Jews had become totally fair prey; people felt entitled to treat them as they pleased with impunity.

"Jew-houses" were not the only springboards for deportation; camps and barracks for Jewish forced laborers, who had been evolving more and more into slaves since June 1941, acquired the same role. By the outset of the offensive against Russia, the number of Jewish slave laborers had climbed to as many as fifty-three thousand, roughly one-third of the remaining Jewish population of the Reich. At first the forced-labor camps (each housing some five thousand Jews)[33] were used to banish Jews from city centers; the decision to deport them from Germany came later. There was also found a political and economic advantage to having the camps: the longer the war lasted, the more legitimate it appeared to exploit the Jews' economic value as slaves; concentrating them in camps was supposed to make this abuse more efficient. In the middle of 1941, the labor exchanges were tasked with the administrative organization of this forced labor. The costs were borne by the "employers" and firms such as Siemens in Berlin and Zeiss-Ikon Werke in Dresden, which paid the RSHA a certain sum per laborer. The encampment and gradual curfewing of the Jewish slaves served primarily to place the Jews under tighter control and magnify their humiliation. Slave labor in the armaments industry was an utterly cynical act of revenge against the Jews, one that forced them to participate in manufacturing instruments for the military victory that was considered a condition for the "Final Solution." However, the wish to get rid of all of German Jewry surfaced even before Operation Barbarossa, especially in the thinking of Joseph Goebbels. Therefore, Goebbels repeatedly pressed to dispense with Jews in the armaments industry and, instead, to expel them from Berlin and the Reich.

In March 1941, Adolf Hitler himself alluded to the "right" priority between economic utility and a "totally Judenfrei Reich." It happened in a different context, when Franz Seldte, the Reich Minister of Labor, and Arthur Greiser, Reich Governor of the Warthegau, decided to send seventy-three thousand Jews from the Warthegau—that is, those who until 1918 were partly German Jews and now had become so again as inhabitants of the expanded German Reich—to the "Altreich" for slave labor. Hitler ruled out the project because it would increase the Jewish population of the Altreich, contrary to all intentions and goals. With all due obeisance, the Minister of Labor issued on April 7, 1941, an urgent missive canceling the order that he had issued only three weeks earlier.

But the question remained: What should be done with Jews who were employed in "essential war industries" when the transports to the east began? In a meeting on October 23, 1941—shortly after the deportations began—with the participation of a representative of the Wehrmacht supply and armaments office; the Interior Ministry's Jewish affairs expert, Bernhard Lösener; and Adolf Eichmann, it was decided to spare "armament Jews" from deportation. Although Heydrich approved the decision at the Wannsee Conference on January 20, 1942, the Gestapo behaved differently: from the spring of 1942 onward, the posting of German Jews to slave labor, encamped or not, ceased to assure their being allowed to remain in Germany. On September 22, 1942, Hitler made it clear to Fritz Sauckel, the General Plenipotentiary for Labor Deployment, that he favored the termination of Jews' labor in the armaments industry and their deportation to the east.[34] Goebbels greeted this news with satisfaction: "The Führer again expressed his unmitigated resolve to remove the Jews from Berlin no matter what. Even when our economic experts and manufacturers say that they cannot do without what they call the 'excellent Jewish labor,' it makes no impression on him."[35] By January 1943, only some fifty-one thousand Jews remained in Germany; of them, around twenty-one thousand were slave laborers. In February 1943 at the latest, the Jew-purging policy superseded all other considerations when, as part of the "factories operation" (Fabrikaktion), all Jews working in armaments plants in greater Berlin and other cities were "gathered" and deported to the east.[36]

I now return to the decision to deport the Jews of Germany. In early August 1941, Hitler still rejected Heydrich's proposal to start banishing the Jews to the east forthwith. Heydrich then settled on a less grandiose scheme: partial evacuation from the large cities, since there Nazi stalwarts such as Goebbels (Berlin), Kaufmann (Hamburg), and others competed with each other in Jew purging. In September, however, against the military and psychological background described above, compounded by the growing spillover of cruelty from the eastern front into the Reich, came the decision to mark the German Jews and, ultimately, to deport them en masse.

The pretext that turned Hitler toward favoring a radical move was a measure invoked by the Soviet authorities. On August 28, the Soviet government mandated the forced relocation of four hundred thousand Germans from the Volga area for security reasons; it completed the displacement on September 15. In this context, Hitler said over dinner on September 9, "If anyone is justified in carrying out an evacuation—it is us after all, since we have evacuated our own people again and again. Eight hundred thousand people were evacuated from Eastern Prussia alone [because of the Versaille Treaty 1919] . See how softhearted we Germans are: The liberation of our land from 600,000 Jews seems to us an act of extreme brutality, whereas we related without objection to the evacuation of our people as though it were necessary."[37] This remark illustrates the gap between Hitler's stance on the Jewish matter and public opinion—a problem that he had had to bear in mind thus far and had resolved to surmount.

On September 13, Rosenberg's Ministry for the Eastern Occupied Territories issued guidelines for appropriate radio broadcasts in response to the deportation of the Volga Germans: "The Jews in the German-ruled territories will pay tenfold for this crime." A day earlier, Rosenberg told his diary, "If this mass murder takes place, Germany will make the Jews of Central Europe pay for it." Convinced, in his own words, that the exiling of the Volga Germans effectively spelled their murder, Rosenberg's allusion to what the Jews of the Reich would "pay" for it is clear.[38]

By now, Hitler and Rosenberg construed the "Jewish conspiracy" as something very real and actionable. The popular press (e.g., the *Berliner illustrierte Zeitung* on several occasions in August–September) was in any case severely outraged over church desecrations that had come to light during the campaign in the east; thus, they appealed to Christian antisemitic sensitivities. Rosenberg even raged about Moshe Shertok (head of the Jewish Agency Political Department and, as such, the "foreign minister" of the Jewish community in Mandate Palestine) for allegedly having said, at a "conclave of Jews," that the Jews had a special interest in the formation of an alliance among Moscow, London, and Washington. On September 14, Rosenberg told his diary that Hitler had personally recommended that the information on the Jewish question be disseminated among British and French war prisoners, evidently to convince them of the rectitude of his policy on this matter.

Rosenberg did not limit his initiative to threats or guidelines for radio propaganda. He sent Otto Bräutigam, formerly of the Foreign Ministry and now the liaison of the Ministry for the Occupied Eastern Territories with the Wehrmacht, to Hitler in order to convince him of the need for an immediate decision on this "punishment." According to Bräutigam, as evidenced in his diary, he had gone on September 14 to Hitler's headquarters at the Wolfslair but was initially treated unenthusiastically by the officers who were supposed to set up a meeting between him and Hitler. The next day, however, Hitler's adjutant, Colonel Rudolf Schmundt, suddenly told him that Field Marshall Keitel had found the idea worthy of mulling with Hitler but first wished to explore it with the Foreign Ministry. Therefore, Bräutigam turned to Walther Hewel (the Foreign Ministry liaison at Hitler's headquarters), who in Hitler's absence on the same day (!) referred him to Gustav Adolf Steengracht, the Deputy State Secretary of the Foreign Ministry, who reported that Foreign Minister Ribbentrop would take it up with Hitler personally when back in the Wolfslair.[39]

Apparently, then, to spare themselves from international attention as to the nature of the measure in formation, the system put the Foreign Ministry to work. In fact, after meeting with Reich Governor of Hamburg Karl Kaufmann and his ambassador in Paris, Otto Abetz, Hitler met with Foreign Minister Ribbentrop before concluding the round with a talk with Himmler. Thus it was these meetings, on September 16 and 17, *that led to the decision on the Final*

Solution for German Jewry. It was on September 17 that Hitler decreed the deportation to the east of the German Jews, who just then had been marked with the yellow star. The next day, Himmler issued Arthur Greiser, Reich Governor and Gauleiter of the Warthegau, with the following order: "It is the Führer's wish that the Altreich and the Protectorate be cleared of and liberated from Jews, from the west eastward, with all possible celerity. . . . [The Jews must] be transferred, before year's end if possible . . . as a first stage, to . . . the new areas that have been added to the Reich in the east, and afterwards deported farther to the east next spring."[40]

A moot question is whether the penny dropped because Hitler now expected the campaign against Russia to end soon after the great battle at Smolensk on August 8 and the defeat of three Soviet armies on August 16, or whether it was the other way around—because he or his intimates reasoned, given the complicated military situation in the month preceding the decision, that it was pointless to dither until the final triumph—"after the war"—to rid Germany of its Jews. The latter alternative seems more reasonable. According to the *Meldungen aus dem Reich* (no. 218), which tracked the state of public morale, it appeared on September 8, immediately preceding the decision to deport the Jews of Germany, that the war would not be over that winter and that "the end . . . is not in sight." As for Hitler's state of mind on the night of September 17, one may infer it from a comment he made at his conversation over dinner: that even ten years of war were preferable to a peace conference.

To carry out Hitler's wish to empty Germany of its Jews, Himmler intended to begin by deporting sixty thousand from the "Altreich" and the Protectorate to Łódź, in the Warthegau, after receiving from his confidante in that district, Wilhelm Koppe, relevant information about the Łódź ghetto. Greiser's objection to this was characteristic of a material problem that beset "solving the Jewish problem" in the "Altreich" generally. The Reich's overseers in the occupied territories in the east—the Warthegau, the Generalgouvernement, the Baltic countries, and Belarus—were loath to turn their territories into reception camps for Jewish deportees from Germany because they were attempting at this time to deport and murder "their own" Jews and make their provinces Judenrein. After all, Greiser saw it as his principal task to "Germanize" the area under his control and had been toiling diligently and cruelly toward this end for the two years since the annexation of the Warthegau. Hitler's order, however, was unimpeachable; Greiser could engage only in containing the damage. Thus, the planned number of deportees fell to twenty-five thousand, and, in his ensuing discussions with Himmler, Greiser reached an agreement about the need to liquidate tens of thousands of Jews in the Warthegau who were unfit for labor.[41] Thus a connection between deportation and systematic extermination took shape.

The deportations began in October 1941. On the first of that month, specifically on Yom Kippur, representatives of the Berlin Jewish community—Moritz Henschel, Philip Kotzover, and Martha Mosse—received notice about the impending transport, which was to be coordinated with the planned evacuation of "Jew-houses." Now, even more than in mid-September, when the decision was made, "after the war" seemed nigh. After Hitler's speech on October 4, upon the inauguration of "winter aid," it was felt that Moscow would soon fall. At a press conference on October 9, Otto Dietrich, the propaganda chief, insinuated that the Soviet Union had indeed been militarily obliterated—an announcement that is considered one of the greatest blunders the Nazi propaganda system ever made. These events generated "excessive optimism" in the ensuing days, as the author of a report several days later pointed out.[42] It was against this manic-depressive German background that the trains with their deportee cargoes began to roll eastward, and it was then that Himmler forbade Jewish emigration from the Reich henceforth.

The first train left Vienna for Łódź on October 15, 1941. On October 16, two trains, from Prague and Luxemburg, followed. The first train from Platform 17 of Grunewald Station in Berlin, carrying one thousand Jews destined to Łódź, set out on October 18. By November 1, additional transports in the so-called first wave had hauled more than twenty thousand Jews out of the "Altreich," Ostmark, and the Protectorate.

The destinations of the "second wave" of deportations were the ghettos of Riga, Latvia, and Minsk, Belarus. On October 10, Heydrich presented his own program, by which fifty thousand Jews from the Reich were to reach each of these cities the very next week. The Reichskommissar Baltenland (Reich Commissar for the Baltic countries), Hinrich Lohse, and Alfred Rosenberg, Minister for the Eastern Occupied Territories, chafed at these measures for the same reason that prompted the Governor of the Generalgouvernement, Hans Frank, and his counterpart in the Warthegau, Greiser, to feel the same way even though they had to defer to Hitler's will. On October 24, after a ten-day postponement, the chief of the Order Police fired the opening shot: "Between November 1 and November 4, 1941 . . . 50,000 Jews shall be deported to the east, to the vicinity of Riga and Minsk . . . in Reichsbahn freight cars, 1,000 persons per transport. The freight trains shall depart from Berlin, Hamburg, Hanover, Dortmund, Münser, Düsseldorf, Köln, Frankfurt am Main, Kassel, Stuttgart, Nuremberg, Munich, Vienna, Breslau, Prague, and Brno."[43]

In October, when Reich Commissar Lohse protested the mass executions by firing squad—lamenting the loss of a valuable labor force—he received instructions about how the system was supposed to work: the local Jews should be murdered and their dwellings confiscated for Jews from the Reich, who, after a short spell, should also be shipped to death. As I explain below, this had nothing to do with a "preference" for German Jews; it was a tactic meant to sustain the impression in the Altreich that authentic resettlement was taking place, thwarting manifestations of resistance among the Jewish candidates for evacuation and their "Aryan" relatives and preventing hard feelings among other Germans.

On October 25, 1941, Rosenberg's ministry issued the following "soothing" instruction: camps would be built in Minsk, to which, if necessary, Jews from the Altreich could be sent as well. "In these very days, Jews are being evacuated from the Altreich . . . and are to reach Litzmannstadt [the German name for Łódź] whence they shall be sent, insofar as they are able-bodied, to labor camps." Jews unfit for labor, the letter continued, "shall be liquidated using Brack's auxiliary device"[44]—meaning they would be murdered in gas chambers and gas vans, as disabled and mentally ill persons were being murdered under Viktor Brack's "euthanasia" program. Thus, a direct association with murder by gas came about at this very initial stage of the deportation of the German Jews.

No one can see the murder of German Jewry and other Jews in Europe as anything but the consistent outcome of a steadily radicalized intention of getting "rid" of the Jews, in which the possibilities of implementation became more and more real. In no manner, however, may one speak here about a systematic phased plan. The vacillations among the "Third Reich" leadership in the autumn of 1941 concerning "solving the Jewish question" were associated with Hitler's decision-making process, vagueness about exactly when the oft-announced "after the war" period would begin, and power struggles among National Socialist leaders as Rosenberg, Himmler, Kube, Lohse, Greiser, the Einsatzgruppen, and many others wished to play first violin. Thus matters snowballed, among other things, to the first executions by gunfire of Jews from the Reich, without systematic advanced planning. Since coordination between the *transportmeisters* in Germany and the competent authorities in the east was inadequate, the bloodthirsty Einsatzgruppen swiftly "settled" matters their own way. From their standpoint, there was no difference whatsoever between Jews from the Reich and those from Poland. Those at the top of the murder pyramid, Himmler and Heydrich, had attended Hitler's dinner talk on October 25, 1941, only ten days after the transports to the east began and three months after mass murder in the east commenced, and had heard him say, "So they shouldn't tell me: we can't send them to the marshes! And who's looking out for our own people? It's good if we sow fear ahead of us until we wipe out Judaism. The attempt to establish a Jewish state [possibly in reference to Lublin, Madagascar, or Palestine] will lead to failure." A tenor of apologia crept into his rhetoric: "Even facing the Jews I long had to remain inactive," but not forever. With utterances as sweeping as these, the Jews of Germany also had no chance. Hitler's uninhibitedly antisemitic eruption ten days later, again over dinner ("We can live without the Jews but they can't live without us") shows that his practical murderous intent had ceased to be a momentary flicker of passion by this stage of the war.[45]

The first five transports from the Reich—departing from Berlin, Frankfurt, Munich, Vienna, and Breslau—that were originally destined to Riga were diverted to Kaunas (November 17–25, 1941). The large share of Lithuanian Jews who had been living in the sealed "large ghetto" of that city since August were murdered by gunfire at Fort IX on October 25 and October 29, 1941. All the German Jews who reached Kaunas on November 21–28, 1941, were not taken to the ghetto at all; instead, they were delivered straight to Fort IX and murdered. Among them were three hundred children and Willy Cohn, whose diary I quote at some length. The force behind these executions was Friedrich Jeckeln, "Higher SS and Police Leader in the Northern Russia and Ostland Sphere."

Those sent out in the first transport that reached Riga, having left Berlin on November 27, were also murdered shortly after their arrival, on November 30 at dawn, at the initiative of the local Einsatzkommandos. Their death preceded that of the Jews of Latvia, whose turn came later that day—the Bloody Sunday of Riga—evidently because "room" for them had not yet been prepared. Himmler reprimanded those responsible for this operation for having ignored the rules that he had laid down: not to kill Jews from the Reich "immediately" but to intern them first. These rules, of course, had been established not for humanitarian reasons but for tactical ones, lest disquiet erupt in the rear and among the remaining German Jews in the Reich. Indeed, on December 19, Himmler's hypothesis about the "tender" sentiments of the Volksgemeinschaft in the Reich found confirmation. Himmler met with the Jewish affairs expert at the Ministry of the Interior, Bernhard Lösener, who had heard from an eyewitness about the mass execution in Riga and was horrified. Thus, either way, the first organized mass murder of German Jews occurred in Kaunas and Riga in late November 1941[46]—making these Jews, too, victims of systematic execution shortly after the onset of the deportations.

The "second wave" of transports from the Reich to Riga continued to roll. In all, it delivered some thirty thousand German Jews to the Baltic lands, "compensating" in a sense for the Baltic ethnic Germans who had been evacuated to the German Reich under the Ribbentrop-Molotov pact.

Approximately eighteen thousand people reached Minsk in the transports; initially they were housed in the "large ghetto" and then were murdered in the adjacent forests. The trains were supposed to make their way to Minsk between November 8, 1941, and January 20, 1942, with a moratorium between Christmas and New Year's Day. Some nineteen thousand Jews from Belarus were murdered before the German Jews arrived. Ultimately, however, "only" around seven thousand Jews from the Reich—from Hamburg, Bremen, Berlin, Düsseldorf, Frankfurt, Vienna, and Brno—reached Minsk by the end of 1941 and received housing in the so-called Hamburg ghetto.[47] One of the main reasons for this paucity of deportees was the campaign against Moscow, which forced the Reichsbahn to make room for Wehrmacht soldiers on its eastbound trains. Many Jews were murdered near Minsk on arrival. Wilhelm Kube, the Generalkommissar (head of the German civil administration) in Belarus, initially took exception to the murder of German Jews.[48] Products of "our culture," he reasoned, should not be compared to "the bestial rural herds" of the Ostjuden. This aside, Kube was born in 1887 and was raised and educated in the Kaiser's Reich. Thus, even though he was a radical antisemite, it upset him to find veterans of World War I and people "with Aryan blood" among the German Jews who had been deported to his sphere of control. At day's end, however, these circumstances served him as nothing more than justification for a measure of "essential" humanness; they did not give him sufficient reason to refrain from murdering these German Jewish deportees.[49] By February 1942, the murder of the German Jews who were living in the Minsk ghetto, along with others, had begun. Although these Jews were overlooked in the massacres of March 2–3, 3,500 of their number were murdered in July with Kube's consent and 2,600 others met this fate in March and September 1943.[50] From July 1942 to after January 1943, transports from the Reich that were destined for Minsk and Belarus no longer reached the ghetto. Some twenty thousand German Jews were murdered upon arrival. Of the more than thirty-five thousand German Jews who were "evacuated" to Minsk by October 1942, only ten survived to witness the liberation of the city by Red Army forces.

Another destination of resettlement was in the Protectorate of Bohemia and Moravia and, therefore, officially in Reich territory: Theresienstadt. On October 10, 1941, Heydrich, Chief of the RSHA and Acting Reich Protector of Bohemia and Moravia, advised representatives of the Jewish communities that a temporary holding camp would come into being in Theresienstadt. By May, some thirty thousand Jews from the Protectorate had been sent there. On October 23, however, Eichmann proposed to turn Thesienstadt also into a Ghetto for the elderly. At the Wannsee Conference on January 20, 1942, Theresienstadt was already mentioned as a ghetto for German Jews aged sixty-five and over.

In late May 1942, Eichmann advised the Reichsvereinigung of an impending evacuation to Theresienstadt, and on June 19, 1942, the Gestapo explained to the heads of the Berlin Jewish community exactly who should be sent there: Jews or frail individuals aged sixty-five or over, disabled war veterans, and people considered "Jewish by upbringing" (*Geltungsjude*) even if they were Mischlinge.[51] Here again, the main purpose was to mislead: Theresienstadt was presented as a solution in order to dissuade the deportees or their relatives from asking how even children and the elderly were being deported for resettlement and strenuous labor in the ghettos of the east.

Again the Third Reich's mechanism of dispossession sprang into efficient action. German Jews designated for resettlement in Theresienstadt were compelled to execute "homebuying contracts" with the Reichsvereinigung. These documents, by directive of the RSHA on August 28, 1942, were phrased identically throughout the Reich: against their savings, these Jews were to receive a dwelling for life in so-called shared neighborhoods in their new place of residence. Since Theresienstadt was in Reich territory, title to the Jews' property would not be transferred to the Reich automatically in the event of resettlement. This made the deal look reasonable even in the eyes of those designated for "resettlement." In reality, it was robbery in broad daylight. The Jews were ordered to deposit their wealth in a special Reichsvereinigung bank account, effectively turning it over to the Jewish affairs department of the RSHA (thus outwitting the state treasury, too), and to forfeit their entitlement to pensions and similar forms of social security. When they reached Theresienstadt, of course, no dwelling was waiting for them other than housing worthy of a concentration camp. The term "change of place of residence" that appeared in the contracts was a mere euphemism.

Summing up the first two "waves" of deportation, one gets the following picture: twenty transports were sent to Łódź between October 15 and November 3, 1941; seven to Minsk on November 8–28, 1941; five to Kaunas on November 17–25; and ten to Riga between November 27 and December 15, 1941. Between January 9 and February 21, 1942, ten additional transports set out for Riga. Thus, more than fifty thousand Jews in all—most from Vienna and Berlin[52]— were exiled. In the next chapter, I ask how the German Jews who were not murdered upon arrival in the east went about their lives in the ghettos in the east to which they were sent.

By April 1942, only 121,500 Jews—*Rassejuden* ("Jews by race") in the language of the German authorities—remained in Germany. That month, a group of German Jews was gassed to death within the confines of the Reich: Jewish prisoners in the Neuengamme concentration camp near Hamburg, who were sent to Bernburg, a "euthanasia" institution that was equipped with gas chambers.[53] The next "wave" of deportations, launched in July 1942, was essentially destined straight to Auschwitz or Theresienstadt. By January 1943, only around 51,000 Jews remained in Germany.[54] When the deportations began, some 165,000 had been there, including 70,000 in Berlin. Eighteen months later, on March 31, 1943, the count was down to 31,907, inclusive of 18,515 in the Reich capital. On June 20, 1943, when the Reichsvereinigung and the Berlin Jewish community were dissolved and the city was declared "Judenfrei," only some 15,000 Jews remained there. In October 1941, members of the aging Jewish community could still avail themselves of 231 welfare institutions, old-age homes, public kitchens, and the like. Some 60 percent of the Reichsvereinigung's total budget went for welfare. Growing numbers of elderly had to crowd into fewer and fewer old-age homes that were sustained by steadily shrinking staffs. A special problem in administering the Jewish welfare system was how to maintain hygiene in all these institutions. In addition, Conrad Cohn, Director of Welfare for the Reichsvereinigung, was arrested in March 1942 for sloppy reportage of old caches of soap and was replaced by Dr. Paul Eppstein—another example of the narrow line that the "dying" Jewish community had to walk.

As the welfare recipients were gradually deported, the buildings that housed the old-age homes, the children's residences, the shelters for the disabled, and the Jewish societies fell into the clutches of the rivaling Nazi authorities—the state welfare system, the Hitlerjugend, municipal councils, tax authorities, the Lebensborn ("Fount of Life") program for German women (as in the case of the Jewish hospital in Munich), and, foremost, the RSHA. The plundering of German Jewry knew no limits.[55] Competition between the RSHA and the SS, and at times the Wehrmacht as well, on the one hand, and the civilian tax and other authorities, on the other, was effectively resolved in favor of the former.[56] The looters' immense distrust among each other often came to light. When the Jews of Erfurt were deported in the spring of 1942 and their apartments became "vacant," for example, the mayor—evidently not without reason—believed that "the Gestapo desired to finally take control of these apartments for the needs of its followers, or to assign them as the Gestapo desired to privileged parties of their preference." He approached the Ministry of the Interior; this made the municipal police take these "rather strong complaints" seriously.[57]

From the onset of the deportations, the question of the role of the Reichsvereinigung and the Jewish communities as "collaborators" in the "Final Solution"

process surfaces with growing intensity. H. G. Adler assumes as a point of departure that the Reichsvereinigung was a tool in the Gestapo's hands and even
accuses the association's statistics department of diligently gathering the data
that were needed for the deportation, thus helping the RSHA to organize it.[58]
Esriel Hildesheimer, in contrast, states with emphasis that the documents—
questionnaires with exact personal particulars and details of property and
dwellings—were always filled out at the behest of the authorities, which in any
case could rely on their own statistical data for their needs. One does get the
impression that the authorities repeatedly instructed the Reichsvereinigung
and the communities to prepare lists either to harass them or due to indo-
lence. Instead of processing the data that they possessed in their own files, they
insisted that the frightened Jews bring the information up to date by themselves. It stands to reason that even without the Reichsvereinigung's statistics
department, the deportations would have proceeded with no efficiency lost.[59]
One should, however, bear in mind a remark by Beate Meyer: "The Reichsvereinigung's efforts to investigate Jews who went underground or disappeared,
in order to produce a 'new Jew-catalogue' for the Gestapo, seem highly problematic after the fact."[60] These investigations, however, did not take place until
the second half of 1943, when all that remained of the Reichsvereinigung was
a Gestapo-appointed rump that went by the name of the "New Reichsvereinigung," a body headquartered at the Jewish hospital in Berlin that engaged,
practically speaking, only in obliterating the last vestiges of Jewish affairs, a
matter to which I will return in chapter 6.

Even more complex is the question of the involvement of Reichsvereinigung
and community officials in compiling deportation rosters and their role in "delivering" Jews to the staging points. In this matter, despite Raul Hilberg's pun-
gent remarks,[61] Esriel Hildesheimer found no allusion in the existing minutes of
the Reichsvereinigung—apart from one case in late 1942—to any participation
in preparing deportations. Martha Mosse attended the meeting of the Berlin
Jewish community leaders, Kotzover and Henschel, with the Gestapo on October 1, 1941—the meeting where they were advised of the decision to deport the
Jews—and described the Gestapo's directives, although her credibility is dubious: "The Jewish community should ensure that the participants in the transport
be well dressed; it should see to adequate food and equipment in the railroad
cars that the Gestapo will provide." Namely, the Jewish community had not
been tasked with carrying out the selection. "Despite the many reservations,"
she continues, "it was decided nevertheless to play a role in the resettlement—
at the request of the Gestapo—in the hope of being able to improve the participants' conditions to the extent possible."[62] After the fact, one may of course

dispute the logic of helping to improve the conditions of people who were doomed to death when it was clearly known that this would be their fate. It should be borne in mind, however, that death at the end of the road was not a foregone conclusion; the cynical Nazis went to unlimited lengths to confuse the matter. In some cases, however, the community did more than alleviate the conditions of the deportation. In Würzburg, the community also had to draw up the deportation list. Sixty years after the events, Charlotte Knobloch, subsequently leader of the Jews of Germany in the Federal Republic, remembered that deportation notices were always served by the head of the Jewish community administration in Munich, Theodor Koronchik. "Even though he did only what the Nazis forced him to do, I consider him the embodiment of evil because I had heard that it was he who had prepared the deportation lists."[63] Thus these individuals became hostages, willing or not, of the agents of malfeasance.

Obviously, it was the Gestapo that ensured that community leaders would personally advise victims of their impending deportation: "By order of the Gestapo, we had to inform them that they and their children were designated for participation in a transport to the east."[64] It was also the Gestapo that had ordered the formation in Berlin and Munich of a department of Jewish order-keepers for the transports. And it was the Gestapo that prepared the lists. Camille Neumann, in her memoir about her time in hiding and her rescue, expressed it thus: "The Jewish community was just a department of the Gestapo."[65] Jacob Jacobson, Director of the General Archive of German Jewry, described the situation of the German Jewish leadership more empathetically: a "mousetrap." Jacobson, who himself had taken part in "delivering" Jews to a transport, asked himself—albeit long afterward—whether the Reichsvereinigung should have refused to help implement deportation orders. Even in retrospect, however, he could not answer with certainty. That is, he did not know whether the "Final Solution" would have claimed fewer Jewish victims had the Jewish leadership collaborated less. The collaboration allegation is a familiar and controversial one, raised by Raul Hilberg and Hannah Arendt in their postwar writings. Arguing from his personal vantage point, Jacobson claimed that the Jews whom he had "delivered" to the transfer were appreciative that he, and not the SS, was with them as they packed their belongings and had their last meal at home.[66] Control of the staging point—or local transit camps—and the process shortly before the train was boarded, however, belonged entirely to the SS and representatives of the tax authorities. In these camps, there were extreme conditions that depended solely on the camp commander, as the example of the holding camp at 26 Große Hamburger Straße in Berlin attests. In late 1942, Alois Brunner, no less, was brought in from Vienna to run this camp with greater cruelty than were applying the Gestapo people of Berlin, who were replaced due to their involvement in corruption as the transports were being organized.

At the collection points or camps from which deportees set out to the east with up to fifty kilograms of luggage and one hundred Reichsmarks per person, meticulous inspections were performed and woe to anyone found in possession of a fork or knife instead of the lonely spoon that they were allowed, or who had rolled up more than one blanket (maximum seventy centimeters long and thirty centimeters in diameter) among their belongings. Afterward, securities and cash were collected and the sixty-Reichsmark transport fare was stolen. A body search was conducted to make sure no valuables of any kind were concealed and to further humiliate the passengers. Finally, work permits, ration cards, and other documents were confiscated and passports were rubber-stamped with the word "Evacuee."[67] Volksgenossen ran the whole procedure; representatives of the Jewish community were allowed to take care only of supplies, slices of bread, and helping the infirm to board the train. An integral part of the method was the exploitation of the inspections by those who conducted them—Gestapo men and members of the Bund Deutscher Mädel ("League of German Girls")—for personal gain. To answer succinctly the question of Jewish community leaders' contributory responsibility, it is worth resorting to a summary by Beate Meyer, whose book about this affair gives the latest authoritative word: the Jewish functionaries, Meyer writes, tried to slow the dynamic of the Jewish policy by invoking Prussian bureaucratic practices, placing arrangements or concessions in writing, upholding transparency, and adhering to working procedures. Ultimately, the path led most of them to Theresienstadt and afterward to death.[68] This conclusion, a far cry from that of Hilberg and Arendt, does justice to the special plight of the Jewish leadership in Germany of the deportation era.

Further on the role of the Jewish leadership, it is best to notice that even if the leadership of the Reichsvereinigung and its successor, the New Reichsvereinigung, was exclusively male, at least four women held responsibility under the Reichsvereinigung for important matters that pertained to most of the Jews in the Reich (which by then had a significant female majority in any case). It was yet another absurdity of the time that, in this state of affairs, the emancipation of the Jewish woman found meaningful expression in the community's rearguard struggle.

Cora Berliner (b. 1890), a doctor of economics and from 1919 onward an economist at the Ministry of Economic Affairs, and from 1930 a professor at the Technical College (Berufspädagogisches Institut) in Berlin, was dismissed on April 7, 1933, under the "Restoration of the Professional Civil Service Law." From then on, she oversaw the most overburdened section of the Reichsvertretung der Deutschen Juden, the Emigration and Welfare Department. She was considered a member of the Reichsvertretung board, although she held no official appointment to that panel. In 1938 and even in 1941, she could have exploited an invitation from her brother to emigrate to the United States but made a point of remaining in Germany for reasons of loyalty to her mission. On June 22, 1942, she was sent to the Mali Trostinec extermination camp near Minsk.

Paula Fürst (b. 1894), a teacher by profession, had been in charge of the Reichsvereinigung Education Department since 1939, a time when Jewish education verged on a mission impossible. On June 22, 1942, she was sent to Auschwitz. Hannah Karminski (b. 1897) had run the Reichsvereinigung Welfare and Emigration Counseling Department since "Kristallnacht." Previously she had been a social worker and an activist in the Jewish Women's League (Jüdischer Frauenbund), under the influence of Bertha Pappenheim, editor of the *Frauenbund* newspaper from 1925 to 1938. Karminski, too, refused to emigrate or escape and on December 9, 1942, was sent to Auschwitz (about half a year after her partner, Paula Fürst) as a hostage for functionaries who had managed to go underground and was murdered on June 11, 1943.

One who survived the war after being sent to Theresienstadt was Martha Mosse (b. 1884), a PhD who in 1933 was dismissed from a high-ranking post with the Berlin police for being Jewish. Representing the Reichsvertretung and later the Reichsvereinigung, she was in charge of housing the Jews, a duty that made her central in managing transports within limits that the Gestapo had set for the Reichsvereinigung. She was sent to Theresienstadt only when it came time to liquidate the community, in June 1943, and there she was given responsibility for the Jewish criminal police. After the war, she was placed on trial before the Jewish community of Berlin for collaboration but testified at the Wilhelmstraße trial in Nuremberg just the same.

From the safe retrospective gaze of observers who in greater part consider themselves towering savants, it is also customary to disregard the uncertainty that surrounded the word "evacuation" in 1941 and 1942. The guidelines that Eichmann laid down in his cable of January 31, 1942, illustrate the expectations that he wished to evoke among the Jews of Germany: "[Jews] who work in essential war enterprises, Jews aged sixty-five and over, especially frail Jews aged 55–65" are not to be evacuated. "Jewish spouses, one of whom is older than age sixty-five and one younger than sixty-five, may be evacuated if . . . they have medical confirmation of being fit for labor."[69] These guidelines were meant to give Jews the impression that they were being sent to the east for forced labor and not for certain death. Among Klemperer's acquaintances, people imagined being transported to Minsk in order to rebuild the place.[70] When his directives were not properly obeyed, Eichmann warned his people—according to a report of March 9, 1942—to comply unreservedly with the guidelines pertaining to aged and morbidity so that no one might be deported "unjustly," as had happened in one of the transports to Riga. The illusion had to be perfect. The growing burden on the Jewish old-age homes was a by-product of this masquerade that necessitated the further deceit, mentioned above, of the Theresienstadt model ghetto for elderly Jews. The existence of Theresienstadt made the decision to evacuate Jews aged sixty-five and below to the east for labor purposes seem more credible. The "Third Reich" could create the same impression for foreign consumption, too; it was expressed euphemistically in a 1944 film about Theresienstadt, produced under Eichmann supervision, that was later known as *Der Führer schenkt den Juden eine Stadt* (The Führer gives the Jews a city).[71]

Two additional instructions from Eichmann at the aforementioned meeting on March 9, 1942, demonstrate how finely tuned the fraud was. First, Jews were forbidden "in any manner to know . . . about the preparations for evacuation; therefore, absolute secrecy must be maintained," and second, commanders of details that escorted transports of Jews had to make sure "that the freight cars [carrying the deportees' luggage] from the Altreich be transported back immediately after [!] they reach their destination."[72] The smokescreen took precedence over saving on the round-trip transport of a railroad car packed with suitcases.

On October 23, 1941, a week after the deportations from Germany began, Himmler officially prohibited the emigration of German Jews. There was a slight lag; between October 29 and November 3, 150 additional Jews managed to depart for America via Spain and Portugal. Afterward, legal emigration was totally prohibited. On January 3, 1942, Himmler linked the prohibition to the concept of the "Final Solution": "Since the Final Solution of the Jewish problem is steadily approaching, we forbid the emigration of Jews who hold German citizenship . . . from the Reich." The familiar wording of the Wannsee Conference of January 20, 1942—"Evacuation of the Jews to the east, subject to prior approval of the Führer, supplants [!!] emigration as an additional potential solution"—is plainly addressed to the Jews of Germany. It confirms the Jewish policy that had been practiced in Germany since October 1941. The person who had heard Hitler on the night of January 24 at the Wolfslair had no need to interpret the Führer's intentions: "It is useless for me to pull one tooth a few centimeters out once every three months—once the tooth is out, the pain goes away. The Jew must be tossed out of Europe. . . . I'll say only this: he's got to go.

If he's annihilated as that happens, I can't help them. I see only this: absolute annihilation if they don't go willingly."

He knew to whom he addressed the illusion about such an alternative: those good burghers who were asking, "What's happening to the Jew?"[73] Only on January 31, 1942, however, by which time tens of thousands of German Jews had already been exiled, did the RSHA issue a circular that made explicit reference to the onset of the Final Solution of the Jewish problem. The signatory to this document was Eichmann: "The recent evacuation of Jews to the east from several areas in the Reich is but the beginning of the Final Solution of the Jewish problem in the Altreich, Ostmark, and the Protectorate of Bohemia and Moravia."[74]

The two anti-Jewish measures that the "Third Reich" instituted against the Jews of Germany after the onset of Operation Barbarossa—the identifying mark and deportation to the east—were augmented on November 25, 1941, by the Eleventh Regulation to the Reich Citizen Law, one of the two "Nuremberg Laws." To obliterate German Jewry lawfully and murder them civilly, the regime added a legal and formal measure. At the early going of December 1940, it was proposed at the Ministry of the Interior to revoke the Jews' citizenship and relegate them to the status of "protected subjects of the German Reich." This new status, however, was rejected, if only due to the impression that its title created; no one, after all, intended to protect Jews.[75] Thus, in January 1941, officials from various ministries (including Hans Globke, later to serve as Secretary of State at Adenauer's postwar chancellery) met at the Ministry of the Interior in order to revoke the rights of the German Jews by turning them stateless. Here was formed the basis for the aforementioned Eleventh Regulation to the Reich Citizen Law, promulgated on November 25, 1941, after much debate and vacillation and after Hitler's direct intervention: "A Jew shall be automatically deprived of his German nationality (Staatsangehörigkeit) . . . if he has established his residence outside of Germany." The regulation went into effect retroactively, and coercion as the reason for a person's establishing residence abroad was immaterial.

By January 1941, bureaucrats were acting on the assumption that the Jews of Germany would be expelled, be it to Madagascar or to the east. In November, the authors of the regulation discovered not only that all the Jews of Germany were earmarked for expulsion, making discussion of the status of the Jewish inhabitants of the Altreich—protected or not—effectively unnecessary, but also that most deportees to the east were doomed to certain death whether they were German citizens or stateless. Even Jews who had emigrated or been banished before November 25, 1941, forfeited their German nationality after this imposed fact. At issue here were neither statistics nor formalities nor rituals but rather a definitely practical outcome: "The property of a Jew shall be seized upon the loss of his nationality . . . and placed in the hands of the Reich."[76]

The preparations for the promulgation of the regulation dragged on not only because a decision had to be made on the nature of the "Final Solution" to the Jewish problem and when "after the war" would begin, followed by the onset of the campaign against the Soviet Union. Where "miscegenation" and "Mischlinge" were concerned, the questions of pension and benefit rights for Jewish former civil servants and even the definition of the occupied territories as part of the Reich or as "outside of Germany" were also problematic and had an inhibiting effect in the matter at hand. At its base, the criminal Nazi regime was incomparably fussy about matters of law. This aside, struggles ensued over the official pocket or account that would receive the seized property. As mentioned above, the Ministry of Finance competed with the SS for the loot. Ultimately, the Jews of Germany lost their German nationality when they crossed the border, as though they had done this of their free will, particularly since the word "residence," as in "residence outside of Germany," was also a euphemism in most cases.

Not only were the state and the SS interested in the Jews' property; so were private individuals whose positions gave them an opportunity to enrich themselves from the Jews' eviction. Gestapo operatives exploited apartment searches to "equip" themselves with sundry objects; various functionaries allowed Jewish subordinates to give them "gifts"; the Chief of Police in Berlin, Count Wolf-Heinrich Graf von Helldorf, blackmailed affluent Jews by forcing them to raise a contribution to a "Helldorf Foundation." This aside, there were "pirate" self-enrichment incidents at Jewish deportees' expense at transport departure points and even destinations. The SS donated pilfered fur coats, watches, and children's clothing to guards and to its members' families. Even ordinary Volk profited from the murder of the Jews. Public auctions of Jewish deportees' possessions took place in villages and cities. A suitable example of this was displayed at an exhibition titled *Legalized Burglaries: The Fiscal Exploitation of Jews in the State of Hesse, 1933–1945* (2002): shortly after the deportation of the Grünbaum family from Espa, a village in Hesse, tax officials from the city of Wetzlar sealed the family home, but only after removing some laundry for the army's use. Afterward, in the courtyard of the home itself, cattle, household effects, and furniture were auctioned off; several villagers even managed to appropriate some of the Grünbaums' household effects tax-free. One member of the family still lived there and had to observe the auction; he was exiled to Theresienstadt two months later.[77]

The provenance of the auctioned objects—from valuable paintings and silver Judaica (*Judensilber*) to a desk or a suit—was known to one and all. The plunder of Jewish-owned works of art by the Nazi high and mighty, foremost Hitler and Göring themselves but also by German museums, was also no secret. Notices about auctions appeared in the newspapers in inexorable succession: "On Thursday and Friday, December 11 and 12, 1941, I will voluntarily offer for auction the following objects in good condition, some originating in non-Aryan property: four men's smoking parlor sets . . . a bedroom set of linden wood . . . clothing, shoes, German rugs, a vacuum cleaner, etc."[78] Especially telling was the popular observation that "simple housewives . . . were suddenly wearing fur coats, bartering coffee and jewelry, buying ancient furniture and rugs." Professor Wolfgang Dreßen, who took part in a documentary film on the topic, sarcastically called it "Germans utilizing their Jewish neighbors."[79] Jews' persecution nurtured the inventiveness of the Volksgemeinschaft. In Berlin, for example, several Jews were promised deletion from the deportation lists for five thousand Reichsmarks.[80]

Private individuals who snapped up things on the cheap at auctions or exploited Jews in other ways, however, were not the main profiteers. Those were the institutions that pocketed most of the money—the tax authorities, the party, the National Socialist welfare system, the Haupttreuhandstelle Ost (HTO) (the Main Trustee Office for the East, Altreich desk), and many others. The "little man" justified his pilfering by noting that deportees' bank accounts, securities, and other assets had also made their way to the exchequers of the banks and the state. The Volksgemeinschaft was also mindful of corruption charges that various official institutions leveled against each other. Below is one example of many, harvested from a report from the SD in Minden on December 19, 1941: "Especially here in Minden, we have a situation where the Revenue Office, to which the right of [sale] of furnishings can be transferred, is now [selling] the apartments for itself. Since in this procedure there is no approval by the Party, the general suspicion is that within the ranks of the officials in the Revenue Office, a system of favoritism is developing."[81]

Irrespective of the Eleventh Regulation to the Reich Citizenship Law, the sundry ministries and authorities continued to expand the suite of regulations that made the lives of the dwindling Jewish population unendurable. On June 12, 1942, Jews were required to surrender bicycles, typewriters, and optical instruments, and in the ensuing months of that year, their food rations were trimmed again.

In October 1941, as the deportations began, there were still 6,742 pupils in seventy-four Jewish schools. The Gestapo applied pressure to fire more and more teachers and slash the budget in order to harass the Jews; ultimately, its objective was the money that it would obtain at the end of the transports. The schools' efforts to continue giving physical education (*Turnen*) lessons, for example, surely seemed unnecessary to the Gestapo in view of the impending "Final Solution." In June 1942, when 2,583 pupils still attended forty-six Jewish schools, a decision in principle was made to outlaw the education of Jewish children. Even under these circumstances, however, the Jews of Germany re- fused to surrender their right to educate. Now Jewish youngsters could receive an even better education than before, a private one, and all were educated well. So Eric H. Boehm interpreted in 1949 a remark by Leo Baeck in *We Survived*. Even in the east, after deportation, the Jews hoped to sustain systematic teach- ing activity. Accordingly, Jewish teachers in Hamburg who faced deportation requested a special permit for one hundred additional kilograms of textbooks per teacher. To keep up the deceptive nature of the deportation system, such a permit was actually issued.[82] The Jüdische Hochschule in Berlin, which was allowed to call itself only a "teaching institute" from 1934 onward and still had thirty-one students at the beginning of the war, was closed down in June 1942, at the end of a semester that featured one lecturer—Rabbi Leo Baeck—and three students.[83]

The question of why the remaining Jews had not emigrated while they still could seems to have become moot once emigration was prohibited. Still, it is worth asking on a hypothetical basis in this context, and the answer may be edifying.

On November 28, 1941, about a month after the emigration ban went into ef- fect, a letter from a Jew in Berlin named Stamuel (or Samuel), dated November 19, 1941, to the preacher Katzenstein of Essen was quoted in a Gestapo report. The letter evidently described a transport of Berlin Jews to Minsk, and the Gestapo quoted it in order to reflect the German Jews' state of mind:

> Why didn't we rescue ourselves in time from the clutches of this hell? . . .
> We . . . certainly had numerous reasons to stay on here. But it is clear that
> these were foolish sham reasons which we should have seen through for
> what they in reality were. We foolishly did not believe that such a thing was
> possible. As if, especially in a horrible war, there was anything impossible for
> the dehumanized fighters. We were blind and deaf and listened to the voices
> of Sholomm [peace] as in the time of Jeremiah [justifying exile among pious
> Jews, cf. Jeremiah 29:7]. . . . We from the Altreich should have all been saved.
> We could have all been saved.[84]

That day, Victor Klemperer—who as an intermarried Jew in Dresden was still spared from the direct experience of deportation—mulled the possibility of escape as a real alternative. He summarized his situation as follows: "Everything uncertain, changing daily." But his answer was "We weighed matters up again. Result as always: stay. If we go, then we save our lives and are dependents and beggars for the rest of our lives. If we remain, then our lives are in danger, but we retain the possibility of afterward leading a life worth living."

From our retrospect, this picturing of "afterward" may be said to have been based on utter ignorance. As the entry continues, Klemperer attests to something else that he could not know: "Going hardly depends on us anymore." Therefore, he treated the question rather fatalistically: "Everything is fate. . . . If, e.g., we had moved to Berlin in spring, then by now I would probably already be in Poland"[85]—as though the Jews of Berlin really faced resettlement and not transport to death. Important, however, is the bourgeois stance that his words reflect—namely, more fear of a life of destitution than of outright death.

According to a starkly contrasting charge that was repeatedly brought against the Jews of Germany ex post, they were overly obedient and did not participate actively in resisting the Third Reich. The question is what they could have gained from such resistance,[86] and the Herbert Baum affair answers with terrifying clarity. On May 18, 1942, the so-called Baum group, a communist-oriented resistance cell led by Herbert Baum and composed largely of Jews, mainly workers at Siemens plants, carried out a firebomb attack at "the Soviet Eden," a special anti-Soviet exhibition sponsored by Goebbels. Fourteen people were injured in the attack, and the exhibits sustained damage. In its reprisal, the regime targeted more than the group itself. That is, Baum and twenty-one associates (although Goebbels mentions only twelve), seven of whom were Jewish or "half-Jewish," were arrested and placed before a special court (*Volksgericht*). The entire Jewish population absorbed an eruption of fury. Even though the Gestapo considered not Baum but the non-Jewish Joachim Franke the leader of the group, Goebbels wished to do away with all the Jews of Berlin at once. Even if matters did not go that far, ten days after the attack, 500 Jews were selected arbitrarily and sent to Sachsenhausen; 250 of them were murdered that very day, and the others shared this demise later on. Goebbels's press muzzled the whole affair, although one could read about it in the *New York Times*.

The police not only apprised the leadership of German Jewry of the Baum group's deed and its punishment but also advised it vehemently to warn Jews against doing anything similar. Therefore, after the attack, Leo Baeck tried to contact the communist resistance in order to forestall additional attacks, which due to their catastrophic outcomes he considered acts of madness. In fact, the Baum group's operation and the assassination of Heydrich on May 27, 1942, did furnish an excuse to expedite the deportations. As always, and to marshal support for the measure, the anti-Jewish operations were presented as responses to Jewish provocation. "[The Baum group's attack] is further proof that the Jews of Berlin should be evicted no matter what," Goebbels explained to his office staff on May 23, 1942, in a direct reference to revenge against the Jews. By now, all Jews could see that "they will be deported one day and may die as a consequence." At issue, Goebbels explained, were forty thousand people, inclusive of twenty-five thousand healthy and strapping Jews who had nothing to lose. Plainly, these Jews in the Reich capital, Berlin, "are more dangerous than 25,000 Englishmen circulating freely, because the English know that [their] endangerment is a situation that will end at the end of the war, whereas Jews know that nothing whatsoever can save them now."[87] Goebbels's assessment, however, was based on his knowledge of the nature of the "Final Solution," whereas the victims could not imagine it. Even if the assessments of the Jews' despair were mistaken, such cases unquestionably provided grist for supporters of faster deportation. If so, resistance by the Jewish population was almost totally irrational because the system knew how to exploit such cases to prove the veracity of the prejudices that the propaganda disseminated and to justify even more radical policies toward the Jews. In addition, the National Socialist terror apparatus did not wait for more extreme acts of resistance and sabotage to invoke the most brutal measures. The aforementioned deception tactic that was employed shortly after the deportations began was gradually set aside because it became unnecessary as time passed. On October 20, 1942, several months after the Baum group's operation, a selection was conducted for the purpose of slashing the staff of welfare workers. Those dismissed were designated for deportation; several of them apparently knew the fate that awaited them and therefore attempted to go underground. In response, twenty Jews were taken hostage, including Hannah Karminski, the director for relief and welfare, and were executed by gunfire or deported as an object lesson.[88]

The problem of resistance found its way to the agenda not in only extreme cases, such as the Baum group attack, but also at the quotidian level. The question we asked above about ostensible collaboration by the Reichsvereinigung and the community leadership in implementing the deportation policy is also, ultimately, a question of plausible resistance. "Would there have been fewer victims" had these entities refused to collaborate? Jacob Jacobson, quoted above, asked. His answer—that the fate of Dr. Otto Hirsch was definitely a warning signal—is indicative of the entire context. As will be recalled, Hirsch, a member of the Reichsvereinigung board, was imprisoned in February 1941 and murdered in Mauthausen for having protested against the deportation of the Jews of Baden. When Jacobson reported this after the war, it was known only that of the thirteen main representatives in the Reichsvereinigung leadership, only two—Leo Baeck and Moritz Henschel—survived the war. Before his deportation, Jacobson himself faced the dilemma of how to behave toward people who visited his archive and asked him to conceal "inculpating records" concerning their Jewish origins. "I could not know if those who expected me to play this dangerous game were informers."[89]

This aside, some individuals personally resisted the abjection that accompanied their deportation. Jews who reached a collection camp, wherever it was—on Levetzowstraße or on Große Hamburger Straße in Berlin, at the large market hall in Frankfurt, in front of the Freemasons House on Moorweidenstraße in Hamburg, or at a school in Mainz—underwent humiliation and torment. An example cited by Beate Meyer demonstrates the utter hopelessness of any attempt to salvage self-respect. At the party conference site of the collection camp in Nuremberg, a Gestapo man ordered the prisoners in the camp, for the sole purpose of depredation, to race around a table with chairs in hand as he filmed them. One dignified banker, not wishing his humiliation to be documented, attempted to dodge the camera. For this, the Gestapo operative broke his teeth. Were that not enough, he was locked into the latrine and a sign was posted on its door: "Kohn Bank, Closed." The footage also documents the banker exiting the latrine mortified. His attempt to salvage a shred of his lost dignity as a decent and respectable human being thus ended in mortification even more extreme.[90]

At this stage, with the number of "full Jews" in Germany plummeting initially due to emigration and then on account of deportation, the regime was increasingly occupied by the question of where to draw the line between "Aryan" and "Jew." According to the May 1939 population census, there were 72,738 "Mischlinge of the first degree" and 42,811 "Mischlinge of the second degree" in Germany, 0.09 percent and 0.05 percent of the total population, respectively—a small if not negligible minority. The classification in these statistics, however, had ceased to be theoretical and no longer pertained only to access to university, military service, managerial posts, and pension rights; it had become a matter of life and death. It is no wonder that by the middle of 1941, 9,636 individuals attempted, by applying to Hitler, to "upgrade" themselves from "considered Jewish" (Geltungsjude) to "Mischlinge of the first degree" or from "Mischlinge of the first degree" to "Mischlinge of the second degree." Only 263 such applications were requited. One of the paradoxical phenomena were "Mischlinge" who served as soldiers in the "Third Reich." At the beginning of the war, "Mischlinge of the first degree" were still being inducted. Only on April 8, 1940, did the Wehrmacht high command, by decree of Hitler, discharge them by secret order along with other soldiers "from the tribe of the Jews." After the campaign in Russia began, Hitler took a more radical turn and rejected all special appeals. Just the same, no few "Mischlinge" remained in the Wehrmacht. Thus, at first—but not in every case—they could protect their Jewish parents against deportation. There were also totally absurd cases in which a "Mischling" son was inducted and fought for Germany while his Jewish father, deported to Poland in 1938, fell in the Warsaw ghetto uprising.[91]

The minutes of the January 20, 1942, Wannsee Conference show that the pretext for the thoroughgoing debate there was neither the decision in principle to commit mass murder nor the question of coordinating the transports nor other logistical matters but rather the fate of "Mischlinge" living in the Reich. This consideration was expressed even more clearly when the invitations to Wannsee were sent out on November 29, 1941. With the deportations already underway, not only Heydrich but also the Ministry of the Interior needed a new, practical, and explicit definition of the term "German Jew." The awareness of the purpose of the impending conference—to discuss the fate of the Jews of Germany—slipped into the background due to the postponement of the gathering, caused by the United States entering the war, from December 9, 1941, to January 20, 1942.[92] The views of the Reichssippenamt (the Reich Kinship Office, an auspice of the Reich Ministry of the Interior) and of other authorities, jurists, and the courts all had to be reconciled with those of the SS and the police in this matter. By January 1942, enough experience with "origin claims" had accrued and enough attempts to cleanse "half-Jews" of legal Jewishness had been carried out. "Mischlinge" and "miscegenational" spouses often invoked legal methods to save their lives or, at least, to avoid statutory restrictions. Many made humiliating attempts to prove that they had been born out of wedlock and not to a Jewish father. Racial theory experts were called in to confirm or disprove this by observing outer indications.[93] En passant, verdicts in "race defilement" trials might also depend on the legal opinions of "race scientists."[94]

The fear among "Mischlinge" of being deemed equal to "full Jews" was eminently justified. On August 21, 1941, the RSHA and the government ministries reached a consensus about their fate. Bormann advised Heydrich of Hitler's intention of dropping the distinction between "half-Jews" and "full Jews." This recommendation was not effective immediately because the deportation of the former might have an adverse effect on "Mischlinge of the second degree" (offspring of persons designated for deportation) who were serving in the Wehrmacht.[95] Just the same, the danger to those defined as "Mischlinge" mounted in 1941. The SD in Minden summarized public opinion on the topic in a report: "Whether a Jew or a half-Jew, it's all the same, they're all the same sort."[96]

After Walther Gross, head of the Nazi Party Office of Racial Policy, again broached the question of principle in view of the looming "Final Solution," the Party Bureau, the Office of Racial Policy, and the RSHA sought to equalize the legal status of Jews and "Mischlinge." The racial affairs expert at the Ministry of the Interior, Bernhard Lösener, fearing that it would now become part of the official policy to consider German "Mischlinge" simply "Jews"—as though they were East Europeans—successfully opposed this and demanded the enactment of regulations that would take "full Aryan" family relations into consideration. The solution of forced sterilization appears to have failed. It was taken up again at the second and third "Final Solution conferences," on March 6 and October 27, 1942, where it was resolved to allow "Mischlinge of the first degree" to remain in the Reich after sterilization and to treat "Mischlinge of the second degree" like Germans. Even the sterilized, however, were not exempt from slave labor.[97]

On the agenda next to the "Mischlinge" question stood the problem of "miscegenation." The number of "miscegenational marriages" had dropped from 20,454 in 1939 to 16,760 in December 1942 and only 12,487 in April 1943. The decline traced not only to factors such as natural mortality but also to political and social pressure on members of this group. "Privileged [priviligiert] miscegenational marriages," a class that Göring had established on December 28, 1938, pursuant to a decision by the Führer, were defined as a status in the Tenth Regulation of the Reich Citizenship Law; the term recurred in orders, regulations, and court rulings. Steadily escalating pressure, however, was aimed mainly at "nonprivileged miscegenational marriages," in which the Jewish spouse was the husband or the children had received a Jewish upbringing. About one-fifth of "miscegenational marriages" ended in divorce in the first years of the war. Attesting to the meaning of the expression "political and social pressure" is the fact that roughly one-fourth of these divorces coincided with internment in a concentration camp or a prison. Ordinary arguments hardly played a role in the divorce proceedings of miscegenational couples. If the Jewish husband had been dismissed from his job, was preparing to emigrate (up to October 1941), or had received a deportation order, he was always found at fault for the divorce.[98] From October 1941 on, a non-Jewish wife who wished to divorce her husband effectively signed the latter's death warrant.

It was not only the RSHA that promoted the extreme line at this time. The questions of "Mischlinge" and "miscegenation," with which the Wannsee Conference, headed by Heydrich, had dealt at such length led to Eichmann's aforementioned telegram ten days after the conference, in which these additional guidelines were set forth. Evacuation applied to all Jews apart from

"Jews living in German–Jewish miscegenational marriages."[99] It was the Council of German Communities (Deutscher Gemeindetag), of all elements, that pressured to extend the measures of persecution to Jews in miscegenational marriages—not so much for ideological reasons as due to financial outcomes. The council wished to reserve welfare and relief money for the destitute and roll the expenses onto the Reichsvereinigung. The council, however, had only partial success in attaining its goals in September 1942: only after the death of the non-Jewish spouse or the dissolution of the miscegenational marriage would the Jewish spouse be disentitled to welfare. The same logic was used in decisions relating to Jews' deportation to the east. From July 1942 onward, many Jewish spouses from dissolved "privileged miscegenational marriages" found themselves in transports. The struggle over the next steps was waged ruthlessly.[100]

The aforementioned "factories operation" (Fabrikaktion) on February 27, 1943, may be considered the climax of the "miscegenational marriage" struggle. Some twenty thousand "armament Jews" were arrested at their workplaces in German cities—mainly Berlin, where the operation lasted several days. The operation had been planned out by the RSHA in coordination with the enterprises in order to hold the menace to continued production to a minimum. In addition, Eichmann suspended the deportation of Jews in "privileged miscegenational marriages" and the offspring of "Aryan" families who were "considered Jews" (Geltungsjuden). Thus, detainees who had not participated in "miscegenational marriages" were sent to Auschwitz, while about two thousands Jews who lived in "miscegenational Marriages" were trucked to the Berlin Jewish community building at 2–4 Rosenstraße. "The conditions at Rosenstraße are unimaginable," one of the prisoners said. "Latrines in indescribable condition. One who needs them has to queue for three hours or so and, most humiliatingly, men and women have to use the same stalls, the doors of which cannot be closed."[101] Scholars disagree about whether "privileged" prisoners on Rosenstraße were designated for transport from there to Auschwitz or were singled out as replacements for "full Jews" who had been fired from their jobs with the Jewish community and deported to Auschwitz. They also disagree about whether the "Aryan" women's demonstration in front of the building, a wholly commendable feat—"Give us back our men!"—indeed spared their husbands from deportation to Auschwitz.[102] One thing, however, is clear: the more imminent the deportation of "full Jews" became, the more the policy of persecution escalated. Even though those interned at Rosenstraße were released two weeks later, the turn of "Mischlinge" and Jews in "miscegenational marriages" was bound to come sometime. Goebbels, reporting to his diary, wrote about "disagreements" because "at first Jews and Jewesses in privileged marriages were arrested as well." What bothered the Minister of Propaganda was not the wish to deport these Jews but the excessive fear and embarrassment that this specific move stirred among "Aryans."[103] Apparently, however, no embarrassment welled up in early 1943, when Jews in "miscegenational marriages" were dismissed from their factory jobs and put to grueling labor in construction, road building, and cleaning.[104]

Attentive Germans were not oblivious to the imminence of the assault on the USSR even before the middle of 1941. Ruth Andreas-Friedrich, a journalist with good contacts at the Foreign Ministry, advised her Jewish friend Emma Lehmann of this possibility, probably in the hope that the campaign would prove to be the regime's downfall. In Andreas-Friedrich's words, Mrs. Lehmann replied, "Anything but [war] against America! . . . If America enters the war, they'll kill us all."[105] The salvation that German Jewry obtained via the assault on the USSR came much too late, of course. By the time the Red Army reached Germany in 1945, almost all the Jews who had been alive in Germany in June 1941 had been murdered. The American enlistment in the war against Germany in December 1941 actually contributed—as I showed above—to the demise of the National Socialists' last inhibitions in their treatment of German and European Jewry.

NOTES

1. Joseph Goebbels, *Tagebücher 1923–1945*, ed. Elke Fröhlich (Munich: Institut für Zeitgeschicht, 1993–2007), entry of August 20, 1941.

2. Joseph Walk, ed., *Das Sonderrecht für die Juden im NS-Staat Eine Sammlung der gesetzlichen Maßnahmen und Richtlinien—Inhalt und Bedeutung*, 2nd ed. (Heidelberg: C. F. Müller, 1996), 347.

3. Otto Dov Kulka and Eberhard Jäckel, eds., *The Jews in the Secret Nazi Reports on Popular Opinion in Germany, 1933–1945* (New Haven, CT: Yale University Press, 2010), 568.

4. Walk, *Das Sonderrecht für die Juden*, 343.

5. Ibid., 371.

6. Ibid., 344.

7. Victor Klemperer, *I Will Bear Witness: A Diary of the Nazi Years, 1933–1941* (New York: Random House, 1998), 417, entry of July 9, 1941.

8. Walk, *Das Sonderrecht für die Juden*, 350.

9. Klemperer, *I Will Bear Witness*, 426, entry of August 10, 1941.

10. Kulka and Jäckel, *The Jews in the Secret Nazi Reports*, 568.

11. Walk, *Das Sonderrecht für die Juden*, 363–66.

12. Klemperer, *I Will Bear Witness*, 451, entry of December 22, 1941.

13. Abraham Margaliot and Yehoyakim Cochavi, eds., *History of the Holocaust: Germany* (Hebrew) (Jerusalem: Yad Vashem, 1998), 770–825.

14. Jacob Tsur, "The Orthodox Jews," in Margaliot and Yehoyakim Cochavi, n. 13, 905–8.

15. Eric A. Johnson, *Nazi Terror: The Gestapo, Jews, and Ordinary Germans* (London: John Murray, 2000).

16. Walk, *Das Sonderrecht für die Juden*, 344.

17. Beate Meyer, Hermann Simon, and Chana Schütz, eds., *Jews in Nazi Berlin: From Kristallnacht to Liberation* (Chicago: University of Chicago Press, 2009), 94–95.

18. Kulka and Jäckel, *The Jews in the Secret Nazi Reports*, 543.

19. Anna Georgiev, "Zur materiellen Geschichte des 'Judensterns,'" *Zeitschrift fuer Geschichtswissenschaft* 7, no. 8 (2018): 623–39.

20. Arnd Müller, *Geschichte der Juden in Nürnberg 1146–1945* (Nuremberg: Selbstverlag der Stadtbibliothek, 1968), 276; cf. Marlis Buchholz, *Die hannoverschen Judenhäuser Zur Situation der Juden in der Zeit der Ghettoisierung und Verfolgung 1941–1945* (Hildesheim: A. Lax, 1987), 16ff.

21. Klemperer, *I Will Bear Witness*, 431, entry of September 17, 1941.

22. Walk, *Das Sonderrecht für die Juden*, 66.

23. Kulka and Jäckel, *The Jews in the Secret Nazi Reports*, 538, 543, Security Police report, September 25, 1941.

24. Walk, *Das Sonderrecht für die Juden*, 57.

25. Konrad U. Kwiet, "Nach dem Pogrom: Stufen der Ausgrenzung," in Wolfgang Benz, ed., *Die Juden in Deutschland 1933–1945 Leben unter nationalsozialistischer Herrschaft* (Munich: Beck, 1988), 610.

26. Alexandra Przyrembel, *Rassenschande Reinheitsmythos und Vernichtungslegitimation im Nationalsozialismus* (Göttingen: Vandenhoeck & Ruprecht, 2003), 248, 461, 468, 471–74.

27. Jürgen Matthäus and Frank Bajohr, eds., *Alfred Rosenberg Die Tagebücher von 1934 bis 1944* (Frankfurt a.M.: Fischer, 2015), 405.

28. Susanne Willems, *Der entsiedelte Jude Albert Speers Wohnungsmarktpolitik für den Berliner Hauptstadtbau* (Berlin: Hentrich, 2002).

29. Buchholz, *Die hannoverschen Judenhäuser*, 30.

30. Kulka and Jäckel, *The Jews in the Secret Nazi Reports*, 551–52.

31. Buchholz, *Die hannoverschen Judenhäuser*, 169.

32. Przyrembel, *Rassenschande Reinheitsmythos*, 475ff.

33. Gruner, *Jewish Forced Labor under the Nazis*, 75.

34. Ibid., 21–27, 77.

35. Goebbels, *Tagebücher 1923–1945*, entry of September 30, 1942.

36. Cf. Wolf Gruner, "Terra incognita? Die Lager für den jüdischen Arbeitseinsatz 1938–1943," in Ursula Büttner, ed., *Die Deutschen und die Judenverfolgung im Dritten Reich* (Frankfurt: Fischer, 2003), 172–85.

37. Henry Picker, *Hitlers Tischgespräche im Führerhauptquartier 1941–1942* (Stuttgart: Seewald, 1963), 31.

38. Ernst Piper, *Alfred Rosenberg: Hitlers Chefideologe* (Munich: Blessing, 2005), 583; Jürgen Matthäus and Frank Bajohr, eds., *Alfred Rosenberg Die Tagebücher von 1934 bis 1944* (Frankfurt: Fischer, 2015), 393–409.

39. H. D. Heilmann, *Das Kriegstagebuch des Diplomaten Otto Bräutigam, Biedermann und Schreibtischtäter* (Berlin: Rotbuch, 1987), 145. The same day Keitel decreed that no Jew may serve as soldier in the armed forces of foreign countries fighting alongside Germany. This may explain his change of mind concerning the meeting of Bräutigam and Hitler.

40. H. G. Adler, *Der verwaltete Mensch Studien zur Deportation der Juden aus Deutschland* (Tübingen: Mohr, 1974), 173.

41. Epstein, *Model Nazi*, 185–86.

42. Heinz Boberich, ed., *Meldungen aus dem Reich*, No. 228, October 17, 1941, 182.

43. International Military Tribunal, vol. 33, 535ff. Quoted from Buchholz, *Die hannoverschen Judenhäuser*, 38ff.

44. Piper, *Rosenberg*, 585.

45. Werner Jochmann, ed., *Adolf Hitler: Monologe im Führer-Hauptquartier 1941–1944* (Hamburg: Albrecht Knaus, 1980), 106, 130–31.

46. Christopher R. Browning, *The Origins of the Final Solution: The Evolution of Nazi Jewish Policy, September 1939–March 1942* (Lincoln: University of Nebraska Press, 2004), 302–5, 329–33, 361–74.

47. Cf. Christian Gerlach, *Kalkulierte Morde: Die deutsche Wirtschafts—und Vernichtungspolitik in Weißrußland 1941 bis 1944* (Hamburg: Hamburger Edition, 1999), 2 Aufl Studienausgabe, 2000, 748–52.

48. Piper, *Rosenberg*, 593.

49. Joseph Tenenbaum, *Race and Reich: The Story of an Epoch* (New York: Twayne, 1956), 373.

50. Gerlach, *Kalkulierte Morde*, 755.

51. Margaliot and Cochavi, *History of the Holocaust*, 363.

52. Browning, *The Origins of the Final Solution*; Alfred Gottwald and Diana Schulle, *Die "Judentrasportation" aus dem deutschen Reich 1941–1945* (Wiebaden: Marixverlag, 2005), 84–136.

53. Christoph Kreutzmüller, *Ausverkauf, Die Vernichtung der jüdischen Gewerbetätigkeit in Berlin 1930–1945* (Berlin: Metropol, 2012), 361.

54. Bruno Blau, "The Jewish Population of Germany 1939–1945," *JSS* 7 (1950): 161–72.

55. Rivka Elkin, *The Heart Beats On: Continuity and Change in Social Work and Welfare Activities of German Jews under the Nazi Regime, 1933–1945* (Hebrew) (Jerusalem: Yad Vashem, 2004), 261–340; Gruner, *Öffentliche Wohlfahrt*, 295–307.

56. Avraham Barkai, "The Struggle for Economic Existence 1933–43," in Margaliot and Cochavi, *History of the Holocaust: Germany*, 585ff; Adler, *Der verwaltete Mensch*, 562–63.

57. Kulka and Jäckel, *The Jews in the Secret Nazi Reports*, 588.

58. Adler, *Der verwaltete Mensch*, 871.

59. Esriel Hildesheimer, *Jüdische Selbstverwaltung unter dem NS-Regime* (Tübingen: Mohr, 1994), 208–12.

60. Beate Meyer, *"Jüdische Mischlinge": Rassenpolitik und Verfolgungserfahrung 1933–1945* (Hamburg: Dölling and Galitz, 1999), 54.

61. Raul Hilberg, *The Destruction of the European Jews* (New York, London: Holmes & Meier), vol. 1.

62. Hildesheimer, *Jüdische Selbstverwaltung*, 217.

63. Doris Seidel, "Die jüdische Gemeinde Münchens 1933–1945," in Angelika Baumann and Andreas Heusler, eds., *München arisiert Entrechtung und Enteignung der Juden in der NS-Zeit* (München: Beck, 2004), 44.

64. Hildesheimer, *Jüdische Selbstverwaltung*, 219.

65. In Monika Richarz, ed., *Jüdisches Leben in Deutschland*, vol. 3 (Stuttgart: Deutsche Verlags-Anstalt, 1982), 413.

66. Jacob Jacobson, "Bruchstüke," in Avraham Barkai, *Leo Baeck, Leadership and Thought, 1933–1954* (Hebrew) (Jerusalem: The Zalman Shazar Center / Leo Baeck Institute, 2000), 100ff.

67. Browning, *Origins of the Final Solution*, 385.

68. Meyer, *A Fatal Balancing Act*, 292–96; Marion Kaplan, *Der Mut zum Überleben Jüdische. Frauen und ihre Familien in Nazideutschland* (Berlin: Aufbau Verlag, 2001), 263ff.

69. Longerich and Pohl, *Die Ermordung der europäischen Juden*, 166.

70. Klemperer, *I Will Bear Witness*, 443, entry of November 9, 1941.

71. Lara Pelner, Hans-Georg Soeffner, and Marija Stanisavljevic, eds., *Theresienstadt - Filmfragmente und Zeitzeugenberichte* (Wiesbaden: Springer, 2021).

72. Longerich and Pohl, *Die Ermordung der europäischen Juden*, 168ff.

73. Jochmann, ed., *Adolf Hitler: Monologe*, 228–29.

74. Hildesheimer, *Jüdische Selbstverwaltung*, 215; Longerich and Pohl, *Die Ermordung der europäischen Juden*, 165.

75. Cf. Uwe Dietrich Adam, *Judenpolitik im Dritten Reich* (Düsseldorf: Droste, 1972), 294ff.

76. Joseph Walk, *Das Sonderrecht für die Juden*, 357, Section 3 of the 11th Regulation; cf. Essner, *Die "Nürnberger Gesetze,"* 292–305.

77. Susanne Meinl and Bettina Hindemith, eds., *Legalisierter Raub Der Fiskus und die Ausplünderung der Juden in Hessen 1933–1945* (Exhibition catalogue: Spangenberg, 2002), 23ff.

78. Ibid., 63.

79. Frank Bajohr, *Parvenüs und Profiteure Korruption in der NS-Zeit* (Frankfurt: Fischer. 2001), 120–36; Cf. Wolfgang Dreßen, *Betrifft: Aktion 3 Deutsche verwerten jüdische Nachbarn* (Berlin: Aufbau, 1998).

80. Kulka and Jäckel, *The Jews in the Secret Nazi Reports*, 574, Berlin Gestapo report, January 12, 1942.

81. Ibid., 567.

82. Joseph Walk, "Jewish Education in Nazi Germany," in Margaliot and Cochavi, *History of the Holocaust: Germany*, 677–95.

83. Ernst Simon, *Aufbau im Untergang Jüdische Erwachsenenbildung im Nationalsozialistischen Deutschland als geistiger Widerstand* (Tübingen: Mohr, 1959), 63.

84. Kulka and Jäckel, *The Jews in the Secret Nazi Reports*, 562.

85. Klemperer, *I Will Bear Witness*, 446, entry of November 28, 1941.

86. Buchholz, *Die hannoverschen Judenhäuser*, 18.

87. Longerich and Pohl, *Die Ermordung der europäischen Juden*, 170.

88. Elkin, *The Heart Beats On*, 297.

89. Jacob Jacobson in Monika Richarz, *Jüdisches Leben in Deutschland*, 403.

90. Beate Meyer, "Handlungsspielräume regionaler jüdischer Repräsentanten (1941–1945). Die Reichsvereinigung der Juden in Deutschland und Deportation," in Birthe Kundrus and Beate Meyer, eds., *Die Deportation der Juden aus Deutschland. Pläne–Praxis–Reaktionen 1938–1945* (Göttingen: Wallstein, 2004), 77.

91. Meyer, *"Jüdische Mischlinge": Rassenpolitik und Verfolgungserfahrung*, 230ff.

92. Cf. Christian Gerlach, "Die Wannsee-Konferenz, das Schicksal der deutschen Juden und Hitlers politische Grundsatzentscheidung, alle Juden Europas zu ermorden," in *Werkstatt Geschichte*, October 1997, 9–11.

93. In her diary, Ruth Andreas-Friedrich describes the case of her dentist, Dr. Jakob. See Ruth Andreas-Friedrich, *Der Schattenmann Schauplatz Berlin: Tagebuchaufzeichnungen 1938–1948* (Frankfurt: Suhrkamp, 1986), 87, entry of February 23, 1942.

94. Alexandra Przyrembel, *Rassenschande Reinheitsmythos*, 491–94; Essner, *Die "Nürnberger Gesetze,"* 203.

95. Wolf Gruner, *Jewish Forced Labor under the Nazis: Economic Needs and Racial Aims, 1938–1944* (New York: Cambridge University Press, 2006), 85ff.

96. Kulka and Jäckel, *The Jews in the Secret Nazi Reports*, 576.

97. Meyer, *"Jüdische Mischlinge,"* 97–100, 162–65.

98. Ibid., 24–25, 72–73, 78–79.

99. Longerich and Pohl, *Die Ermordung der europäischen Juden*, 166.

100. Wolf Gruner, *Öffentliche Wohlfahrt und Judenverfolgung Wechselwirkung lokaler und zentraler Politik im NS-Staat 1933–1942* (Munich: Oldenbourg, 2002), 303–5.

101. Konrad U. Kwiet, "Nach dem Pogrom: Stufen der Ausgrenzung," in Benz, ed., *Die Juden in Deutschland 1933–1945*, 593ff.

102. Cf. Nathan Stoltzfus, *Widerstand des Herzens Der Aufstand der Berliner Frauen in der Rosenstraße 1943* (Munich/Vienna: Carl Hanser, 1999); Wolf Gruner, *Widerstand in der Rosenstraße Die Fabrik-Aktion und die Verfolgung der "Mischehen" 1943* (Frankfurt: Fischer Taschenbuch, 2005).

103. Goebbels, *Tagebücher 1923–1945*, entry of March 11, 1942.

104. Gruner, *Jewish Forced Labor under the Nazis*, 28.

105. Andreas-Friedrich, *Der Schattenmann Schauplatz Berlin*, 77, entry of March 28, 1941.

FIVE

—ᴧᴧ—

LOST IN THE EAST

WHEN THE DEPORTATION OF GERMANY'S Jewish population began in
October 1941, most Jews who had lived in Germany in 1933 were abroad, inclusive of the occupied territories in Western Europe. In the ensuing months, the
deportation of German Jewry resolved itself via "resettlement" in the eastern
Reich-controlled territories and only occasionally in immediate death. Here
the deportees had to start anew, albeit for a short time only. The lives of the
Jews of Germany in the east and their attempts to survive form the theme of
the chapter that follows.

Even after the decision in principle to deport these Jews was handed down
and the order to implement the deportation was given, the *responsables* did
not know exactly what the "final goal" of the planned transports was and how
the fulfillment of the "Final Solution of the Jewish problem" was supposed to
look in practice. The "final goal" and the "Final Solution"—the idea of extermination camps and systematic murder by toxic gas—crystallized gradually in
November–December 1941 as long-term substitutes for the mass starvations
and executions by gunfire that had been predominant in the occupied Soviet areas, since these, as Himmler had said, overly burdened the murderers' psyches.[1]
As mentioned above, the key but nebulous timing of "after the war" was an
alibi for the regnant lack of systematicness. Antipodally, in view of pressure on
Hitler from National Socialist leaders in the "Altreich," in Vienna, but also in
the Wartheland and the Generalgouvernement, to deport the Jews as swiftly as
possible, never mind where to, the possibility of avoiding a decision no longer
existed. Thus, transports of German Jews reached Łódź, which had been annexed to the Reich; Lublin and Warsaw in the Generalgouvernement; Kaunas
and Riga in the Baltic lands; and Minsk in Belarus—where those transported

either lingered for a while or died in idleness. Only too late has historical research begun to examine the lives that German Jews shared with the traditional objects of their derision, the "Ostjuden."

The history of the Jews of Germany in the ghettos of the east is more than a prequel to their murder; it also substantiates the abyss between myth and reality in the case of German Jewry, the tension within Jewry at large, and the heterogeneity of the Jewries of Europe and Germany. Only according to the National Socialist racial ideology was a monolithic "international Jewry" or "world Jewry" presumed to exist; only in National Socialism's antisemitic eyes were the Jews of Germany a slightly more refined version of "world Jewry." One may already find evidence of the heterogeneity of Jewish population groups in the customs and outlooks of Christians whom the National Socialist system had expelled from Germany as "full Jews." These people did not consider themselves Jews and, being far from their fatherland, remained tethered to each other and united in Christian congregations. Also for most German Jews who had not been associated with any Jewish community or had not been numbered directly among the Orthodox minority (i.e., liberal Jews), the sojourn in Poland, Belarus, and the Baltic countries among or alongside the "native" Jews of those lands was a stint amid a totally foreign society, not only due to differences in language and culture. "Ostjuden" who had once lived as citizens in Germany and had now become deportees, in contrast, often had another bond with the Jews of Eastern Europe and could usually communicate with ghetto inhabitants in Yiddish, Polish, or some other East European tongue. Even they, however, were a heterogeneous group. In Germany, "Ostjuden" were sometimes the "most German" Jews in Germany. One may surmise that the perpetrators deliberately planned the forced stay of German Jews in the ghettos of the east as a means of abjection because it forced them to surrender their claim to a German identity, which the imposed Jewish identity now crowded out.

By the spring of 1942, an estimated twenty-five thousand German Jews and a similar number from Austria and Bohemia—15 percent of the Jews who had lived in the greater German Reich when the war began—reached the aforementioned ghettos and thus temporarily avoided summary murder.

Before October 1941, the number of German Jews who had been deported eastward to the Nisko, Lublin, and Kielce districts was small, tension between Jews of the east and those of the west was minimal, and the local Jews greeted the German Jews cordially despite all the hardships. Therefore, blatantly overt complaints about the absence of bourgeois virtues such as precision or the presence of primitive sanitary conditions were not audible at first. After all, "[what]

Viennese Jew would give up his bed to others! Even as poor and filthy as they are, these people are lovely in their naturalness."[2]

The onset of ghettoization and mass deportation from the Reich in October 1941, however, thoroughly changed the relations between these groups. The Prague publicist Oskar Singer, deported to the Łódź ghetto in the autumn of 1941, profiled the basic stances of the Jews of east and west:

> The Eastern Jew ... couldn't forget a thing ... about the malice and contempt with which the Western Jew [i.e., those arriving from Germany] had treated him.... He responded with pride and loathing and bided his time.... And his time arrived indeed. The Jew from the West had not come to the east of his free will ... but had reached the Ostjuden as an imperiled dependent. Arriving at the ghetto, he became doubly dependent: on the supervising authorities here and on Jewish rule there.[3]

In the ghetto of Łódź, part of the Reich-annexed Wartheland, where 143,000 Jews from the city and its vicinity eked out an agonizingly penurious living, the deported German Jews experienced their first intake camp. Between October 16 and November 4, 1941, transports reached this location nearly every day. Readying the ghetto to receive 20,000 Jews from the Reich, including 9,441 from the "Altreich," was a mammoth task. Hitler's intention of exiling sixty thousand Jews to Łódź, as mentioned in chapter 4, was utterly unrealistic in view of the prevailing conditions in the ghetto. On September 23, 1941, shortly before the German Jews arrived, the Judenälteste (chair of the Jewish council) of the ghetto, Chaim Rumkowski, was instructed to make room for the new inhabitants. In response, he closed down the schools for use as housing. Then came an extreme measure by the Gauleiter, Greiser: the establishment of an extermination camp for tens of thousands of Jews who were ill or not "able-bodied"—Chełmno (Kulmhof). The idea of using industrial methods to exterminate Jews had germinated on July 16, 1941, in the mind of SS-Obersturmbannführer Heinz Höppner, the chargé for population exchanges in the Wartheland. To solve the feeding problem that would arise in the area in the approaching winter, Höppner recommended the use of a "fast-acting humane method": obliterating anyone unfit for labor. He articulated the concept, based on the assumption that death by starvation is inhumane, in a letter to Adolf Eichmann. It fit the agreement that Greiser and Himmler had worked out after the September 18, 1941, letter that had announced the transport of tens of thousands of Jews to Łódź concerning the need to liquidate thousands of unproductive ones. One may definitely concur with the assessment of Greiser's importance in the history of the Holocaust as the man who "initiated the first mass gassing of Jews." The connection between this decision and its underlying precipitant—the decision to deport the Jews of Germany—is noteworthy.[4]

The first transports to arrive were five from Vienna, five from Prague, and four from Berlin. Two additional transports came from Köln, one from Luxembourg, one from Frankfurt, and one from Düsseldorf. Unlike the Polish Jews, who had been herded into the ghetto from its close vicinity, the German, Austrian, and Czech Jews arrived well-dressed and with relatively capacious luggage. Upon arrival, they were dealt a shock: tramping through mud and muck under Gestapo inspection and being housed in "collectives"—unheated mass accommodations that lacked running water and latrines. The ghetto was a wretched place even by the standards of the "Jew-houses" or barracks in Germany. These western Jews had not foreseen such ghastly conditions. In addition, they were dependent on the local ghetto population, itself struggling for survival, for help. After they reached the ghetto, they were grouped in collectives of roughly one thousand persons each—approximately the size of the transports—that were named for their cities of origin. The head of each collective and his deputy had been appointed by the Gestapo back in Germany, and they, in turn, appointed order keepers and liaison officers whose task it was to maintain daily life and settle internal affairs. One of the main tasks of the collective heads was to look out for the many who were ill.[5]

When the first reports about the conditions in the ghetto reached Germany, the remaining Jews there tried to help the deportees by sending not only money but also parcels and mattresses. At first, the new arrivals could make do by consuming the supplies they had brought; afterward, they starved together with the rest of the ghetto inhabitants. The daily bread ratio was 286 grams. The money they had brought was confiscated by the German administration. Thus it became their main task, one that required brazenness, to obtain food and other essentials they had not been able to bring. Prices on the black market spiraled endlessly. From then on, German Jews endured by barter, surrendering the scanty belongings they had managed to salvage for toilet paper and bread. In their foreign surroundings, the newcomers were plainly at a disadvantage. In their first half year in the ghetto, three thousand of those deported from the Reich and Luxembourg—more than 15 percent—died. Their death was "natural" (i.e., induced mainly by starvation and illness). Suicide augmented the numbers. In percentage terms, the mortality rate among this population was twice that of other groups in the ghetto that had not been placed in mass housing and were better prepared—psychologically and also practically—for the conditions.

The aforementioned Oskar Singer, seated in the office of the ghetto statistics department, explained the plight of these people several months after they reached the ghetto: "Mass housing, in comparison with which the boiler decks of immigrant vessels in the worst of times were cushy palaces. . . . No shower room for a thousand people. How long would it take Europeans under such conditions to shed their cultured veneer?"[6]

The East European inhabitants of the ghetto were totally foreign to the Jews of Germany. Contemporary chronicles attest to this repeatedly. The newly arrived tried to distance themselves from the "Ostjuden" in the ghetto in various ways. Sometimes they took matters to absurd lengths, for example, refusing to replace their made-in-Germany yellow stars with those of local manufacture.

Rumkowski did not annex German Jews to his administration even though the German commander of the ghetto, Hans Biebow, explicitly demanded that he do so "because they are well acquainted with the German taste and the German work ethic."[7] After the ghetto was sealed in April 1940, Rumkowski geared his strategy to saving "his" Jews by means of labor—that is, by making them useful if not crucial to the Germans. Since 60 percent of the newly arrived were over the age of fifty or younger than fifteen, they had little "added value" for him. Those obliged to work did not always manage to carry out their tasks—often not only for health reasons, as many claimed: "Mr. Lawyer from Frankfurt or Mr. Banker from Berlin did not manage to hitch himself to the heavy vegetable wagon with true conviction." Only slightly more than fifty deportees had been laborers or artisans. "Some of the new ghetto inhabitants refuse to understand the meaning of life in the ghetto and comport themselves arrogantly. . . . I still have to deal with my brethren from the Reich, who think they can introduce here the rules to which they are accustomed. They think they're the smartest and the finest of them all, the chosenest of the chosen!" noted Rumkowski in an aggressive speech in November 1941.[8] Ultimately, the German Jews were employed at the cultural center as librarians or musicians, haulers of garbage and human waste, or—as in the case of former officers—members of the ghetto Jewish police.

From an economic standpoint, the Reich Jews were initially helped by being able to receive money from their blocked accounts through relatives and acquaintances. In fact, this was the only reason to maintain postal contact at all, since they were not allowed to forward information. Thus, they became postal beggars. "I'm not proud anymore!" was the last sentence in one of these letters.[9] By August 1942, some four million Reichsmarks had reached the ghetto. Two-thirds of the sum was expended on rent and the like, and 10 percent was withheld as a tax for the Judenälteste's exchequer. Since Łódź and the "Warthegau" belonged to the Reich, German Jews could be exploited in this manner, too, without limit.

Focal in the literature on the lives of the Reich Jews in the ghetto is the tension between the Jews of the east, meaning Eastern Europe, and those of the west, Germany. Accounts of this relationship, relying on the records of contemporary chronicles and other witness reports, emphasize the stereotypical confrontation and the mutual prejudices that existed. Mentioned repeatedly are the German Jews' elegant appearance and visits to the barber, the stamp collections and photos of Kaiser Wilhelm that they had brought along,[10] their obedient ways, and their conceit. Indeed, there are testimonies of the self-image of "us Germans" among the deportees in encounters with "the Poles" (i.e., the Ostjuden).[11] One doubts the accuracy of such generalizations, however, given the material changes that had taken place in the living conditions and habits of German Jewry between 1933 and 1941. The binary of German Jews and Polish Jews had been something of an ideological construct to begin with, because the "Warthegau" was home to many Jews who had been raised in the German Reich before World War I and because some deportees from the "Altreich" were Ostjuden themselves. There were enormous differences between German Jews and Czech Jews, particularly in their different kinds of rapprochement with local Jews. Briefly put, the stereotyped image of the bourgeois and assimilated German Jew who encountered the "unwashed" Ostjude in the ghetto does not apply sweepingly. One thing, however, is clear: the Jews' persecutors wished to fan the tension into confrontation and sow the encounter with humiliation in order to corroborate what the antisemitic ideology and propaganda had always stressed—that the Jews of Germany have no share in Germanness and demonstrate the truth of the antisemitic clichés about Jewishness. The tragedy and irony here is that the German Jews—as I show below—were considered simply "Germans" in the eyes of various groups in the ghettos and were judged similarly by immigrants in New York or Jerusalem and were rejected contemptuously as such.

For 10,900 Jews from the "German Reich," the interlude in Łódź drew to a close by May 1942. After the deportations from the "Altreich" began, the authorities made room for them in the ghetto by murdering the quarter's original inhabitants. From Łódź alone, from January 16, 1942, onward, some forty-five thousand residents were sent to death at the Chełmno death camp. The German Jews were initially spared from this fate, apparently due to the authorities' wish to maintain the illusion of resettlement for the vestiges of Jewry in Germany and the non-Jewish German population. By mid-1942, no more than eighty thousand Jews remained in the "Altreich." As the German population, increasingly numbed emotionally by the ravages of war on the battlefield and bombardments of its homes and towns, accustomed itself to silent acquiescence in the deportations, the need for this caution gradually disappeared. The path was also now open to the systematic murder of German Jews as well—by gas, in accordance with the October 26, 1941, letter from the Jewish affairs expert at Alfred Rosenberg's Ministry for the Eastern Occupied Territories, Erhard Wetzel, concerning the use of "Brack's auxiliary device."[12] Evidently, Himmler gave an order on April 17, 1942, to kill all German Jews in the Łódź ghetto who were "unfit for labor."[13] The murder took place a few weeks later in Chełmno, on "German" soil.

Included in the twelve transports from Łódź to Chełmno on May 4–15, 1942, were only Reich Jews who were living in the ghetto. It is not known whether Rumkowski or the Gestapo made this decision. Either way, Rumkowski knew what awaited those who were being transported. By directive, he spared from deportation "wounded war veterans who received the Iron Cross or decoration of honor, and also workers." This circumscription alerted anyone with the slightest sense to the advantage and privilege of remaining in the ghetto. The next day, this wording disappeared from the notices. The German administration apparently realized that by issuing exceptions to its rules it would divulge the purpose of the transports and might exacerbate agitation. The intention of the transports, however, was revealed again in the ensuing days, when Reich Jews who were working, along with disabled and decorated war veterans, were indeed left off the transport lists. The treatment of the deportees at the railroad station also revealed the true destination: they were deprived of their twelve and a half kilograms of permitted luggage and were loaded aboard the third-class cars empty-handed. In observers' eyes, the stereotyped image of German Jews played a role even as they were being deported: "The people reached the gathering place on the dot. The 'yekke,' as German Jews are derisively called here, brought with him the discipline that is customary in his milieu. He makes no attempt whatsoever to hide and evade his fate. Everyone shows up, because order must be maintained."[14]

Here as everywhere else, the German Jews' first thought was to behave in a way that would look dignified and restrained, avoiding displays of emotion and hysteria as indignities that should not take place in the persecutor's presence. This approach was definitely not understood in other cultural circles. Peculiar attitudes such as these, however, could not be kept up for long. By the time of the displacement in September 1942 and the liquidation of the ghetto in the summer of 1944, the Jews of the German Reich had been totally "assimilated."

Even before October 1941, German Jews had been deported to Polish areas that had not been annexed to the Reich (i.e., the Generalgouvernement—Lublin District—and to Warsaw as well). In February–March 1941, some five thousand Jews from Vienna and Stettin reached Opole, Kielce, and other cities even before those localities were equipped with ghettos. From the standpoint of the fanatic implementers of the racist antisemitic policy, whose prime desiderata it was to cleanse the Reich of Jews, this displacement to the Generalgouvernement, from October 1941 onward at the latest, was another step toward deportation to the annexed areas in the eastern reaches of the Reich.

In the first half of October 1941, the Chief of Police in Lublin, SS-Gruppenführer Odilo Globocnik, faced roughly the same situation that Gauleiter Greiser of the "Wartheland" had to cope with: transports from the west and Slovakia were expected to arrive, and their "continuing transport" to the east would have to wait for the vague era known as "after the war." It was systematically concluded that some form of demographic "relief" that would square with the idea of Germanizing the area had to be found. The radical outcomes in this case were the Bełżec and Sobibór extermination camps, which in effect were "pressure release stations."[15] Apart from those sent to labor camps, the Jews were shipped after a brief stay in the ghettos of the district to these two camps and to Majdanek. The same fate befell fifteen thousand German Jews who reached Lublin District in the spring of 1942 and were sent straight to the gas chambers with no stopover.

The German Jews evidently found life even harder in this part of Poland than in the "Wartheland." Those from Stettin who had been exiled to this area in early 1940 openly expressed their culture shock: "Relieving oneself is a special torment. In the open air, in nature, because these people leave the latrines in a ghastly state."[16] Extremely harsh living conditions, hunger, and distress were typical of the ghettos in the Lublin area, as of other transit ghettos in the east. The ghetto in Izbica, which in 1942 did serve as a transit station to Bełżec and Sobibór (and a smokescreen against discovery of the final destination of the transports by relatives back in the Reich), was a macabre arena of confrontation between Jews from the Reich and those from Poland. Here, much as in Łódź, the deportees from the Reich met not only with total revulsion in the eyes of Christians of Jewish origin but also, and mainly, with complaints about their ostensible wealth and the preferential treatment they received from the ghetto administration. But from April 1942 onward, at the latest, the SS had been confiscating all luggage that the deportees from the Reich had brought. Therefore, once again the prejudices against the German Jews were plainly counterfactual for the additional reason that the German overlords cynically added fuel to the flames of the contrasts and thus set their victims against each other. The ghettos of Lublin District provided almost no labor opportunities for German Jews, and in May 1942 postal contact was terminated, meaning that parcels (i.e., food

supplements) ceased to reach the east. In the eyes of the local Jewish population, however, the German Jews were not only exploiters—they were said to
work less—but simply "the Germans." A survivor from the ghetto expressed
this in his testimony: "These Germans, they're literally Jewish Gestapo men....
You mustn't let them into your home."[17] Here, too, the German Jews' restrained
comportment on their way to death was misconstrued as a manifestation of
stupidity. A rare letter from a German Jew who had been smuggled back from
Izbica to Germany to the deportee's spouse reveals the mindset: "Everything is
filthy and infested.... Now there were three different categories [of Jews] here:
Germans, Poles, Czechs. The German character you know: military discipline,
reliable, hardworking. The Pole is the opposite: ill-disciplined, lazy, dirty, un-
comradely, very good at business.... There is a Polish Judenrat, whose leader
has managed to seize most of the power.... It's very hard for us Germans." This
deportee realizes, however, that the many transports out of Izbica were leading
to an even worse future.[18]

The transit ghettos in Lublin District were liquidated in October–November
1942. Only around three hundred "able-bodied" German Jews were sent to labor camps instead of extermination camps. There, German origin and language
did confer an advantage and placed these individuals in a relatively superior
stratum. Just the same, few survived.

Fewer German Jews were deported to Warsaw than to Łódź, Lublin, or
Riga, and they were deported much later. It is true that German "Ostjuden"
had already reached Warsaw in the deportation of Polish and stateless Jews in
October 1938; it is also the case that Jews from the Wartheland, some of whom
had been German Jews until 1918, were evacuated to Warsaw in the first year of
the war. Only in April 1942, however, did Jews from the German Reich in the
narrow sense of the term (the Altreich)—approximately four thousand people
from Hanover, Gelsenkirchen, and Berlin—first arrive in Warsaw.

There, too, German Jews, although an inconsequential minority and one
that was housed outside the ghetto, encountered stereotypical prejudice on
the part of the Polish Jews. These biases may have spread with the arrival of the
"Ostjuden" from Germany before the war. From the standpoint of the Bundists,
supporters of the Jewish labor movement, and of Orthodox Jews, the image of
the deportees from the Reich always reduced itself to the same traits: orderly,
clean-shaven, well-dressed, assimilated, distant, and favored by the German
administration. For the Jews of Warsaw, too, the importation of yellow stars
from Germany was an attempt to demonstrate preferential status. What is
more, German Jews who were assigned to factory labor were accused of beating
even their Polish Jewish brethren. It also seems that in Warsaw, as elsewhere,

there was a recurrent scene of Polish Jews outwitting "naïve" German Jews in bartering belongings they had salvaged from Germany.

Adam Czerniaków, chair of the Warsaw Judenrat, was willing, as were other objective contemporary chroniclers, to correct his prejudices after the initial difficulties, especially in view of the German Jews' efficient, assiduous, and modest ways but also in light of what he and others saw as their placid demeanor. Here, their serenity as they marched to death impressed even the critics. The witness Yehoshua Perle captured it in a nutshell: "They were Germans."[19]

For both classes of Jews, however—Varsovians and others deported to that city—extermination camps awaited as "pressure release stations" because neither the "after the war" era nor further deportation eastward was foreseeable for the time being. Accordingly, the German Jews' stay in Warsaw was relatively short; by July 1942, they were sent to Treblinka as a group and were murdered there by gas. Apparently they were the first to go because they had been housed outside the ghetto, in the hospital building on Leszno Street and in a synagogue, even though the commander of the ghetto, Heinz Auerswald, definitely wanted initially to accommodate them in the ghetto. Being a German Jew conferred no advantage in this case.

North of the Polish territory occupied in 1939 lay the Baltic countries, which the Germans conquered from June 1941 onward. Now German Jews were deported to these lands as well, ostensibly ahead of deportation farther east. The first Reich Jews who reached this area did so only forty days after a similar group arrived in Łódź. As mentioned in the previous chapter, however, by October 10, 1941, Heydrich had decided to favor this destination. Riga and Minsk were to alleviate the "pressure" on Łódź. And to Rosenberg, Reich Minister for the Eastern Occupied Territories, it was clear by November 1941 that, once the winter would pass, the Reich Jews should be deported from "his" territory to places farther east.[20] The first transports from Vienna, Berlin, Munich, and Frankfurt set out on the week of November 21–28, 1941, first to Kaunas, because room for German Jews in Riga had not yet been "prepared." As I noted above, those who reached Kaunas were immediately murdered by the Einsatzkommando at the Fort IX. Here, the ghetto inhabitants knew exactly what awaited the German Jews. When the new arrivals passed the ghetto and asked, in a whisper, where they were marching to, however, the locals failed to muster the courage to answer truthfully. As for whether the German Jews resisted their murderers at the Fort IX, there are conflicting testimonies.[21]

As noted, the sequence of events in Riga was the usual one: room for new arrivals was made in the ghetto by the murder of earlier inhabitants. Thus, all thirty thousand residents of the "large ghetto" of Riga, including Simon

Dubnow, the noted Jewish national historian, were murdered by Einsatzgruppen in the Rumbula forest by December 9. Reichsbahn freight trains from Berlin, Nuremberg, Stuttgart, and other German cities reached the Riga station from November 30 onward—that is, even before the murder operation against the Baltic Jews was over. Apparently for this reason, the SS executed the passengers aboard the first train, around one thousand Berlin Jews, as soon as they had arrived—the famous case in which Himmler's order "Do not eliminate!" (*Nicht liquidieren*) arrived too late. In the Reich, in the meantime, rumors spread about the massacre in Kaunas within several days of its occurrence, including allegations about the deportation from the Reich even of war veterans and Mischlinge. This, it seems, is why Himmler sought to halt the killings of German Jews. By the time his order reached the Police and SS Commander, Friedrich Jeckeln, however, these Jews were already dead, as stated. Therefore, the next four thousand German Jews who were deported to Riga were given provisional housing, men and women separately, in granaries or shacks or on the grounds of the Jungfernhof estate, five kilometers out of town. One of the Jews from Hamburg who reached Jungfernhof was Rabbi Joseph Carlebach; he even conducted religious services there.

Several hundred German Jews among the four thousand mentioned above were put to work building the Salaspils concentration camp, some twenty kilometers from Riga. Those taken to the Riga ghetto were housed in Latvian Jews' apartments that had been vacated after their prior tenants had been murdered, some still stained with the victims' blood. As many as nine hundred people died from hunger and cold in the first months. That the Germans did not make use in Riga of the "cheap" solution of sending the German Jews straight to their death—except in the case of the first transport from Berlin—was a corollary of Himmler's decision, which flowed not from compassion but from practical calculus:[22] the remaining Jews in Germany and the sensitive "Volksgenossen" must not be jolted out of their placidity. After all, word of the killing by gunfire of the Berlin Jews on November 30 had spread right away, even reaching candidates for deportation in ensuing transports.[23] The aforementioned March 9, 1942, meeting at the RSHA shows that despite the aspiration to "a final solution of the Jewish problem," the National Socialists took care not to foment resistance among the population: "In regard to the transport to Riga, the Gauleiters Lohse and Meyer forwarded to SS-Obergruppenführer Heydrich a complaint from the elders of the Jews in Riga about some forty to fifty men who had been unlawfully evacuated [because they were over sixty-five years of age or were in 'privileged' mixed marriages]. . . . Accordingly, the aim should be to avoid such complaints at any price."

By February 1942, thirteen additional transports from Reich territory had arrived at the large ghetto in Riga; and in September–October, three more from Berlin and Insterburg (East Prussia) did the same. Most of the thirteen thousand or so Reich Jews who reached the ghetto were still alive when the ghetto was liquidated in November 1942. Some, however, succumbed to mass execution by gunfire. Approximately two thousand were murdered later on, not in the ghetto but in the Riga concentration camp. Around two thousand others, mainly elderly and children, were sent to Auschwitz.[24]

For the German Jews who had been exiled to Riga and its vicinity, this meant—unless they had starved or been shot to death back in early 1942, like the 1,500 elderly who had been murdered in the Bikernieki forest—an extra eighteen months of life in the ghetto, on average, relative to most of those who had been deported to Łódź or other destinations in the "east." Since the original ghetto residents were but a rump population and the German Jews lived in a separate part of the ghetto, matters between them did not escalate into east–west tension of the kind encountered in Łódź, Lublin, and Warsaw. In Riga, command headquarters deliberately discriminated in favor of the German Jews because, unlike the Latvian ghetto population, they did not organize an uprising. They had more than a separate administration, "the Ältestenrat of the Reich Jews in Riga," a Jewish order police force with a blue armband, a job placement center, and a school where sports instruction was given. They were even able to conduct public worship; observe festivals;[25] and hold concerts, plays, and sports competitions. In addition, the authorities strove to give the ghetto grounds a typical local atmosphere by dividing the area into streets that were named for the origin cities of the Jews living on them—Berlin Street, Köln, Prague, Leipzig, and so on. Those displaced from Köln were considered the most privileged of all in the ghetto. One survivor had the impression that "they [let] the German Jews believe that 'this' was the portion of the Ostjuden only, but never of them themselves."[26] Ultimately, however, "this" was also their portion, albeit a belated one.

Chronologically, Minsk, capital of an area that before 1941 had belonged to the Soviet Union, was the second destination of the transports of German Jews. By October 10, a few days before the transports to Łódź began, Heydrich chose the ghettos of Minsk and Riga as the next targets for transports from Germany. Seven transports with seven thousand Jews aboard—fewer than initially planned for this period—reached Minsk between November 11 and December 1941. Two had originated in Hamburg. By October 1942, eight additional transports from Reich territory reached Minsk. Altogether, around 35,500 Jews were deported from the Reich to the Minsk ghetto, the population of which was kept steady at around 7,000. Thus, many were summarily murdered, most shot to death by the Waffen-SS in pits that had been excavated around twenty kilometers out of town. Here, as in all the ghettos in the east, room for those allowed to survive for the time being was created by murdering previous inhabitants. That the German Jews were initially kept alive was due, here again, to tactical considerations and not to humaneness toward or respect for these groups. The entire police system, and surely the other administrative organs as well, wished to forestall overly vehement responses among Jews and non-Jews back in the Reich. Aware of the problem of the "Mischlinge" and their kin, they may even have considered this an easier way to loot what remained of living Jews' property.

In the Minsk ghetto, Reich Jews were fenced off from Russian Jews in the area known as the "Hamburg ghetto." Here, in contrast to Łódź, they could not even speak with the rest of the ghetto population. Their only interaction with the Russian Jews, in fact, was via "trade"—bartering their belongings for food. The Judenrat of the "Hamburg ghetto," a much smaller place than the Russian ghetto, numbered seven Jews from Hamburg and a subordinate Jewish police force. Outwardly, and as it seemed to the Russian Jewish residents of the ghetto, the German Jews enjoyed preferential discrimination; here, too, the imported made-in-Germany Judenstern became an absurd status symbol. The application of reverse discrimination toward German Jews by Wilhelm Kube, Commissioner General for "White Ruthenia," may have played a role in this. The German Jews themselves entertained the self-image of a "vanguard" population and hoped that, as Germans, they were being kept around for a fate other than that intended for the "Ostjuden." The first chairman of the Judenrat, Edgar Frank, and the commander of the Jewish police, Karl Loewenstein, had themselves served in the Freikorps after World War I, meaning they were flush with German nationalist beliefs.

Here, however, as with all the extermination operations, deception was at work. Ultimately lurking behind the attitude toward the German Jews was the criminal cynicism of the National Socialist system. No other epithet can possibly fit the establishment of the German Jewish orchestra, for example, that had to accompany the Russian Jews from the Minsk ghetto as they set out for their death. It is not known whether the omission of the German Jews from the early March 1942 massacre was also a cynical ploy or a corollary of Kube's inhibitions. Either way, most of these Jews were shot to death on July 28–31, 1942. The others were sent to Auschwitz in May 1943 or were murdered or dispatched to labor camps when the ghetto was liquidated in September 1943.[27]

Overcrowding in the ghettos due to the first wave of deportations from Reich territory, the unexpected prolongation of the campaign in Russia, and the entry of the United States into the war were definitive catalysts in the decision to send Jews to extermination camps, where they would be put to death first by labor and afterward by gas. Auschwitz, after all, had been established "only" as an extermination camp for Russian prisoners of war. Six days after the Wannsee Conference, Himmler, in a letter to the General Inspector of the Concentration Camps, Richard Glücks, offered a makeshift explanation: "Since Russian prisoners should not be expected soon, I am about to send to the camps a large number of Jewish men and women who are being forced to emigrate [!] from Germany. . . . In the coming weeks, 100,000 Jewish men and as many as 50,000 Jewish women will have to be received in the camps. Great economic tasks."[28]

Thus, for most German Jews who had been deported to the east, the ghetto became a hellhole of torments that sapped not only their physical strength but also their spiritual gird as a prelude to their brutal demise.

A special chapter in the history of the deported German Jews is reserved for the Theresienstadt ghetto. This ghetto evolved out of the deportation policy into the largest concentration of German Jews—along with those from Vienna and the Bohemian areas—in the so-called Greater German Reich.

As noted above, the idea of establishing a ghetto for the elderly dated to the very onset of the deportation of German Jewry. A fortnight after Heydrich decided (on October 10, 1941) to turn Theresienstadt into a transit camp for Jews in his protectorate—that is, just as the deportation of the German Jews started—Eichmann came up with the idea of using Theresienstadt as a ghetto for elderly Jews. Several months into that operation, on March 9, 1942, Eichmann explained what he had in mind: "[The idea is] to lull them [!], because those Jews who remain in the Altreich will be deported by the summer or the autumn to Theresienstadt, which is intended to become a 'ghetto for the elderly.'" Indeed, contrary to his directives, zealous Gestapo commanders had begun to "deport also the elderly Jews, who were burdensome to them," together with the others, to the east.[29] Eichmann had no sympathy for these elders; instead, he was aware of the conclusion that any thinking person would draw about the purpose of their deportation for "labor" in the east.

By the end of May 1942, some twenty-nine thousand Czech Jews had been "resettled" in Theresienstadt. From June onward, forty-two thousand others from the Altreich and fifteen thousand from "Ostmark" joined them. In and after 1943, more German Jews were living in Theresienstadt than had lived in the entire "Altreich" and "Ostmark." Thus, from mid-1942 onward, the demographic epicenter of German Jewry, which was less and less protected from physical extermination, shifted to Theresienstadt.

To fool the Reich Jews who were designated for transport to Theresienstadt, the authorities replaced the word "evacuation" with the officious phrase "relocation of place of residence." When the "elders' ghetto" was established, the Jews were not only misled about what awaited them but also dispossessed of what they still owned. "To implement his measures [the establishment of the elders' ghetto], the commander of the Security Police and the SD uses [!] mainly the National Association [the Reichsvereinigung]," the Ministry of Finance noted on December 14, 1942. "A Jew earmarked for resettlement in Theresienstadt signs with the Reichsvereinigung a contract concerning his accommodation in the Theresienstadt elders' ghetto (a contract for admission to the elders' home). . . . In the contract, the Reichsvereinigung undertakes to support the Jew in Theresienstadt to the end of his days. In return, the Jew transfers his property in the form of cash, bank accounts, securities, and promissory notes, to the Reichsvereinigung."[30]

The money (deposited in "special accounts" H and W), of course, made its way not to the Judenälteste in Theresienstadt, as had been agreed, but to the RSHA. When they arrived, the deportees realized they had also been duped about the living conditions in Theresienstadt. Instead of being housed in apartments as they had expected, they were packed into cramped and unheated barracks, fifty to sixty to a room. One of the survivors described the newcomers: "A certain kind of people. Especially when they had diarrhea because of food they were not used to, inhuman scenes took place there. On every floor there was only one bathroom . . . cold water only . . . fleas, gnats, and lice."[31] In 1942, the ghetto had a 50 percent mortality rate, cresting in September and receding afterward. Due to the high average age and, undoubtedly, their weakened immune system in the foreign surroundings, the German Jews in Theresienstadt had greater propensity to illness than did the Czech Jews in the same location.

Bad as the conditions were in Theresienstadt, the deported German Jews apparently believed at first that they surely stood a better chance of survival in Theresienstadt, not far from the classical metropolis of the First German Reich, than elsewhere in the east. That Theresienstadt could also serve as a stopover en route to Auschwitz seems not to have occurred to them for a while. To alleviate crowding in the ghetto, however, the Nazis acted in their usual way, by shipping the overflow to Auschwitz. On December 16, 1942, as these transports were being prepared, the Gestapo Commander Heinrich Müller revealed, in a letter to Himmler, the considerations in selecting the victims: "Those designated for the transports, as has been thus far, [!] are Jews who have no special connections and no decorations whatsoever."[32] Even a year after the deportations began, the authorities tasked with the "Final Solution" for German Jewry tried to avoid complaints or troublesome questions by deportees' relatives or acquaintances in the Reich.

Theresienstadt also served as a camp for "prominent" individuals—this was the official term—who could be used as hostages for exchange deals with the Allies. Such inmates lived under better conditions than did the rest and enjoyed sundry privileges as well as superior medical care. So aberrant was their treatment that a train carrying 1,200 privileged Jews set out from Theresienstadt to Switzerland on February 5, 1945. Many of the "prominent," however, had not been so privileged as to avoid the autumn 1944 transports; they had gone to death in Auschwitz together with other Jews from the ghetto.

From early 1943 on, by order of Eichmann, German Jews were appointed to the Theresienstadt administration. Thus Rabbi Leo Baeck, deported to this camp on January 28, 1943, along with the top echelon of the Reichsvereinigung and the community administration, served as the ghetto's "spiritual pastor" until the Red Army liberated the ghetto. Paul Eppstein headed the Ältestenrat (council of elders) from January 31, 1943, until he was murdered on September 28, 1944.[33] His successor was Rabbi Benjamin Murmelstein of Vienna. The German Jewish leadership seemed to be the group best suited to the use of Theresienstadt as a propagandistic model ghetto. In the estimation of Hans-Günter Adler, the Czech Jewish survivor and historian of the ghetto, Eppstein was feeble relative to his predecessor, Jacob Edelstein, a Polish Jew, who before being sent to Theresienstadt had chaired the Jewish community in Prague: "Courage was not one of [Eppstein's] characteristics. . . . The impression was he represented the Jews vis-à-vis the SS weakly and unresistingly." In addition, he was said to have entangled himself in "shameful love affairs"—which also gave Leo Baeck sufficient cause to keep him at arm's length.[34] Eppstein was a controversial figure in Theresienstadt, as he had been in Berlin, his experiences with the SS perceptibly filling him with fear or realism. In the judgment of the archivist Jacob Jacobson, however—himself from Berlin—Eppstein was actually beloved in Theresienstadt, especially among the German Jews. His credentials as a social scientist and an administrator were undisputed.

During his stint as the Judenälteste of Theresienstadt, Paul Eppstein managed to stabilize ghetto life, relatively speaking. Although the transports to Auschwitz continued—he cannot be faulted for this—the ghetto inhabitants were able to organize welfare for the ill, employment, youth work, and other fields. In the view of historian Wolfgang Benz, Eppstein played a double game—obtaining aid for the Jews in return for obsequy toward the tyrant's authorities. The historian and expert on the history of the Jewish leadership in the Third Reich Beate Meyer disagrees and rightly so: Eppstein sought not the authorities' favor but a certain amount of predictability and security. Meyer deftly explains the difficulty that Eppstein, like the entire German Jewish leadership, faced in Theresienstadt and before: they attempted to translate the "enemy's order" into Prussian rules of bureaucracy in the hope that the Nazi regime would obey them, too. This strategy of collaboration, Meyer reminds us, ultimately cost these Jewish leaders and activists their lives. Again, too, they were unable to do a thing amid the Nazi "crisis of civilization."[35]

As the masses of German Jews in Theresienstadt grew, the ghetto increasingly became the center of the German Jewish culture. For example, a modicum of research activity persisted there as rabbis Leo Baeck and Leopold Lukas continued to work on their history of the Jews, evidently in order to ready it for publication after a successful coup against Hitler.[36] Also active was a leisure culture department, initially headed by Otto Zucker of Prague and then by the Breslau attorney and erstwhile member of the Reichsvereinigung board Moritz Henschel. Theresienstadt had a German theater for German Jews and a Czech theater for Czech Jews; an opera and singing department; a library with some sixty thousand volumes; and soccer, volleyball, handball, basketball, and table tennis championships. There was even a two-division soccer league stocked mostly with teams that represented various vocations: electricians, gardeners, cooks, and youth welfare workers, but also teams that called themselves the Vienna Football Club or Hagibor Theresienstadt.[37] A cabaret was run by the famous actor and director Kurt Gerron in the finest German tradition. Four hundred eighty-nine speakers gave 2,309 recorded lectures on matters of history, literature, and religion but also on topics such as "Which wine is appropriate for Viennese schnitzel?"

Academics, artists, and intellectuals were strongly represented in the Theresienstadt ghetto, starting with Professor Maximilian Adler, who had instructed in Halle and afterward at the German University in Prague, and Emil Bacher, who had taught at the Talmud Torah school in Hamburg, and culminating with Ludwig von Blumenthal, professor of mathematics and erstwhile lecturer in Göttingen. The sociologist Paul Eppstein also lectured in Theresienstadt, for example, on the contribution of demography to the sociology of the Jews. Rabbi Regina Jonas of Berlin, while not recognized as a rabbi by the German administration of the ghetto, lectured on women's role in Jewish life. Jacob Jacobson did research for the SS on Jewish genealogy and lectured on family tree studies. The ghetto inhabitants saw leisure culture as the only way to maintain their human image. The German ghetto administration expressed its awareness of this by canceling leisure events as punishment for attempts to escape from the ghetto.

Life in the Theresienstadt ghetto was not free of tension, largely between national-minded Czech Jews and German or German-speaking Jews, but also between young and old or between "nonworkers" and laborers.[38] German was the official language of the ghetto, used for orders, posters, and minutes. Accordingly, non-German Jews viewed German Jews as somehow representative of the loathed authorities. Adler remarks:

> There were Czech Jews who said they had been sent to the ghetto wrongfully because they were not Jewish. All the guilt was borne by those who were simply called "Germans." Had the Jews of the Czech land not spoken German since time immemorial, Hitler would never have found an excuse to occupy their country and all the mayhem would have been avoided. Now and then things turned into heightened hostility among the Czech-speaking Jews toward the German-speaking Jews.[39]

Thus in Theresienstadt, too, German Jews were linked with the German perpetrators as "the Germans," irrespective of the fact of their being victims themselves. Concurrently, national-minded German Jews who had been deported to Theresienstadt alleged, quite absurdly, that "the Jews are guilty of everything that happens even here." Thus, inadvertently, they identified with their oppressors. Beyond this, German Jews suffered from the familiar stereotype that other Jews continually used to take their measure: "They were not bright and they had less of an understanding than [the others] of what was happening ... and they took almost everything too seriously. They lacked what the rest of European Jewry had: the capacity for alert self-defense and the flexibility to adapt to the risks that they encounter."[40]

One unique German cultural asset that survived the ghetto was the film *Theresienstadt: A Documentary Film from the Jewish Settlement Area*, subsequently euphemistically titled *The Führer Gives the Jews a City*. In the summer of 1944, while the movie star Heinz Rühmann stood before the camera to help create the film *Die Feuerzangbowle* (Tongs of fire) back in Berlin, Kurt Gerron, Rühmann's acting partner back in 1930, in the popular film *Die Drei von der Tankstele* (The threesome from the gas station), directed the Theresienstadt film at the authorities' command. The ghetto documentary was presented in the manner of a Potemkin village: Jews working, Jews reading, Jews playing.[41]

In June 1944, a mission from the International Committee of the Red Cross (sent to probe the conditions of the Danish Jews in the ghetto) was shown a fiction of normal life in Theresienstadt. Even Eppstein instructed those who were in on the secret not to tell them the truth. As evidence of the success of the deception, the Swiss representative of the International Committee of the Red Cross reported, "The Theresienstadt ghetto is a communist society led by an immensely valuable 'Stalin': Eppstein." At roughly that time, Eichmann's men in Prague decided to produce in Theresienstadt, from August 16 to September 11, 1944, the aforementioned propaganda film in order to mislead the public or the politicians abroad, before or after the expected end of the war. The scriptwriter and director Kurt Gerron created a superb professional product, planned meticulously and implemented efficiently. Erstwhile famous personalities from the German cultural world took part in the film as extras in order to insure themselves temporarily, so to speak, for their survival. Gerron sought out the "super-famous" in order to present them sitting at a table on a balcony: Dr. Georg Gradnauer, formerly a minister in the Reich government; Dr. Alfred Meissner, erstwhile Minister of Justice in the Republic of Czechoslovakia; Léon Mayer, once the French Minister of Trade; and Dr. Fritz Rathenau, cousin of Walther Rathenau and once the director general of a government office. Also shown were well-known professors enjoying a lecture at the community center: Professor Dr. Emil Utitz, once a lecturer at the German University in Prague; Adler, the ghetto historian; and Professor Dr. Alfred Klang, formerly of the University of Berlin. What the SS wanted to achieve by means of these scenes is clear. Unclear, however, was what Gerron had in mind by going along with this deceit. May he have sought, as an experienced cinema man, to insert a subversive message in this work? The question recurs in view of his stage instructions for a scene at a dental clinic: "In addition, I would like to send an ultraviolet lamp with several cute children, but not blond ones [!]."[42] Many participants in the film, as well as Gerron himself, were sent to Auschwitz after the job was done and were murdered there. Afterward, the film was reedited. The new version was never shown publicly; instead, it was excerpted in newsreels so that viewers could see the café scene accompanied by the following explanatory remarks: "While in Theresienstadt Jews sit for afternoon coffee and cake and do some afternoon dancing, our soldiers are struggling under the burden of the terrible war"—exactly in accordance with the Third Reich's familiar propaganda technique, which reverses the roles of perpetrators and victims.

Some tried to reveal the truth to the world. Their fate was as bitter as Gerron's. Jewish painters who furtively sketched the actual conditions of life in the Theresienstadt ghetto were interrogated on July 17 by Adolf Eichmann and the camp commanders. Found guilty of "atrocity propaganda," they were sent to Auschwitz or Sachsenhausen.[43]

Absurdly but typically, the National Socialist policy contributed nothing whatsoever to the "fortification of German-ness" in the Protectorate; instead, perversely, it abetted the destruction of everything German in that region. In the course of the war, German and German-speaking Jews were murdered in Theresienstadt or sent to Auschwitz. Some of the best-known representatives of German-ness who perished in Theresienstadt, apart from the many academics and artists mentioned above, were athletes. The most famous of them, beyond doubt, were two Jewish gymnasts who had won a gold medal and a silver medal for Germany in the first modern Olympic Games (1896)—Alfred and Gustav Flatow. Alfred died in the ghetto on December 28, 1942; his cousin Gustav passed away on January 29, 1945.

It is no wonder that, after the war, everything German was reviled in Bohemia, and the Czechs, instead of distinguishing between Germans and Germans, expelled the entire German minority. Even German Jews there could no longer nurture their German-ness. Hans-Günter Adler, an inmate at Theresienstadt and an important historian of the ghetto after the war, as noted, tellingly summarized matters after 1945: "I was not Czech. I belonged to the German culture and German no longer had a place in post-war Czechia."[44]

Paul Eppstein, who saw collaboration with the National Socialists' deception tactics as an instrumentality of rescue and survival, delivered a speech in Theresienstadt on September 19, 1944, on the occasion of the Jewish New Year. Centering on the topic of the impending end of the war, his address was perceptibly different from the anodyne rhetoric documented in the film about Theresienstadt. Defying Leo Baeck's counsel, Eppstein spoke openly about "[his] thoughts on the occasion of Rosh Hashana"—specifying, among other things, the true destination of the deportations. The speech was evidently one of the reasons for his murder by the Germans on September 28, 1944.[45]

In the autumn of 1944, after the Red Cross mission left Theresienstadt and the propaganda film was created, a great wave of deportations from Theresienstadt to Auschwitz ensued. Including those murdered in the camp, it took some fifty-one thousand lives. The ghetto, however, continued to exist until the end of the war and even served as a destination for many death marches. Overall, 5,120 Jews were liberated in Theresienstadt in 1945—more than the number of German Jews who were freed in the entire "Altreich."

NOTES

1. Cf. Christian Gerlach, *Kalkulierte Morde: Die deutsche Wirtschafts—und Vernichtungspolitik in Weißrußland 1941 bis 1944* (Hamburg: Hamburger Edition, 1999, 2 Aufl Studienausgabe, 2000), 646.

2. Quoted in Avraham Barkai, "Deutschsprachige Juden in osteuropäischen Ghettos," in idem, *Hoffnung und Untergang Studien zur deutsch-jüdischen Geschichte des 19 und 20 Jahrhunderts* (Hamburg: Christians, 1998), 203ff.

3. Ibid., 198–99.

4. Peter Klein, "Die Rolle der Vernichtungslager Kulmhof (Chełmno), Bełzec (Bełżec) und Auschwitz-Birkenau in den frühen Deportationsvorbereitungen," in Dittmar Dahlmann and Gerhard Hirschfeld, eds., *Lager, Zwangsarbeit, Vertreibung und Deportation Dimensionen der Massenverbrechen in der Sowjetunion und in Deutschland 1933 bis 1945* (Essen: Klartext, 1999), 474ff; Michael Alberti, *Die Verfolgung und Vernichtung der Juden im Reichsgau Wartheland 1939–1945* (Wiesbaden: Harrassowitz, 2006), 402–32; Phillipe Burrin, *Hitler und die Juden* (Frankfurt: Fischer, 1993), 139; Catherine Epstein, *Model Nazi: Arthur Greiser and the Occupation of Western Poland* (Oxford: Oxford University Press, 2010), 185, 190.

5. Andrea Löw, *Juden im Ghetto Litzmannstadt. Lebensbedingungen, Selbstwahrnehmung, Verhalten* (Göttingen: Wallstein, 2006), 247ff.

6. Quoted from Avraham Barkai, "Zwischen Ost und West Deutsche Juden im Ghetto Łódź," in idem, *Hoffnung und Untergang Studien zur deutsch-jüdischen Geschichte des 19 und 20 Jahrhunderts* (Hamburg: Hamburger Beiträge zur Sozial- und Zeitgeschichte, 1998), 241.

7. Löw, *Juden im Ghetto Litzmannstadt*, 240, 258.

8. Barkai, "Zwischen Ost und West Deutsche Juden im Ghetto Łódź," 243–45; Löw, *Juden im Ghetto Litzmannstadt*, 245, 254.

9. Barkai, "Zwischen Ost und West. Deutsche Juden im Ghetto Łódź," 250.

10. Dina Porat, "The Legend of the Struggle of the Jews from the Third Reich in the Ninth Fort near Kovno 1941–1942," in *Tel Aviver Jahrbuch für deutsche Geschichte* 20 (Tel Aviv: The Minerva Institute for German History, 1991), 366.

11. Roseman, *Past*, 190.

12. See p. 87 in this book, and cf. Hans Mommsen, *Auschwitz 17. Juli 1942. Der Weg zur europäischen "Endlösung der Judenfrage"* (Munich: Deutscher Taschenbuch, 2002), 142ff.

13. Löw, *Juden im Ghetto Litzmannstadt*, 247.

14. Ibid., 278.

15. Klein, "Die Rolle der Vernichtungslager Kulmhof (Chelmno), Bełzec (Bełżec) und Auschwitz-Birkenau in den frühen Deportationsvorbereitungen," 474ff; Michael Alberti, *Die Verfolgung und Vernichtung der Juden im Reichsgau Wartheland 1939–1945* (Wiesbaden: Harrassowitz, 2006), 476–78.

16. Robert Kuwalek, "Das kurze Leben 'im Osten': Jüdische Deutsche im Distrikt Lublin," in Birthe Kundrus and Beate Meyer, eds., *Die Deportation der Juden aus Deutschland. Pläne–Praxis–Reaktionen* (Göttingen: Wallstein, 2004), 116.

17. Ibid., 125.

18. Roseman, *Past*, 186–90.

19. Lea Preis, "The 'Other' Jews in the Warsaw Ghetto: The Discourse about the German Refugees in Warsaw Ghetto April–July 1942," in *Dapim. Studies on the Shoah* 20 (2006): 125–45.

20. Christopher R. Browning, *The Origins of the Final Solution: The Evolution of Nazi Jewish Policy, September 1939–March 1942* (Lincoln: University of Nebraska Press, 2004), 324ff.

21. Dina Porat, "The Legend of the Struggle of the Jews," 367.

22. Christopher R. Browning, *The Origins of the Final Solution: The Evolution of Nazi Jewish Policy, September 1939–March 1942* (Lincoln: University of Nebraska Press, 2004), 330ff.

23. Andrej Angrick and Peter Klein, *Die "Endlösung" in Riga: Ausbeutung und Vernichtung 1941–1944* (Darmstadt: Wissenschaftliche Buchgesellschaft, 2006), 217ff.

24. Sworn deposition of Alfred Winter, 1947, in Longerich and Pohl, *Die Ermordung der europäischen Juden*, 157–59.

25. "The Religious Life of the Deportee from Germany in the Ghetto: From the Diary of Karl Schneider," in Netanel Katzberg, *Pedut, Rescue in the Holocaust Texts and Studies* (Hebrew) (Ramat Gan: Bar-Ilan University Press, 1984), 131–44.

26. Avraham Barkai, "German-Speaking Jews in the Ghettos of Eastern Europe," in *Hope and Destruction: Studies of the History of German. Jews in the Nineteenth and Twentieth Centuries* (Hebrew) (Jerusalem: Leo Baeck Institute, 2009); Abgrick and Klein, *Die "Endlösung" in Riga*, 212–45.

27. Barkai, "German-Speaking Jews."

28. Klein, "Die Rolle der Vernichtungslager," 482.

29. Longerich and Pohl, *Die Ermordung der europäischen Juden*, 68.

30. H. G. Adler, *Die verheimlichte Wahrheit. Theresienstädter Dokumente* (Tübingen: Mohr [Siebeck], 1958), 89.

31. Ruth Elias in Longerich and Pohl, *Die Ermordung der europäischen Juden*, 178ff.

32. Ibid., 176.

33. Adler, *Die verheimlichte Wahrheit*, 131ff.

34. Ibid., 116ff.

35. Beate Meyer, *Paul Eppstein—Eine tödliche Gratwanderung* (Mannheim: Mannheimer Abendakademie und Volkshochschule GmbH, 2013), 34–36.

36. Arnold Paucker, "Resistance of German and Austrian Jews to the Nazi Regime, 1933–1945," *LBYB* 40 (1995): 8.

37. Adler, *Die verheimlichte Wahrheit*, 248; Stefan Zwicker, ed., *Frantisek Steiner. Fußball unterm gelben Stern* (Paderborn: Schöningh, 2017).

38. Anna Hájková, *The Last Ghetto: The Everyday History of Theresienstadt* (New York: Oxford University Press, 2020).

39. H. G. Adler, *Theresienstadt 1941–1945. Das Antlitz einer Zwangsgemeinschaft: Geschichte, Soziologie, Psychologie* (Tübingen: Mohr, 1960), 303.

40. Ibid., 304.

41. Lara Pellner, Hans-Georg Soeffner, and Marija Stanisavlievic, eds., *Theresienstadt-Filmfragmente und Zeitzeugenberichte* (Wiesbaden: Springer, 2021).

42. Adler, *Die verheimlichte Wahrheit*, 310, 312, 328, 344; cf. Karel Margry, "Theresienstadt (1944–1945): The Nazi Propaganda Film Depicting the Concentration Camp as Paradise," *Historical Journal of Film* 12 (1992): 2.

43. Hannelore Dauer, "Kunst im Schatten des Todes," in Richard Albrecht and Otto R. Romberg, eds., *Widerstand und Exil 1933–1945* (Frankfurt, New York: Campus-Verlag, 1986), 170.

44. Adler, *Theresienstadt 1941–1945*, 191.

45. Elena Makarova et al., eds., *University over the Abyss: The Story behind 520 Lecturers and 2430 Lectures in KZ Theresienstadt 1942–1944* (Jerusalem: Verba, 2000), 184.

SIX

—◆—

MISCHLINGE, "DIVERS," AND VIRTUAL JEWS

ACCORDING TO REICHSVEREINIGUNG STATISTICS, IN October 1941—before the deportations began—Reich territory was home to a vestigial population of 163,696 "Jews by race" (*Rassejuden*). In January 1942, after the first wave of transports, this number fell to 130,823. Given the original intention of banishing all Jews from the Reich by the end of 1941, the data demonstrate the relative inefficiency of the deportation mechanism. Even though the evictions continued systematically in the course of 1942, the end of that year still found 51,257 Jews in the Reich. For the Jews of Berlin, February 1943—immediately after the surrender of the Sixth Army in the Battle of Stalingrad—was particularly harrowing because Goebbels, henceforth in charge of the "total war" policy, decided at long last to make his Gau (district) Judenfrei. Thus, 7,973 people were deported directly to Auschwitz and 1,259 others to Theresienstadt. By the summer of 1943, shortly before the Reichsvereinigung was dissolved, the number of Jews in the "Altreich" shrank to 31,807. Most of them—17,375 individuals to be more precise—did not wear the Judenstern. Namely, before 1933 they had not belonged to Jewish communities or had not considered themselves Jews. (This is not to say that all "star-wearing" Jews had self-identified as Jews before 1933.) Others were defined as Mischlinge or as "privileged" or "nonprivileged" miscegenational spouses. From this standpoint, it is somewhat consistent to use the term "Judenfrei," since most people who were defined as Jews in 1943 in Germany were Jewish not in their own eyes but only under the criteria that the racist regime had imposed on them.

In the course of 1942, the Jewish population of Germany fell to less than one-tenth of what had been in 1933. Nevertheless, the regime continued to churn out anti-Jewish rules and edicts. The pleasure derived from the "war on

134

Judaism" within the Reich had not waned; as long as people defined as Jews remained alive on German soil, party functionaries, bureaucrats, and various hangers-on persisted in their efforts to make these people's lives even more detestable and to protect the Volksgemeinschaft against what they called the "Jewish mess." Accordingly, additional enactments against the residual Jewish population substantiate the unmatched petty vileness of National Socialist antisemitism. The February 15, 1942, directive, requiring the marking of Jewish names in telephone books with the Star of David, served only the purpose of gratuitous humiliation. It pertained mainly to "miscegenational" Jews, since all the others were already enjoined against owning telephones. Additional orders came in swift succession. From March 24, Jews' use of public transport was limited even further. Even within their cities, they were allowed to use the tram only with written permission from the police. On May 26, the party bureau promulgated a ban on selling traditional German clothing to Jews. On June 6, the Ministry of Transport forbade Jews to use waiting rooms at railroad stations. From June 11 onward, Jews were denied tobacco rations—an especially nasty stricture in wartime—with only severely disabled veterans and Jews in "mixed marriages" excepted. Two months later, another loophole was detected and closed in Dresden: when writing to the authorities, Jews were not allowed to use previous titles such as "attorney" or "doctor." Also in August, the RSHA ruled that Jews might no longer buy postcards. In October, Jews were denied the additional pleasure of shopping in bookstores.

As absurd as it may seem, the transformation of the "Altreich" into a "Jew-free zone" meant that Jews were no longer tolerated even in the concentration camps in Germany. The few remaining Jewish prisoners in these camps, who in any case had been prime targets for harassment if not extortion by "green-triangle" inmates (i.e., "professional criminals") began to be sent to the east by order of Heinrich Himmler in the summer of 1942. On October 5, 1942, Himmler ordered "all concentration camps in Reich territory [to] be made free of Jews."[1] The Jewish prisoners were earmarked for deportation to Auschwitz. Foreseeing their bitter fate, Jewish inmates in the Sachsenhausen concentration camp attempted to resist deportation, unavailingly. Not all the deportees, however, were sent to immediate death; some were posted to labor in the construction of Auschwitz III or industrial plants in the district. Those not protected by accepted safeguards for criminal prisoners did not die from "natural causes" but were murdered in the course of "Sonderbehandlung [special treatment] 13f14" (gassing to death in "euthanasia" facilities). Above I mentioned the removal of Jewish prisoners from the Neuengamme concentration camp in April 1942 to extermination in Bernburg. Here, however, an absurd turning point took place: given the growing influence of the SS main office on the economy and the administration, Jews were sent not only from German concentration camps to slave labor in the east but the other way around: some Jews in the east were delivered to the German Reich to perform slave labor there. For economic reasons, a forced "remigration" of Jews to Germany ensued in the spring of 1944, marking the start of a strange and unique chapter in the history of the "Jews in Germany": thousands of Jewish prisoners from the east were put to work under inhumane conditions in underground aircraft manufacturing plants—turning out the so-called wonder weapon (the V-2 rocket), clearing rubble, and performing other tasks. In Mauthausen (Austria), there were only nineteen Jewish prisoners in February 1944, but in September one could find more than eleven thousand Jews there. In Buchenwald, the population of Jewish inmates ballooned from 220 in July 1943 to almost 12,000 in September 1944. Most of the newly arrived were East European Jews, many of whom would remain in Germany after the war as displaced persons. However, a small number of them were German Jews who had been sent back from Łódź, Auschwitz, and other camps. Their itinerary demonstrates once again the absurdity of the National Socialists' Jewish policy.[2]

Since the number of "full Jews" in Germany had contracted so severely since 1942, the new rules pertained more and more to "Mischlinge." On February 26, 1943, several days after the defeat in Stalingrad and eight years after the adoption of the appropriate definitions under the "Nuremberg Laws," it became forbidden to employ domestics "of German blood" in the homes of Jews, "Mischlinge of the first degree," and "miscegenational marriages."[3]

The inventive capacity of antisemitism in a Germany that had already been declared "Judenfrei" is demonstrated by a rule enacted on September 28, 1943, forbidding state officials to marry any woman who had formerly been married to a Jew—as though contact with Jews truly caused incurable contagious diseases! A year earlier, the RSHA dealt with dead Jews in its own way: the SD complained on June 22, 1942, that "pictures and prints by Jewish artists . . . [are being] dealt with commercially without any restrictions. . . . At [one] auction, three paintings by Max Liebermann were purchased."[4] That dead Jews remained a possible topic of conversation was evidenced by the farce that surrounded the publication of an obituary notice in an SS newspaper in December 1942 when it turned out the deceased was Jewish.[5]

In the Third Reich's ecosystem of murder and robbery, it was evidently still possible to find places to hide, and plugging them up seemed to be an imperative among regime-loyal Volksgenossen. Since the deportations began, as noted, automatic confiscation of deportees' property had been standard practice. In the summer of 1943, the rare possibility that a Jew would some-how remain in Germany and leave considerable wealth on German soil after his or her death was also dealt with. On July 1, the Thirteenth Regulation to the "Nuremberg Laws" established that the property of a deceased Jew would be turned over to the Reich. On June 10, the Reichsvereinigung was disman-tled and its property—that is, the remaining collective property of German Jewry—was divided between the tax authorities and the RSHA. To facilitate supervision of the vestigial Jewish presence in the Reich, particularly in Berlin, it was decided on August 3, 1943, that the Reichsvereinigung would continue to exist for the time being. The duties of this rump entity, known as the "New Reichsvereinigung," will be discussed below.

To persecute the Jews, all inhibitions were abandoned and a special bureau-cratic and administrative dynamic was set in motion. Anti-Jewish rules were enacted even after June 1943. This should not be surprising: especially after Stalingrad, the propaganda machine stepped up its scapegoating of "the Jew" to distract attention from the Wehrmacht's defeat and the generally wretched state of supplies. On April 29, 1943, the press was instructed to deal with the Jewish question "continually." Even soccer fans had to read about it at this time. On June 3 and 4, 1943, Otto Nerz, coach of the national team until 1936, wrote in the Berlin newspaper 12Uhr Blatt about how "performance has improved since the Hebrews were banished." Against the background of the war that the Jews had fomented, "the peoples of Europe," Nerz wrote, "may see from up close the pow-erful momentum of German sports, which have been Judenfrei since 1933. . . . One after another, the nations are shaking off the yoke of the Jews. Ultimately, we look forward to a Judenfrei Europe and Judenfrei sports."[6] Unsurprisingly, then, loyal Volksgenossen sought to avenge themselves against "the Jew" with full force by making new rules and overseeing their implementation.

The police finally put an end to this torrent of regulations, which had become increasingly absurd but were no less cruel on that account. On March 10, the Chief of the Security Police appealed to the zealous bureaucrats: "The evacu-ation and isolation of the Jews . . . have made the promulgation of old-style special regulations valueless and it must stop."[7] In fact, in July 1944, according to statistics kept by the New Reichsvereinigung, no more than 14,529 live Jews remained in all of Germany, and even this figure, as stated, was based only on the racist definition of the term. By using the euphemisms "evacuation" and "isolation," Ernst Kaltenbrunner, Heydrich's successor after the latter's assas-sination, honored the instruction of the Party Bureau Chief, Martin Bormann, of July 11, 1943, against talking about a final solution in any public discussion of the Jewish problem. Despite the directive, Alfred Rosenberg revealed, in a speech on October 13, 1943, that "Germany today has solved the Jewish question," referring in this context to Germany and not to Europe, and spoke of a "biological purge" that had not been attained "by small measures."[8] Thus he acknowledged the systematic murder of German Jewry. Hitler himself, meeting with senior officers in Obersalzberg on April 26, 1944, mentioned the "distancing" of the Jews from Germany. This, he said at this late phase of the war, had eliminated the menace of a fifth column in Germany itself.[9] As time passed, the schizophrenic inclination of this attitude became increasingly clear: on the one hand, as "lackeys of international Jewry," the Jews of Germany were the ultimate lightning rod, making the struggle against them more existential than ever. On the other hand, the looming defeat, which must not be acknowledged, made it necessary to tread carefully and kindled fears of revenge and retribution after the war. On February 16, 1945, the Ministry of Economic Affairs ordered all files pertaining to anti-Jewish activity to be destroyed "lest they fall into enemy hands."[10]

The prime cause of the decline in Germany's Jewish population after October 1942 was deportation, of course. The operations attending to this endeavor became more and more extreme from October 1942 onward. Now, officials of the Jewish communities and the Reichsvereinigung were also expelled from Germany. Alois Brunner, stationed in Berlin, introduced for the purpose of "cleansing of Jews" methods that had already been applied in Vienna: dragnets for Jews in city streets and workplaces. These persecutions crested with the "factories operation" (Fabrikaktion) that began on February 27, 1943, in which all Jews still employed in manufacturing, including the armaments industry, were abruptly rounded up from their workplaces for deportation. Targeted in the operation were what remained of "full Jews" in Germany, particularly those in "miscegenational marriages," who until then had been exempt from deportation due to their spouses and their contribution to the war economy. The operation took place throughout the Altreich—in Dresden, Hamburg, and Breslau, among other places. Within a few days, some eleven thousand Jews, including more than seven thousand in Berlin alone, were deported. It was this Aktion, mentioned in chapter 4, that triggered the "Aryan wives" demonstration on Rosenstraße. Ultimately, whether or not their intervention led to the liberation of their husbands and saved them from death is neither here nor there;[11] either way, the Fabrikaktion, as an anti-Jewish measure that directly affected the Volksgenossen, substantiates the difficulties that arose in implementing the racial policy consistently.

The limits of the totalitarian method and policy toward the Jews come to light here: at day's end, matters escalated to the point of a public demonstration but also to a wave of "diving" or "submerging" (going underground). Thus, according to various estimates, about one-third of the potential victims, as many as seven thousand people, managed to evade the clutches of the police. Since such an operation (i.e., deportation) could not be kept secret, many Jews were forewarned and decided to "dive." By February 1943, not only the police but also the Jews knew the name "Auschwitz";[12] it was the direct destination of the transports out of Berlin between late 1942 and October 1944.

Deportation and natural morbidity among the older-than-average Jewish population, however, do not fully explain this population's rapid contraction at this stage of the war. (The number of Jews who managed to cross into Switzerland was inconsequentially small.) Any observer notices the very high number of suicides that accompanied the deportation waves. From October 1941 to the summer of 1943, three thousand to four thousand Jews, about 2 percent of the remaining Jewish population that was threatened with deportation, took their lives. An estimated one-quarter of recorded deaths in Berlin at this time were by suicide. In 1941, 18 percent of all suicides were among Jews. From October on, when the deportations got underway, the rate escalated to 40 percent. In the third quarter of 1942, after the destination of the transports became known, it climbed to as much as 75 percent according to police statistical data.[13] The cemetery in the Weissensee quarter of Berlin received 59 suicides for burial in 1940, 254 in 1941, 811 in 1942, 314 in 1943, and only 34 in 1944, after Berlin had been declared Judenfrei. The total number of suicides between 1933 and 1945 was 1,907. "There were weeks," the Jewish cleric Martin Riesenburger wrote, "when there were so many suicides that we were kept busy burying [them] until the evening hours."[14] The average age of Jews who took their lives was roughly sixty-five. Those up in years were unwilling to leave their accustomed environment and start over, or die, in an unknown place. "Diving" was more suitable for young people, which is not to say they found it easy.

For many Jews, persecution and humiliation were sufficient reason to "choose" suicide over continuing to live. The suicide rate among German Jews, inordinately steep even before the deportations began, attained new heights in many cities due to a wave of suicides in 1941–1942, even though at first there was no talk of gas chambers and no rumors about mass murder.[15] The Orthodox Jew Willy Cohn, fifty-two, told his diary on September 30, 1941, under the impression of the Judenstern decree and the evacuation of apartments in Breslau: "My nervous reserves are at an end, and yet large reserves are what are needed to face what lies ahead of us. Sometimes I think to myself that it would be better if I no longer existed, but when you have such small children it is impermissible even to think such a thing."[16]

Two weeks later, the deportations started and many could no longer avoid thinking about "such a thing." "Neither of us is young and healthy enough," wrote the author of a typical farewell letter on July 1, 1942, "to endure life without care, without proper and adequate food, in cold and filth, imprisoned with masses of people in a narrow space and suffering from brutal treatment."[17] "It would be something of a paradox to go mad due to fear of death," wrote another, in a common way of expressing resistance to suicide.[18] Ultimately, fear of torture, humiliation, and uncertainty did prompt many to take their own lives. As more and more reports about goings-on in the east filtered into Germany despite all attempts to repress them, this dread seemed increasingly justified. The American journalist Howard K. Smith, still in Germany in October 1941, attempted to interpret this phenomenon: "They were facing death either way; the discerning preferred the easy and quick way over the difficult and slow one."[19]

Suicide was not only a way to evade humiliation, deportation, and murder in the east; it was also an act of defiance and resistance as well as an expression of the wish to deny the Nazis authority over one's life. Willy Cohn expressed the basic attitude tellingly: "But I believe that . . . we will be forced to tread the same path that so many others have before us. The main thing is to do it with dignity and not to lose one's nerve."[20] The tranquility that was displayed at the time of the deportation and even at the time of suicide reflected an attempt to preserve dignity. In his work *We Survived*, Leo Baeck remarks in amazement about the ability among the Jews to maintain restraint: although the transports aroused fear and anxiety in the Jews, they did not want to give the SS men satisfaction and make a scene.

Many went to their death with the help of Veronal, a powerful sedative in pill form for which some sold their remaining property. Others opened their gas jets, fulfilling a wish that Hitler had expressed in *Mein Kampf* twenty years earlier. Most made the difficult decision when deportation or roundup loomed. Others attempted suicide at the staging point: "Many suicides took place right there," Herta Pineas, a food supplier at one of the gathering camps, related. Since the expulsion of Jews was officially and formally an "evacuation" and their dispatch to death had to take place in a controlled way, absurd guidelines in the event of a failed suicide were laid down: "Anyone who did not succeed was punished for attempting suicide! Those who recovered in the hospital—in a special ward under police observation—were sent out in the penal department of the next transport. . . . It was also forbidden to feed them."[21] "My colleagues at the internal-medicine department," recounted the neurologist Dr. Pineas, who practiced medicine at the Jewish hospital in Berlin until March 1943, "were of two minds about whether it was better to save these patients or let them go to sleep in peace."[22]

Jews who "chose" suicide were punished not because Jewish lives had special value but because thus they had managed to evade the regime's directives. Even the decision to read *Faust* or *Hamlet* before dying was an act of resistance because it signified an attempt to nullify the reader's exclusion from German culture.[23] Men who pressed to their chests the First Class Iron Cross before taking Veronal protested not only against the injunction against wearing decorations of valor but also, generally, against their banishment from German society.[24]

Several suicides of Jews who had escaped from Germany are relatively well known: Kurt Tucholsky, Stefan Zweig, Walter Benjamin, and Ernst Toller. Only a few of the many suicides on German soil remain in the collective memory. Martha Liebermann and the popular actor Joachim Gottschalk and his family are among them. Martha Liebermann, widow of the famous painter Max Liebermann, took Veronal in March 1943 at the age of eighty-five, when she received the order to prepare for deportation, and Gottschalk, who refused to divorce his Jewish wife despite pressure from Propaganda Minister Goebbels, chose suicide on November 6, 1941, as did his wife and their son, because the danger of deportation loomed over both spouses. The reason for the death of the thirty-seven-year-old actor was concealed at the time. Only Kurt Maetzig's 1947 film *Ehe im Schatten* (Marriage in the shadows) divulged his bitter fate to millions of viewers *after* the Third Reich fell. In Berlin, one also recalls the author Jochen Klepper, who died of suicide on December 11, 1942, along with his Jewish wife, Hani *née* Gerstel, and their daughter, Renate, because he saw no way to save them. Klepper had become famous mainly for his novel *Der Vater: Roman des Soldatenkönigs* (The father: A novel of the soldier-king), in which he tells the story of Friedrich Wilhelm I and describes him as an exemplary God-fearing and modern Prussian ruler. Klepper's diary entries in 1932–1942 were published in 1956.[25]

As stated above, the regime spent its last two years trying to stamp out even the last tatters of the phenomenon of a "Jew" in Germany. Jews who had "Aryan" spouses belonged to the "tatter" class, and now I wish to summarize the relevant concrete measures that pertained to them. From 1933 on, the regime saw "Mischlinge," the natural outcomes of "miscegenation," as a special problem. At the Wannsee Conference on January 20, 1942, and at additional conclaves on March 6 and October 27, 1942, representatives of the party, the SS, and the senior bureaucracy debated their fate intensively. The discussion concerned the 115,000 or so "half-Jews" and "quarter-Jews" who accounted for slightly more than one-thousandth of the German population. The discussants at these get-togethers mulled both the sterilization and the deportation of the people in question. According to the "Third Reich" racists' logic, the indiscriminate murder of "Mischlinge" also constituted an offense against "German blood." Those who were "considered Jews" (*Geltungsjuden*; i.e., "Mischlinge of the first degree" who had been raised and schooled as Jews) could be "upgraded," so to speak, to "plain" "Mischlinge of the first degree" by ad personam decision of Hitler and thus be protected from deportation among lesser troubles. At the "Final Solution conference" in October 1942, it was decided that "Mischlinge of the first degree" would be allowed to remain in Germany after being sterilized, whereas "Mischlinge of the second degree" should be treated as of German blood.[26] The participants decided—with sublime cynicism—no longer to allow exceptions for "Mischlinge of the first degree": they were to be mustered out of the Wehrmacht. This made it impossible to protect a Jewish parent against deportation as long as the son was fighting for Germany. By decision of Hermann Göring in the autumn of 1943, after their discharge from military service, "Mischlinge" would be assigned to slave duty in the labor brigades of "Organisation Todt." Despite harsh working conditions, the members of "Sonderkommando [Special Unit] J" were considered "highly fit" and motivated. Managers of armaments plants often declared skilled Jews definitively crucial in order to retain them in a "normal" workplace. In October 1944, Himmler ordered an end to exceptions of this kind even though there were no worthy substitutes for these Jews and the Jews' deportation would crimp the arms industry somewhat. By then, with the Reich in retreat, a combination of signs of decline and ideological radicalization had set in. In addition, the bureaucracy now dealt continually with personal requests for "upgrades" from "Mischlinge of the first and second degree" to "person of German blood" or at least "Mischlinge of the second degree." The entire affair ultimately illustrates both the madness and the absurdity of the racial policy and the nearly inconceivable radicalization that had occurred in the treatment of people who carried the "taint" of Jewishness in National Socialist eyes.[27] Thus James F. Tent summarizes the history of the Mischlinge in the Third Reich: "The Gestapo-led actions in the final winter of the war of rounding up all Jews in 'privileged mixed marriages,' all so-called *Geltungsjuden*, and all male *Mischlinge* first degree demonstrated that all organizations under the umbrella of the SS were continuing . . . their irrational and perverted attempts to create a Germany that was *judenfrei*."[28]

Science, too, with or without scare quotes, was allowed to continue dealing with the question of Jews and "virtual Jews" long after most German Jews had been deported to the east and murdered along with fellow Jews already there. Wilhelm Grau, until 1942 director of the Institute for the Study of the Jewish

Problem in Frankfurt, acting in the service of Rosenberg, published in 1943, in the "Kleine Weltkampfbücherei" (Little Library) series of the newspaper *Weltkampf*, his lecture about "historical attempts to solve the Jewish question," which concluded with the following warning: "We, too, must not allow the new and never-to-recur historical possibility of totally solving the Jewish question to slip away without exploiting it or letting it be solved halfway. . . . The twentieth century, which at its inception saw the Jew at the peak of his power, will no longer see Israel at its end because by then the Jews will have disappeared from Europe."[29]

The Jews of Germany indeed "disappeared" from the standpoint of the other Germans, having been exiled to and murdered in the east. Wilhelm Grau, Rosenberg's lackey historian, knew this well. Intensive research on the Jewish matter, however, took place not only at the academic level—for example, by Professor Günther Franz of the Reich University in Strasbourg, Alsace; Walther Frank of the Reich Institute for the History of the New Germany; Fritz Arlt in his dissertation on Judaism; and numerous authors who placed critical articles and writings in the highly important scientific journal *Historische Zeitschrift* and with Rosenberg's Institute for the Study of the Jewish Problem—but also at the RSHA. Rosenberg's Ministry for the Eastern Occupied Territories and the RSHA both established mammoth Judaica libraries by looting public and private Jewish collections. The theologian and historian Johannes Pohl, appointed chief librarian at Rosenberg's institute in Frankfurt in 1941, confiscated the public and private libraries of deported Jews from all over Europe but mainly in Germany, whereas the "rival" institution in Berlin, the RSHA, seized the libraries of the Reichsvereinigung, the Jewish Theological Seminary of Breslau, and the Jewish communities in Berlin, Hamburg, and Vienna as the deportations proceeded.

Fate, however, treated the matter with a bitter guffaw: not only Jews but also their books were destroyed—albeit against the Nazis' wishes. The RSHA's collection succumbed to an aerial bombardment of Berlin in November 1943, as did Rosenberg's library in March 1944 in Frankfurt.[30]

The question of why the SD maintained a special department (Amt II) for "ideological study of the adversary," headed by Professor Franz Six, arises after the fact not only because another department at the RSHA—Eichmann's Bureau IV B 4—was dealing with a practical solution to the Jewish problem but also because the "adversary" continued to be "studied" even after it had ceased to exist in the territories ruled by the Third Reich. The reason, apparently, is that the Jews outside the Reich had yet to be "dealt with." What is more, I note en passant, other ministries also engaged in "Jewish studies."[31]

The RSHA's department for research on the Jews, inaugurated in December 1941, marked VII B II and run by Dr. Heinz Ballensiefen, looted Jewish libraries to establish a central Judaica library, published a journal titled *Sources and Studies on the Jewish Question*, and researched "historical attempts to solve the Jewish problem." It also asked the "professional," Adolf Eichmann, to propose ideas for projects. Eichmann made available to "researchers of the adversary" a "library squad" (*Bibliothekskommando*) of Hebrew-speaking Jews for VII B II until they were sent to Auschwitz as part of the Fabrikaktion. With immense grotesquerie, Eichmann had the opportunity to engage in separate "Jewish studies" of his own because he had the greatest experts in the field at his beck and call. As mentioned above, rabbis Baeck and Lukas, both of them prisoners in Theresienstadt, wrote a history of the Jews' legal status on Eichmann's orders, a work subsequently presented as an act of conspiracy. In Prague, he ordered the establishment of a Jewish museum in order to showcase the legacy of the vanished Jews. From 1943 onward, by which time few Jews remained in Germany, Ballensiefen's bureau issued fortnightly "information reports on the Jewish question," including a review of the Jewish press abroad. The recipients of these reports were high-ranking police and government officials. Until the demise of the Third Reich, Jews were objects of National Socialist research, with former German citizens replaced by "virtual Jews" as "virtual" objects of study.

The final act of German Jewry on "Altreich" soil, performed mainly in Berlin and lasting almost two years, was essentially limited to the last bastion of Jewish life in that city, the Jewish hospital.[32] Only in this facility, on Iranische Straße in the Wedding quarter of the city, could Jewish men and women still receive medical care. There, too, since June 1943, by authorization of the Minister of Finance in an order dated August 3, the rump Reichsvereinigung and its sixty-four-member staff had their last headquarters, engaging mainly in taking care of the Reichsvereinigung's property. To manage this last vestige of the Reichsvereinigung, the Reich authorities appointed Dr. Walther Lustig, the husband of an "Aryan" woman. Lustig had only the faintest knowledge of Jewish customs and displayed characteristic willingness to collaborate with the Gestapo. Subordinate to his management were forty-one leaders of the rump community, whose main duties were taking care of "miscegenational" Jews. Essentially, Lustig decided on his own which of the patients and hospital staff would appear on the transport rosters. (Three hundred employees of the hospital had already been deported to the east in the "Hospital Aktion" of February 27–March 7, 1943.) Dr. Lustig, strongly remembered by many Jews as a "determined Jewish antisemite" who maintained "pleasurable relations with the nurses,"[33] was executed after the war by the Soviet occupation forces for having collaborated with the Nazis. In Hamburg, too, a physician at the Jewish hospital, Martin Corten, was designated a "representative of the New Reichsvereinigung." In Munich, the Director of the Reichsvereinigung district office appointed Theodor Koronchik as its "representative."

In March 1943, three transports, 1,700 Jews in each, were still put together in Berlin, whereas from August onward there were fewer than one hundred persons in each transport and, in October, fewer than fifty. The hospital staff had to evict Jews from their apartments and deliver them to the collection camp, which had been relocated from Große Hamburger Straße to the lot on Iranische Straße. In the hospital itself was a well-guarded police station, where patients "who had attempted suicide due to fear of being deported" received treatment.[34] Obersturmführer Walter Dobberke, the Gestapo commander of the collection camp, organized the transports and acted as "master of life and death" until the last moments of the war.

In the final year of the war, most Jews remaining in Germany lived in hiding. The number of those who went underground, aka "divers" (in German, the word has both literal and figurative meaning) is estimated at eight thousand (five thousand to seven thousand of whom in Berlin), of whom some two thousand managed to survive. Jews who went over to "illegal" life found it difficult to arrange hideouts and essential necessary documents, including ration cards. The population was eagerly willing to denounce any suspicious person (a fortiori a suspected Jew) to the police and the Gestapo, as the Jews knew at the time and as ex post historical research confirms. However, the longer the deportations continued and as certainty mounted that death awaited them at the end of the journey, the more willing were young people or families with children to take the risk of "diving" anyway. Practically speaking, the very possibility of "diving" was limited to the major cities, foremost Berlin. The recently researched case of Munich corroborates this. There, although an estimated one hundred Jewish townspeople "submerged," in 1941–1942, only twenty-two cases are known in detail, among a remaining Jewish population of only some 3,200. Rescuers of Jews in Munich were of various and sundry kinds. At one extreme, one finds General Franz Ritter von Epp, the Reichsstatthalter (Reich commissioner) of Bavaria for the Nazi Party, who extended his patronage to one of his former officers, a Catholic of Jewish origin.[35] A large city provided more opportunities for "diving" because informers had less influence among masses of people and anonymity helped to mask a false identity. Possibly, too, the city's proletarian environment made people somewhat less willing to collaborate with the authorities, giving "submerged" Jews a better periphery than

they could have found elsewhere. Furthermore, as the bombardments escalated, the chaos they caused made a false identity easier to pass off. Just the
same, exceptional cases of "diving" in small localities are known. In the Rhe-
ineland village of Herbern, Heihrich Aschoff concealed Marga Spiegel and her
mother with the help of additional farmers in the vicinity for the last two years
of the war. The 2009 film *Unter Bauern: Retter in der Nacht* (Among farmers:
Rescuers in the night) made the case famous.

Even amid the ongoing deportations, "diving" was a hard decision for individual Jews to make. "How many cases do we know," Hermann Pineas wrote
after the liberation, "of people who made all preparations for submerging and
still could not resolve to do it and thus fell prey to the roundup?" To keep Jews
from going underground on the verge of their deportation, the Gestapo did not
serve notice of evacuation in a timely way. Reluctance to "submerge" was also
associated with the question of the ability to do it, of course. The preparations
were dangerous even for those who had friends who could keep the secret:
"Think of how hard it was just to obtain passport photos. With the Judenstern
on your jacket lapel, asking a photo shop to make [such a photo] was grounds
for a complaint to the police. Therefore, it had to be done in the following way:
Go to a faraway shop, leave the jacket with the star along the way with some-
body reliable, enter the photo shop wearing a jacket with no star, and hope that
no one identified you en route and would not identify you in the shop."

This is only an example to prove the point. Another example is the story of
Franz Kaufmann, who ran a network of at least forty-two aides and was murdered by the Gestapo in February 1942.[36] The complications and perils that
arose in helping "divers" are excellently demonstrated in the diary of Ruth
Andreas-Friedrich, who did much to help the "submerged"; in the story of
Marianne Strauss; and in Marie Jalowicz Simon's tell-all autobiography. They
reveal the difficulty, the importance of which was belittled after the fact, of the
impossibility of knowing when the war would finally end. The potential "diver"
asked herself: How long must I prepare for? And what if the regime survives?
Although by September 1944, one could hope that Germany would lose the war
very soon, by December 9, Ruth Andreas-Friedrich ceased to believe that the
end was imminent.[37] On March 31, 1945—only a few weeks away from the end
of the war from our point of view—so many fugitives went underground that
their helpers found it hard to cope. By then, the National Socialist system was
gripped with madness and more dangerous than ever. The chances of survival
depended less on the mercies of non-Jews than on their widespread and fortu-
nate ignorance of the regime's full collection of anti-Jewish rules. On the basis
of this surprising realization, Marie Jalowicz Simon reached the conclusion

that her "submersion" might succeed even if she would come into incidental daily contact with her surroundings.

It took audacity to go underground, and Jews who were unprepared for the adventure quickly abandoned the idea, accepting deportation to the east or preferring suicide. For many, life in the underground posed a dilemma of conscience because at any moment it could end in disaster for other Jews or for their non-Jewish rescuers. In the aforementioned October 1942 "community transport," which swept up most functionaries of the Berlin Jewish community and the Reichsvereinigung for deportation, "a few managed to evade their fate. The result was that four community officials . . . as well as four members of the Reichsvereinigung board . . . were executed by gunfire, even though they were totally innocent and could not have prevented the disappearance of these people in any way."[38]

The Mishnaic aphorism "all Jews are each other's guarantors" was fulfilled in the "Third Reich" in a manner that made all Jews hostages in life and death.

Given the very dynamic and consistency of "cleansing" a place of Jews, the Gestapo aggressively continued trying to track down the few remaining Jewish "divers" even after the Fabrikaktion. Shortly after that operation, unwilling to rely only on informers and German police, it activated a "Jew-Scouting Service." In Berlin, some thirty "scouts" or "trappers" were involved in arresting divers. The Gestapo strove in particular to employ former staff members of Jewish authorities or the Jüdischer Kulturbund as Jew-hunters because their wide circle of acquaintances made them especially suitable as snitches. The reason is that the trappers' activity focused not on one-off denunciation of other fugitives, as often happened when a "diver" was captured and tortured, but on systematic manhunting. A "scout" (*Greifer*) received payment, ration cards, and permission to circulate without the yellow star, all of which was instead of being shipped to Auschwitz. In the historical literature, as noted, the Reichsvereinigung, the Judenräte, and the "deliverers to the transports" are all roundly criticized for being collaborators. The "Jew-Scouting Service," however, was the most radical example of the erosion of Jewish solidarity and betrayal of "our own." Yet it also gives further evidence of the terrifying circumstances that the regime imposed on the Jewish minority. Here the police invoked a tactic they would ordinarily use to penetrate a crime organization or an espionage agency: blackmailing a member of the target entity in order to "turn" him or her and make him or her collaborate. Even the most famous/infamous "trapper," Stella Ingrid Goldschlag, aka Stella Kübler-Isaaksohn, the beautiful daughter of a composer and, for a while, a singer, whose story would be retold in investigative and biographical writings, was mobilized for this purpose.[39] Arrested and tortured in 1943, she worked for the Gestapo from September 1943 on. Her motive, she said, was her wish to spare her parents from deportation.

"Of some 8,000," however, "there were sixty in all," reported a prisoner at the collection camp at the time. "All the others preferred to be sent to Auschwitz and not to help to track down relatives, acquaintances, or co-religionists."[40] Although the accuracy of this statement cannot be known, one thing is absolutely clear: suitable candidates who balked at collaborating had to join the transport.

The Jewish "scouts" facilitated the Gestapo's work and delivered fugitives to the agency's clutches. The crucial point is that they, too, were hostages, wedged between hammer and anvil, and those who had made them so could construct fictitious turfs in which they could operate. Some "scouts" definitely plunged into the work enthusiastically and fell prey to the illusion of having power. A few wore black Gestapo jackets and sometimes even went about armed and, when arresting their "co-racials," cried not only "I'll call the Gestapo" but also, sometimes, "We are the Gestapo!"[41] At all times, they carried green ID cards of Gestapo issue. They enriched themselves by blackmailing hiding Jews. Others conducted private selections and warned a few fugitives against impending arrest. In a few words, at a time when being Jewish had in effect become a crime and Jews could be "struggled" against without inhibition, the relationship between police and Jews increasingly resembled one between police and an underworld.

Snitches and "scouts" had to do various things. They postured as prisoners and tried to milk real prisoners for information, say, about "divers." At their own initiative, they searched for hideouts of Jews and participated in arrests and raids. The fear they sowed crested in inspections of public places: trams, exits from the metro, cafés, theaters, and opera houses ("divers" did not forgo this "normalcy"). At shelters and ration stations for Jews, they snooped for Jews of their acquaintance and surrendered them to the Gestapo. If their quarry tried to escape, it sufficed to cry "Catch the Jew!" to galvanize passersby to chase the victim down.[42]

When Greifers were detected in Jewish circles, as some eventually were, they were threatened, and some faced attempted murder. After the war, several were brought to trial, for example, Stella Kübler-Isaaksohn and her assistant husband (October 1944 onward), the document forger Rolf Isaaksohn. Stella was sentenced to ten years in prison, which she spent in Sachsenhausen, Torgau, and Hohenschönhausen—infamous Soviet camps. After discharge, she was retried for the same crimes, this time in West Berlin, and given a ten-year prison sentence that was set aside due to time served. By then, however, it was too late to determine the extent of her guilt and that of the other "scouts" for the arrest, torture, and deportation of eight hundred or, perhaps, more than one thousand Jews. These Jewish Jew-hunters undoubtedly made a meaningful contribution to the mere 25 percent average survival rate among Jewish "divers."

The deportations continued until the spring of 1945, when the Thousand-Year Reich was in its death throes. The last transport from Hamburg set out for Theresienstadt on February 14, and the last out of Berlin rumbled toward Theresienstadt and Sachsenhausen in late March.[43] After the war, around one thousand Jews were living on the grounds of the Jewish hospital in Berlin; only about one-third of them were patients. They were the remnants of what had been the largest Jewish community in Germany. Some 1,500 Jews surfaced from sundry hideouts. In Hamburg, approximately 700 Jews survived, of whom 631 were in "privileged" or "nonprivileged" mixed marriages and 59 had "submerged." Only 115 were "star-wearers." Of a Jewish community that had numbered twenty thousand before 1933, fewer than a hundred of those who had not emigrated in time came out alive.[44]

If so, the "Third Reich" had indeed cleansed itself of the German Jews. A few of those who had "submerged" and survived would become famous public figures in Germany, such as the emcee of West German TV amusement shows Hans Rosenthal, the journalist Inge Deutschkron, and the writer Ralph Giordano. Their memoirs and those of the people who had helped them, such as Ruth Andreas-Friedrich, substantiate the immense difficulty and danger that Jews who "submerged" undertook. The ideology and the persecution mechanism of the "Third Reich," as well as the snitches and most of those swept up in the regime's wake, had created an almost insurmountable hurdle.

It is worth noting again that, ultimately, it was the National Socialist regime itself that thrust the wheels of the cleansing policy into reverse: from April 1944 onward, Jewish men and women were sent from Eastern Europe to the Reich, which had been declared Judenrein, for war-economy considerations. From mid-January 1945, too, the SS led evacuees from camps in the east back to the Reich on death marches. The story of the Bergen-Belsen Aufenthaltslager ("holding camp"—its official name) from June 1943 onward also illustrates this paradox. Himmler wished to incarcerate several thousand influential Jews there as hostages to be swapped for Germans in Allied hands. On the day of its liberation, April 15, 1945, however, the camp held approximately sixty thousand prisoners, most of them Jews who had been sent there from every direction as the "Third Reich" imploded. More than thirty-five thousand of them did not live to experience the liberation, including the teenagers Margot and Anne Frank, who had had to flee from Frankfurt to Amsterdam, whence they were transported via Westerbork and Auschwitz to Bergen-Belsen. After the liberation, fourteen thousand additional people died as a consequence of their imprisonment. Many of the survivors, however, remained in Germany, initially as displaced persons and then as citizens, including some German Jews who had had to march from the Netherlands or Auschwitz to Bergen-Belsen. The stations in the life of Trude Bürger—born in Frankfurt, childhood and teen years in Memel, migration to Kaunas after the "return" of the Memel district to the Reich in 1939, afterward transfer to the Kaunas ghetto, deportation to the Stutthof concentration camp, and finally, in the last days of the war, relocation to western Germany, Frankfurt, and emigration to Mandate Palestine a year after the end of the war—exemplify the paradox of the National Socialist regime. Its internal dynamic did not stop after it had made Germany "Judenfrei"; instead, it ultimately abetted the resumption of Jewish life on German soil. On the day of Germany's defeat, there were roughly as many Jews in the territory of the quondam Reich as there had been when the deportations began. Few of them, of course, had appeared as German Jews in the 1933 population census.

Even more paradoxical is the presence, from 1944 onward, of Jewish soldiers in the Allied armies in Germany, including former German Jews and some from German-speaking areas who had left Europe as refugees. In Camp Ritchie, a military intelligence training center in Maryland, they and some non-Jewish soldiers received training in psychological warfare. The group included, among others, the writers Stefan Heym and Klaus Mann, Hans Habe, the director Hans (Hanus) Burger, German literature professor Guy Stern and the historian Werner Angress. The Allies gave them missions that entailed fluency in German: writing leaflets, distributing disinformation behind German lines, and interrogating war prisoners and deserters. Together with their colleagues at the Office for Strategic Services (the OSS, forerunner of the CIA) and the British SOE (Special Operations Executive), they made a definitive contribution to both the military success and the manhunt for and punishment of Nazi criminals. Some became famous due to the film *Monuments Men*. One of them was Harry Ettlinger, who had fled Germany as a boy in 1938 and returned as the war wound down to locate works of art that the Nazi regime had plundered and cached. Some 6,700 Jewish refugees served in the British Army alone. Inducted in Palestine, a Jewish brigade, to which a special unit of erstwhile German Jews belonged, first fought under the Union Jack on the Italian front and reached Germany at the end of the war.[45] Some of them were making their way through Germany to seek revenge for the Nazi crimes against the Jews.

Hans Spear was born in Hessen as Hans Spier and fled from Germany in 1938; his brother was murdered by the Nazis. In the following, he summed up his feelings as an American soldier on German soil: "I was moved to the depths of my soul and it saddened me greatly that to return to the land of my fathers I had to go to war with it."[46]

NOTES

1. Detlef Garbe, "Absonderung, Strafkommandos und spezifischer Terror: Jüdische Gefangene in nationalsozialistischen Konzentrationslagern 1933–1945," in Arno Herzig and Ina Lorenz, eds., *Verdrängung und Vernichtung der Juden unter dem Nationalsozialismus* (Hamburg: Hans Christians, 1992), 190.

2. Ibid., 193–99.

3. Joseph Walk, ed., *Das Sonderrecht für die Juden im NS-Staat Eine Sammlung der gesetzlichen Maßnahmen und Richtlinien—Inhalt und Bedeutung*, 2nd ed. (Heidelberg: C. F. Müller, 1996), 395.

4. Otto Dov Kulka and Eberhard Jäckel, eds., *The Jews in the Secret Nazi Reports on Popular Opinion in Germany, 1933–1945* (New Haven, CT: Yale University Press, 2010), 594.

5. Ibid., 607.

6. Nils Havemann, *Fußball unterm Hakenkreuz. Der DFB zwischen Sport, Politik und Kommerz* (Frankfurt: Campus Verlag, 2005), 280.

7. Bruno Blau, *Das Ausnahmerecht für die Juden in Deutschland 1933 bis 1945* (Düsseldorf: Verlag Allgemeine Wochenzeitung der Juden in Deutschland, 1954), 116.

8. Ernst Piper, *Alfred Rosenberg: Hitlers Chefideologe* (Munich: Blessing, 2005), 595.

9. Cf. Ian Kershaw, "Hitler's Prophecy and the 'Final Solution,'" Lecture at the Raul Hilberg Holocaust lecture series, University of Vermont, December 5, 2001.

10. Walk, *Das Sonderrecht für die Juden*, 406.

11. Nathan Stoltzfus, *Widerstand des Herzens. Der Aufstand der Berliner Frauen in der Rosenstraße 1943* (Munich, Vienna: Hanser, 1999), particularly 285–371; cf. Wolf Gruner, *Der Geschlossene Arbeitseinsatz deutscher Juden. Zur Zwangsarbeit als Element der Verfolgung 1938–1943* (Berlin: Metropol, 1997).

12. Beate Meyer, *"Jüdische Mischlinge": Rassenpolitik und Verfolgungserfahrung 1933–1945* (Hamburg: Dölling and Galitz, 1999), 57–62.

13. Christian Goeschel, "Suicides of German Jews in the Third Reich," *German History* 25 (2007): 1: 34ff.

14. Hermann Simon, "Die Berliner Juden unter dem Nationalsozialismus," in Arno Herzig and Ina Lorenz, eds., *Verdrängung und Vernichtung der Juden unter dem Nationalsozialismus* (Hamburg: Hans Christians, 1992), 263; cf. Anna Fischer, *Erzwungener Freitod. Spuren und Zeugnisse in den Freitod getriebener Juden der Jahre 1938–1945 in Berlin* (Berlin: Textpunkt, 2007).

15. Kulka and Jäckel, *The Jews in the Secret Nazi Reports*, 439.

16. Willy Cohn, *No Justice in Germany: The Breslau Diaries, 1933–1941*, ed. Norbert Conrads, trans. Kenneth Kronenberg (Stanford, CA: Stanford University Press, 2012), 382, entry of September 30, 1941.

17. Konrad U. Kwiet, "Nach dem Pogrom: Stufen der Ausgrenzung," in Wolfgang Benz, ed., *Die Juden in Deutschland 1933–1945: Leben unter nationalsozialistischer Herrschaft* (Munich: Beck, 1988), 652.

18. Camilla Neumann's diary in Monika Richarz, ed., *Jüdisches Leben in Deutschland*, vol. 3: *Selbstzeugnisse zur Sozialgeschichte 1918–1945* (Stuttgart: Deutsche Verlags-Anstalt, 1982), 418.

19. Howard K. Smith, *Last Train from Berlin* (New York: Knopf, 1942), 138.

20. Cohn, *No Justice in Germany*, 393, entry of November 1, 1941.

21. Hermann Pineas in: Richarz, *Jüdisches Leben in Deutschland*, 431.

22. Ibid., 433.

23. Cf. Käte Mugdan, ibid., 396.

24. Cf. Marion Kaplan, *Der Mut zum Überleben: Jüdische Frauen und ihre Familien in Nazideutschland* (Berlin: Aufbau, 2001), 258.

25. Jochen Klepper, *Unter dem Schatten deiner Flügel. Aus den Tagebüchern der Jahre 1932–1942*, ed. Hildegrad Klepper (Stuttgart: Deutsche Verlags-Anstalt, 1956).

26. Cf. Beate Meyer, *"Jüdische Mischlinge": Rassenpolitik und Verfolgungserfahrung 1933–1945* (Hamburg: Dölling and Galitz, 1999), 98ff.

27. Cf. ibid.

28. James F. Tent, *In the Shadow of the Holocaust: Nazi Persecution of Jewish-Christian Germans* (Lawrence: University Press of Kansas, 2003), 193.

29. Wilhelm Grau, *Die geschichtlichen Lösungsversuche der Judenfrage* (Munich: Heneichen, 1943).

30. Cf. Alan E. Steinweis, *Studying the Jew: Scholarly Antisemitism in Nazi Germany* (Cambridge, MA: 2006), 92–130; and articles in Fritz Bauer Institut, ed., *"Beseitigung des jüdischen Einflusses…": Antisemitische Forschung, Eliten und Karrieren im Nationalsozialismus* (Frankfurt: Fritz Bauer Institut, 1999).

31. Cf. Dirk Rupnow, "'Arisierung' jüdischer Geschichte. Zur nationalsozialistischen 'Judenforschung,'" in *Leipziger Beiträge zur jüdischen Geschichte und Kultur* 2 (2004): 349–67; cf. also Carsten Schreiber, "Generalstab des Holocaust oder akademischer Elfenbeinturm? Die Gegnerforschung des Sicherheitsdienstes der SS," in *Jahrbuch des Simon Dubnow Instituts* 5 (2006): 327–52.

32. Cf. Rivka Elkin, *Das Jüdische Krankenhaus in Berlin zwischen 1938 und 1945* (Berlin: 1993); idem, "The Survival of the Jewish Hospital in Berlin 1938–1945," *LBYB* 38 (1993): 157–92; idem, "Was He Indeed 'a Man after Their Own Heart'? Directors of the Jewish Hospitals in Berlin and Vienna in the Shadow of the Nazi Regime," *Moreshet* 5 (Summer 2008): 82–112.

33. Hermann Simon, "Die Berliner Juden unter dem Nationalsozialismus," in Arno Herzig and Ina Lorenz, eds., *Verdrängung und Vernichtung der Juden unter dem Nationalsozialismus* (Hamburg: Hans Christians, 1992), 261.

34. Bruno Blau's diary in: Richarz, *Jüdisches Leben in Deutschland*, 460ff.

35. Susanna Schrafstetter, "Submergence into Illegality: Hidden Jews in Munich, 1941–1945," in Susanna Schrafstetter and Alan E. Steinweis, eds., *The Germans and the Holocaust: Popular Responses to the Persecution and Murder of the Jews* (New York, Oxford: Berghahn Books, 2016); idem, *Flucht und Versteck. Untergetauchte Juden in München* (Göttingen: Wallstein, 2015), 57ff.

36. Hermann Pineas in ibid., 434; see also Katrin Rudolph, *Hilfe beim Sprung ins Nichts. Franz Kaufmann und die Rettung von Juden und "nichtarischen" Christen* (Berlin: Metropol, 2005).

37. Ruth Andreas-Friedrich, *Der Schattenmann. Schauplatz Berlin Tagebuchaufzeichnungen 1938–1948* (Frankfurt: Suhrkamp, 1986), 181; Marie Jalowicz Simon, *Untergetaucht. Eine junge Frau überlebt in Berlin 1940–1945* (Frankfurt: Thomas Medicus Frankfurter Allgemeine Zeitung, 2014); Mark Roseman, *The Past in Hiding: Memory and Survival in Nazi Germany* (London: Penguin, 2000).

38. Bruno Blau in: Richarz, *Jüdisches Leben in Deutschland*, 461.

39. Peter Wyden, *Stella* (New York: Simon & Schuster, 1992). Since 2016, the Neuköllner Opera Berlin has been presenting the musical *Stella* by Wolfgang Böhmer (music) und Peter Lund (text).

40. Doris Tausendfreund, *Erzwungener Verrat. Die Verfolgung "illegal" lebender Juden in den Jahren 1943–1945 in Berlin und Wien durch den jüdischen Fahndungsdienst* (Berlin: Metropol, 2006), 74.

41. Ibid., 99.

42. Cf. ibid., 69–123.

43. Alfred Gottwaldt and Diana Schulle, *Die 'Judentrasportation' aus dem deutschen Reich 1941–1945* (Wiesbaden: Marix, 2005), 467; Wolf Gruner, *Judenverfolgung in Berlin 1933–1945. Eine Chronologie der Behördenmaßnahmen in der Reichshauptstadt* (Berlin: Hentrich, 1996), 99, 101.

44. Ina Lorenz, "Das Leben der Hamburger Juden im Zeichen der 'Endlösung,'" in Herzig and Lorenz, *Verdrängung und Vernichtung der Juden*, 239.

45. Cf. Dorit Orgad, *Orders in a Foreign Tongue: The Story of the "German Unit"* (Hebrew) (Jerusalem: Domino, 1991).

46. Christian Bauer and Rebekka Göpfert, eds., Die Ritchie Boys. Deutsche Emigranten beim US-Geheimdienst (Hamburg: Hoffmann und Campe, 2005), 166; Robert M. Edsel, Monuments Men: Allied Heroes, Nazi Thieves and the Greatest Treasure Hunt in History (New York: Center Street, 2009).

SEVEN

—ᘛ—

"THE JEWS WERE OUR
MISFORTUNE"

WHEN GERMANS WERE CONFRONTED WITH the Nazis' crimes after the war, the common stereotyped response was "We knew nothing about it!" This apologetic denial steadily descended into incredulity and sounds downright ridiculous today. One may, however, fine-tune the question and ask, "About *what* did we know nothing?" That is, what did or could "the Germans" know? After all, the collective noun pertains in this case to the average German, not only to the police, party members, and associates of other Nazi organizations in the "Third Reich." Exactly what is it that they profess not to have known back then? Within the contours of this book, we skirt the trite general question, "What did people know about Auschwitz or the Holocaust?" Instead, we ask—we need to ask—what they knew or could have known about the fate of the Jews of Germany, their neighbors, and what they thought about it.

Fritz Süllwold (1927–2010), professor emeritus at the Institute for Psychology at Johann Wolfgang Goethe University in Frankfurt, did not believe in the structure of "collective repression." Half a century after the war, he interrogated 137 witnesses born in 1907–1927 in the hope of forming a "more realistic" impression of the opinion of the normal citizen under the "Third Reich." Of the 194 questions he asked, or 157 in other cases, 25 concerned attitudes toward Jews. From his research, Süllwold inferred that "most normal citizens at the time were largely marginally or partially aware of Jews and Jewish affairs." According to a tally of the results, 64 percent of those questioned professed scanty interest in the Jewish question or an interest that came up in exceptional cases only; 60 percent considered the slogan "The Jews are our misfortune" propaganda or nonsense, and only 3 percent remembered responding derisively or insultingly at the sight of Jews wearing the yellow star. Some 82 percent believed that the regular population interpreted the deportation of the Jewish population to the east as an act of resettlement, and 91 percent assumed that buying Jewish property in auctions was not widely known.[1]

If these findings are correct, the question is not only how things reached the point where some two-thirds of the population was only "marginally" aware of the ghastly policy toward the Jews but also how it happened that the SD put out such detailed and frequent reports about the connection that public opinion saw between the pogrom against the Jews and the bombardment of German cities or between the fate that awaited the defeated Germans and the annihilation of the Jews. Perhaps people did not care much about the fate of German Jewry, and their awareness was indeed marginal. However, *information* about the German Jews' fate—from exclusion up to extermination— definitely existed and was widely circulated. On March 31, 1945, for example, the Wehrmacht propaganda office, based on a rumor making the rounds in Berlin, reported that "in Aachen and Köln [conquered by the American army] the heads of leading Party members were shaved . . . and they were led in the streets" as the Jews' revenge for "having been marked in Germany with the Judenstern." On November 6, 1944, the SD reported the reaction to newspaper photographs of atrocities against Germans: "Everyone [!] thinks" immediately about the atrocities "that we ourselves committed . . . even in Germany. Did we not slaughter Jews in the thousands?" A simple soldier asked his mother to throw out his party uniform because "the Jews will be out for bloody revenge, especially against Party members."[2] In Schweinfurt or Bad Brückenau, the SD heard "over and over" in 1943 and 1944 that "the terror attacks [i.e., the aerial bombardments of Germany] are reprisals for the Judenaktion in 1938." Even Rosenberg, in a conversation with Himmler on February 6, 1939, said, "The pogrom of the Jews truly harmed the State. . . . We had to pay for everything that G[oebbels] did. It's horrible, terrible."[3] By October 3, 1939, reported the SD, "older persons" were pronouncing the war "a punishment for the way Jews were being treated."[4] As we know, people take revenge or reprisal into account when they believe they have been wronged or are seen by others as having been wronged. By inference, then, information about the wrong done to "our" Jews (i.e., *the Jews of Germany*) before and during the war was diffuse enough to evoke gnawing fear of revenge or even pangs of conscience.

"In Ochsenfurt, it is widely rumored that enemy aircraft will not attack Würzburg because in Würzburg not even one synagogue was set afire." Such a rumor reeks of the traditional antisemitic canard about revenge as a cardinal principle in Judaism, a corollary of the "an eye for an eye, a tooth for a tooth" rule. Those who believed in a "Jewish" imperative such as this could turn the matter around and demand that, in response to the destruction of German cities, "all Jews still living in Germany should be hanged." Such remarks were expressed by newspapers that were read in Germany. Johannes von Leers, a professor and at the same time a journalist in the service of Goebbels's Ministry of Propaganda, in an article that he published on June 7, 1943, headlined "The Jew and the Terror of the Bombardments," understood the causal relation thus: "Responsibility [for the bombardments and the war] should be imposed on [the Jews], and their annihilation is the only possible atonement for this global-scale crime."[5] Others managed to interpret the causal relation inversely, speculating that "if the German side had not attacked the Jews, we would already have peace."[6] All these points make it clear that the "Jewish matter"—be it in reference to German Jewry or to European Jewry—was discussed with total openness in the Third Reich media, in Germany in any case, and occupied the Germans, albeit at the level of presumed rumor.

Shortly before Germany was declared "Judenfrei," sounds of regret were already being heard, although they had very little to do with sympathy for the Jews: "The Jews should not have been allowed to leave the Reich. . . . Had we held the Jews as hostages, we would have had an effective guarantee against the air raids." People took account of the possibility of reprisals—not only for crimes against "our" Jews, those of Germany, "when the Jews return to Germany," as references to the pogrom that night in 1938 and the introduction of the yellow star in 1941 make clear, but also to the persecution of Jews at large. The SD quotes an opinion expressed in Kitzingen in September 1943, three months after Germany had been declared "Judenfrei": "The rotten thing about our leaders is that after they exterminated the Jews, they pounced on their homes. . . . It is after all well known how in the dead of night they hauled the expensive carpets, furniture, and silver from the Jewish homes."[7]

Here, unequivocally, is talk about murder, not "resettlement," and about the looting of German Jewry. In addition, by May 1943, the party bureau admitted that the Auschwitz concentration camp was "generally well known in the East."[8] Indeed, even Victor Klemperer had heard of it back in March 1942 as the embodiment of the worst thing imaginable.

The assertion "We knew nothing about it!" needs exacting scrutiny. Since the Jewish population in Germany—that is, those whom the Germans called *Rassejuden* ("Jews by race")—numbered less than half a percent of the total population in late 1938, obviously not all non-Jewish Germans came into direct contact with German Jews and their persecution. Even if ten non-Jews insulted, denounced, and tortured every remaining Jew, only 5 percent of the population would be implicated. Even the circulation of the leading antisemitic newspaper,

Der Stürmer—473,000 copies before the war and 380,000 in March 1944[9]—justifies the assessment that radical and obsessive occupation with "solving the Jewish problem" was relatively limited, even if we assume that more than one German read each copy. The public bulletin boards on which *Der Stürmer* was posted also had an effect, and newspapers such as *Der Angriff* indulged in extreme antisemitic demonization. Just the same, the presence of the "Jewish question" in the public scene was such as to allow an inference to be made about how people actually knew or conjectured about what they claimed ex post not to have known. Whether people smiled or frowned on what they knew is a totally different question, which we take up below. Ralph Giordano, in his novel *The Bertini Family*, posed the question tellingly in the form of Roman Bertini's response to the argument expressed by the Mitläufer Herbert Mörtling, who wishes to adopt ex post the image of an opponent of the regime: If you knew nothing—what did you want to oppose?[10]

Having said that regular personal contact with Jews was a marginal phenomenon, we must first identify Germans' sources of information about the fate of German Jewry. The possibilities—beyond kinship relations with Jews or random encounters with Jews in the market, the street, or government offices—included conversations about the topic in places where people socialized, along with institutes of science that dealt with the "Jewish question" or Jewish history and schools and party bureaus. Conversely, they also included unofficial information and rumors that circulated in the media and the public sphere. Foreign newspapers and networks, to which few had access, reported on what was being done to the Jews, to the regime's immense irritation. These sources of information have been intensively researched in recent years. My late colleague at the Hebrew University of Jerusalem, Otto Dov Kulka, was the pioneer of research on the attitude toward the Jewish question in German public opinion, and his pupil David Bankier followed his lead. In the past thirty years, occupation with the topic has expanded enormously. The works of Bankier (1992), Peter Longerich (2006), Frank Bajohr and Dieter Pohl (2006), Jeffrey Herf (2007), Bernward Dörner (2007), Frank Bajohr and Christoph Strupp (2011), and Nicholas Stargardt,[11] as well as relevant articles by Bajohr and Wolf Gruner in Schrafstetter's and Steinweis's much up-to-date book (2016), prove that there was definitely no shortage of "real-time" information about goals and actions. Within the frame of this study, however, we must distinguish carefully between Germans' information about "their" Jews and information about the Holocaust at large. As stated, the question that usually occupies researchers relates solely to "what the Germans knew about the Holocaust." From our standpoint, however, the question is relevant only in the context of the persecution and murder of the Jews of Germany and within the broader contours of knowledge about events *in Germany itself*.

How should one approach the "Jewish question," and what answer should one expect to find? The answers were already well known not only among adolescent members of the Hitlerjugend and the Bund Deutscher Mädel ("League of German Girls") but also among adults who partook of activities of the party, the SS, and other organizations, along with readers of *Der Stürmer* and other relevant newspapers. The education they received could not have been served up without some connection with reality. At rallies, assemblies, and public appearances, politicians and functionaries often addressed themselves to things that had actually happened or were happening to Jews. Some of these events were mentioned in radio broadcasts; speeches that referred to them were printed fully or partly in the newspapers. Goebbels's policy was to use newspapers and newsreels as (controlled) media for such information. Two months after the 1938 pogrom, the Prime Minister of Bavaria said, as mentioned above, "The daily discussion of the Jewish Question in the radio before the latest news broadcast has proven to be an excellent means of instruction."[12] And whatever failed to make its way to the print, broadcast, or cinematic media, the public discovered via rumors.

Below we focus on *information* pertaining to four topics: (1) the November 1938 riots; (2) statutory persecution, including the yellow-star rule; (3) the deportations; and (4) the murder of German Jewry.

1. *The nighttime pogrom in 1938* was reported on at length in the German and foreign media. The Reich Ministry for Public Education and Propaganda issued an unequivocal order after the murder in Paris: "The assassination perpetrated by the Jews will by necessity have exceedingly grave implications for the Jews in Germany." Accordingly, Goebbels's newspaper, *Der Angriff* (Attack), demanded "fierce responses." Therefore, the public was prepared for the pogrom, which was euphemistically called an act of "reprisal" or "punishment." Accordingly, the riots were presented as justified expressions of the "rage of the masses" and not as something organized from the top down. To avoid the impression of a centrally orchestrated pogrom, the ministry ordered the media to refrain from overreporting the event (i.e., to keep it off the front page, provide no photos, and limit detailed reportage to the local press). Either way, however, news about the torched synagogues, the looted shops, and the arrested Jews appeared in all newspapers and even non-eyewitnesses received more detailed reports than the ministry intended. The *Völkischer Beobachter*, the official party newspaper, used gangster language that brooked no misinterpretation: "Shattered window and display panes are the new calling cards of Jewish shops."[13] Many

photographs document not only synagogues going up in flames and Jews being arrested during the pogrom but also the onlookers themselves.[14]

All organs of the regime spoke openly, of course, about the decisions that were made at the meeting with Hermann Göring on November 12, 1938, and the rules enacted shortly afterward. The newspapers also ran items about successful implementation. Thus, on November 12, the *Niederdeutscher Beobachter* reported from Mirow, "The business that had been in Jewish hands until now ... has been sold ... for the price of 27,000 Reichsmarks. ... Thus, the last representatives of the Jewish mischpoke have left our town at long last. Therefore, the foot of the curly-haired Jewish low-life ... and of his Jewess will no longer trample our city. The population in Mirow will see to it." Sometime later, the same newspaper, reporting from Röbel, noted, "The Jewish synagogue has been serving as a garage for several weeks now."[15] Newspaper readers in Leipzig encountered a notice in a relatively large format: "Demolition: the synagogues on Gottschedstraße and Apels Garten. Some 200,000 bricks, un-dressed, price per thousand units: 15 Reichsmarks." They discovered in this manner not only that the synagogues would not be rebuilt but that the proceeds of the sale of the bricks would accrue to the H.Fr. Seydel construction company and not to the victims of the arson.[16]

2. For several months after November 1938, the German political constellation and public devoted special intensity to their occupation with the Jewish matter. The November 9 Judenaktion "represents perceptible progress toward the total solution of the Jewish problem," remarked the SD. In other words, rioting was not the right way to fight the Jews, but the legislative measures that followed were considered a worthy modus operandi. One may even construe the intensive public attention to these measures as an instrument of repression because the riots had evoked such disgust simply by being riots. Protected by this camouflaging of the anti-Jewish campaign that followed the pogrom, one could promote "Aryanization" vigorously. Even if not all Germans participated actively in purging the German economy of Jews (*Entjudung*), the public was undoubtedly familiar with the process. The torrent of successive regulations provided a continual pretext for new ideas and discussions about the Jewish issue in Germany. A case that took the lawyers' guild by storm shows how absurd and cynical the discussions could be. A Jewish woman was acquitted of violating Section 218 of the Penal Code, which forbade abortion, on the grounds that German law should not defend the bequeathing of Jewish blood.[17] The guild found especially challenging a discriminatory rule that resulted in exoneration instead of even graver punishment of Jews, as was customary. The case described, however, is the exception that proves the rule: the plight of

German Jewry worsened, and the public could learn a great deal about it from the media, directly or otherwise, even if the assaults on these Jews waned three or four months later, as Hitler's speech of January 30, 1939, signaled. From then on, the object of the antisemitic propaganda transmogrified from the battered Jews of Germany to so-called world Jewry, because thus the regime could justify its aggressive foreign policy. The abuse that the German Jews continued to experience no longer made headlines even though the German media attacks on "world Jewry" actually targeted the Jews who inhabited the German Reich until the war began.

The intensification of anti-Jewish measures in the "Altreich" after the outbreak of the war was background static for most Germans. Victor Klemperer, describing the visit of a retired high school principal from Köln—a Catholic and "a highly vehement opponent of Hitler"—with relatives in Dresden, remarked, "[I] had no notion of all the restrictions placed on non-Aryans." Klemperer also encountered ignorance at the Pensions Office: "I thought [blurted an official there] you as a veteran . . ."[18] This comment, however, indicates that the official knew about discrimination against Jews who had *not* served on the front. Thus, his great amazement may have been a pretense, but since the edicts were advertised in the *Jüdische Nachrichtenblatt* more frequently than in the general press—although even there not always—the chaotic nature of the orders remained opaque to most people who had no personal stake in them. Regulations read out in synagogues were not addressed to the public at large, of course, and did not find their way to them.[19] This turned out to be useful in a way: the widespread unfamiliarity with the anti-Jewish enactments, as I noted in the context of Marie Jalowicz Simon's remark, opened the way for Jews who "submerged" and evaded the fate of the rest.

The introduction of the yellow star, however, made a public impact that may be likened only to that of the pogrom three years earlier. First of all, the instigator of this demarche, Propaganda Minister Goebbels, promulgated it with enormous fanfare. He ordered the distribution to all households of a leaflet titled "When You See This Mark," by which he meant the Judenstern. Second, the marking of Jews made them conspicuous to everyone except in places that were "Judenfrei." "Among us in the Reich," a German soldier wrote from Romania on July 26, 1941, "one can hardly encounter any more Jews."[20] Now, in contrast, the few remaining Jews were visible to one and all. The metastasizing fear in Germany that German Americans would similarly be ordered to wear swastika armbands or patches, or the opposite rumor, that Germany had introduced the yellow star in response to the United States, where "Germans have been made to wear a swastika and an armband bearing the word 'Nazi,'"[21] also attests to the public's awareness of this measure against Jews in Germany. A week before it went into effect, placards appeared with the slogan of the week that the Ministry of Public Education and Propaganda had chosen: the infamous quotation from Hitler's speech on January 30, 1939. The yellow star was supposed to reveal the identity of the Jews who had thrust Germany into war, and from September 13, 1941, on, the newspapers doubled down on this message.[22]

3. Unlike the yellow star, the deportations of Jews that began in October 1941 were not publicly announced in writing or orally. For the Jews and those in their immediate surroundings, they were no secret, of course. After all, the Reichsvereinigung and the various Jewish community institutions had been mobilized against their will to prepare for and be involved in them. People knew that the deportation was destined to end "in the east," and no one fooled himself about what awaited the passengers there, even before the murder-by-gas industry evolved. Willy Cohn in Breslau already knew on September 20, 1941, that one thousand Jews from his hometown were to be deported by the end of that month.[23] After the war, a Jew who had lived in Breslau at the time remembered that the schoolteacher would ask whether a student who missed a class was ill or had been deported.[24] What the Jews knew, however, was not necessarily known to the non-Jewish population, which after all had not been advised of it by the official and semiofficial media. Historians sometimes mention the fact that the SD reports deal only marginally with deportations as proof that most of the population knew nothing about them. A report dated December 16, 1941, from Bielefeld, relating to a deportation to Riga that had taken place five days earlier, refutes this as well: "Even though the police kept this operation secret, word about the transport of the Jews was widely known among all [!] circles of the population." In Göttingen, the matter was widely reported even before the planning stage (December 19, 1941). It was further insinuated by the huge number of new applications for allocation of housing that were submitted just then—a response that only the imminent deportation of Jews would allow. A vulture circling over its carrion surely knows what is about to transpire. In Münster, too, the planned deportation "to large labor camps in the east" was a topic of conversation in social encounters and even of gossip; it was mentioned in the context of "a plan to ease the housing shortage."[25]

Reportage on the deportation of Jews could spread before or after the fact. Not only the small circle of participants' acquaintances knew what was up; so did neighbors and observers of the star-wearing and baggage-laden Jews who made their way to the collection yard in groups; so did tram drivers and tram passengers as they passed the staging point; so did the schoolchildren, be they in Hamburg or Lower Franconia, who cheered as they escorted the convoys of Jews. "Those living around the train station on Putlizstraße crowded on the bridge stretching over the rails and contemplated these transports as they arrived at the station and the trains as they pulled out," reported Herta Pineas, who worked for the emergency supply services of the Jewish community of Berlin. "Noteworthy are the young girls whom the Gestapo men brought. Always only one of them was busy as a stenographer; the others came to watch the whole process."[26] Those caught complaining and not cheering were interrogated by police.[27] Probably, too, the things Richard Lichtheim knew in real time (at the time working for the Jewish Agency in Geneva) were also known to a core of cognoscenti in Germany; otherwise, whence did he obtain his information? Lichtheim warned in November 1941 about mass deportation from the Reich, knew about deportations to Theresienstadt in March 1942, and was the first to report in July 1942 about the systematic mass-murder operations in the east—a matter discussed in the next paragraph.[28]

4. By the time the deportations began, the war had already accustomed Germans to an anomaly in peacetime, the routine spectacle of masses of people in transit. Trains sagging with soldiers heading eastward and groups of ethnic Germans moving from here to there (the Baltic countries, the Generalgouvernement, Bessarabia, Bukovina, or the southern Tyrol, and adolescents in children's transports to the countryside) were daily occurrences. However, reports about "resettlement" of Jews were associated ab initio with unhappy consequences for them. This was assured not only by the state's language of Jew hatred. Neither was it something that first had to gain acceptance in 1941. Heydrich's instruction of November 19, 1938, to the State Attorney's Office, decided on in counsel with the Ministry of Justice, according to which killers (of Jews) in the course of the "Judenaktion" would be prosecuted only if they acted for "selfish motives," sent a clear message even before the war: anyone who killed a Jew for purely antisemitic reasons would be treated with impunity. What every lawyer now knew by force of an official guideline also soon became common public knowledge. On November 24, 1938, the SS newspaper *Das Schwarze Korps* wrote overtly about obliterating the "Jewish underworld" "by fire and sword" and about "the practical and final end of Judaism in Germany and its total annihilation." Even if this message was aimed primarily at the readers of this newspaper, it probably made its way into broad public circles.

The infamous quote from Hitler's January 30, 1939, speech is widely proffered as proof that the public knew about and supported an "extermination program" or an "eliminationist intent." The ordinary newspaper reader, however, surely construed the speech differently. A typical Nazi newspaper that published the speech in its entirety headlined it "The Whole World Has Heard the Führer."

Even Countries that Frown on National Socialism Must Recognize in the Peace Speech [!] the Historical Greatness of Adolf Hitler." Only the thirteenth subhead, "The Truth about the Jewish Question," touched on the Jewish issue and was followed in a smaller font: "Plain Words to the Churches."[29] Given the ordinary way of grasping political speeches, even the potential victims were essentially unable to understand the infamous statement or take it literally. Victor Klemperer responded to it with one sardonic sentence but in no way was worried: "Hitler once again turned all his enemies into Jews and threatened the annihilation of the Jews in Europe if they were to bring about war against Germany."[30] Willy Cohn, the Jewish historian from Breslau, did express his concern about the ferocity of the threat but stressed, "we are harvesting more than a few things that we sowed, and the incitement abroad is making matters even more difficult for us." Thus he, too, believed the allegations that Goebbels's propaganda diffused and that the public accepted as fact.[31]

As we know, it took Hitler until 1941 to repeat this "prophecy."[32] Therefore, one might maintain that before the war he had not meant words like "extermination" and "elimination" seriously, that no one took them at face value, and that, accordingly, they were not perceived as an operative policy. At least among the leadership, however, the nexus of war and a brutal solution to the Jewish problem had already taken shape. At the aforementioned November 12, 1938, meeting, about three months before Hitler's speech, Göring stated, "If the German Reich finds itself in a confrontation in the foreseeable future, it is plain and self-evident that we in Germany will seize the opportunity foremost for a fundamental reckoning with the Jews." In the very same breath, he mentioned Madagascar. Furthermore, accustoming oneself to turns of phrase and rhetorical metaphors is a major event. Thus, when the context changed in the course of the war—especially after the all-out assault on the Soviet Union began—these words gradually acquired practical significance, certainly for the victims but also for the perpetrators and the indifferent or collaborating public. The words legitimized the actions even before the actions were taken. In a struggle that prompted them to acquiesce ab initio in unprecedented harshness and the death of millions of people, there was, in a certain sense, something "normal" about the implementation of threats against the German Jews; it was nothing more than a footnote. The decision to deport German Jewry, and afterward European Jewry, to places where individuals' lives would become valueless was probably perceived, at least implicitly, as the decision to kill most of the deportees. Even if they had no concrete information about whether the deportees were being interned in concentration camps or being killed off by hard labor, ghastly living conditions, or even gunfire, even if they still did not know about the mass executions by gunfire or gas, people could surmise, as Willy Cohn did shortly after the deportations began, that "they [the Jews of Berlin] were probably taken to the larger ghettos in the East, where there isn't anything to eat to begin with. . . . They are sent to Litzmannstadt [Łódź]!"[33] Most Jews who faced the menace of deportation almost certainly understood this, but so did non-Jews who knew about those operations. How else could they have construed Josef Goebbels's remarks on November 16, 1941, published in the newspaper *Das Reich* and broadcast over the radio: "We are now observing the practical application [!] of this prophecy [of Hitler's]. . . . World Jewry is now experiencing a process of gradual extermination"?[34] There was no hint that the Jews of Germany might avoid the fate of "world Jewry." It was on this very point that Goebbels, familiar as he was with the national pulse, dwelled in his article. The Volk must express no compassion toward an elderly Jewess wearing the yellow star because her kin in America are collaborating with the German-hating Jew Nathan (Goebbels made up this Jewish name, as in the case of the Jewish Chief of the Berlin Police, Isidor) Kaufman. I take up the matter of this Kaufman below. If such was the case in November 1941, it was so a fortiori afterward.

As for how quickly they could accustom themselves to the new lethal praxis, soldiers had an advantage over civilians in the rear: "Here [in Romania] the Jewish question is solved differently from among us. The Romanians group all the Jews together and shoot them to death," a soldier wrote home.[35] The addressees of such letters—relatives of soldiers on the front—were thus the first people in the "Altreich," Ostmark, and Bohemia who could accustom themselves to this "logic." People noticed the deportation of the Jews, and most of them identified its "advantages" and occasionally even exploited the deportees. For the most part, too, they strove to think as little as possible about the fate that awaited the deportees at the end of the trip. That the certain destination of the transport must be the murder of the Jews—most people could not know in the first months of the deportations, as mentioned above; at the utmost, they could assume or surmise it. Years later, a Jewish attorney related what he imagined when he read his deportation notice in November 1941: "We thought that in Poland it would surely not be so comfortable, but it would be possible to live."[36] In December 1941, after having successfully emigrated in October of that year, Elisabeth Freund, niece of the Nobel Prize laureate Fritz Haber, wrote down her fresh memories of the deportations and asked a central question for my purposes: "Exactly what are they doing with the camp prisoners? Look, the Nazis cannot kill them in their thousands! It is inconceivable that Germans would kill their fellow citizens, who fought with them shoulder-to-shoulder in 1914." In the autumn of 1941, these thoughts still retained some connection with reality because even then the "Final Solution" for German Jewry had not yet been decided on in the sense of systematic extermination; thus, one might give the threats unleashed in the public arena a somewhat lenient exegesis.[37] However, the Freunds owed their ability to emigrate to a neighbor of theirs, who had been instructed by her husband, a sentry at a concentration camp in the east, to urge them to make sure "to get out, the faster the better."[38] Elisabeth Freund did not know what a seventeen-year-old member of the Hitlerjugend knew in October 1941: that "the Jews . . . [were] being shot to death after they left the territory of the German Reich."[39]

By the summer of 1942 at the latest, the fate of the Jews of Germany in the east must have been clear to them as well as to the German public at large. True, even in July 1942 most German Jews could still believe in resettlement and not in transport to death. This is traceable to the media embargo imposed on the Jews, but it may also be understood as a psychological defense mechanism against the inevitable. People were "tired of struggling."[40] Also, the German Jews were not as close to the scene of the murder as was Chaim Kaplan, who kept his diary in Warsaw and knew by June 3, 1942, that tens of thousands of Jews from Lublin were being shipped by train to their death and informed his diary on July 10 about a "mass-murder enterprise" in Sobibór. What, however, should the readers of the *Völkische Beobachter* have thought several months earlier, on November 7, 1941, when they read the article "The Jews in Wartime," which reported the Führer's resolve "to wipe out this pestilence once and for all"? How should they have understood Hitler's repeated threat "to destroy the Jews," as expressed, for example, in his speeches of January 30, 1942; September 30, 1942; and February 24, 1943? The reaction to the murder by gunfire of the passengers in some of the early transports of German Jews to the east also indicates that the rumor about mass murder could not be kept from spreading even under conditions of deliberate gagging from above. Soldiers returning from the east on furlough described what they had seen. A salient example is the inclusion of the topic of murder of the Jews in the antiregime manifesto of the White Rose resistance group in Munich in June 1942. The city of Munich provides rare evidence of the limited ability to thwart information bleed: a group of Jewish women industrial workers, reaching a linen weaving factory from Łódź in December 1941, were able to report, at that early stage, what was happening in their city of origin as the first transports of Jews from Germany arrived.[41]

Were it not for the certainty that steadily solidified over time, the notary who deleted an evacuated Jew from the population registry in early 1943 could not have claimed that "by the term 'evacuation' one should understand the loss of the head of the person at issue."[42] Absent this certainty, *Der Stürmer*, too, could not have seen fit to ask its readers, in early 1943, whether "one should say, as has been said thus far, that the Jews *are* our misfortune! or whether the Jews *were* our misfortune." This adage was still festooned in bold print on the front page of the paper, and by "our misfortune" it meant Germany's. One reader of the newspaper suggested that the expression, no longer relevant to Germany, be amended to read: "The Jews are humankind's misfortune!"[43] The multitudes of Volksgenossen who got word of the auctioning of deported Jews' property thought exactly the same way. After Stalingrad, it was certainty about what was transpiring in the east that amplified fear of "the Jews' revenge." Remarks by a tailor's apprentice at the Vaterland Café in Berlin to two SS men on May 10, 1943—"With us in Germany, it's no different [from Katyn, where Soviet police murdered thousands of Poles] that here [i.e., in Germany!] they executed ninety-nine percent of the Jews by gunfire"[44]—were but a natural outcome of the confluence of threats, rumors, and concrete information. It was for this reason that Bormann, on July 11, 1943, promulgated Hitler's ban on public discussion of the "Final Solution" in Germany.[45]

After the fact, the number of Germans who had information cannot be calculated, and the quantity and nature of the information they possessed cannot be precisely assessed. However, if we may hypothesize via data on the circulation of newspapers and journals, the number of radio listeners, and visitors to movie theaters, and also on the basis of the number of denunciations of Jews or other sources, the relevant question concerns not information per se but the awareness and internalization of the information. In Nicholas Stargardt's words: "What was being created was a sense of 'knowing without knowing.'"[46] This leads at once to the question of the Germans' opinions and positions. The fact that the German Jews were being hounded, tormented, and deported was evidently known to one and all. Most of the anti-Jewish measures were fairly overt and verbalized. As for what was happening abroad, however, (i.e., in the east after their deportation—namely, whether the Jews were dying of hunger, gunshots, or gas) about this most could only hypothesize. Shortly after the deportations began, those who had had Jewish acquaintances received desperate letters from the ghettos in the east or soon noticed that correspondence with the deportees had been cut off.[47] One may, as noted above, adduce the acuity of uncertainty about the destination and absoluteness of the deportation by the lively involvement of "little people" in the auctioning and looting of property that the Jews had left behind. There is no telling, however, how many people took particular interest in the fate of their country's erstwhile Jewish citizens so much as conjectured about them. The historian Peter Fritzsche gave the Germans' knowledge of this subject a telling epithet: "Babi Yar, but not Auschwitz."[48]

Finally, beyond the question of *what* was known, the question about *public opinion* (i.e., the overall *attitude* toward the fate of German Jewry) arises. Since our sources provide no representative opinion polls but only impressions gathered from memoirs, letters, and the sort of input harvested from foreign elements (diplomats or exiled dissidents), and, antipodally, reports from the SD, the historian can only make an "educated conjecture." In the absence of systematic coeval research on public opinion, information that ostensibly speaks for itself is highly dubious, as Schrafstetter and Steinweis warn in their collection *The Germans and the Holocaust.*

During the war, Victor Klemperer drove to the heart of the matter when he tried to obtain information and take the public pulse by means of rumors, street talk, and other ways (he had no access to radio, of course): "Who can judge the mood of 80 million people, with the press bound and everyone afraid of opening their mouth?" he wrote two days before the war began.[49] "Always the question: What is the mood of the people, who can account for it?" he asked a month before the onset of Operation Barbarossa.[50] The historian David Bankier gave painstaking attention to the question of the reliability of the sources from which we expect an answer to emerge. The SD reports were tendentious and worded so as to reinforce the conventional view about the public mood. So also, to a large extent, were reports from diplomats or members of the Social Democratic opposition outside Germany, from which Frank Bajohr harvested additional information. This is not to mention the abrupt dwindling of these testimonies once the war began (i.e., in the main period of concern in this book). Contemporary witnesses tend to remember selectively, rationalize, and suppress or repress unpleasant recollections, whereas foreign espionage services depend on the "hidden agenda" of their sources of information or the institutions for which they work. Just the same, the information accessible to historians not only corroborates the assumption that the fate of the German Jews between 1938 and 1943 was widely known; it even confirms the hypothesis that the non-Jewish German population at the time, for the most part, took what may best be described as a reserved stance toward the Jews. Stargardt's conclusion: "For non-Jewish Germans . . . the deportation and murder of the Jews was neither very secret nor very significant."[51] In the historians' dispute over the most common response to the anti-Jewish measures—was it "indifference" or "tacit consent"?—the historian Wolf Gruner adds an important element by emphasizing responses that reduce the numbers of those usually described as bystanders—snitches on the one hand and those who defied the anti-Jewish measures on the other.[52]

In my attention to the public *mood*, below I focus on four topics of concern above: the November pogrom, legislative persecution and the Judenstern decree, deportations, and the murder of German Jewry.

1. I referred to the public's attitudes after the November pogrom in chapter 2. It is worth noting the precedents to which Wolf Gruner calls attention: anti-Jewish violence as a product of the assumption that the regime gave this practice its backing. By the summer of 1938, preceding Kristallnacht, there was already much violence of this sort. What made the November event special was its scale and intensity. On the one hand, there was broad assent to the Judenaktion, as it was called at the time (the term "Kristallnacht" came along later): "All these operations enjoyed the consent of the masses that gathered," the SD reported from Vienna. "Compassion about fate of the Jews was hardly heard anywhere, and when such compassion nevertheless dared to raise its voice in trepidation, the crowd immediately opposed it vigorously; several onlookers who expressed too much sympathy toward the Jews were arrested."[53] Conversely, shaking of heads was also observed, as was lack of understanding about the nature of the "reprisal action." That is, the shattered display windows troubled the good bourgeois civilians who favored law and order. "The population's stance toward the operations," reported another agent in a tendentious SD report, "which was initially supportive, turned around totally once the property damage became visible." Gauleiter Streicher already felt obliged on November 10, 1938, to give a speech in Nuremberg in which the message was "there is no need to have such great pity for the Jews."[54] Catholics "plainly" objected to the operations against synagogues. Liberal circles pronounced the riots "irresponsible." In addition, the SD reported, the idea of collecting donations under the auspices of the National Socialist welfare system was rejected due to the disgraceful nature of the "Jews' Action."[55] On November 10, Hitler gave a speech to newspaper editors in which he managed to concentrate on the Munich agreement that he had signed a month earlier while totally avoiding any mention of the Judenaktion that had taken place the night before.

2. Although the number of critics of the November 1938 riots is unknowable, the regime's exertions to counter them prove that they had reached a critical mass. One could crack down harshly on individuals. Thus, on November 11, 1938, "the insurance agent Gustav Gellner [stood] in front of a Jewish shop and cried: 'The Jews are our [good] fortune.' When two SA men demanded that he explain himself, he told them, 'You are asses.' Gellner was arrested."[56] This,

however, did not attenuate the menace of widespread dissatisfaction. "Day after day, a respectable share of the population sang a lament for the decent Jews who had not harmed a soul and were incomparably honest," a small-town gendarmerie reported. "Many Berliners, as we can learn from police logs . . . reacted with critique, protest, and even resistance."[57] As we know, even a "normal" person of bourgeois upbringing who is disgusted by cockroaches finds the spectacle of crushed cockroaches even more repulsive. Accordingly, now even the most consistent antisemites warned against another pogrom on German soil.[58] The historian and journalist Lothrop Stoddard, an American racist who visited Germany in late 1939 as a correspondent for the North American Newspaper Alliance, rightly "got the impression that, while the average German condemned such methods [pogroms], he was not unwilling to see the Jews go and would not wish them back again." Himmler personally informed him that "we are even marking out a place [in East Europe] for the Jews where they may live quietly unto themselves."[59]

3. By accusing the Jews of espionage, the authorities revealed something of the mood at the beginning of the war. We already mentioned Klemperer's fear that "we Jews will [be] put up . . . against the wall yet—ten Jews for every German who would fall." Here the Jews are shoved into the familiar role of scapegoats.[60] Reports from occupied Poland about the persecution of ethnic Germans, connected with the Jews who were living there, and, of course, the attempt to blame the Jews for the attempted assassination of Hitler on November 9, 1939, helped to foul the general anti-Jewish mood. However, however small the Jewish minority in Germany had become, the readers of Der Stürmer continued to notice the existence of amicable relations between non-Jews and Jews and demanded that the former be shunned and punished. "I ask you to properly reprimand and censure [Brandmarken], in your newspaper, the girl Klute" (due to "lively relations with the Jewess Marcus"), the manager of a local branch of the Nazi Party in Southern Westphalia demanded on October 9, 1939. A farmer who had not contributed to the Winterhilfe project but gifted a Jew with a goose received proper defamation in Der Stürmer for so doing.[61]

From the onset of the war to the beginning of the campaign against Russia, the German Jewish question was no longer a hot topic; instead, it had its ups and downs. During this period, one could detect occasional sympathy and compassion for the Jews of Germany along with the opposite.[62] However, the presence of German soldiers in occupied Poland and their encounters there with "real Jews, bearded and befouled" or "bearded and [wearing] a kapota," yielded pejorative conclusions about the German Jews. Even from the occupied Netherlands, soldiers could post to Germany not only information but also appropriate opinions: "That the Jews . . . should honor other regions with their presence . . . in Europe, that's over; Asia is open to them," a soldier wrote home in August 1940. This impression gained strength after the offensive against Russia began: "In the Main area, we could not form a correct idea about Judaism. But here in the east . . ."[63] Such testimonies were greeted with nodding heads in the "Altreich."

The basis for this consonance took shape in the first year of the war in various ways, including one worthy of special scrutiny. The Minister of Propaganda, Joseph Goebbels, was of course known for his special interest in the cinema as the most effective way to instill values and views. This medium belonged to his fiefdom, and when it is mentioned in the context of our topic, something immediately comes to mind: the film that was presented as a "documentary" and approved in late November 1940, *Der ewige Jude* (The eternal Jew). Apart from likening Jews to rats, one scene signaled the "authentic" origin of the Jew who lurked behind the image of the modern German and West European specimen of the race. In the soundtrack, use was made of an excerpt from Hitler's January 30, 1939, speech, in which the Führer spoke of the Jews' impending annihilation. After this scene in the film appeared, "an outburst of enthusiastic applause" erupted in the cinema hall in Munich, the SD reported on January 20, 1941.[64] The movie may have even reminded Hitler of the speech, which he had delivered so long ago as to have forgotten it.[65] "This . . . film, evidently very nasty and launched with the greatest ballyhoo, has incidentally disappeared here again after less than a week," Victor Klemperer remarked in contrast.[66]

The realization that a documentary film about Jews might miss its target was evidently the reason for the relatively scanty exposure of the topic in the cinema logs of September–October 1940 and onward.[67] The fictive film, in contrast, played an indirect but effective role in enhancing Volk awareness of the "Jewish matter" and disseminating the views that the regime wished to spread. When the documentary film *The Eternal Jew* was shown, "word-of-mouth propaganda" against it was voiced, reported the SD, but antisemitic fictional movies did not have this effect. Although not many movies devoted to the Jewish topic appeared in 1939–1940, the few relevant works were significant enough, and the masses got the message. Not only Goebbels but any run-of-the-mill propagandist knew that the impact of fictional movies shown to viewers who are mentally unprepared to resist their message outweighs that of straightforward propaganda vehicles.

It was in 1939 (i.e., after the November pogrom) that moviegoers encountered anti-Jewish tropes in a fictional film. *Robert und Bertram* is a comedy that recounts two nineteenth-century crooks who "save" a German family from an assimilated Jew. In one scene, Herr Ipelmeyer admits, "I'm a Jew," and his obese interlocutor replies, "I've got a secret, too: I have a belly." The viewers, identifying Ipelmeyer as a Jew and despising him on the basis of the familiar derogatory clichés, must have found the scene especially funny. The fact that the scoundrels in the film reach the Garden of Eden instead of being punished for having destroyed a Jew's life may have been interpreted at this time as an allusion to the appropriate treatment of the Jews of Germany (per Heydrich's aforementioned directive) shortly before the war began. Namely, one can wrong a Jew with impunity because it isn't wrong at all.

Leinen aus Irland (Linen from Ireland), first shown in October 1939, shortly after the war began, exploits a similar antisemitic meme. Over a three-decade period, a Jewish boy named Cohn rises to the top of a linen trading firm and wants to be "the linen king of the whole world" at the expense of the national linen industry and the local spinners. July 1940 saw the debut of *The Rothschilds' Shares in Waterloo*, which reckons with the theme of "Jewish greed" and for this purpose is set against an anti-English background. Incidentally, the actor Herbert Hübner, who appeared in both *The Rothschilds* and *Robert and Bertram*, did not flinch from carrying on with his career after 1945. Neither did the director of *The Rothschilds*, Erich Waschneck, who before the Nazis' accession to power had arranged for cinema, and had done the filming of, a story by Kurt Tucholsky, or the director of *Linen from Ireland*, Heinz Helbig. Irene von Meendorff, who acted in *Linen from Ireland* and subsequently in *Kolberg*, also continued to perform after the war. Although these films were meant to prepare the Germans for the anti-Jewish measures to come, their cast would be considered innocent props and naïve artists as opposed to criminals.

After the debut showing of *Jud Süß* (The Jew Süss) at the Venice film festival on September 5, 1940, and its first screening in Germany on September 24, the impact of antisemitic fictional cinema could no longer be doubted. Goebbels was elated: "An antisemitic film of the kind that we could only have imagined. I'm pleased with it."[68] Cinema critics and viewers gushed about it, too. This film was "many times more convincing than *The Rothschilds*," Klemperer remarked.[69] In response to the scene of the Jews entering Stuttgart, matters repeatedly escalated into overt demonstrations against "Judaism." In Berlin, for example, cries such as "Banish the Jews from Kurfürstendamm! Rid Germany of the last of them" were heard.[70] By order of the Reichsführer SS on November 15, 1940, all German police were given until the end of the winter of 1940–1941 to see the film. The idea was to disabuse those who would be in charge of deporting and plundering the Jews of hesitations and pangs of conscience—insofar as they still had any—in their treatment of the Jews of

Germany. Indeed, the concluding scene, depicting the deportation of the Jews from Stuttgart, making it Judenfrei forever, definitely spurred the perpetrators of the deportations a year later. Notably, even the director of this immensely influential antisemitic film, Veit Harlan, was allowed to continue directing films after the war, although not without opposition.

Once the offensive against the USSR began, antisemitic propaganda became, by orders from above, "the dominant trend in the German press."[71] The likening of Jews to Bolsheviks was effective and lethal. Detailed reportage from the Ministry of Propaganda about "Bolshevik atrocities" and photos published about "the Bolshevik terror in Lemberg [Lwów]" were exploited not only against Jews who lived in Russia. It being believed that "the Jews are the real ones pulling the strings behind the scenes, demands are being voiced in some quarters that the Jews in the Reich [!] be dealt with in a radical way."[72] An SD report from Bielefeld demonstrates the potential import of this practice: since the Jews, according to the rapporteur, had indulged in provocative behavior, it was decided to ban Jews from the markets "in order to prevent brawls." Even the rapporteur knew for sure that the cowed Jewish minority would not even dare to think about behaving provocatively. The Jews of Germany—Jews in Germany—also fell prey to reports from the eastern front and pressure from party leaders and were taken hostage by the canard of an all-out effort by the Jews to destroy Germany.[73]

Accordingly, according to the SD reports, the introduction of the Judenstern was widely greeted with such "contentment" and "great satisfaction" that people even criticized the exemption of "miscenegational" Jews from the edict or demanded the placement of an additional star on Jews' backs so they could be identified from behind as well. However, some resisted this (e.g., in the Catholic Church against the idea of singling out Catholic Jews at mass). In Breslau, Willy Cohn observed, "This morning when I went to get the milk, I saw that, if anything, the Aryans will find it more awkward than we do! . . . The public's behavior was irreproachable. . . . The badge has had the opposite effect that the regime had intended."[74]

This disapprobation was not the product of pity alone; it also stemmed, as stated above, from fear of revenge against Germans in America, where, according to the rumors, the intention of marking them with a swastika was gaining currency.[75] Even Goebbels noticed "sentimental objections" among the population and tried to take countervailing measures:[76] a week after the yellow-star rule went into effect, manifestations of compassion among "good strata" toward the Jews over the marking were reported at a propaganda meeting of the Ministry of Public Enlightenment and Propaganda. Thus, displeasure with and even rejection of this measure—evidently due to the method of discrimination as opposed to discrimination per se—were truly widespread. I cannot determine whether reports in letters and diaries about Germans' demonstratively greeting or helping star-wearing Jews attained a critical mass and whether an American correspondent in Berlin spoke the truth when he termed the yellow star a "colossal failure." Clearly, however, the level of disgust surpassed the expectations of Goebbels and the party institutions. Goebbels even complained about it to Hitler: "The nation simply isn't ripe."[77] This led to the promulgation of a new enactment rendering punishable any display of personal sympathy for Jews.

3. The historian Ian Kershaw speaks about a fundamental apathy among Germans to the fate of the Jews. Otto Dov Kulka believes that even the deportation stage was greeted not with indifference but, in fact, with tacit consent. New continuing research gives evidence of lively interest in the matter, ranging at its extremes from active consent to the measures to overt revulsion. The SD reports describe a difference between the "politically knowledgeable," who welcomed the evacuation, marveled at the roundup of Jews under the luxurious conditions of "amazingly well equipped city buses," and wondered ruefully why the whole thing had not happened fifty years earlier, and those circles, mainly Christian, who were loath to surrender their Jewish employees for reasons of pity or even friendship.[78]

A famous letter from the editor of the SS newspaper *Das Schwarze Korps* to Rudolf Brandt, a member of the SS commander's personal staff, shows, on the one hand, how widespread the information about the deportations was and, on the other, what it was that decent German civilians opposed. The editor describes a scene that preceded the transport of Jews from the Fabrikaktion on March 4, 1943: many employees and executives at the newspaper's publishing house looked on as someone flogged Jewish men and even women with babes in arms for no reason. The SS man's grievance, he writes in his letter, "has nothing or half of nothing to do with humaneness or sentimentalism"; instead, it originates in the attitude toward the event as something "irreconcilable with a German position. After all, ultimately we do not wish to give the impression that we are savage sadists." The SS man knew in early 1943 what many others knew, but he raged not about the "what" of it but rather about the "how," not as a human being but as a German.[79]

The aforementioned "sentimental objections" among the Volk gave Goebbels sufficient cause to order, on August 21, 1941, "[the] use against the Jews [of] everything that can be used against them." Given his feeling that the public was insufficiently enthusiastic about the just-begun deportation of the Jews, he placed two articles in the newspaper *Das Reich* (on November 9 and 11), headlined "The Jews Are Guilty," in which he warned explicitly against all contact with German Jews. "The Jewish question has been spoken of at more than two hundred rallies around town,"[80] reported Elisabeth Freund in December 1941, two months after having emigrated to Cuba by the skin of her teeth. The American author Theodore N. Kaufman's book, *Germany Must Perish*,[81] mentioned above en passant, served as an ideal gimmick for Goebbels's tactic: Kaufman was presented as a Jew who pulled Roosevelt's strings; the wording of the title of his book was construed as a threat to bring physical annihilation upon the Germans as America's goal in the war (which the United States had not yet joined at the time). Thus Goebbels could turn the propaganda tables upside down in regard to sterilization and extermination:[82] it was the Jews who had started the whole thing; the Germans were merely hitting back. At the end of this chapter, I revisit this tactic and the role of Kaufman's book in detail.

4. From October 1941 onward, the topic of inquiry changes. At issue now is the Germans' attitude both toward the deportation and murder and toward the few Jews who remained, or were allowed to remain, in the Reich. According to an SD report, in February 1942, the vigorous struggle against the Jews was publicly construed as meaning "soon the last Jew will be expelled from European soil."[83] In a report dated February 21, 1942, the SD stated, "If you talk with combat soldiers from the East, you'll see that the Jews here in Germany are still being treated far too humanely."[84] In other words, all the Jews in Germany should be killed. The exact fate of Jews being deported from Germany was not widely known then, as noted. As the war continued and the de facto cleansing of Germany of its Jews (*Judenbereinigung Deutschlands*) progressed, views became even more radical. One soldier wrote in April 1944, "Dear Mom! Your position on the Jews has changed perceptibly. Didn't you once pity them? And now you even want to help pummel them."[85] The disappearance of Jewish neighbors and their succession by the "abstract Jew" as the object of animus made further radicalization of this kind possible.

Peter Longerich, who dealt intensively with the question of public opinion, concluded—as did David Bankier years earlier and Frank Bajohr subsequently— that the many and varied reports, diary entries, and writings reveal clashing outcomes: manifestations of sympathy along with much estrangement, apathy, and hate. Ultimately, any attempt to weight and quantify all of this would be irresponsible. One who wishes to tally the many personal cases finds oneself disregarding the specific context of the reports and writings. Furthermore, 1941 cannot be compared with 1943 in any sense. "From the methodological standpoint, this is a cul de sac," Longerich admits. Even the personal cases in themselves do not speak unequivocally. Consider the September 1942 report about an incident in the Berlin metro, in which a young girl ordered an elderly Jewish woman wearing the Judenstern to surrender her place: "The matron stood up and no one paid the episode any attention."[86] How should one interpret the response of those who witnessed it—as proof of widespread animus toward Jews, tacit consent to the deportations, or indifference?[87] Or might it have been simply fear of the terror, denunciation, and castigation of the loyal Volksgemeinschaft? To resolve the hermeneutic difficulty, one should ask whether anyone today can possibly interpret metro passengers' passive treatment of attacks on women or the elderly as consent to or sympathy for the offenders.

As paradoxical as it may sound, it is precisely the leading antisemites, Hitler and Goebbels, who can help us, ex post, to answer the question about the general state of mind. In May 1942, nearly a year into the offensive against USSR and many months after the deportation of German Jewry began, Hitler vented on the topic in one of his "table talks" (Tischgespräche): "That Jew who back then stabbed the nation in the back, what's called today our bourgeoisie laments when they deport him to the east."[88] He must have been familiar with the February 1942 jeremiad of the Gestapo Commander Müller, who alleged that objections against the Jewish policy were being expressed "in anonymous letters sent relentlessly to almost all bureaus in Reich territory."[89] In July 1942, Hitler said, "After the war ends, he will claim vehemently that city after city should be pounded unless all the befouled Jews exit and emigrate to Madagascar or to some other Jewish nation-state."[90] Thus, the Führer himself admitted that the public was displeased by the deportations, passed the blame to the bourgeoisie, and still assumed in July 1942 that even his intimates had no idea where the deportations were headed. Two months later, Goebbels, too, reported the existence of objections or at least displeasure: "They [the Jews in the war industry] are not as crucial as our intellectuals claim. . . . The outstanding Jewish worker has become . . . a permanent argument of philosemitic intellectual propaganda. Here we see again that we Germans tend too easily to excessive decency."[91]

Goebbels took appropriate propaganda measures: at a secret conclave at his ministry on August 13, 1942, he instructed reportage on progress in the new wave of deportations to be placed mainly in the bourgeois press, as a preventive measure against "Jews' atrocities" abroad.[92] Repeatedly faulting the oppositionist intellectuals who invoked war-economy logic to resist the wholesale deportation of Jewish professionals, he remarked several months later, after the Fabrikaktion: "Unfortunately, it has been proved here, too, that the elite circles, particularly the intellectuals, do not understand our policies toward the Jews and even take their side."[93] The civilians who in late 1941 already objected to the deportations, as reported by the Swedish banker Jacob Wallenberg,[94] belonged to those circles that Hitler and Goebbels decried.

Those affiliated with the resistance movement that would be identified with the assassination attempt on July 20, 1944, knew what was happening to the Jews. Back in early 1941, in his programmatic memo *Das Ziel* (The goal), Carl Friedrich Goerdeler demanded the nullification of the anti-Jewish enactments but nevertheless argued in favor of deporting from Germany such Jews as were socially unassimilated. In March 1943, Helmuth von Moltke assumed that most of the population still thought the Jews could carry on with their lives in the east and, accordingly, saw no need to protest against their fate. That month, another member of the resistance movement spoke about a concentration camp in Upper Silesia that had a monthly killing capacity of three thousand to four thousand persons.[95] Many members of this anti-Hitler group took a dichotomous position on the Jewish question, believing in the Jews' "otherness" and accepting the idea of expelling them, although not of murdering them. Frank Bajohr reaches the same conclusion about German society at large: "It was not anti-Jewish policy as such that marked a rupture in the social consensus, but rather the mass murder."[96]

Valid evidence of the Germans' representative attitude may be harvested from public opinion polls that the American military administration in Germany conducted among Germans in the American occupation zone immediately after the war. In these surveys, stereotyping of Jews and acceptance of the National Socialist stance toward them are reflected with statistical certainty. Less than half a year after the end of the war, one-fifth of Germans expressed being in favor of the manner in which Hitler had "dealt with" the Jewish problem, whereas about half rejected it. In 1946, 18 percent of respondents were still found to have extreme antisemitic views, 39 percent antisemitic views, and 61 percent racist views (the data for Berlin were lower and those among women considerably higher).[97] Some 14 percent thought the Jews alone had benefited from the war, and only 59 percent admitted that Germany had tortured and murdered millions of Jews. If we bear in mind that two years of postwar reeducation programs must have made some impression on the population and that some respondents guessed what the purpose of the questions was, then David Bankier's conclusion—that most of the population tended to open hostility toward the Jews—is essentially confirmed.[98]

Nevertheless, not all non-Jewish Germans were eliminationist antisemites (if I may adopt Daniel J. Goldhagen's term). The various measures that were brought against German Jewry always demanded an excuse that might serve as grounds or justification. The dictum "the Jews are our misfortune" was common more than half a century before the Nazis rose to power. Had it not been concretized, however, automatic sweeping consent to practical antisemitic steps would not have been given. As described above, the recourse to steadily escalating measures was repeatedly greeted, despite all attempts at justification, with condemnation and even resistance in relatively broad circles. Had the regime not employed the tactic of blaming the Jewish population itself for these measures, the displeasure with this policy would probably have been even stronger. The nature of this tactic was plain: anti-Jewish measures were always presented and justified to the public as *responses* to Jewish provocations—"eye-for-an-eye" reprisals, as it were.[99]

Thus, the 1938 "Judenaktion" was portrayed as retribution for the assassination of a German diplomat in Paris by "the Jews" (and not by a young Jew) and the escalating ferocity of measures against German Jewry once the war began as reprisals for Chaim Weizmann's ostensible declaration of war on Germany. As the campaign against Poland wound down, it was stated, "Jews and convicts murder Germans in Warsaw."[100] When the war in the west lasted longer than expected, allegedly by fault of "the Jews," Klemperer expressed the fear that "we Jews will [be] put up . . . against the wall yet."[101]

When the war on the Soviet Union began, this tactic was wielded even more bluntly. On July 9, 1941, Goebbels's newspaper, *Der Angriff*, published matching snipings by Robert Ley under the headline "This Is the Jews' Plan": "There's no way back from here. . . . We have crossed the Rubicon. . . . The Jew seeks his revenge against the German people. . . . The God of the Jews is a God of vengeance. . . . He destroys and consumes." If Germany loses, Ley warned, the Jew will rape and murder the women and enslave the men. "This war is incomparably cruel. . . . It is the Jews' wish to destroy us, the Germans, until not a trace remains." Two weeks later, he added, "The world has discovered that the Jew is its enemy. . . . If this struggle is determined by the Jews to be a struggle of life or death, then we Germans will remain alive and the Jew will be destroyed this time." A week later, this time in response to the American Kaufman's book, Ley exhorted, "Free yourselves of the Jews! Peoples of the world, unite and batter the Jews wherever they may be!" In the same vein, he wrote in August, "[The Jews' god] is a bloodthirsty god. . . . Therefore, Judea and its world must be annihilated." Weizmann was mobilized for the campaign, too: "So the world isn't perfect without a solution to the Jewish problem, Weizmann claims?—He's definitely right about that," Ley retorted sarcastically.[102] Thus the radicalization of the Jewish policy to the point of extermination was justified as a preventive or retributive measure, and the hope was expressed that the world would acknowledge its necessity.

The Judenstern edict was also presented in Germany as an appropriate response—that is, as retribution for the atrocities that, ostensibly, had been discovered in the Soviet Union and in the territories that had been occupied since 1939. Against the background of atrocity stories from the east, it was alleged, this is how a German should identify the Jew in Germany as well. In the media, but also in letters from soldiers on the front, "Bolshevik Jewish atrocities" such as the murder of eight thousand civilians at the prison in Lwów and of two thousand ethnic Germans in Tarnopol were reported. "Thus far, we have sent 1,000 Jews to the afterworld," a soldier quipped sarcastically in an attempt to persuade his family that the Jewish menace existed in Germany, too.[103] The next step—the deportation of German Jewry from October 1941 onward—was also put forward as a reprisal operation, this time in response to the expulsion of Germans from the Volga region. The confiscation of deported Jews' apartments and homes, in turn, was depicted as payback for the bombardment of German cities. The extension of this tactic to the world outside Germany was already phrased in Goebbels's November 16, 1941, article, quoted above: the sentence "World Jewry is now experiencing a gradual process of extermination" concludes with the words "the very process that it had intended for us."[104] By this reasoning, the Jews were being annihilated in response to, or in self-defense against, Jewish exterminationist schemes. "The Jews wanted this war" was heard in late 1943, when Germany's defeat began to loom.[105]

Several times above, I mentioned Theodore N. Kaufman's book *Germany Must Perish*. Now it is time to elaborate. The work, published in the United States in early 1941, played a special role in shifting the blame to the Jewish population and presenting the deportation and murder of German Jewry as a mere reprisal. As noted, too, the concentration of the Jews of Hanover in Jewhouses in early September 1941 was presented explicitly as a response to this book. "[Under the heading 'Houses for Jews and Casualties of Bombardments,'] the Gauleiter mentioned that this war was that of Judaism, i.e., the Jews, against the German people and again described the sadistic intent of the American Jew Kaufman to obliterate the [German] people by means of sterilization."[106]

This argument was possible mainly because Goebbels had long treated the nexus as a gimmick for his antisemitic propaganda *en bloc*.

To give wider circulation to the reports on "Bolshevik-Jewish atrocities" in the east, Goebbels suddenly began in June 1941 to use Kaufman's slender opus, which had already been published at least four months earlier, as conclusive proof of a Jewish-plutocratic conspiracy against Germany. Kaufman, an unimportant figure himself, was portrayed as a Roosevelt confidante and his scheme as American policy. Kaufman's point of departure—half a century before Daniel Goldhagen—was that "Hitler is no more to be blamed for this German war than was the Kaiser for the last one. Nor Bismarck before the Kaiser. These men ... were merely the mirrors reflecting centuries-old inbred lust of the German nation for conquest and mass murder."

To forestall future wars, Kaufman offers the prescription "Germany must perish forever." Germany's total war should be countered by total punishment: dividing the country among its neighbors and applying "[the] modern method, known to science as Eugenic Sterilization." The fact that Goebbels and other National Socialist propagandists pounced on this pamphlet, calling for the bio-logical extermination of the Germans, like a treasure is as plain as Kaufman's inanity. It gave Goebbels's tactic fertile soil. "From this pamphlet," he told his diary on August 29, 1941, "even the stupidest of the stupid can understand the immensity of the menace if we display weakness." A German who accepted the contents of Kaufman's book as Goebbels intended could not, it seems, but assent to the most vigorous measures against Jews everywhere, starting with those in Germany itself. This German citizen received the appropriate infor-mation in the newspapers, in a pamphlet by Wolfgang Diewerge, an official in Goebbels's office who specialized in matters concerning antisemitism, and in the leaflet "When You See This Mark," which by order of Goebbels was distrib-uted in the millions ahead of the introduction of the yellow star.

The very fact that one could derive rationally from this leaflet the Jewish population's guilt for its own extermination was shown by none other than the Nazi arch-criminal Adolf Eichmann. In his postwar memoirs, he wrote,

Today I believe that this Kaufman-plan may have been nothing but a provocation meant to cause a violent eliminationist policy against the Jews and promote the establishment of a Jewish state under international guarantee as a countermeasure. . . . If this scheme was indeed meant to serve as a provocation, then one cannot but say that the Jews attained their goal. Presumably the Kaufman plan gave the highest circles of our leadership an impetus for the extermination measures that we adopted.[107]

Thus after the war, too, Eichmann invoked Goebbels's old tactic by blaming the murder of the Jews on a specific group of Jews, the Zionists. They, he said, had triggered the extreme German reaction in a sophisticated way that would bring on the establishment of a Jewish state.

When reports about the murder of Jews in the east became frequent in Ger-many, as happened about a year after the deportations began—either due to the onset of reportage about it abroad or because German soldiers were sending home photographs of Jews being executed—Goebbels deliberately switched to "a large-scale propaganda campaign to cleanse of responsibility," Longerich reports—that is, preventive blaming of Jews, British, and Americans for atrocities. Accordingly, for example, the order was handed down: "The press shall deal with a report on Emil Ludwig Cohn's demand to disarm Germany and use it to sustain the antisemitic momentum so that the imminent evacuations of the Jews will not spread false sentimentality among the public."[108]

This weapon of reprisal (in German: *Vergeltungswaffe* or, in short, "V-Waffe") targeted Jews long before the V-1 and the V-2 rockets (V standing for *Vergeltung*) were manufactured to target Britain and Belgium. It was a weapon, however, that deliberately provided grounds for payback. Joseph Goebbels, the consummate cynic, explained his tactic back in early September 1940: given that the world attacks Germany's antisemitism relentlessly, why should we not at least take advantage of these assaults and, for example, banish the Jews from the theater, the film industry, public life, the public bureaucracy, and so on? Responsibility for this "payback" was charged to the Jews' international propaganda. When others condemn this policy, the condemned will be able to answer with a clean conscience, "It paid off."[109]

The "payback" policy and the mentality that came with it took yet another step forward. When displeasure in Church circles was noticed, when protest on religious grounds stirred because the idea of reprisal and revenge against the Jews was not greeted with enthusiasm—as many in Goebbels's habitus thought—the propagandists turned their eyes toward Islam. Back in 1937, Nazi Germany had switched to the Arabs' side in the Middle East because "the Jews" in Palestine were planning the "violent Judaization of Palestine," as Alfred Rosenberg put it. Furthermore, they were ready to erase the word "antisemitism" from the dictionary because Arabs were considered Semites. They were even willing to present Muhammad, instead of Jesus, as the portender of the National Socialist ideology. Not only had the Muslim prophet banished the Jewish Quraysh tribe from the Arabian Peninsula, but he had slaughtered them "because the Jews entered into an alliance with our enemies." The new Quraysh were the Jews of Germany, some of whom had already fled to Palestine by the time this warning was sounded, in December 1942.[110] Here the tried-and-true tactic—foisting the blame on the Jews and thus establishing the right to exact revenge against them—was taken to absurdity in the additional sense of using the Islamic tradition, something totally foreign to German society, to justify the murder of the Jews by Nazi Germany.

NOTES

1. Fritz Süllwold, *Deutsche Normalbürger 1933–1945. Erfahrungen, Einstellungen, Reaktionen. Eine geschichtspsychologische Untersuchung* (Munich: Herbig, 2002), 116, 123, 208–12.

2. Walter Manoschek, ed., *"Es gibt nur eines für das Judentum: Vernichtung!": Das Judenbild in deutschen Soldatenbriefen 1939–1944* (Hamburg: Hamburger Edition, 1995), 74.

3. Cf. Hans-Günther Seraphim, ed., *Das politische Tagebuch Alfred Rosenbergs* (Munich: Deutscher Taschenbuch, 1964), 81.

4. Otto Dov Kulka and Eberhard Jäckel, eds., *The Jews in the Secret Nazi Reports on Popular Opinion in Germany, 1933–1945* (New Haven, CT: Yale University Press, 2010), 476.

5. Bernward Dörner, *Die Deutschen und der Holocaust: Was niemand wissen wollte, aber jeder wissen konnte* (Berlin: Propyläen, 2007), 185.

6. Kulka and Jäckel, *The Jews in the Secret Nazi Reports*, 622: General Guidance of the Press, May 22, 1943.

7. Ibid., 634; cf. 613, 618, 632, 645, 650ff.

8. Ibid., 624.

9. Cf. Fred Hahn, *Lieber Stürmer. Leserbriefe an das NS-Kampfblatt 1924–1945* (Stuttgart: Seewald, 1978), 149.

10. Ralph Giordano, *Die Bertinis* (1982, *The Bertini Family*).

11. Cf. David Bankier, *The Germans and the Final Solution: Public Opinion under Nazism* (Oxford: Blackwell, 1992); Frank Bajohr and Dieter Pohl, *Der Holocaust als offenes Geheimnis. Die Deutschen, die NS-Führung und die Alliierten* (Munich: Beck, 2006); Peter Longerich, *"Davon haben wir nichts gewußt!" Die Deutschen und die Judenverfolgung 1933–1945* (Munich: Siedler, 2006); Jeffrey Herf, *The Jewish Enemy: Nazi Propaganda during World War II and the Holocaust* (Cambridge, MA: Harvard University Press, 2006); Dörner, *Die Deutschen und der Holocaust*; Frank Bajohr and Christoph Strupp, eds., *Fremde Blicke auf das "Dritte Reich": Berichte ausländischer Diplomaten über Herrschaft und Gesellschaft in Deutschland 1933–1945* (Göttingen: Wallstein, 2011); Nicholas Stargardt, *The German War: A Nation Under Arms, 1939–1945* (New York: Basic Books, 2015); Frank Bajohr, "German Responses to the Persecution of the Jews as Reflected in Three Collections of Secret Reports"; Wolf Gruner, "Indifference? Participation and Protest as Individual Responses to the Persecution of the Jews as Revealed in Berlin Police Logs and Trial Records, 1933–45," in Susanna Schrafstetter and Alan E. Steinweis, eds., *The Germans and the Holocaust: Popular Responses to the Persecution and Murder of the Jews* (New York: Berghahn, 2016).

12. Kulka and Jäckel, *The Jews in the Secret Nazi Reports*, 389.

13. Cf. Longerich, *"Davon haben wir nichts gewußt!"* 124–29.

14. Cf. Bajohr and Pohl, *Der Holocaust als offenes Geheimnis*, 42–46. For an example of a small village, see Sven Felix Kellerhoff, *Ein ganz normales Pogrom* (Stuttgart: Klett-Cotta, 2018).

15. Karl Heinz Jahnke, "Die Vernichtung der Juden in Mecklenburg," in Arno Herzig and Ina Lorenz, eds., *Verdrängung und Vernichtung der Juden unter dem Nationalsozialismus* (Hamburg: Hans Christians, 1992).

16. Manfred Unger and Hubert Lang, eds. *Juden in Leipzig. Eine Dokumentation zur Ausstellung anläßlich des 50. Jahrestages der faschistischen Pogromnacht* (Leipzig: Ausstellungszentrum der Karl-Marx-Universität, 1988), 163.

17. Kulka and Jäckel, *The Jews in the Secret Nazi Reports*, 402, SD report of January 13, 1939.

18. Victor Klemperer, *I Will Bear Witness: A Diary of the Nazi Years, 1933–1941* (New York: Random House, 1998), 357, entry of September 27, 1940.

19. Cf. Willy Cohn, *No Justice in Germany: The Breslau Diaries, 1933–1941*, ed. Norbert Conrads, trans. Kenneth Kronenberg (Stanford, CA: Stanford Studies in Jewish History and Culture, 2012), 271–76, entries of September 1–14, 1939.

20. Manoschek, ed., *"Es gibt nur eines für das Judentum,"* 38.

21. Cohn, *No Justice in Germany,* 384, entry of October 9, 1941.

22. Cf. Longerich, *"Davon haben wir nichts gewußt!"* 168ff.

23. Cohn, *No Justice in Germany,* 379–80, entry of September 20, 1941.

24. Ken Arkwright, "Das Ende der jüdischen Schule in Breslau," in *Mitteilungen des Verbandes ehemaliger Breslauer und Schlesier in Israel* (March 1972): 8ff.

25. Cf. Kulka and Jäckel, *The Jews in the Secret Nazi Reports,* 571, 575.

26. Monika Richarz, ed., *Jüdisches Leben in Deutschland*, vol. 3: *Selbstzeugnisse zur Sozialgeschichte 1918–1945* (Stuttgart: Deutsche Verlags-Anstalt, 1982), 430.

27. Cf. Bajohr and Dieter, *Der Holocaust als offenes Geheimnis,* 47–50. Cf. also Dörner, *Die Deutschen und der Holocaust* (Berlin: Propyläen 2007), 344, 437.

28. Raya Cohen, "Confronting the Reality of the Holocaust: Richard Lichtheim, 1939–1942," *Yad Vashem Studies* 23 (1993): 335–68.

29. *Volksstimme*, February 1, 1939.

30. Klemperer, *I Will Bear Witness,* 293, entry of February 5, 1939.

31. Cohn, *No Justice in Germany,* 236, entry of January 31, 1939.

32. Ian Kershaw, "Hitler's Prophecy and the 'Final Solution," lecture at the Raul Hilberg Holocaust Lecture Series, University of Vermont, December 5, 2001.

33. Cohn, *No Justice in Germany,* 389–90, entries of October 21 and 26, 1941.

34. Bajohr and Pohl, *Der Holocaust als offenes Geheimnis,* 57; cf. Dörner, *Die Deutschen und der Holocaust,* 431.

35. Manoschek, ed., *"Es gibt nur eines für das Judentum: Vernichtung!"*

36. Cf. Beate Kosmala, "Zwischen Ahnen und Wissen. Die Flucht vor der Deportation (1941–1945)," in Birthe Kundrus and Beate Meyer, eds., *Die Deportation der Juden aus Deutschland. Pläne–Praxis–Reaktionen* (Göttingen: Wallstein, 2004), 144.

37. Bajohr and Pohl, *Der Holocaust als offenes Geheimnis,* 59.

38. Elisabeth Freund in: Monika Richarz, ed., *Jüdisches Leben in Deutschland,* 381.

39. Dörner, *Die Deutschen und der Holocaust,* 336.

40. Ibid., 438; cf. Kosmala, "Zwischen Ahnen und Wissen," 148. Hermann Samter, a member of the Jüdische Nachrichtenblatt staff, still believed on November 30, 1941, in the possibility of returning "within a few years." A year later to the day, he wrote in a letter that Germany's defeat was imminent and, thus, "our stay in the east is becoming shorter and shorter." Cf. Daniel Fraenkel, ed., *To Be a Jew in Berlin: The Letters of Hermann Samter, 1939–1943*, trans. Bronagh Bowerman (Jerusalem: Yad Vashem, 2012).

41. Schrafstetter, *Flucht und Versteck,* 53.

42. Dörner, *Die Deutschen und der Holocaust,* 345.

43. Fred Hahn, *Lieber Stürmer. Leserbriefe an das NS-Kampfblatt 1924–1945* (Stuttgart: Seewald, 1978), 82, 167.

44. Dörner, *Die Deutschen und der Holocaust,* 351.

45. Bankier, *The Germans and the Final Solution,* 149.

46. Stargardt, *The German War,* 248.

47. Kosmala, "Zwischen Ahnen und Wissen," 143.

48. Peter Fritzsche, "Babi Yar, But Not Auschwitz: What Did Germans Know about the Final Solution?" in Susanna Schrafstetter and Alan E. Steinweis, eds., *The Germans and the Holocaust* (New York, Oxford: Berghahn, 2016).

49. Klemperer, *I Will Bear Witness*, 306, entry of August 29, 1939.

50. Ibid., 386, entry of May 24, 1941.

51. Stargardt, *The German War*, 259.

52. Cf. Bankier, *The Germans and the Final Solution*, chapters 6–7, 101–38; and Marlis G. Steinert, *Hitlers Krieg und die Deutschen. Stimmung und Haltung der deutschen Bevölkerung im Zweiten Weltkrieg* (Düsseldorf, Vienna: Econ, 1970), 26; Gruner, "Indifference? Participation and Protest as Individual Responses to the Persecution of the Jews as Revealed in Berlin Police Logs and Trial Records 1933–1945," 59–84.

53. Hans Safrian and Hans Witek, eds., *Und keiner war dabei. Dokumente des alltäglichen Antisemitismus in Wien 1938* (Vienna: Picus, 2008), 278.

54. Hahn, *Lieber Stürmer*, 91.

55. Kulka and Jäckel, *The Jews in the Secret Nazi Reports*, RSHA report, December 7, 1938; cf. ibid., 357, 376.

56. Manfred Unger and Hubert Lang, eds., *Juden in Leipzig. Eine Dokumentation zur Ausstellung anläßlich des 50. Jahrestages der faschistischen Pogromnacht* (Leipzig: Karl-Marx-Universität, 1988), 177, police report.

57. Gruner, "Indifference? Participation and Protest as Individual Responses to the Persecution of the Jews as revealed in Berlin Police Logs and Trial Records 1933–1945," 67.

58. Cf. Ian Kershaw, *Popular Opinion and Political Dissent in the Third Reich, Bavaria 1933–1945* (New York: Clarendon Press of Oxford University Press: 1983), 269.

59. Theodore Lothrop Stoddard, *Into the Darkness: Nazi Germany Today* (Newport Beach, CA: Noontide Press, 2000; facsimile reprint of the original 1940 edition).

60. Kulka and Jäckel, *The Jews in the Secret Nazi Reports*, 476.

61. Hahn, *Lieber Stürmer*, 237–43.

62. Longerich, *"Davon haben wir nichts gewußt!"*

63. Manoschek, ed., *"Es gibt nur eines für das Judentum: Vernichtung!"* 14–17, 40.

64. Kulka and Jäckel, *The Jews in the Secret Nazi Reports*, 516.

65. Hans Mommsen, "Hitler's Reichstag Speech of 30 January 1939," *History and Memory* 9 (1997): 1–2, 150–53.

66. Klemperer, *I Will Bear Witness*, 364, entry of December 10, 1940.

67. Cf. Longerich, *"Davon haben wir nichts gewußt!"* 155.

68. Joseph Goebbels, *Tagebücher 1923–1945*, ed. Elke Fröhlich (Munich: Institut für Zeitgeschicht, 1993–2007), entry of September 18, 1940.

69. See n. 63.

70. Kulka and Jäckel, *The Jews in the Secret Nazi Reports*, reports from September 1941.

71. Longerich, *"Davon haben wir nichts gewußt!"* 160.

72. Kulka and Jäckel, *The Jews in the Secret Nazi Reports*, 527, 530ff, July 10, 1941.

73. Ibid.

74. Cohn, *No Justice in Germany*, 379–80, entries of September 19, 20, and 23, 1941.

75. Kulka and Jäckel, *The Jews in the Secret Nazi Reports*, reports from September 1941, 529, 564.

76. Goebbels, *Tagebücher 1923–1945*, entry of August 20, 1941.

77. Longerich, *"Davon haben wir nichts gewußt!"* 172–78.

78. Kulka and Jäckel, *The Jews in the Secret Nazi Reports,* 557, 565ff, reports of November 11 and December 12–16, 1941.

79. Peter Longerich and Dieter Pohl, ed., *Die Ermordung der europäischen Juden Eine umfassende Dokumentation des Holocaust 1941 bis 1945* (Munich: Piper, 1989), 163–65.

80. Elisabeth Freund in Monika Richarz, ed., *Jüdisches Leben in Deutschland,* vol. 3: *Selbstzeugnisse zur Sozialgeschichte 1918–1945* (Stuttgart: Deutsche Verlags-Anstalt, 1982), 381.

81. Cf. Wolfgang Benz, "Judenvernichtung als Notwehr? Die Legenden um Theodore N. Kaufman," *VfZ* 29 (1981): 615–29.

82. Longerich, *"Davon haben wir nichts gewußt!"* 167.

83. Kulka and Jäckel, *The Jews in the Secret Nazi Reports,* 575.

84. Ibid., 576.

85. Manoschek, ed., *"Es gibt nur eines für das Judentum: Vernichtung!"* 72.

86. Longerich, *"Davon haben wir nichts gewußt!"* 248–50.

87. Cf. Bankier, *The Germans and the Final Solution,* 129–30.

88. Andreas Hillgruber and Henry Picker, eds., *Hitlers Tischgespräche im Führerhauptquartier 1941–1942* (Munich: Deutscher Taschenbuch, 1968), 145, entry of May 15, 1942.

89. Longerich, *"Davon haben wir nichts gewußt!"* 435; cf. Christian Gerlach, "Die Wannsee-Konferenz, das Schicksal der deutschen Juden und Hitlers politische Grundsatzentscheidung, alle Juden Europas zu ermorden," *Werkstatt Geschichte* 18 (October 1997): 16.

90. Hillgruber and Picker, *Hitlers Tischgespräche,* 250, entry of July 24, 1942.

91. Goebbels, *Tagebücher 1923–1945,* entry of September 30, 1942.

92. Cf. Willi A. Boelcke, ed., *"Wollt Ihr den totalen Krieg?" Die geheimen Goebbels-Konferenzen 1939–1943* (Stuttgart: Deutsche Verlags-Anstalt, 1967), 271.

93. Goebbels, *Tagebücher,* entry of March 2, 1943.

94. Bankier, *The Germans and the Final Solution,* 106ff.

95. Cf. ibid., 102, 112.

96. Cf. Christof Dipper, "Der deutsche Widerstand und die Juden," *Geschichte und Gesellschaft* 3 (1983): 349–80. Cf. also Bankier, *Die öffentliche Meinung im Hitler-Staat*; Susanna Keval, *Die schwierige Erinnerung. Deutsche Widerstandskämpfer über die Verfolgung und Vernichtung der Juden* (Frankfurt, New York: Campus, 1999), 23, 95; and Frank Bajohr, "German Responses to the Persecution of the Jews as Reflected in Three Collections of Secret Reports," in Schrafstetter and Steinweis, *The Germans and the Holocaust,* 52.

97. Cf. Anna J. Merritt and Richard L. Merritt, eds., *Public Opinion in Occupied Germany. The OMGUS Surveys, 1945–1949* (Urbana: University of Illinois Press, 1970), 105, 146ff; David Bankier ed., *Probing the Depths of German Antisemitism. German Society and the Persecution of the Jews, 1933–1941* (Jerusalem, New York, Oxford: Yad Vashem, Leo Baeck Institute and Berghahn Books, 2000), 279.

98. Bankier, *The Germans and the Final Solution,* 121.

99. Kulka and Jäckel, *The Jews in the Secret Nazi Reports,* 574.

100. Klemperer, *I Will Bear Witness,* 312, entry of September 18, 1939.

101. Ibid., 343, entry of June 11, 1940.

102. "Das ist der Plan der Juden!" *Der Angriff,* July 9, 1941, "Das Wettringen. Schicksalswende," July 7, 1941; "Befreit Euch von Juden!" July 30, 1941; "Die hässliche bolschevistische Fratze," August 13, 1941; August 22, 1941, "Einer trägt die Fahne," September 9, 1941; Longerich, *"Davon haben wir nichts gewußt!"* 160ff.

103. Manoschek, ed., *"Es gibt nur eines für das Judentum,"* 31, 33.

104. Bajohr and Pohl, *Der Holocaust als offenes Geheimnis*, 57.

105. Kulka and Jäckel, *The Jews in the Secret Nazi Reports*, 626.

106. Marlis Buchholz, *Die hannoverschen Judenhäuser Zur Situation der Juden in der Zeit der Ghettoisierung und Verfolgung 1941–1945* (Hildesheim: A. Lax, 1987), 45ff.

107. Theodore N. Kaufman, *Germany Must Perish* (Newark, NJ: self-published, 1941), 99. Cf. Jeffrey Herf, *The Jewish Enemy: Nazi Propaganda during World War II and the Holocaust* (Cambridge, MA: Harvard University Press, 2006), 110–15; Wolfgang Benz, "Judenvernichtung als Notwehr? Die Legenden um Theodore N. Kaufman," *VfZ* 29 (1981).

108. Longerich, *"Davon haben wir nichts gewußt!"* 260ff.

109. Boelcke, *"Wollt Ihr den totalen Krieg?"* 290–305.

110. Moshe Zimmermann, "Mohammed als Vorbote der NS-Juden-politik?" *Tel Aviver Jahrbuch für deutsche Geschichte* 33 (2005): 290–305.

EIGHT

—ᗑ—

JEWS AS EXPATRIATE GERMANS

SINCE ONLY THE NATIONAL SOCIALIST state saw matters through the prism of "Jews *in* Germany," the Jews who were forced to leave Germany should be considered German Jews or Jewish Germans and not only "Jews *from* Germany." Until October 1941, Jews *of* Germany, excluded and isolated since January 1933, were allowed to emigrate from their country of birth. By the time war broke out in 1939, most Jews who had been living in Germany in 1933 had already left. As growing numbers of Jews were murdered in the east after the onset of Operation Barbarossa, one could increasingly apply the epithet "German Jews" to those who had managed to emigrate or flee to countries not occupied by National Socialist Germany. I speak not only of the literal migration of German Jews to the four corners of the earth but also of the emigration of a population that could characterize itself outside of Germany as representative of German Jewry and German culture or collectively considered itself German Jewish and behaved as such.

Most statistical data about German Jews who had been deported to other lands should be considered rough estimates that deserve the most cautious treatment.[1] The various conceptual definitions of a "Jew" sow imprecision before anything else can be considered. The statistics are also hard to assess because surveys pertaining to Jews, including those who had emigrated, do not always relate solely to the so-called Altreich after the Reich annexed Austria and Bohemia in 1938 and 1939. In Europe, some five thousand Jews were saved by having fled to Sweden via Denmark or Finland; around sixty-five thousand, including more than twelve thousand children, reached Britain, Ireland, and Iceland in the Kindertransports that began in November 1938 (including more than eleven hundred Christian children of Jewish origin to England); and some twenty-five thousand Jews made their way to Switzerland. Due to the neutrality and diplomatic activities of Turkey during World War II, Jews who fled to that country could also survive. More than one hundred thousand Jewish refugees, not only from the Reich, escaped via Portugal and Spain, mainly to North and South America. German Jews who fled to European countries such as France, Belgium, or the Netherlands (including more than three thousand children in the Kindertransports) were again snared in the National Socialists' web during the war and were evacuated to the east along with Jews in the countries that hosted them; there, they were murdered as were the German Jews who had been shipped from Germany straight to the east.

In northern Africa, Morocco and Algeria served as stopovers for German Jewish emigrants; in this sense, there is nothing fictional whatsoever about the 1942 film *Casablanca*.[2] Several thousand managed to flee to South Africa, Kenya, or Liberia. The story of Stefanie Zweig, who in childhood had to escape with her parents to Kenya, became famous worldwide in 2001 due to the film *Nirgendwo in Afrika* (Nowhere in Africa); it shows that even migrants in Britain's African colonies, far from Europe, did not surrender their Germanness. Another exotic destination was China: nearly twenty thousand Jews, two-thirds of them from the Reich, found refuge in Shanghai. In 1943, however, they were placed in a ghetto of sorts—the rundown Hongqiao quarter, a fenced-in compound four square kilometers in area—that the Japanese, Germany's allies, had established.

Around ten thousand Jews, more than half of them from Germany, plied the even longer route to Australia and New Zealand, and several thousand made their way to Japan or Singapore. The three most important centers of Jewish emigration from Germany and Central Europe, however, took shape in North America (around 130,000 individuals, roughly half in New York),[3] South America (approximately sixty thousand, half settling in Argentina), and British Mandate Palestine (another seventy thousand).

The meaning of living as a German Jew in a new homeland, or developing a Jewish version of Germanness outside Germany, may be illustrated by parsing each German Jewish émigré society in this respect. In Shanghai, "the émigrés spoke only German to each other" because they were less than fluent in English, let alone in Chinese.[4] From 1939 onward, a German-language newspaper, the *Gelbe Post*, appeared in that city, reporting inter alia on Chinese culture, offering advice on day-to-day survival, and explaining matters such as "dirt in China." The owner and editor of the paper, A. J. Storfer, wrote about "the word 'Jud' in the German vernacular." He urged his readers to "disengage from the past" because "some of those who were deported from Germany moved upward on the ladder by coming here." By saying this, he intended to refute the conventional wisdom about emigration as claiming a price in social status.[5]

In New York, German Jewish diaspora communities jelled in Washington Heights ("Frankfurt on the Hudson")[6] and on the Upper East Side. There, it was thought virtuous not to become too American. Only one-third of the refugees who married up to 1945 took an American spouse. The regnant point of view was "we don't dress better than or worse than others—just other." It was commonly said that the émigrés from the Reich always set their tables grandly, gracing the scene with china dishes and fresh flowers in a vase. "The Polish and Russian Jews were 90 percent Jews and 10 percent Poles or Russians. The German Jews were 100 percent German," quipped Quack.[7] Klaus Mann elaborated on this: "Look, most of our émigrés were good burghers who thought of themselves primarily as 'good Germans' and only afterwards as Jews."[8] "In different cities, German Jews clung to the habits and symbols of their previous lives in a surprisingly similar way." They spoke about their *Spazierengehen* (easygoing stroll), met for afternoon *Kaffee und Kuchen* (coffee and cake), and said *Fußball* instead of football.[9] The phenomenon per se, however, was more complex. The later the Jews left Germany and the more traumatic their experience there had been, the more likely they were to develop ill regard for the German language, customs, and habits.[10] When war in Europe broke out at the latest, many wished to disconnect from their "German" profile. Thus, the "German Jewish Club" became the "New World Club," and the newspaper *Aufbau* subtitled itself "Dedicated to the Americanisation of the Immigrants." Like those in America, German Jews in Australia formed a distinct and visible group, "a microcosm of German Jewry," and congregated in specific neighborhoods such as Kings Cross in Sydney and St. Kilda in Melbourne.[11]

Also repeatedly mentioned are the numerous celebrities who emigrated/escaped, foremost to Britain and America.[12] In his 1970 book *Germany without Jews*, Bernt Engelmann put together a list of artists, doctors, professors, politicians, and other notables and described comprehensively the process by which this group was cut off from the German society and culture, to the immense detriment of cultural life in Germany. Sixteen percent of the skilled German Jews who reached America were academics, a high proportion for the 1930s. More than one-third of all scientists, professors, and artists who had been forced out of Germany settled in America.

By focusing on the academic discipline of history alone, in which Jews in Germany were rather scantily represented—just ten "full" Jews by the racial definition served in German universities—one gets a clear sense of how much the German historians' guild lost due to the dismissal of these historians and how much academic life abroad gained. Enumerated among these expatriates are the full professors Ernst Kantorowicz, Hans Rothfels, Guido Kisch, and Eugen Täubler, who emigrated to America; the associate professors Richard Koebner, dean of historians in Israel, and Arthur Rosenberg, known for his critical analysis of the history of the Second Reich and the Weimar Republic; and the lecturers Hajo Holborn and Hans Rosenberg, who from their new perch in America strongly influenced German historiography after the war. Additional émigrés became important historians only after settling abroad (e.g., Felix Gilbert, Fritz Stern, and George Mosse in the US, and Jacob Katz, Walter Grab, and Jacob Toury in Israel). Collectively they substantiate the brain drain that the Nazis had set in motion. And even if not all the renowned historians can be noted in this discussion, I should expand the list by adding the names of scores of less-known historians who in exile made an important contribution to their discipline.[13]

The names of celebrities among the German Jewish refugees are repeatedly emphasized[14]—writers such as Else Lasker-Schüler, Anna Seghers, Leon Feuchtwanger, and Max Brod; architects such as Erich Mendelsohn and Munio Gitai Weinraub; composers such as Arnold Schoenberg and Kurt Weil; the conductor Otto Klemperer; stage directors such as Max Reinhardt, Fritz Kortner, and Billy Wilder; actors such as Elisabeth Bergner, Elise Bassermann, and her husband, Albert, who, although not of Jewish origin, emigrated with his Jewish wife; physicists such as Albert Einstein and James Frank; the psychoanalyst Sigmund Freud; and intellectuals such as Ernst Cassirer, Herbert Marcuse, and Theodor Adorno. Athletes are well represented, too: the high-jump champion Gretel Bergmann, the German footballer Gottfried Fuchs, and innumerable others who found refuge mainly in Anglo-Saxon countries. The multitudes of Jewish scientists, artists, and cultural personalities who were murdered or forced to emigrate provide, in fact, the most conspicuous proof of the insanity that marched hand-in-hand with the inhumanity of the "Third Reich." If so many Nobel Prize laureates—foremost Albert Einstein, mocked in the Nazi film *Der ewige Jude* as "Einstein, the Relative Jew"—had to exile themselves from racist Germany, then the common sense of non-Jewish Germans at large, not only of avowed National Socialists, is all the more questionable. Today, however, it goes without saying that, in relating to the degree of dastardliness employed in persecuting and exterminating Jews, it matters not whether the victims belonged to the cultural elite or the "simple" class.

Generally speaking, the host countries—including those that still allowed migrants to enter at all—were not passionately eager to receive the refugees. From 1939 onward, Jewish refugees from the Reich in France languished in *camps de concentration* that, after the defeat of France in 1940, became traps from which the exit eventually led to Auschwitz. In May 1940, when intense fear of sabotage erupted in Britain, large numbers of nonresidents, including thirty thousand persons defined as "friendly enemy aliens," mainly German and Central European Jews, were interned. Some eight thousand of them were sent to Canada and Australia. Although this was usually a temporary measure, it prompted some to take their lives. In Australia, Jews as "enemy aliens" had to surrender their binoculars, cameras, and drivers' licenses. Even in the US, German Jews were essentially suspect in the military's eyes, impeding their enlistment. Admittedly, the American attitude toward them was nothing like that toward citizens of Japanese descent or "persons of color."

Antisemitism was not an unfamiliar phenomenon outside of Germany; it could be encountered in the countries to which German Jews migrated. The German Foreign Ministry, aware of this, saw the diffusion of antisemitism as an important goal of German foreign policy. Explicit evidence of this emerges in the aforementioned memorandum that the ministry's Jewish affairs expert, Emil Schumberg, produced as a summary of events in 1938. Between 1933 and 1941, more than one hundred antisemitic organizations were established in what is taken to be the epitome of an open society, the United States, as against only five such entities in all of American history until then. American antisemitism crested in the 1938–1945 period. Between 1939 and 1942, the Christian Front acted to "liquidate" American Jewry. On November 18, 1938, nine days after the nighttime pogrom in Germany, the respected Senator William A. Borah spoke out against easing the immigration laws. Two days later, the racist Catholic priest Charles Coughlin unleashed an especially ignoble radio assault on the Jews. Public opinion polls found 70–85 percent of Americans opposed to the idea of greater flexibility in immigration options for refugees. As for the practical question of whether the US should take in more Jewish exiles from Germany, in 1938, 37 percent said no. Antisemitic attitudes gained strength in the course of the war.[15] Many articles in the German Jewish immigrant newspaper *Aufbau* document American antisemitism and its effects. Sinclair Lewis's dystopian novel *It Can't Happen Here* (1935) left no room for illusions concerning American antisemitism. The film *Crossfire* (1947) portrays animus against Jews in the military; the successful Hollywood vehicle *Gentleman's Agreement* (also 1947) exposes latent antisemitism among ostensibly liberal and tolerant Americans. Philip Roth, in his novel *The Plot against America* (2004), describes the way discrimination in the US metamorphosed into militant antisemitism during World War II.

Indeed, the United States was known as a bastion of freedom. The most vehement protests against the "Third Reich's" Jewish policy from 1933 on took place there; demonstrations and boycott exhortations were regular fare. However, due to antisemitism or fear of being accused of "Judaizing," the American social and political spheres failed to act effectively against the persecution of the Jews and did not promote a more beneficent immigration policy. That the Hollywood film industry refrained from turning out anti-German works even though its greatest moguls were Jewish—Louis B. Mayer and the Warner Brothers come to mind—was due also to direct pressure from Germany. Jewish or not, but for very few exceptions the moguls have taken care, before the United States entered the war in 1941, to avoid the topic of the Third Reich and, a fortiori, to steer clear of any criticism of that entity, lest they be plastered with the charge of acting against American interests and suffer on the bottom line. Another reason for soft-pedaling the Jewish topic until the United States entered the war in late 1941 and even afterward, however, was fear of the audience's antisemitic response and the antisemitic argument that the war was being prosecuted on behalf of Jewish interests.[16] In another example, after the German heavyweight boxer Max Schmeling defeated his rival, the dark-skinned ("Brown Bomber") Joe Louis in 1936, Schmeling was supposed to fight the world champion, James Braddock, in America. The Anti-Nazi League tried to prevent this, and in January 1937 in New York, the *Daily News* published critical letters from readers in the spirit of "God help the German Jews if the Schmeling-Braddock fight is called off due to the calls for a boycott." What the German Jews have suffered so far, another reader predicted, would be "nothing" compared with the assaults that would follow if Schmeling were denied an opportunity to snatch the title. The boycott committee, he continued, should organize evacuations of all German Jews if it continued to insist on a ban. Such a warning had a dire effect on German Jews in America, even as the cancellation of the match had not elicited special reactions in Germany. On April 29, shortly before the second Louis–Schmeling fight in the United States, Joe Jacobs, Schmeling's Jewish manager, interpreted the situation in Germany in accordance with Goebbels's propaganda line: "Most of the problems of the Jews there are the making of the Jews here."[17]

Even without overt antisemitism, the immigrants found it hard to integrate into society. Here, too, Hollywood may be considered a test case. Fortune did smile on several German émigré directors and actors in Hollywood, a place where Jewish moguls figured importantly. The scriptwriter and director Billy Wilder was one such success story. Of few others, however, could this be said.

Unaccented English was a sine qua non for acceptance. With a German accent, one could get secondary roles at best, mostly—in a monumental historical irony—playing Nazis.

However, it was not only non-Jewish society that slowed integration and crimped behavior in the context of Germany and its emigrants. The Jewish minority itself did its share. Even in Palestine, since 1948 in Israel, like anywhere else, there were perceptible tensions between German Jews and the majority of Jews, who were of East European origin.[18] The emphasis on German virtues—precision, order, discipline, compliance with authorities, and strict upholding of formalities, along with pleasant demeanor and demonstrative respect for the German classics at home, in the synagogue, and in the public domain served the Jews of Germany in the New World as a way of isolating themselves from the Ostjuden. As paradoxical as it sounds, German Jews defined their Jewishness in their destination countries by means of typical German customs and habits.[19]

Obviously, I do not wish to sketch the entire history of the German Jewish dispersion in this chapter, nor can I. What is more, a surfeit of literature specific to the topic exists today.[20] What I want in this chapter is to emphasize that the history of German Jewry also became, upon the community's emigration and deportation, the history of expatriate Germans (*Auslandsdeutsche*)—even though this term denoted only non-Jewish Germans at the time and was put to maximum use by an organization of such Germans on behalf of the Nazi Party (the AO—Auslandorganisation—which operated from 1938 onward as a division of the German Foreign Ministry). As the Israeli author of this book, I wish here to focus, as a representative group, on the German Jews in the land of Israel, the so-called Yekkes.[21] The history of this diaspora population has also been privileged recently with meticulous and comprehensive, sometimes nostalgic, attention, so the chapter here is set aside for one specific topic within that broader context: the identification of Jews as German Jews even after they were excluded from German society and banished from Germany, and the *problematique* that this caused.

"Yekke" is a derisive term that East European Jews coined for their German compatriots. It appears to trace to the jackets (*Jacke* in German) that German Jewish men wore, as opposed to the kaftan or cape that East European Jewish males donned. (Some claim that the East European Jews identified those of Germany with the *Jeck* of the carnival in the Rhineland.) Around the year 1933, the Yishuv—Jewish society in Mandate Palestine—adopted the mocking epithet and used it to demean this group even in its new place of refuge, the Jewish homeland. At that time, "Yekke" meant lack of Jewishness, vigorous exactingness, and pedanticism. Sometimes it even denoted a western Jew who looked down on "Ostjuden." An expert in a very narrow professional field, a poor fit for a state-in-the-making that needed occupational flexibility, might also be called a "Yekke." In the opinion of the historian Kurt Jakob Ball-Kaduri, the attitude toward the German Jews turned around by 1945, when Sammi Gronemann's *Memoirs of a Yekke* appeared in Hebrew and became a best seller.[22] It would be more correct, however, to speak of a process that persisted long afterward. In today's Israeli society, "Yekke" is a neutral term that may even express esteem; accordingly, henceforth I use it without the scare quotes.

In a recent work that deals with the café culture of Tel Aviv, a Jewish woman born in Mandate Palestine of the 1930s is quoted as saying, "The German immigrants surrendered neither their habits nor their principles. Their café catered to people who got together to converse, consult, and sometimes just gossip. . . . The matrons here had not parted with their furs, nor had the men with their ties. Few native-born visited the place."

A local newspaper complained that "in our surroundings [at Café Sapir] German is in all mouths, on the plates, in the glasses of tea, and obviously in the air, too." Another newspaper remarked, "At the cafés they don't turn to the customers in Hebrew at all [but in German] . . . 'Vhat vould you like? Cake or vhipped cream?' as if we weren't sitting on Allenby or Eliezer Ben-Yehuda Street but on Kurfürstendamm in Berlin."[23] M. Hanfling, owner of Curso, a café-restaurant on 83 Allenby Street in Tel Aviv, touted his establishment as follows: "Lunch and dinner are famed for their quality. Strictly kosher—German cuisine. A choice Viennese café."[24]

The cafés in Jewish Mandate Palestine were a microcosm of daily life. Jews who had been deported from the German Reich neither could nor wished to surrender their attachment to bourgeois, political, and cultural German traditions. In this respect, they mirrored the German Jewish expatriates in America. The National Socialist system of injustice could revoke their German citizenship but not their inherent affinity for the so-called German cultural sphere. This was also true of the neo-Orthodox German Jews, affiliates of the *Torah 'im Derekh Eretz* teachings of Samson Raphael Hirsch, who are mistakenly thought of as having failed to attain social integration in Germany. A future candidate for the Nobel Prize in literature, Yehuda Amichai, reached Palestine from Würzburg in childhood as Ludwig Pfeuffer and attended a synagogue where his rabbi, Dr. Wolff of Köln, gave sermons in German. The Yekkes paid a price for all this, as did the German Jews in the ghettos of Eastern Europe and the various diaspora centers. On the one hand, Yishuv society was largely of East European origin even after 1933; thus it was estranged, if only for historical reasons, from the German Jews and their traditions. In America, German Jews had preceded the "Ostjuden," arriving in the middle of the nineteenth century and therefore belonging to the Jewish establishment. The German Jews who reached Palestine from 1933 onward, in contrast, found it difficult to cope with the hegemony of East European Jews in the well-established political and cultural institutions that the latter had created in the country. Furthermore, given its focus on building a culture that would be literally Hebrew, Yishuv society dismissed the Yekkes' attitude as non-Zionist, tainted by adherence to their own culture and seemingly unwilling to leap into the social melting pot.

The veteran Jewish society's estrangement toward, if not rejection of, the Yekkes has been comprehensively documented.[25] At assemblies, on leaflets, and in press articles, it repeatedly denigrated Yekkes for their habits, their seeming wealth, and their alleged individualism, but also for their social-democratic affinities and their obeisance, conceit, and stubbornness—everything that squared with the clichés about Germans and German Jews.[26] Furthermore, from 1933 onward and particularly after the 1938 nighttime pogrom, the Jewish national society contemptuously rejected anything German, extending its struggle against National Socialist Germany to the German culture and language. Within the Zionist community, the response of the nationalist revisionists was the most extreme of all, assailing the immigrants from Central Europe as carriers of the German cultural bacillus. German films, German theater, gatherings conducted in German (including a birthday party for Kaiser Wilhelm, then living in exile in the Netherlands), and other matters were boycotted or even resisted violently. In the early going of May 1933, a leader of the *HaPoel HaTzair* movement unburdened himself on the topic:

> Our resurrection movement is now facing great danger from "Hitler's Zionists" . . . in our country [in contrast to Zionists of inner persuasion]. If they settle in concentrated neighborhoods of their own . . . it is not out of the question that here, too, they will develop German schools, publish a German newspaper, and preach assimilation. . . . It should be ensured, first of all, that assistance be given only to the sort who belonged to the Zionist movement before Hitler's strong hand shoved them out.[27]

This attitude turned increasingly extreme over time, and its argumentation acquired a harder and harder edge once the war began. For some Yekkes, the rhetoric sounded familiar—it reminded them of the way the antisemites in Germany spoke.[28] It also led to real threats, such as that brought against Stella Kadmon: "If you allow speeches in German to be given on the roof of your house, the roof and all the accursed onlookers will be tossed into the air."

The war on German culture in Jewish Mandate Palestine, however, could not be waged with absolute consistency. First, potential protesters could not keep abreast of everything that the Yekkes were up to. Sammy Gronemann and Else Lasker-Schüler recited their works at German-language literary evening events.[29] In Tel Aviv, Jerusalem, and Haifa, plays in German were put on in Yekke circles. Second, the German culture was treasured not only by Yekkes; Friedrich Schiller was the most popular poet among East European Jews, too. Furthermore, even before 1933, East European intellectuals translated German literary works, including plays, into Hebrew. Between 1939 and 1945, more than 130 German-language books received this treatment, more than in the entire preceding half-century. Among them were not only works by German Jewish authors but also children's books such as Wilhelm Busch's *Max und Moritz* (1939) and Erika Mann's *Muck, der Zauberonkel* (Muck the magic uncle, 1943). Alongside German classics such as Schiller's *Kabale und Liebe* (Intrigue and love, 1939), Goethe's *Faust* (1943), and Kant's *Kritik der reinen Vernunft* (Critique of pure reason, 1944) stood contemporary opuses such as Brecht's *Mutter Courage und ihre Kinder* (Mother Courage and her children, 1940), Anna Seghers's *Das siebte Kreuz* (The seventh cross, 1945), and political literature such as Friedrich Engels's *Der Ursprung der Familie* (Origin of the family, 1940), Konrad Heiden's biography of Hitler (1941), and Hermann Rauschning's *Gespräche mit Hitler* (Conversations with Hitler, 1941). As a rule, the repression of cultural life in Germany enraged not only Yekkes but also the Jewish population at large, as though it were their own. So remarked the historian Na'ama Sheffi, who researched German literature in Hebrew translation. In the newspapers' culture columns, one could plainly sense esteem for the pre-1933 attainments of German culture along with anguish over the more recent events in Germany. After the war, it was not only German Jews who had to cope with the question that the émigré from Hamburg, the intellectual and physician Isaiah Aviad (Oskar Wolfsberg), asked: "How does one explain the ghastly, horrifying contradiction of a nation that fathered artists and sophisticates such as these ... becoming the nation that sired generations that devastated the world, destroyed every treasured possession, and blasphemed God?"[30]

Soon after the outflow from Germany to Mandate Palestine began—the "Fifth Aliya," not just immigration, in Zionist historiography—the newly arrived German Jews established a German-language newspaper called *Das Mitteilungsblatt* that attained a print run of 3,500 copies by the mid-1930s. In October 1942, after much hesitation, the Central European immigrants also founded a political party, Aliya Hadasha (New immigration), for purposes that included a less nationalistic brand of Jewish politics than that espoused by the other large parties.

Behind the formation of Aliya Hadasha was the sense among Yekkes that they were underrepresented in the leadership of the largest party, Mapai (Worker Party). Several of their number did manage to break into the highest ranks of Mapai—foremost Fritz (Peretz) Naphtali, an erstwhile important member of the German Social Democratic Party—but in no way did this amount to adequate representation. Furthermore, the problem was not limited to party positions. In December 1940, S. Z. Rubashov, an East European Jew who had spent years living in Weimar Republic Germany and would become the third president of the state of Israel as Zalman Shazar, explained the matter typically: "There's something ridiculous about the wish of the German *Landsmanshaft* [immigrants' association] to serve as a guide for the whole Yishuv and teach it how to behave and live. These immigrants have just arrived and are not yet adequately immersed in [Yishuv] life; most do not yet know our language. This young immigrant population still needs a great deal of care."[31]

In December 1942, the dean of prestate Zionism, David Ben-Gurion, purported to know the spirit of the German immigration and deem it foreign to true Jewish peoplehood not only in its political attitude but in its entire way of life.[32] Thus it is no wonder that the response to this confusion of center with periphery—as if Germany had not been the center of modern Jewry and an important Jewish cultural hub up to 1933—came in the form of creating a new party.

As the rejection of the German language gathered strength, in 1944 Aliya Hadasha established a Hebrew-language newspaper, *Amudim*, and from that year on it held its conferences in Hebrew. This, however, did not doom the German tradition to disappearance. In Hebrew, the Yekkes exerted ongoing influence because among them were the publishers of the country's two most important newspapers, *Ha'aretz* and *Yedioth Ahronoth* (and subsequently *Ma'ariv*): Gershom Schocken, son of the owner of the famous department store in Chemnitz, and Azriel (Esriel) Carlebach, son of the town rabbi of Leipzig and an avowed anticommunist. In the early years of this century, the Central European *Landsmanshaft* in Israel undertook to rekindle interest in the Yekkes' long-term impact on preindependence Jewish and Israeli society. The *Ben-Yehudastraße Dictionary*, published in 2012, is a pronounced example of this effort.

From April 1942 to February 1943, a group on the political left congregated around another German-language organ in Palestine, the weekly journal *Orient*. Also beset by a sense of exile, they adhered to the German language and culture more intensively than did the majority of Yekkes, who affiliated with Aliya Hadasha or the General Zionist Party and Mapai. Although the titular chief at *Orient* was the author Arnold Zweig, the actual editor was Wolfgang Yourgrau, a quondam member of the Socialist Workers' Party in Germany (SAPD) who wrote explicitly about the German Jews' basic problem in Palestine. In his article "Homeland or Refuge," Yourgrau conjectured that "[apart from] the Zionist cadre, the German Jew [before 1933] was simply a German Jew . . . often nationalistic in his views. . . . Those German Jews left their homeland because they had been banished. . . . [and] found refuge in Palestine. . . . The German Jew had sunk roots in his old homeland and did not find a new homeland."

The immigrants' task, he continued, is to "make the refuge into a homeland," whereas the long-tenured residents need to be told that German Jews "are a sector of the Yishuv, admittedly different . . . but belonging nonetheless." Yourgrau knew exactly how hard this was; he spoke of "humiliating accusations," "heinous ridicule," "unfriendliness toward the German Jews," and a "petty urge for vengeance" due to "the German Jews' treatment of their East European brethren, which was not always especially beneficent," in pre-Hitlerite Germany.[33] The offensive that *Orient* absorbed was waged to some extent by self-appointed defenders of the Hebrew language but mostly, it seems, by its critical attitude toward the hegemonic tendency in Zionism. The print shops that turned out the journal were torched. Jewish ultra-rightists brutally broke up an open conference in Tel Aviv where Arnold Zweig spoke, battering the participants with batons and injuring many seriously enough to be rushed to hospital. This violent defense of Hebrew, or the violent struggle against German, proved victorious in February 1943 when a bomb demolished *Orient*'s new printing facility, eventually forcing the weekly to shut down.

The German Jews' advantages and training found expression in economic affairs and other areas of activity in Mandate Palestine. Capital inflow, creation of industry, and development of medicine are quintessential examples. More than half of all immigrant engineers and two-thirds of doctors came from Central Europe, although some had not been born there. Here the establishment was unable, and apparently unwilling, to thwart the Yekkes' success. In the final reckoning, Youth Aliyah was one of the original ideas of the Zionist movement and the Jewish national settlement venture in the land of Israel. In rural settlement and even in the kibbutz movement, too, the German imprint was far from nil; it appeared in Kefar Shmaryahu, Kibbutz Hazorea (founded by Werkleute people), and a religious kibbutz such as Tirat Zvi.

Apart from their personal distress, the German Jews in Palestine took a special interest in the fate of the Jews under National Socialist rule, the course of the war in Europe, and the question of its end—victory—in Europe and

Palestine alike. The Yishuv's Hebrew-language newspapers, maintaining contact with Germany as long as they could or using German newspapers as sources of information, had no illusions about the future of the Jews who remained in Germany. On November 13, 1938, the bourgeois newspaper *HaBoker* reported in detail on the outcome of the meeting with Göring a day earlier—the gathering that sealed the fate of German Jewry and, in fact, dealt with the "Final Solution" for that community. On December 1, 1938, in an exposé about goings-on in the Reich, there appeared a summary of interviews with Jews who had been released from the Buchenwald and Dachau concentration camps. Their stories were characterized as "indescribable." The socialist newspaper *Davar* carried especially detailed eyewitness testimonies from Dachau.[34]

On December 7, 1938, *HaBoker* published another "letter from Germany" with details about the public humiliation of Jews. Readers of *Hatzofe*, the newspaper of the religious Zionists, learned on December 14, 1938, about "the Amalekites' scheme"—that is, the call for the obliteration of German Jewry as described in the SS newspaper *Das Schwarze Korps* on November 5 and 24, 1938.

For German Jews who had emigrated to Palestine, there was nothing abstract about such reports. *Ha'aretz* advised its readers that thousands of German Jews now in Palestine were suffering terribly due to reports they had received from their families back in Germany. According to the paper, things went so far as causing two suicides in the days following the pogrom due to inability to help relatives who had been interned in concentration camps in Germany.[35] The German immigrants' *Landsmanshaft* was in a dire state. The erstwhile German Social Democrat Fritz Naphtali envisaged Palestine as the spearhead of the antifascist struggle. Siegfried Moses, in contrast—chair of the Zionist Federation of Germany in the first years of National Socialist rule—understood that German Jewry had been taken hostage and preferred concrete actions over grandiose rhetoric.[36] Either way, the Yishuv as such was generally rather indifferent to the catastrophe because it had set its sights mainly on local struggles with the Arabs of the country and with the mandatory power, Britain.[37]

When the war erupted in September 1939, a relatively large number of Yekkes in Palestine volunteered to serve in the British Army in order to fight Germany.[38] "The Jews' fate will be decided on the banks of the Rhine!" prodded Gustav Krojanker, a leading personality among the Yekkes, in the Hebrew-language newspaper *Ha'aretz*. The German and Austrian Landsmanshaft in Palestine demanded unequivocal identification with Britain, something not self-evident among the Jews of the country due to the contents of the white paper that the British had published shortly before the war. Given the obvious implausibility of sympathizing with Germany or Italy, most of the Jewish

establishment focused on expanding its own military potential—that is, illegally arming the *Hagana* militia and preparing it for struggle against the Arabs
and the British, instead of serving in the British Army. Even before the end of
the "phony war," the Yekkes tried to explain to the Zionist leadership that the
Jewish national home in Palestine was one of the targets of Hitler's threats and
that, accordingly, the idea of enlisting in the British forces should be disseminated as a top priority. In 1941 and 1942, as Rommel's divisions crouched at
the gates of Palestine with the aim of occupying the country, the Yekkes were
proved right. It is estimated that more than 60 percent of Jews in Palestine
who volunteered for service in His Majesty's army at the beginning of the war
were from Central Europe. Their share in the Jewish population was hardly
20 percent, meaning that the majority viewed the war differently. For Yekkes,
however, fighting under the British colors involved an additional risk: if they
were taken prisoner, they might be separated from other POWs and taken to a
special camp or to a concentration camp. Many Jewish soldiers from Palestine
were captured in Greece, for example, as readers of the newspaper *Das Reich*
in Germany also discovered in July 1941.

At first, the British military commanders opposed the mobilization of German Jews for a different reason: concern that the Gestapo and German intelligence had slipped agents into the population of refugees from Germany. Only
sometime later were German Jews from Palestine placed in special commando
units that operated behind German military lines in northern Africa. The Yishuv's elite fighting unit, the Palmah, also had a "German company" that would
have been sent into action if Rommel had managed to occupy Palestine. After
Rommel's defeat in Al-Alamein, it prepared for war in Europe. German Jews
were particularly motivated to participate in the fighting there because by doing so they might find out what had become of their loved ones. As mentioned
in chapter 6, several German Jews in the Allied armies did go all the way back
to Germany, albeit only as the war wound down.

It was in a state of utter helplessness—"numbed and indifferent . . . mentally
spent . . . almost apathetic"—that the Yekkes greeted the news from occupied
Europe that reached Palestine in late 1942. "A demarche unknown to the public
is unfolding today: . . . Behind the curtain that blankets the land east of the
Wisła, they are murdering, murdering the Jewish people," wrote Arnold Zweig
in an article titled "Silence," shortly before Hitler's Sixth Army surrendered in
Stalingrad.[39] Like him, few Yekkes deluded themselves about what they could
contribute to Germany's defeat. Zweig, of all people, now placed his trust in the
United States, evoking metaphors from the European history of the Christian-
Muslim confrontation in the Middle Ages: "To defeat the new Islam—if I may

so call Hitler's movement without offending that great religion—that storming of savage peoples from the lush forests of the German psyche—we need a new Charles Martel and new Franks. These new Franks . . . are the men and women of the United States."[40]

The ultimately futile attempt of the weekly *Orient* to remain evenhanded toward Germany—in contrast to the understandable anti-German tenor of the Hebrew-language press, *Das Mitteilungsblatt*, and the journal *Aufbau*, founded in the United States in 1934—is important as evidence of the continued existence of German Jewry even in its expatriated state. In September 1942, as reports on the magnitude of the crimes against the Jewish population gradually began to spread in the West, Schalom Ben-Chorin, a noted German-speaking Jewish philosopher of religion and after the war a prominent representative and exponent of Israel–German and Jewish–Christian relations, took a clear stance in response to a speech by the famous German Jewish literary critic Alfred Kerr on the topic of "Germany—Tomorrow": "That Hitler should write his memoirs in Huis Doorn [where Kaiser Wilhelm II languished after being unseated at the end of World War I] . . . must be prevented this time! Those responsible should be stood up against a wall! But then thought should be given to genuine rehabilitation. . . . There are productive elements both in Germany and among the expatriates."[41]

Arnold Zweig, in his article "Antigermanismus," also distinguished between National Socialists and Germans.[42]

The share of Central European Jews in Yishuv society quickly ascended to 15–20 percent, surpassing that of other diaspora-origin communities. In the 1944 elections for the Assembly of Representatives, their party, Aliya Hadasha, received 10 percent of votes cast. Their presence in academia was visibly large: twenty-one of the thirty-five professors at the Hebrew University of Jerusalem in 1939 were from the lands of the Reich. Overall, however, the former German Jewish elites who emigrated to Palestine were a small minority compared to those who emigrated elsewhere. Fewer than 10 percent of professors, scientists, and artists who had emigrated from Germany settled in Palestine, the Jews' national home. This is unsurprising, however, if one recalls that this was a country where the first university—the only one at the time—had been established only eight years before Hitler rose to power. Furthermore, the country had no art scene that could compete with counterparts in Britain or America and was burdened with political instability and a vague future. Thus, the twenty-one professors at the Hebrew University certainly exhausted the country's ability to accommodate senior academics.

Even though relatively few scientists immigrated to Palestine from Germany, they were supremely important in academic life and the development of teaching and research in the new homeland. This is said of mathematics and physics just as it is of medicine and the natural sciences. Again, however, I wish to call specific attention to the humanities: alongside the founder of the general-history discipline in Israel, Richard Koebner, we also find—to name only a few—the important researcher of the Jewish Middle Ages Yitzhak Fritz Baer, the historian of economics Bernhard Weinryb, the social historian Jacob Toury, the historian of medicine and sports Sussman Muntner, and Jacob Katz, born in Hungary and educated in Germany and destined to become the most important researcher of Jewish history in his time. These historians also played prominent roles in the establishment of Israel's archives and libraries.[43] The documentation and interview enterprise that Kurt Ball-Kaduri launched in 1944 was particularly important for the purposes of the present study. Ball-Kadury managed "to induce Jews from Germany to write down what they had experienced during Hitler's era of rule." The treatment of his collection, titled "What Isn't in the Archives," was undertaken by the Yad Vashem memorial and research institute in Jerusalem.[44]

As I insinuated above, when it came to settling the Jewish–Arab conflict in Mandate Palestine, most Yekkes represented a stance that was construed as typically German. Back then, of course, no one had access to the diaries of Joseph Goebbels, who wrote in 1938: "In Palestine, riots with multiple fatalities again, It will never ease off," and "The Arabs admire the Führer as though he were holy." The contents of Hitler's "table talk," as in "The Arabs and the Moroccans turn toward me in their prayers," were also unknown to others.[45] However, there was no need to wait for the Mufti of Jerusalem to meet with Hitler, as he did in November 1941, to realize that a Zionist policy geared to confrontation with the Arabs would ultimately harm the Zionist enterprise, with or without the "Third Reich."

Even before the formation of the Aliya Hadasha Party, the German immigrants' *Landsmanshaft* rejected the stance of the revisionist Zionists, whom it considered representatives of "dangerous non-Jewish nationalism," and advocated compromise with the Arabs instead. The first Yekke party, the short-lived Ahdut ha-'Am (National Unity, 1938), even espoused the idea of a binational state. Fritz (Peretz) Naphtali, an affiliate of the leading party, Mapai, responded to the mandatory government's 1937 partition plan by arguing, "The fact that we have failed to reach an understanding with the Arabs ... has wrought bitter vengeance upon us. . . . It reminds me so much of the days of Versailles in 1919

Germany. . . . The main question for me is . . . whether confrontation with a large Arab minority in a Jewish state will not steer us onto a harmful nationalist path."[46]

The 1937 partition plan soon became a dead letter, but by the time Aliya Hadasha entered political life, the Yekkes evidenced a position that favored partitioning the country into two states. The steep price of a nationalist policy and the honoring of national minorities' demands were matters that the Yekkes knew well from Germany's experience after World War I. David Ben-Gurion showed no empathy for the German Jews' experience and even accused the Yekkes, among all immigrants, of being "the least planted in the sense of peoplehood." The victims of the Germans' "healthy sense of peoplehood" could not leave this charge unanswered, of course.[47] Even Yekkes in Ben-Gurion's party, such as Georg Landauer, did not wholeheartedly embrace the 1942 Biltmore plan and its goal of a Jewish state, preferring cooperation with the British Mandate forces, foremost to rescue Jews from Europe and to forestall a violent standoff with the Arabs such as the 1936–1939 rebellion. Furthermore, per decision of its central committee in 1943, Aliya Hadasha strove to attain a modus vivendi with the Arab population and mutual recognition of rights. The Yekkes criticized the war atmosphere that had gripped the Yishuv, targeting British and Arabs alike. Robert Weltsch reminded the Yishuv that it had survived the war only by virtue of the British Army.[48] This only infuriated Ben-Gurion all the more. Thus, in November 1943, he criticized the German-language *Mitteilungsblatt*, characterizing it as a typical "German" newspaper and not a "German Jewish" vehicle due to what he considered its antistatehood, anti-Jewish, and antihuman stance.

Some Jews from Germany thought differently, of course. A few even belonged to the revisionist movement. One was Georg Kareski, who had emigrated to Palestine after publishing a far-fetched explanation in Goebbels's newspaper *Der Angriff* in Berlin about why the Jews should leave Germany; others were Richard Lichtheim and his circle. Plainly, however, this strain of Zionism gained limited popularity among the immigrants from Central Europe.

Overseas, another German Jewish woman immigrant, also Zionist, Hannah Arendt, took a position similar to that of the prominent representatives of German Jewry in Palestine, both on the conflict with the Arabs and on the nature of the new Jewish society. In 1941, she urged the Yishuv to arm itself but to fight not the Arabs but Hitler and antisemitism.[49] In 1942 and again in 1944, Arendt warned against the use of "the dialectic of Hegelian history," according to which one should accommodate a "relatively small injustice" (against the Palestinian Arabs) in the service of "a higher justice" (toward the Jews). She favored a Jewish home, which, she said, need not be identical to a Jewish state. She categorically rejected the Zionist axiom concerning the land of Israel as the supreme response to antisemitism: "Today [late 1942] . . . antisemitism . . . is the most horrific weapon of the most terrifying imperialism the world has ever known. Today there is no piece of ground protected from it where one can evacuate the Jews."[50] From her perch in America, Arendt, like most Yekkes in Palestine, considered the revisionists the greatest danger to the Zionist movement and idea: "fascists of an oppressed people" who wish to "degrade the hero to the rank of a suicide."[51]

Hannah Arendt developed close relations with Kurt Blumenfeld, the erstwhile leader of Zionism in Germany who immigrated to Palestine in 1933 and became an activist there from then on. In one respect, the two were of one mind. When Arendt asked about "the situation in Israel in the tendencies to ghettoization," Blumenfeld answered from Israel, "I asked [this question] back in my early days as a Zionist."[52] Both were alluding to the nationalist stance, the self-barricading mentality, and the cultural isolation that the German Jews, the victims of German nationalism, saw as the greatest menace to the Zionist project. They also had in mind, however, the attitude toward Germany: "Totally good people," Blumenfeld wrote to Arendt about a decade after the war, "are unable to grasp that the boycott [against Germany] is inhibiting and, in many cases, even reversing Israel's spiritual development. . . . Only a relatively small but important circle of people knows that Israel is a product of the European Jewish question and that the Jews' encounter with German culture was a time of spiritual and human achievements of the highest order."[53]

Blanket rejection of all things German, however, was common not only in Israel and among the Yekkes. In February 1946, after the fate of the German Jewish expatriates' relatives who had remained in Europe became known, a poem appeared in the journal *Aufbau*, published in the United States: "Burn the bridges to the land from which you fled, go forward icy and unrelated or to destruction, there is no third way."[54] Thus the souls of the German Jews in foreign lands—be it the United States, Australia, or Israel—continued to vacillate among tradition, nostalgia, and repudiation.

NOTES

1. Cf. Doron Niderland, *German Jews—Emigrants or Refugees? Emigration Patterns between the Two World Wars* (Hebrew) (Jerusalem: Magnes, 1996).

2. Norbert F. Pötzl, *Casablanca 1943: Das geheime Treffen, der Film und die Wende des Krieges* (Munich: Siedler, 2017).

3. Cf. Sibylle Quack, *Zuflucht Amerika. Zur Sozialgeschichte der Emigration deutsch-jüdischer Frauen in die USA 1933–1945* (Bonn: Dietz, 1995), 75ff.

4. Cf. Michael W. Blumenthal, "Mit 13 Jahren nach Shanghai," in Stiftung Jüdisches Museum Berlin/Stiftung Haus der Geschichte, *Heimat und Exil. Die Emigration der deutschen Juden nach 1933* (Frankfurt: Jüdischer Verlag, 2006), 129.

5. Cf. *Gelbe Post*, July 1, 1939, November 1, 1939, January 27, 1940.

6. Steven L. Lowenstein, *Frankfurt on the Hudson: The German Jewish Community of Washington Heights, 1933–1983; Its Structure and Culture* (Detroit, MI: Wayne State University Press, 1988).

7. Quack, *Zuflucht Amerika*, 150–53.

8. Horst Möller, *Exodus der Kultur. Schriftsteller, Wissenschaftler und Künstler in der Emigration nach 1933* (Munich: Beck, 1984), 56.

9. Atina Grossmann, "Provinzielle Kosmopoliten. Deutsche Juden in New York und Anderswo," in Stiftung Jüdisches Museum Berlin, *Heimat und Exil* (Frankfurt: Juedischer Verlag, 2006), 218ff.

10. Cf. Monika S. Schmid, "'I Always Thought I Was a German, It Was Hitler Who Taught Me I Was a Jew': National-Socialist Persecution, Identity and the German Language," in Christof Mauch and Joseph Salmons, eds., *German-Jewish Identities in America* (Madison: University of Wisconsin Press, 2003), 133–53.

11. Konrad Kwiet, "Die Integration deutsch-jüdischer Emigranten in Australien," in Ursula Büttner et al., eds., *Das Unrechtsregime: Internationale Forschung uberden Nationalsozialismus,* vol. 2 (Hamburg: Christians, 1986), 309–23.

12. Donald Peterson Kent, *The Refugee Intellectual: The Americanization of the Immigrants of 1933–1941* (New York: Columbia University Press, 1953).

13. Cf. Catherine Epstein, *A Past Renewed. A Catalog of German-Speaking Refugee Historians in the United States after 1933* (New York: Cambridge University Press, 1993); and Herbert Strauss and Werner Röder, eds., *International Bibliographical Dictionary of Central European Emigrés* (Munich, New York, London, Paris: K. G. Saur, 1980–1983); Kathleen J. Melhuish, "The German/Jewish Emigration and the Historian's Craft," in Konrad Kwiet, ed., *From the Emancipation to the Holocaust: Essays on Jewish Literature and History in Central Europe* (Kensington, NSW, Australia: University of New South Wales: 1987), 155–65.

14. Cf. Laura Fermi, *Illustrious Immigrants: The Intellectual Migration from Europe, 1930–1941* (Chicago: University of Chicago Press, 1968); and Donald Fleming and Bernard Baylin, eds., *The Intellectual Migration: Europe and America, 1930–1960* (Cambridge, MA: Belknap Press of Harvard University Press, 1969).

15. Cf. Leonard Dinnerstein, *Anti-Semitism in America* (New York: Oxford University Press, 1994), 112–38.

16. Steven Carr, *Hollywood and Anti-Semitism* (New York: Cambridge University Press, 2001); Ben Urwand, *The Collaboration: Hollywood's Pact with Hitler* (Cambridge, MA: Belknap Press of Harvard University Press, 2013).

17. David Margolick, *Beyond Glory. Joe Louis vs. Max Schmeling and a World on the Brink* (New York Knopf, 2005), 206, 254. Cf. the German edition: *Max Schmeling und Joe Louis—Kampf der Giganten—Kampf der Systeme* (Munich: Blessing, 2005), 302, 378.

18. Cf. Rudolf Glanz, "The 'Bayer' and the 'Pollack' in America," *JSS* 17 (1955): 27–42.

19. Cf. Lowenstein, *Frankfurt on the Hudson*, 163–88, 243. Michael N. Dobkowski takes the matter further, titling his article on the German Jews' religious life in postwar America "'The Fourth Reich': German-Jewish Religious Life in America Today," *Judaism* 27, no. 1 (1978): 80–99.

20. See, in particular, Marion Berghahn, *German-Jewish Refugees in England. The Ambiguities of Assimilation* (New York: St. Martin's Press, 1984); Gerhard Falk, *The German Jews in America: A Minority within a Minority* (Lanham: UPA, 2014).

21. Cf. Moshe Zimmermann and Yotam Hotam, eds., *Zweimal Heimat. Die Jeckes zwischen Mitteleuropa und Nahost* (Frankfurt: Beerenverlag, 2005).

22. Cf. Kurt Jakob Ball-Kaduri, *Jüdisches Leben einst und jetzt. Das Calauer Judenhaus* (Munich: Ner-Tamid, 1961), 70.

23. Batya Karmiel, *Tel Aviv Cafés* (Hebrew) (Tel Aviv, Jerusalem: Eretz Israel Museum and Yad Izhak Ben-Zvi, 2007), 105.

24. Cf. photograph in Neima Barzel's article on the German émigrés' attitude toward Germany and Germans, 1945–1954, *LBYB* 39 (1994): 280.

25. Miriam Getter, "The Separate Political Self-Organization of the German Immigrants," *HaTsiyonut* 7 (1981): 240–91.

26. Cf. Tom Segev, *The Seventh Million: The Israelis and the Holocaust*, trans. Haim Watzman (New York: Hill and Wang, 1993), chapter 2.

27. Eliezer Yaffe, "Help for the Jews of Germany," *HaPoel haTzair*, May 5, 1933.

28. Gustav Krojanker, "J'accuse," *Ha'aretz*, March 16, 1941; idem., *Aufstieg und Untergang des deutschen Judentums* (Tel Aviv: 1937).

29. Tom Lewy, *The German Jews and the Hebrew Theatre: A Clash between Western and Eastern Europe* (Hebrew) (Tel Aviv: Resling, 2016), 283–307.

30. Na'ama Sheffi, *German in Hebrew: Translations from German into Hebrew in Jewish Palestine* (Hebrew) (Jerusalem: Yad Izhak Ben-Zvi 1998), 208.

31. Jehuda Riemer, *Fritz Peretz Naphtali, Szialdemokrat und Zionist* (Tel Aviv: Bleicher, 1991), 281–82, minutes of meeting on December 19, 1940.

32. Ibid., 298–99, Mapai Secratariat meeting, December 16, 1942.

33. Wolfgang Yourgrau, "Heimat oder Asyl," *Orient* 27 (October 2, 1942): 1–4. Cf. Adi Gordon, *In Palestine, in Exile: The Weekly "Orient" between Palestinian Exile and German Diaspora* (Hebrew) (Jerusalem, 2004).

34. Cf. "The Hell of Hells," *Davar*, January 11, 1939, 2; January 12, 1939, 2; and March 27, 1939. At the end of the war, Ludwig Bendix (alias Baruch Boker) published his book *I Was in Dachau: Diary Gleanings from a Quarantine Camp in Germany* (Hebrew) (Tel Aviv: 1945)—a diary that describes the author's suffering in the Lichtenberg and Dachau camps up to 1937. Cf. Ilana Bendet-Nowatzki, *Facing Nazism and the Third Reich—The Hebrew Press in Palestine, 1933–1939*. PhD Dissertation, Hebrew University, Jerusalem, 2014.

35. "From the Scroll of Retributions and Torments," *Ha'aretz*, December 1, 1938, 2; December 19, 1938, 2.

36. Yoav Gelber, *A New Homeland—Central European Jewish Immigration to Eretz Israel and Its Absorption 1933–1948* (Hebrew) (Jerusalem: Leo Baeck Institute and Yad Izhak Ben-Zvi, 1990), 518.

37. Cf. "Facing the Catastrophe," *Hatzofe*, November 1938, and Dina Porat, "The Legend of the Struggle of the Jews from the Third Reich in the Ninth Fort Near Kovno, 1941–1942," *Tel Aviver Jahrbuch für deutsche Geschichte* 20 (1991): 363–92.

38. Cf. Yoav Gelber, "Central European Jews from Palestine in the British Forces," *LBYB* 35 (1990): 321–32.

39. Wolfgang Yourgrau, "Not—ohne Ende?" *Orient* 37 (December 18, 1942): 2–6. See also Arnold Zweig, "Schweigen," *Orient* 4/5 (January 29, 1943): 9.

40. Arnold Zweig, "Antigermanismus," *Orient* 37 (December 18, 1942).

41. Schalom Ben-Chorin, "Deutschland—morgen. Antwort an Kerr," *Orient* 23/24 (September 11, 1942): 31ff.

42. Gordon, *In Palestine, in Exile.*

43. Robert Jütte, *Die Emigration der deutschsprachigen "Wissenschaftler des Judentums." Die Auswanderung jüdischer Historiker nach Palästina 1933–1945* (Stuttgart: Steiner, 1991); Shulamit Volkov, "German Émigré Historians in Israel," in A. Daum, H. Lehmann and J. Sheehan, eds., *The Second Generation: Émigrés from Nazi Germany as Historians* (New York: Berghahn, 2015).

44. Kurt Jakob Ball-Kaduri, *Jüdisches Leben einst und jetzt. Das Calauer Judenhaus* (Munich: Ner-Tamid, 1961), 98ff. This documentation was incomparably essential for my book.

45. Goebbels, *Tagebücher 1923–1945*, entries of August 17 and 30, 1938; Werner Jochmann, ed., *Adolf Hitler: Monologe im Führer-Hauptquartier 1941–1944* (Hamburg: Albrecht Knaus, 1980), January 12/13, 1942, 196.

46. Riemer, *Fritz Peretz Naphtali*, 239–40. For the stance of Central European Jewry, see most of the articles in Adi Gordon, ed., *Brith Shalom and Binational Zionism* (Hebrew) (Jerusalem: Carmel, 2008).

47. Gelber, *New Homeland*, 561.

48. Ibid., 567–84.

49. Cf. "Ceterum censeo . . .," *Aufbau*, February 26, 1941.

50. "Neue Vorschläge zu jüdisch-arabischen Verhandlungen," *Aufbau*, August 25, 1944; see also "Die Krise des Zionismus," *Aufbau*, October 22, November 6, November 20, 1942.

51. "Sprengstoff-Spießer," *Aufbau*, June 16, 1944.

52. Kurt Blumenfeld to Hannah Arendt, October 1942, in Ingeborg Nordmann and Iris Pilling, eds., *Hannah Arendt und Kurt Blumenfeld: ". . . in keinem Besitz verwurzelt." Die Korrespondenz* (Hamburg: Rotbuch, 1995), 73.

53. Kurt Blumenfeld to Hannah Arendt, November 22, 1956, ibid., 166–67.

54. Lowenstein, *Frankfurt on the Hudson*, 54.

NINE

LOOKING BACK, LOOKING AHEAD

MY INTENTION IN THIS WORK was not to write an all-encompassing monograph about German Jewry in World War II but to present an essay that summarizes the state of research on a complex slice of history and to sketch its contours
clearly. There is no shortage of reports, documents, and details that I could have
added to this account until it would have ballooned into a thick tome. To give
only two examples, I could have mentioned the German tennis star Gottfried
von Cramm, who in 1938 was sentenced to a year in prison for maintaining a
homosexual relationship with a Jew. His penalty emphasizes the information
already presented in this book about how the regime treated even celebrities
who consorted with Jews. Or I could have reported that in August 1943, twenty-
three German Jews and eighty-six other Jews were sent from Auschwitz to the
Natzweiler concentration camp, where they were gassed to death in order to
become museum exhibits at the Institute of Anatomy at the University of Strasbourg (in conjunction with the Ahnenerbe [Ancestral Heritage] Institute, established by Heinrich Himmler).[1] No torrent of tragic atrocity details, however,
is needed to elucidate the historical essence of German Jewry in the 1938–1945
years. Lacking until now, in contrast, was a synthesis that would focus on the
Jews of Germany. In the fourteen years that lapsed between the appearance of
this book in German and its translation into English, research took additional
strides, and the synthesis had to be updated.

What lesson can and should be learned from this affair, which I defined in
chapter 1 as the finale in the history of German Jewry? Both historians and
nonprofessionals, Jewish and non-Jewish, in Europe and elsewhere, asked
this question even before the curtain fell for good in 1943 (or, at the latest,
in 1945). Those who sought the "solution to the Jewish problem" in the Jews'

emancipation seemed particularly horrified by this historical chapter. That is, not only did advanced, modern Germany repeal the Jews' emancipation; it even expelled its Jews and ultimately murdered them. Certainly this does not bode well for people who pin their hopes on emancipation in other advanced and modern countries, even the land that hosts the largest modern diaspora population, the United States. Zionists, in contrast, interpret this history in a way that confirms their underlying thesis—only the establishment of a state of the Jews, and not the emancipation of the Jews in exile, is the answer to the "Jewish question" and the sole alternative to the "Final Solution." Non-Zionist Orthodox Jews learned their own lesson from this episode: God punished his people, as he had before, for having swerved from the Orthodox way. Thus he settled scores both with Zionism and the "climbing the wall" (a Talmudic expression that anti-Zionists interpret as Zionism's breach of the injunction against mass repatriation to the land of Israel) that typified it and with the majority of German Jews who belonged to the reform movement and made Germany their home. Either way, the various lessons usually share the theme of serving notice against this or that trend of thought in Judaism. They have too little empathy for the victims of this offensive of Germans against Germans and even consider German Jewry the object of a historical experiment. Thus, the truly important question, in my opinion, about the watershed in non-Jewish Germans' attitudes toward their Jewish neighbors has been marginalized even though it is particularly crucial for understanding the post-1938 years and even though from today's perspective it is the most current of questions for Jews, Germans, and people at large.

In an astonishing mechanism that already evolved at a very early stage, the blame for events, even those in which Jews were merely acted upon, was cascaded onto the Jews themselves. It is a familiar tactic among criminals vis-à-vis their victims. In the Third Reich, "world Jewry" was deemed the source of all evil; it was "public enemy no. 1." By this logic, the Third Reich acted in self-defense. World War II—as Hitler, no less, said in his July 1942 "table talk"—had been precipitated by Chaim Weizmann and the World Zionist Congress;[2] thus, Germany had simply "fought back." The famous German historian Ernst Nolte held forth in this manner forty years after the war ended, placing it in writing after a stint in Jerusalem as a guest professor.[3] This tactic targeted not only "world Jewry" but also, from 1933 onward and particularly after 1939, German Jewry specifically. Goebbels's propaganda blamed the Jews for the pogrom that followed Herschel Grynszpan's assassination of Ernst vom Rath in Paris: the Volksgemeinschaft's rage set its sights on the murderers from Paris, it was stated. By holding the Jews themselves liable for all the anti-Jewish

measures—the rules, the yellow star, the deportations—the propaganda allowed the "Volksgenossen" to dodge guilt feelings. To deflect pangs of conscience even after 1945, the tactic remained in use, as proven not only by the
aforementioned case of Nolte but also by the following example: Carl Vincent
Krogmann, a ship owner, banker, and from 1933 to 1945 Mayor of Hamburg, interpreted the November pogrom—thirty years after the event—as follows: "In
any event, the Party leadership and the leaders of the Party organizations had
nothing to do with the matter.... From today's point of view, it cannot be ruled
out that members of the resistance, and perhaps even the Jews themselves, [!]
had an interest in the burning of the synagogues."[4]

This version of events bears strong resemblance to Eichmann's, referenced
above.

The question of what the Germans knew about the Holocaust takes the
phenomenon of guilt deflection to an additional level. More Germans knew
about the treatment of the Jews than participated in it actively, of course. After
the fact, however, the Jews were summoned as state's witnesses in order to give
the population's nonknowledge their seal of approval. In his 2006 book, Konrad
Löw, a retired professor of law, quotes Horst Osterheld, Division Chief at the
office of Konrad Adenauer, the first Chancellor of West Germany, who held
the office on behalf of the Christian Democratic Party: "Back then, even Hans
Rosenthal, Ephraim Kishon, and Abba Eban ... knew nothing about the horrifying Final Solution."[5] If the victims did not know, how could the perpetrators'
brothers-in-arms (e.g., soldiers, police, and bureaucrats stationed in the east, or
their families back home) know? The logical fallacy goes beyond its treatment
of the Final Solution in isolation, as though people knew nothing, or could have
known nothing, about all the phases that preceded and precipitated it. Instead,
the difficulty already lies in the subtitle of Löw's book from which I quoted:
Deutsche und Juden 1933–1945, "Germany and the Jews 1933–1945," as though
it was not Germans who played on both sides of the field. By establishing this
binary, the author relativizes not only the sharing of knowledge but also the
sharing of the crime. Jewish soldiers in the Wehrmacht—"half-Jews," Jewish
denouncers, Jewish "trappers," and others—are exploited ex post to deny the
collective guilt. Then, to amplify the relativization, Löw answers the question
"Is there any country that cannot be linked to weighty crimes in some way?" by
saying, "Let us only mention the United States' war against Iraq in 2003" and
outdoes himself by further noting, "the large majority of German Jews backed
the U.S."[6] Added to this contention is the common reckoning that so enrages
the famous refugee and historian Peter Gay: the (non-Jewish) Germans suffered in the war no less than did the Jews.[7]

Not only did the perpetrator camp foist responsibility and even guilt on the victims, the Jews of Germany, after 1945; this argument was heard in the Jews' own ranks, in variations commensurate with each proponent's ideological or political persuasion: "The Jews themselves are also guilty of the tragic course of events," the Zionist Gustav Krojanker wrote in 1937. True, he related only to the early stage of the murder campaign. "Their guilt was that they wished to be solely Germans and considered Judaism a religion only." In his judgment, the idea of a Jewish nation may serve as grounds for the right way of viewing the situation and attaining salvation.[8]

The question of guilt and the key question for the historian, that of causality, are both answered here in a puzzling way that diverts attention from the real question: How can one explain the paradox of the ability to totally banish, step by step, from economic, cultural, social, and political life, and ultimately from physical life itself, a group of Germans, a group of human beings?

In blaming the victims, the Jews of Germany, for powering this process, the historical literature was overly fixated on the stance of the Jewish leadership echelon, seeing it as long on collaboration and compliance and short on resistance. Raul Hilberg and Hannah Arendt raise this argument in regard to European Jewry at large, but in the German context this criticism had an especially large number of toeholds, so it is claimed. The allegations progressed from one period to the next: before the pogrom, after the pogrom, after the war broke out, after the deportations began. In each phase of its evolution, the question of collaboration or resistance took on a new quality, by which the criticism could be broadened and amplified. The fact that it was usually expressed from a safe geographic and, increasingly, temporal distance does not make it particularly credible. Although it is not the duty of a historical account such as mine to provide an apologia, I wish to propose here an alternative assessment of the leadership of German Jewry, for which Beate Meyer's recent book *A Fatal Balancing Act* furnishes copious factual grist. In the very introduction to her book, Meyer explains en passant that her greatest fear is of "unwanted applause from the wrong side, that is, from those who wish to contend that the persecuted Jews participated in their own murder."[9] Apart from everything else stated above on the topic, one must not forget that most of this leadership could have freed itself of its duty with no difficulty even at a relatively late phase. Leo Baeck, Otto Hirsch, Julius Seligsohn, and others traveled abroad frequently and could have stayed there. That they returned reflected their sense of duty toward their community and not a wish to help the Gestapo. Dr. Joseph Carlebach, the last rabbi of Hamburg, had already been in Palestine, returned to Germany, and was ultimately transported to Riga, where he was murdered. Not only elders acted in this manner. Dr. Bruno Finkelscherer, born in 1906 and summoned to serve as the last rabbi of Munich at the age of thirty-four, retained this post until 1943, when he was sent to and murdered in Auschwitz. Long indeed is the list of Jewish officers who remained in Germany not to quench their thirst for power but mainly due to their consciousness of duty, for which they were murdered in Germany or in the east.

The charge of nonresistance is leveled not only at the Jewish leadership but also—as described in previous chapters—at the individual German Jew, who was ostensibly too compliant or gullible. There is no need here to revisit the Herbert Baum affair or mention the Jews who participated in resistance groups or committed individual acts of defiance, as Wolf Gruner aggregated in his study—Jews who complained to the police or expressed opinions publicly despite the immense risk.[10] Instead, a seemingly trivial example may substantiate what qualified as resistance under National Socialist rule and its cost to those who offered it. The affair of Arnold Reinstein of Würzburg, demonstrating the shrinkage of the Jews' maneuvering room with each passing year, gives the word "resistance" a totally different meaning from that intended by the critics. From 1938 onward, Reinstein labored unavailingly to obtain an emigration permit. "On the one hand, you have to go; on the other, they don't let you in—that's how the history of the world looks to us," he wrote to a friend in December 1940. In May 1941, he finally got a permit to leave for America via Portugal. Instead of Portugal, however, he reached Dachau. The reason: shortly after the war began, he was explicitly enjoined against taking pictures outside his apartment. However, he wished to bring a gift to the guarantor in America by whose dint he had received his exit visa: a photo of his parents' home. Alert townspeople who spotted him taking the picture immediately called the police, whereupon the Gestapo arrested him and shipped him off to the concentration camp. On October 17, 1941, a few days after the deportation of German Jewry began, Reinstein took his life. This example illustrates all the factors that so severely lowered the criteria by which anything a Jew did could be called "resistance": the absurd anti-Jewish rules, the willingness of the Volksgenossen to snitch and serve the regime's goals, and the strict police supervision.[11]

Some after-the-fact critics cannot understand why the Jews did not put up more resistance, or at least more attempts at self-rescue, in view of what they knew about their impending fate. As I pointed out above, the thing the Jews were facing, which they might have foreseen on the basis of existing information, did gain clarity over time. Even by 1942, however, it had not ripened into an unchallengeable certainty. This was assured by the Nazis' tactics of deception and extortion and the potential victims' psychological defense mechanisms, pride, or age. Critics who accept the Monday-morning-quarterback role set out from the premise that the Jews of Germany should have known where the road was heading right after the Nazis rose to power, after the April boycott. The perspective at that time, however, was different. After the war, a German Jewish woman described her shock: "It was the first time a stranger shoved me. That's how it began. In Düsseldorf. In Germany." It had happened to her in 1942, in the staging camp ahead of deportation from Düsseldorf. Until that moment, the narrator of this episode did not understand how far German society had gone in crossing the watershed and had not realized that the process had begun much, much earlier.[12]

In October 1942, a year after the deportations began, one could still hear prognoses such as "rumor has it that you'll have to work there [in the east] under ghastly conditions—lashings and typhus."[13] The Auschwitz murder-by-gas factory was running full steam by then, but a population group isolated from sources of information could not, despite all the rumors, accept the unimaginable as a certainty and respond accordingly. The delusion of "we're Germans and we know the Germans" played a definitive role here. By early 1943, as the truth verged on certainty, things came to the point of a large wave of "diving" or "submerging" (i.e., going underground). How many Jews, however, had enough courageous friends who would agree to help them to do it? In Berlin, one-third of the "divers" survived the war at the most; in small towns, the prospects of Jews who "submerged" were minimal: "In Würzburg, no Jew manages to go underground."[14]

The specific pattern of behavior among German Jews not only affected their decisions in real time but also played a role in retrospect. This group of people, itself German, had a much more complex image of the Germans, of the individual German, and of German history than did non-Germans and, therefore, did not believe in sweeping judgments even after the fact. Ultimately, no one knew non-Jewish Germans better than they did. This is why, among other things, it is possible to quote Jewish newspapers in a way that collectively exonerates Germans of the Third Reich's crimes against the Jews, as I show below. Alfred Neumeyer, a former judge and president of the association of Jewish communities in Bavaria, wrote his memoirs in 1944 while in exile in Argentina; in his memoirs, he describes his last days in Germany before emigrating in February 1941:

> But the strongest impression on us was made by a visit we received at the
> hotel [in Berlin, during the trip]. The elevator was . . . out of order and
> even before we managed to go down to the lobby, the *Geheimrat* whom we

admired, [Max] Planck, approached us. . . . Before our trip, we had parted
with him in writing but he wanted to shake our hand personally. . . . I will
never forget how he spoke simply and profoundly about the era and the forces
at work in it. . . . It was a protest bursting with life against the history of our
time, which, despite his mental composure, was delivered with sizzling spirit
and mind.

Neumeyer, aged seventy-four, was profoundly impressed that "the doyen
of German science demonstrated in front of us, in his simple human way, his
sharing of our fate, and when I try to assess the German character at large, I
always bear that splendorous, conciliatory visit in mind."[15]

Elsewhere in that conversation, Planck also said, "German science is inca-
pable of intervening in politics and, therefore, that is not its role. . . . It tried to
do so once in World War I, when its most prominent representatives wrote a
manifesto aimed at England. It did not help; it only caused great harm." Scientists who realized post factum that the manifesto, which attempted to present
Germany in 1914 as the protector of European culture, made them into fellow
travelers of the regime, skirted all contact with politics from then on. Neumeyer
wrote his memoirs before he knew that Max Planck's son would belong to the
group known for the "July plot," that of July 20, 1944. Neither did he know how
deeply involved German scientists were in the crimes of the Third Reich. All
he and Max Planck could contemplate was the ordeal of World War I, from
which they learned—as often happens—the wrong lesson.

The answer to the question "What did the Germans know?" was also closely
associated with the experience of World War I. In particular, Germany had
fallen prey to Allied propaganda at that time; copious information about "German cruelties" in Belgium, for example, was found after the war to have been
misleading. Consequently, the next time around, in World War II, Germans
and non-Germans treated reports about mass executions, gas chambers, and
so on with a measure of disbelief, regarding them as new iterations of war
propaganda. Now, however, atrocity had become not propaganda but fact. As
representative as Max Planck's gesture may have been, the fate of the Jews was
decided by the very scientists who collaborated with the system and placed
their expertise in the service of its murderous ways. It brings to mind the hero
of Kurt Maetzig's film Council of the Gods (1950): a scientist who asks no questions and discovers afterward that he has provided the regime with a weapon
of mass destruction. Many scientists served the regime knowingly. Just the
same, in judging "the German character at large," it was preferred, even after
the full scale of the "Final Solution" became known, to underscore examples
such as Planck's behavior.

Perhaps it is due to this stance that historians and laypersons in Jewish society generally, and in Israeli society particularly, took some exception to the German Jews' descriptions of Nazism and the Holocaust. They accused these historians and writers of approaching the National Socialists' policies toward the Jews too narrowly. Concurrently and antipodally, however, at least at first, they faulted them for overemphasizing the fate of German Jewry within the general history of the Jews under Nazi rule. Here is a case in point: Shortly before the Eichmann trial, Israel's Minister of Education, Zalman Aranne, set up a committee to determine the materials to use in teaching the topic of "Holocaust and heroism." Two months after the trial, two members of the panel—themselves Holocaust survivors—Arieh Bauminger (from Kraków, director of Yad Vashem in 1962–1964) and Mark Dvorzhetski (a physician from Vilna and a professor of Holocaust studies at Bar-Ilan University)—complained that the provisional curriculum for schools had made excessively broad reference to German Jewish history at the expense of European Jewry. The committee, chaired by the inspector for high schools, Avraham Bartana, an immigrant from Eastern Europe, revised the curriculum accordingly. In the early 1960s, when Holocaust research was still in its infancy,[16] interest in the pre-Holocaust stage—the exclusion of the Jews in Germany up to the night of the pogrom—may have been greater than it is today. The fate of East European Jewry shortly before and then during the Holocaust has been researched with growing intensity over time, and interest in German Jewry has lost ground relative to what the community's weight in Jewish demography would warrant. What prompted me to write this book was the marginalization of the history of German Jewry *after* 1938, as reflected in the public consciousness—a phenomenon that cannot be explained by that population's demographic weight only—and my wish to bring together the findings of the growing number of studies in recent years that deal with partial aspects of this history.

The story of gradual exclusion that lies at the focus of this book, like Holocaust history in general, is incomparably depressing. The German Jewish historian George Mosse, who taught both in America and in Israel—my predecessor as the Richard Michael Koebner Professor of German History—tried to find something positive in it, something associated with Jews who survived the Holocaust: "It was the German-Jewish *Bildungsbürgertum* which, more than any other single group, preserved Germany's better self across dictatorship, war, holocaust, and defeat."

That is, those who were not murdered by the guardians of the German culture in the Third Reich and managed to emigrate to some other country are those who ultimately contributed the most to the safekeeping of the German culture.[17] A poor man's consolation, that. Perhaps this is an overstatement and Germany's "better self" is but a construction, but in this manner the absurdity known as "history of German Jewry in the Third Reich" is made complete.

I return to the questions of what one may learn from this historical episode and what prodded me to investigate it. In retrospect, it seems that the elements of which the Holocaust is composed—the Holocaust of German Jewry in our case—were not necessarily restricted to that event alone. After all, what happened there was the consummation of small steps, sometimes unnoticed, that ultimately added up to total dehumanization. We have seen how neighbors were separated into predators and prey merely because ideology, words, and laws can transform people into monsters and vermin, as the case may be. It is the apparent recurrence of this dynamic and people's predisposition to criminality that makes this chapter in history so edifying.

NOTES

1. Cf. Hans Joachim Lang, *Die Namen der Nummern. Wie es gelang, die 86 Opfer eines NS-Verbrechens zu identifizieren* (Hamburg: Hoffmann und Campe, 2004).

2. Cf. Andreas Hillgruber and Henry Picker, eds., *Hitlers Tischgespräche im Führerhauptquartier 1941–1942* (Munich: Deutscher Taschenbuch, 1968), 250, July 24, 1942.

3. Cf. Ernst Nolte, *Der Europäische Bürgerkrieg 1917–1945. Nationalsozialismus und Bolschewismus* (Frankfurt: Propyläen, 1989).

4. Carl Vincent Krogmann, *Es ging um Deutschlands Zukunft 1932 bis 1939: Erlebtes täglich diktiert von dem früheren Regierenden Bürgermeister von Hamburg* (Leoni am Starnberger See: Druffel, 1976), 341.

5. Konrad Löw, *Das Volk ist ein Trost. Deutsche und Juden 1933–1945 im Urteil der jüdischen Zeitzeugen* (Munich: Olzog, 2006), 214.

6. Ibid., 316ff.

7. Peter Gay, *Verstreut und vergessen. Deutsche Juden im Exil* (Munich: Blanvalet, 2000), 28.

8. Gustav Krojanker, *The Rise and Fall of German Jewry* (Hebrew) (Tel Aviv: Hitachduth Olej Germania, 1937).

9. Beate Meyer, *A Fatal Balancing Act: The Dilemma of the Reich Association of Jews in Germany, 1939–1945*, trans. William Templer (New York: Berghahn, 2013), 1.

10. Cf. Konrad U. Kwiet and Helmut Eschwege, *Selbstbehauptung und Widerstand. Deutsche Juden im Kampf um Existenz und Menschenwürde 1933–1945* (Hamburg: Christians, 1984). Cf. also "Nach dem Pogrom: Stufen der Ausgrenzung," in Wolfgang Benz, ed., *Die Juden in Deutschland 1933–1945. Leben unter nationalsozialistischer Herrschaft* (Munich: Beck, 1988), 545–659; Wolf Gruner, "Expel Hitler," *Yad Vashem Studies* 39, no. 2 (2011): 13–54; Wolf Gruner, "Indifference? Participation and Protest as Individual Responses to the Persecution of the Jews as Revealed in Berlin Police Logs and Trial Records 1933–1945," in S. Schrafstetter and A. Steinweis, eds., *The Germans and the Holocaust* (New York and Oxford: Berghahn Books, 2016), 59–84.

11. Roland Flade, *Die Würzburger Juden. Ihre Geschichte vom Mittelalter bis zur Gegenwart* (Würzburg: Stürtz, 1987), 341ff.

12. Hilde Sherman-Zander, quoted in Andrej Angrick and Peter Klein, *Die "Endlösung" in Riga: Ausbeutung und Vernichtung 1941–1944* (Darmstadt: Wissenschaftliche Buchgesellschaft, 2006), 29.

13. Flade, *Die Würzburger Juden*, 360.

14. Ibid., 359.

15. Alfred Neumeyer in Monika Richarz, ed., *Jüdisches Leben in Deutschland*, vol. 3: *Selbstzeugnisse zur Sozialgeschichte 1918–1945* (Stuttgart: Deutsche Verlags-Anstalt, 1982), 364ff.

16. Hanna Yablonka, *The State of Israel vs. Adolf Eichmann* (New York: Schocken, 2004), 199–200.

17. George L. Mosse, *German Jews beyond Judaism* (Bloomington, IN, and Cincinnati, OH: Indiana University Press and Hebrew Union College Press, 1985), 82.

BIBLIOGRAPHY

Adam, Uwe Dietrich: *Judenpolitik im Dritten Reich*. Düsseldorf 1972.

Adler, H. G.: *Der verwaltete Mensch. Studien zur Deportation der Juden aus Deutschland*. Tübingen 1974.

Adler, H. G.: *Die verheimlichte Wahrheit. Theresienstädter Dokumente*. Tübingen 1958.

Adler, H. G.: *Theresienstadt 1941–1945. Das Antlitz einer Zwangsgemeinschaft: Geschichte, Soziologie, Psychologie*. Tübingen 1960.

Adler-Rudel, Shalom: *Ostjuden in Deutschland 1880–1940*. Tübingen 1959.

Alexander, Gabriel: "Die Entwicklung der jüdischen Bevölkerung in Berlin zwischen 1871 und 1945," *Tel Aviver Jahrbuch für deutsche Geschichte* (1991) S. 287–314.

Altman, Avraham & Eber, Irene: "Flight to Shanghai, 1938–1940: The Larger Setting," *Yad Vashem Studies* 28 (2000) pp. 51–86.

Aly, Götz: *"Final Solution" Nazi Population Policy and the Murder of the European Jews*. New York 1999.

Aly, Götz: *Hitler's Beneficiaries: Plunder, Racial War, and the Nazi Welfare State*. New York 2005.

Aly, Götz & Heim, Susanne: *Architects of Annihilation: Auschwitz and the Logic of Destruction*. Princeton 2002.

Anderl, Gabriele & Rupnow, Dirk: *Die Zenratralstelle für jüdische Auswanderung als Beraubungsinstitution*. Wien 2004.

Andreas-Friedrich, Ruth: *Battleground Berlin: Diaries, 1945–1948*. New York 1990.

Angress, Werner: *Generation zwischen Furcht und Hoffnung. Jüdische Jugend im Dritten Reich*. Hamburg 1985.

Angrick, Andrej & Klein, Peter: *Die "Endlösung" in Riga. Ausbeutung und Vernichtung 1941–1944*. Darmstadt 2006.

Arkwright, Ken: "Das Ende der jüdischen Schule in Breslau," in: *Mitteilungen des Verbandes ehemaliger Breslauer und Schlesier in Israel*. März 1972, pp. 8–9.

Armbruster, Georg et al. (eds.): *Exil Shanghai 1938–1947*. Berlin 2002.

Aronson, Shlomo: *Hitler, the Allies and the Jews*. Cambridge 2004.

Ayalon, Moshe: "Jewish Alltagsgeschichte on the Eve of the Holocaust: Jewish Life in Bresslau," *LBYB* 1996, pp. 323–45.

Backhaus, Fritz & Liepach, Martin: "Leo Baecks Manuskript über 'Die Rechtsstellung der Juden in Europa,'" *ZfG* (2002) pp. 55–70.

Baeck, Leo: "Gedenken an zwei Tote," in: Weltsch, Robert (ed.): *Deutsches Judentum. Aufstieg und Krise*. Stuttgart 1963, S. 307–14.

Bajohr, Frank: *"Arisierung" in Hamburg 1933–1945*. Hamburg 1997.

Bajohr, Frank & Löw, Andrea (eds.): *The Holocaust and European Societies: Social Processes and Social Dynamics*. London 2016.

Bajohr, Frank & Pohl, Dieter: *Der Holocaust als offenes Geheimnis. Die Deutschen, die NS-Führung und die Alliierten*. München 2006.

Bajohr, Frank & Strupp, Christop (Hg.): *Fremde Blicke auf das "Dritte Reich"— Berichte ausländischer Diplomaten über Herrschaft und Gesellschaft in Deutschland 1933–1945*. Göttingen 2011.

Baker, Leonard: *Hirt der Verfolgten. Leo Baeck im Dritten Reich*. Hamburg 1985.

Ball-Kaduri, Kurt Jakob: "Berlin wird judenfrei," *Jahrbuch für die Geschichte Mittel- und Ostdeutschlands* 22 (1973) S. 207–19.

Ball-Kaduri, Kurt Jakob: "The Illegal *Alya* from Nazi-Germany to Palestine," *Yalkut Moreshet* vol. 8 (1968) pp. 130–42 (Hebr.).

Ball-Kaduri, Kurt Jakob: *Jüdisches Leben einst und jetzt. Das Calauer Judenhaus*. München 1961.

Ball-Kaduri, Kurt Jakob: "Zum Leben der Juden in Deutschland während des zweiten Weltkrieges," *Zeitschrift für die Geschichte der Juden* (1973) S. 33–38.

Bankier, David: *The Germans and the Final Solution: Public Opinion under Nazism*. London 2006.

Bankier, David (ed.): *Probing the Depth of German Antisemitism: German Society and the Persecution of the Jews, 1933–1941*. New York 2000.

Barkai, Avraham: "Deutschsprachige Juden in osteuropäischen Ghettos," in: ders.: *Hoffnung und Untergang. Studien zur deutsch-jüdischen Geschichte des 19. und 20. Jahrhunderts*. Hamburg 1998, S. 197–223.

Barkai, Avraham: *From Boycott to Annihilation: The Economic Struggle of German Jews, 1933–1943*. Hanover, NH 1989.

Barkai, Avraham: "Zwischen Ost und West. Deutsche Juden im Ghetto Lodz," in: ders.: *Hoffnung und Untergang. Studien zur deutsch-jüdischen Geschichte des 19. und 20. Jahrhunderts*. Hamburg 1998, S. 225–73.

Barth, Christian T.: *Goebbels und die Juden*. München 2003.

Barzel, Neima: "The Attitude of Jews of German Origin in Israel to Germany and Germans after the Holocaust 1945–1952," *LBYB* 39 (1994) pp. 271–301.

Bauer, Christian & Göpfert, Rebekka (Hg.): *Die Ritchie Boys. Deutsche Emigranten im amerikanischen Geheimdienst.* Hamburg 2005.

Baumann, Angelika & Heusler, Andreas (Hg.): *München arisiert. Entrechtung und Enteignung der Juden in der NS-Zeit.* München 2004.

Beer, Susanne: *Die Banalität des Guten. Hilfeleistungen für jüdische Verfolgte 1941–1945.* Berlin 2018.

Beling, Eva: *Die gesellschaftliche Eingliederung der deutschen Einwanderer in Israel. Eine soziologische Untersuchung der Einwanderung aus Deutschland zwischen 1933 und 1945.* Frankfurt a.M. 1967.

Bendet-Nowatzky, Ilana: *Facing Nazism and the Third Reich: The Hebrew Press in Palestine, 1933–1939.* PhD dissertation, Hebrew U., Jerusalem 2014.

Benz, Wolfgang (Hg.): *Dimension des Völkermords. Die Zahl der jüdischen Opfer des Nationalsozialismus.* München 1991.

Benz, Wolfgang: *Flucht aus Deutschland. Zum Exil im 20. Jahrhundert.* München 2001.

Benz, Wolfgang: *The Holocaust: A German Historian Examines the Genocide.* New York 2000.

Benz, Wolfgang: "Judenvernichtung als Notwehr? Die Legenden um Theodore N. Kaufman," *Vierteljahrshefte für Zeitgeschichte* 29 (1981) S. 615–29.

Benz, Wolfgang: "Theresienstadt in der Geschichte der deutschen Juden," in: Karny, Miroslav et al. (Hg.): *Theresienstadt in der "Endlösung der Judenfrage."* Prague 1992, S. 70–78.

Benz, Wolfgang (Hg.): *Überleben im Dritten Reich. Juden im Untergrund und ihre Helfer.* München 2003.

Benz, Wolfgang & Neiss, Marion (Hg.): *Deutsch-jüdisches Exil—das Ende der Assimilation? Identitätsprobleme deutscher Juden in der Emigration.* Berlin 1994.

Berghahn, Marion: *German-Jewish Refugees in England: The Ambiguities of Assimilation.* New York 1984.

Biggeleben, Christof, Schreiber, Beate & Steiner, Kilian (Hg.): *"Arisierung" in Berlin.* Berlin 2007.

Blasius, Dirk: "Zwischen Rechtsvertrauen und Rechtszerstörung. Deutsche Juden 1933–1945," in: Diner, Dan & Blasius, Dirk, *Zerbrochene Geschichte.* Frankfurt a.M. 1991, S. 121–37.

Blau, Bruno: *Das Ausnahmerecht für die Juden in Deutschland 1933–1945.* Düsseldorf 1954.

Blau, Bruno: "The Jewish Population of Germany 1939–1945," *JSS* 7 (1950) pp. 161–72.

Blumenthal, W. Michael: "Mit 13 Jahren nach Shanghai," in: Stiftung Jüdisches Museum Berlin/Stiftung Haus der Geschichte (Hg.): *Heimat und Exil. Die Emigration der deutschen Juden nach 1933.* Frankfurt a.M. 2006, S. 127–33.

Boberach, Heinz (Hg.): *Meldungen aus dem Reich.* München 1968.

Boch, Volker: *Berlin 1936. Die Olympischen Spiele unter Berücksichtigung des jüdischen Sports.* Konstanz 2002.

Boelcke, Willy A. (Hg.): *"Wollt Ihr den totalen Krieg?" Die geheimen Goebbels-Konferenzen 1939–1949*. München 1969.

Borut, Jacob & Heilbronner, Oded (eds.): *German Antisemitism*. Tel Aviv 2000 (Hebr.).

Brechtken, Magnus: *"Madagaskar für die Juden." Antisemitische Idee und politische Praxis*. München 1997.

Breitman, Richard: *Der Architekt der "Endlösung." Himmler und die Vernichtung der europäischen Juden*. Paderborn 1996.

Bridenthal, Renate et al. (eds.): *When Biology Became Destiny. Women in Weimar and Nazi Germany*. New York 1984.

Broszat, Martin et al. (Hg.): *Bayern in der NS-Zeit. Soziale Lage und politisches Verhalten der Bevölkerung im Spiegel vertraulicher Berichte*. München 1977.

Brothers, Eric: "On the Anti-Fascist Resistance of German Jews," *LBYB* 32 (1987) pp. 369–82.

Browning, Christopher R.: *The Origins of the Final Solution: The Evolution of Nazi Jewish Policy, September 1939–March 1942* (with contributions by Jürgen Matthäus). Yad Vashem Jerusalem 2003.

Bruer, Albert A.: *Aufstieg und Untergang. Eine Geschichte der Juden in Deutschland (1750–1918)*. Köln 2006.

Buber-Agassi, Judith: *The Jewish Women Prisoners of Ravensbruck*. Lubbock 2014.

Buchholz, Marlis: *Die Hannoverschen Judenhäuser. Zur Situation der Juden in der Zeit der Ghettoisierung und Verfolgung 1941 bis 1945*. Hildesheim 1987.

Burger, Reiner: *Von Goebbels Gnaden. Jüdisches Nachrichtenblatt (1938–1943)*. Münster 2001.

Burgess, Greg: *The League of Nations and the Refugees from Nazi Germany*. London 2016.

Burrin, Philippe: *Hitler and the Jews: The Genesis of the Holocaust*. London 1994.

Büttner, Ursula (Hg.): *Die Deutschen und die Judenverfolgung im Dritten Reich*. Frankfurt a.M. 2003.

Büttner, Ursula et al. (Hg.): *Das Unrechtsregime: Internationale Forschung über den Nationalsozialismus*. Hamburg 1986.

Carmiel, Batia: *Tel Aviv's Coffee Houses 1920–1980*. Tel Aviv and Jerusalem 2007 (Hebr.).

Carr, Steven: *Hollywood and Anti-Semitism*. New York 2001.

Cesarini, David & Levine, Paul (eds.): *"Bystanders" to the Holocaust*. London 2002.

Cholavsky, Shalom: "The German Jews in the Minsk Ghetto," *Yad Vashem Studies* 17 (1986) pp. 219–46.

Cochavi, Yehoyakim: "The Hostile Alliance: The Relationship between the Reichsvereinigung of Jews in Germany and the Regime," *Yad Vashem Studies* 22 (1992) pp. 237–72.

Cohen, Raya: "Confronting the Reality of the Holocaust: Richard Lichtheim, 1939–1942," *Yad Vashem Studies* 23 (1993) pp. 335–68.

Cohen, Robert: *Der Vorgang Benario. Die Gestapo-Akte 1936–1942.* Berlin 2016.

Cohn, Willy: *No Justice in Germany: The Breslau Diaries, 1933–1941,* ed. Norbert Conrads, trans. Kenneth Kronenberg. Stanford, CA, 2012.

Conze, Ekart, Frei, Norbert, Hayes, Peter & Zimmermann, Moshe: *Das Amt und die Vergangenheit, Deutsche Diplomaten im Dritten Reich und in der Bundesrepublik.* Munich 2010.

Crane, Cynthia: *Divided Lives: The Untold Stories of Jewish-Christian Women in Nazi Germany.* New York 2000.

Curio, Claudia: *Verfolgung, Flucht, Rettung. Die Kindertransporte 1938/39 nach Großbritannien.* Berlin 2006.

Dahlmann, Dittmar & Hirschfeld, Gerhard (Hg.): *Lager, Zwangsarbeit, Vertreibung und Deportation. Dimensionen der Massenverbrechen in der Sowjetunion und in Deutschland 1933 bis 1945.* Essen 1999.

Dauer, Hannelore: "Kunst im Schatten des Todes. Künstlerischer Widerstand in Konzentrationslagern und Ghettos," in: Albrecht, Richard & Romberg, Otto R. (Hg.): *Widerstand und Exil 1933–1945.* Frankfurt a.M. 1986, S. 169–76.

Dawidowicz, Lucy: *The War against the Jews, 1933–1945.* New York 1975.

Dean, Martin: *Robbing the Jews, 1933–1945.* Cambridge 2008.

Deutschkron, Inge: *Berliner Juden im Untergrund.* Berlin 1980.

Deutschkron, Inge: *Outcast: A Jewish Girl in Wartime Berlin.* New York 1989.

Diehl, Katrin: *Die jüdische Presse im Dritten Reich.* Tübingen 1997.

Diner, Dan: *Beyond the Conceivable.* Berkley 2000.

Diner, Dan & Blasius, Dirk (Hg.): *Zerbrochene Geschichte: Leben und Selbstverständnis der Juden in Deutschland.* Frankfurt a.M. 1991.

Dinnerstein, Leonard: *Anti-Semitism in America.* New York 1994.

Dippel, John Van Houten: *Bound upon a Wheel of Fire: Why So Many German Jews Made the Tragic Decision to Remain in Nazi Germany.* New York 1996.

Dobkowski, Michael N.: "The Fourth Reich. German-Jewish Religious Life in America Today," *Judaism* 27/1 (1978) S. 80–99.

Doescher, Hans-Jürgen: "*Kristallnacht.*" Frankfurt/Berlin 1988.

Dörner, Bernward: *Die Deutschen und der Holocaust. Was niemand wissen wollte, aber jeder wissen konnte.* Berlin 2007.

Dreßen, Wolfgang: *Betrifft: Aktion 3. Deutsche verwerten jüdische Nachbarn.* Berlin 1998.

Drobisch, Klaus et al. (Hg.): *Juden unterm Hakenkreuz. Verfolgung und Ausrottung der deutschen Juden 1933–1945.* Berlin (Ost) 1973.

Dublon Knebel, Irith: *A Holocaust Crossroads: Jewish Women and Children in Ravensbruck.* London 2010.

Dwork, Deborah & Van Pelt, Robert Jan: *Flight from the Reich: Refugee Jews, 1933–1946.* New York 2012.

Eber, Irene: *Wartime Shanghai and the Jewish Refugees from Central Europe: Survival, Co-existence, and Identity in a Multi-ethnic City.* Berlin 2012.

Edvardson, Cordelia: *Gebranntes Kind sucht das Feuer*. München 1989.

Eggers, Christian: *Unerwünschte Ausländer. Juden aus Deutschland und Mitteleuropa in französischen Internierungslagern 1940–1942*. Berlin 2002.

Elkin, Rivka: *The Heart Beats On: Continuity and Change in Social Work and Welfare Activities of German Jews under the Nazi Regime, 1933–1945*. Jerusalem 2004 (Hebr.).

Elkin, Rivka: "The Survival of the Jewish Hospital in Berlin 1938–1945," *LBYB* 38 (1993), pp. 157–92.

Engel, David: *The Holocaust. The Third Reich and the Jews*. New York 2000.

Engelmann, Bernt: *Deutschland ohne Juden. Eine Bilanz*. München 1970.

Epstein, Catherine: *Model Nazi: Arthur Greiser and the Occupation of Western Poland*. Oxford 2010.

Epstein, Catherine: *Nazi Germany—Confronting the Myths*. Chichester 2015.

Epstein, Catherine: *A Past Renewed: A Catalog of German-Speaking Refugee Historians in the United States after 1933*. New York 1993.

Essner, Cornelia: *Die "Nürnberger Gesetze" oder Die Verwaltung des Rassenwahns 1933–1945*. Paderborn 2002.

Feilchenfeld, Werner, Michaelis, Dolf & Pinner, Ludwig (Hg.): *Haavara-Transfer nach Palästina und Einwanderung deutscher Juden 1933–1939*. Tübingen 1972.

Fermi, Laura: *Illustrious Immigrants: The Intellectual Migration from Europe, 1930–1941*. Chicago 1968.

Fischer, Anna: *Erzwungener Freitod. Spuren und Zeugnisse in den Freitod getriebener Juden der Jahre 1938–1945 in Berlin*. Berlin 2007.

Flade, Roland: *Die Würzburger Juden. Ihre Geschichte vom Mittelalter bis zur Gegenwart*. Würzburg 1996.

Flannery, Harry W.: *Assignment to Berlin*. London 1943.

Fleming, Donald & Baylin, Bernard (eds.): *The Intellectual Migration: Europe and America, 1930–1960*. Cambridge, MA 1969.

Fraenkel, Daniel & Avraham, Tamar (eds.): *Pinkas hakehilot—Germany*, vol. D. Northwest Germany, Jerusalem 2007 (Hebr.).

Freeden, Herbert: *Die jüdische Presse im Dritten Reich*. Frankfurt a.M. 1987.

Freier, Recha: *Let the Children Come: The Early History of Youth Aliyah*. London 1961.

Friedenberger, Martin: *Fiskalische Ausplünderung. Die Berliner Steuer- und Finanzverwaltung und die jüdische Bevölkerung 1933–1945*. Berlin 2008.

Friedlander, Albert: *Leo Baeck. Leben und Lehre*. Stuttgart 1973.

Friedlander, Henry: *The Origins of Nazi Genocide: From Euthanasia to the Final Solution*. Chapel Hill, NC, 1995.

Friedländer, Saul: *Nazi Germany and the Jews: The Years of Persecution, 1933–1939*. New York 1997.

Friedländer, Saul: *The Years of Extermination: Nazi Germany and the Jews, 1939–1945*. San Francisco 2007.

Fritsch-Vivie, Gabriele: *Gegen alle Widerstände. Der jüdische Kulturbund 1933–1941.* Berlin 2013.

Fritz Bauer Institut (Hg.): *"Beseitigung des jüdischen Einflusses...": Antisemitische Forschung, Eliten und Karrieren im Nationalsozialismus.* Frankfurt a.M. 1999.

Garbarini, Alexandra: *Jewish Responses to Persecution*, vol. II, *1938–1940.* Lanham, MD, 2011.

Garbe, Detlef: "Jüdische Gefangene in nationalsozialistischen Konzentrationslagern 1933–1945," in: Herzig, Arno & Lorenz, Ina (Hg.): *Verdrängung und Vernichtung der Juden unter dem Nationalsozialismus.* Hamburg 1992, S. 173–204.

Gay, Peter: *My German Question: Growing up in Nazi Berlin.* New Haven, CT, 1998.

Gay, Peter: *Verstreut und vergessen. Deutsche Juden im Exil.* München 2000.

Gelber, Yoav: "Central European Jews from Palestine in the British Forces," *LBYB* 35 (1990) pp. 321–32.

Gelber, Yoav: *A New Homeland: Immigration and Absorption of Central European Jews, 1933–1948.* Jerusalem 1990 (Hebr.).

Gellately, Robert: *Backing Hitler: Consent and Coercion in Nazi Germany, 1933–1945.* New York 2001.

Genschel, Helmut: *Die Verdrängung der Juden aus der Wirtschaft im Dritten Reich.* Göttingen 1966.

Georgiev, Anna. "Zur materiellen Geschichte des 'Judensterns,'" *Zeitschrift für Geschichtswissenschaft* 7–8 (2018) pp. 623–39.

Gerlach, Christian: *Kalkulierte Morde. Die deutsche Wirtschafts- und Vernichtungspolitik in Weißrußland 1941 bis 1944.* Hamburg 1999.

Gerlach, Christian: *Krieg, Ernährung, Völkermord.* Hamburg 1998.

Gerlach, Wolfgang: *Als die Zeugen schwiegen. Bekennende Kirche und die Juden.* Berlin 1987.

Getter, Miriam: "The Separate Political Self-Organization of the German Immigrants," *HaTsiyonut* 7 (1981) pp. 240–91 (Hebr.).

Giordano, Ralph: *Die Bertinis.* Frankfurt a.M. 1982.

Glanz, Rudolf: "The 'Bayer' and the 'Pollack' in America," *JSS* 17 (1955). S. 21–42.

Glanz, Rudolf: *The German Jew in America: An Annotated Bibliography Including Books, Pamphlets and Articles of Special Interest.* Cincinnati 1969.

Goebbels, Joseph: *Tagebücher 1923–1945.* Hrsg. von Elke Fröhlich. München 1993–2007.

Goeschel, Christian: "Suicides of German Jews in the Third Reich," *German History* 25/1 (2007) S. 22–45.

Göpfert, Rebekka: *Der jüdische Kindertransport von Deutschland nach England 1938/39. Geschichte und Erinnerung.* Frankfurt a.M. 1999.

Gordon, Adi: *In Palestine, in Exile: The Weekly "Orient" between Palestinian Exile and German Diaspora.* Jerusalem 2004 (Hebr.).

Gordon, Sarah: *Hitler, Germans and "The Jewish Question."* Princeton 1984.

Gottwaldt, Alfred B. & Schulle, Diana: *Die Judendeportationen aus dem deutschen Reich 1941–1945.* Wiesbaden 2005.

Graml, Hermann: *Reichskristallnacht.* München 1988.

Grau, Wilhelm: *Die Erforschung der Judenfrage. Aufgabe und Organisation.* München 1943 (Kleine Weltkampfbücherei 3).

Grau, Wilhelm: *Die geschichtlichen Lösungsversuche der Judenfrage.* München 1943.

Greif, Gideon et al. (Hg.): *Die Jeckes. Deutsche Juden aus Israel erzählen.* Köln, Weimar, Wien 2000.

Grenville, John: "Die Endlösung und die Judenmischlinge im Dritten Reich," in: Büttner, Ursula (Hg.): *Das Unrechtsregime.* Bd. 2, Hamburg 1986, S. 91–121.

Grenville, John: *The Jews and Germans in Hamburg: The Destruction of a Civilization.* London 2012.

Gross, Leonard: *Versteckt. Wie Juden in Berlin die Nazi-Zeit überlebten.* Reinbek bei Hamburg 1983.

Grossmann, Atina: "Provinzielle Kosmopoliten. Deutsche Juden in New York und Anderswo," in: Stiftung Jüdisches Museum Berlin/Stiftung Haus der Geschichte (Hg.): *Heimat und Exil. Die Emigration der deutschen Juden nach 1933.* Frankfurt a.M. 2006, S. 218–30.

Gruner, Wolf: "Die Berichte über die jüdische Winterhilfe von 1938/9 bis 1941/2," *Jahrbuch für Antisemitismusforschung* 1. Frankfurt a.M. 1992, S. 307–41.

Gruner, Wolf: "Die Berliner und die Judenverfolgung," *Beiträge zur Geschichte des NS* (2011) pp. 57–87.

Gruner, Wolf: "'The Germans Should Expel the Foreigner Hitler.' Open Protest and Other Forms of Jewish Defiance in Nazi Germany," *Yad Vashem Studies* 39/2 (2011) pp. 13–54.

Gruner, Wolf (ed.): *The Greater German Reich and the Jews: Nazi Persecution Policies in the Annexed Territories, 1935–1945.* New York 2015.

Gruner, Wolf: *Jewish Forced Labor under the Nazis. Economic Needs and Racial Aims, 1938–1944.* New York 2006.

Gruner, Wolf: *Öffentliche Wohlfahrt und Judenverfolgung. Wechselwirkung lokaler und zentraler Politik im NS-Staat 1933–1942.* München 2002.

Gruner, Wolf: "Poverty and Persecution: The Reichsvereinigung, the Jewish Population, and Anti-Jewish Policy in the Nazi State, 1939–1945," *Yad Vashem Studies* 27 (1999) pp. 23–60.

Gruner, Wolf: "Vertreibungen, Annexionen, Massenauswanderung. Die NS-Judenpolitik und Evian im Jahr 1938," *Jahrbuch für Antisemitismusforschung* (2019) 15–39.

Gruner, Wolf: "Von der Kollektivausweisung zur Deportation der Juden aus Deutschland 1938–1945," in: Kundrus, Birthe & Meyer, Beate (Hg.): *Die*

Deportation der Juden aus Deutschland. Pläne—Praxis—Reaktionen 1938–1945. Göttingen 2004, pp. 21–62.

Gruner, Wolf: *Widerstand in der Rosenstraße. Die Fabrik-Aktion und die Verfolgung der "Mischehen" 1943.* Frankfurt a.M. 2005.

Gruner, Wolf: *Zwangsarbeit und Verfolgung. Österreichische Juden im NS-Staat 1938–1945.* Innsbruck 2000.

Haase, Norbert et al. (Hg.): *Die Erinnerung hat ein Gesicht.* Leipzig 1998.

Habe, Hans: *Ich stelle mich. Meine Lebensgeschichte.* München 1954.

Hachmeister, Lutz: *Der Gegnerforscher. Die Karriere des SS-Führers Franz Alfred Six.* München 1998.

Hahn, Fred: *Lieber Stürmer. Leserbriefe an das NS-Kampfblatt 1924–1945.* Stuttgart 1978.

Hájková, Anna: *The Last Ghetto: An Everyday History of Theresienstadt.* New York 2020.

Hänschen, Steffen: *Das Transitghetto Izbica im System des Holocaust.* Berlin 2018.

Hassler, Marianne & Wertheimer, Jürgen (Hg.): *Der Exodus aus Nazideutschland. Jüdische Wissenschaftler im Exil.* Tübingen 1997.

Havemann, Nils: *Fußball unterm Hakenkreuz. Der DFB zwischen Sport, Politik und Kommerz.* Frankfurt a.M. 2005.

Hecker, Clara: "Deutsche Juden im Minsker Ghetto," *Zeitschrift für Geschichtswissenschaft* 56 (2008), Heft 10, S. 822–40.

Heim, Susanne & Aly, Goetz: "Staatliche Ordnung und 'Organische Lösung.' Die Rede Hermann Görings 'Über die Judenfrage' vom 6 Dezember 1938," *Jahrbuch für Antisemitismusforschung* 2 (1993) S. 378–404.

Heim, Susanne et al. (Hg.): *Die Verfolgung und Ermordung der europäischen Juden durch das nationalsozialistische Deutschland 1933–1945.* Bd. 2: Deutsches Reich 1938–August 1939, München 2008, Bd. 3: Deutsches Reich und Protektorat September 1939–September 1941. München 2012. Bd. 6: Deutsches Reich und Protektorat Böhmen und Mähren Oktober 1941–März 1943, Berlin 2019. Bd. 11: Deutsches Reich und Protektorat Böhmen und Mähren April 1943–1945, Berlin 2020.

Heim, Susanne et al. (Hg.): *"Wer Bleibt, opfert seine Jahre, vielleicht sein Leben." Deutsche Juden 1938–1941.* Göttingen 2010.

Henschel, Hildegard: "Aus der Arbeit der jüdischen Gemeinde während der Jahre 1941–1943," *Zeitschrift für die Geschichte der Juden* 9 (1972) 1/2, S. 33–52.

Herbert, Ulrich: *Best. Biographische Studien über Radikalismus, Weltanschauung und Vernunft 1903–1989.* Bonn 1996.

Herbert, Ulrich (ed.): *National-Socialist Extermination Policies: Contemporary German Perspectives and Controversies (War and Genocide).* New York 2000.

Herbst, Ludolf & Weihe, Thomas (Hg.): *Die Commerzbank und die Juden 1933–1945.* München 2004.

Herf, Jeffrey: *The Jewish Enemy: Nazi Propaganda during World War II and the Holocaust.* Cambridge, MA, 2006.

Herf, Jeffrey: *Nazi Propaganda for the Arab World.* New Haven, CT, 2009.

Herzig, Arno: *Jüdische Geschichte in Deutschland.* München 1997.

Herzig, Arno & Lorenz, Ina (Hg.): *Die Verdrängung und Vernichtung der Juden unter dem Nationalsozialismus.* Hamburg 1992.

Hesse, Claus: "Bilder lokaler Judendeportationen. Fotografien als Zugänge zur Alltagsgeschichte des NS-Terrors," in: Paul, Gerhard (Hg.): *Visual History. Ein Studienbuch.* Göttingen 2006, S. 149–68.

Heyd, Ludger & Schoeps, Julius (Hg.): *Juden in Deutschland.* München 1994, Kap. IX.

Hilberg, Raul: *The Destruction of the European Jews.* New Haven, CT 1961.

Hildesheimer, Esriel: "Cora Berliner. Ihr Leben und Wirken," *Leo Baeck Bulletin* (1984) S. 41–70.

Hildesheimer, Esriel: *Jüdische Selbstverwaltung unter dem NS-Regime.* Tübingen 1994.

Hillgruber, Andreas & Picker, Henry (Hg.): *Hitlers Tischgespräche im Führerhauptquartier 1941–1942.* München 1968.

Hollstein, Dorothea: *Antisemitische Propaganda. Die Darstellung des Juden im nationalsozialistischen Spielfilm.* München 1983.

Jah, Akim: *Die Deportation der Juden aus Berlin.* Berlin 2013.

Jahnke, Karl Heinz: "Die Vernichtung der Juden in Mecklenburg," in: Herzig, Arno & Lorenz, Ina (Hg.): *Verdrängung und Vernichtung der Juden unter dem Nationalsozialismus.* Hamburg 1992, S. 291–307.

Jalowicz Simon, Marie: *Untergetaucht. Eine junge Frau überlebt in Berlin 1940–1945.* Frankfurt a.M. 2014.

James, Harold: *The Deutsche Bank and the Nazi Economic War against the Jews: The Expropriation of Jewish-Owned Property.* Cambridge 2001.

Jansen, Hans: *Der Madagaskar-Plan.* München 1997.

Jasch, Hans-Christian & Kaiser, Wolf: *Der Holocaust vor deutschen Gerichten.* Ditzingen 2017.

Jochmann, Werner (Hg.): *Adolf Hitler Monologe im Führerhauptquartier 1941–1944.* München 1980.

Johnson, Eric A.: *Nazi Terror: The Gestapo, Jews, and Ordinary Germans.* New York 2000.

Jonca, Karol: "Deportation of German Jews from Breslau 1941–1944 as Described in Eyewitness Testimonies," *Yad Vashem Studies* 25 (1996) pp. 275–316.

Jütte, Robert: *Die Emigration der deutsch-sprachigen "Wissenschaft des Judentums." Die Auswanderung jüdischer Historiker nach Palästina 1933–1945.* Stuttgart 1991.

Kaplan, Marion A.: *Between Dignity and Despair: Jewish Life in Nazi Germany.* New York 1999.

Kaplan, Marion A.: *Der Mut zum Überleben. Jüdische Frauen und ihre Familien in Nazideutschland.* Berlin 2001.

Karny, Miroslav et al. (Hg.): *Theresienstadt in der "Endlösung der Judenfrage."* Prague 1992.

Katzburg, Nathaniel (ed.): *Pedut—Rescue in the Holocaust.* Ramat-Gan 1984 (Hebr.).

Kaufman, Theodor N.: *Germany Must Perish.* Newark, NJ, 1941.

Kellerhoff, Sven Felix: *Ein ganz normales Pogrom.* Stuttgart 2018.

Kent, Donald Peterson: *The Refugee Intellectual: The Americanization of the Immigrants of 1933–1941.* New York 1953.

Kershaw, Ian: "German Popular Opinion and the 'Jewish Question' 1939–1943," in: Strauss, Herbert (ed.): *Hostages of Modernization.* Berlin 1993, pp. 269–79.

Kershaw, Ian: *Hitler, the Germans, and the Final Solution.* Jerusalem 2008.

Kershaw, Ian: "Hitler's Prophecy and the 'Final Solution.'" Lecture at the Raul Hilberg Holocaust lecture series, University of Vermont, 2001.

Kershaw, Ian: *Popular Opinion and Political Dissent in the Third Reich: Bavaria, 1933–1945.* New York 1983.

Keval, Susanna: *Die schwierige Erinnerung. Deutsche Widerstandskämpfer über die Verfolgung und Vernichtung der Juden.* Frankfurt a.M. 1999.

Kieffer, Fritz: *Judenverfolgung in Deutschland—eine innere Angelegenheit? Internationale Reaktionen auf die Flüchtlingsproblematik 1933–1945.* Stuttgart 2002.

Kingreen, Monica (Hg.): *"Nach der Kristallnacht." Jüdisches Leben und antijüdische Politik in Frankfurt am Main 1938–1945.* Frankfurt a.M. 1999.

Klein, Peter: *Die "Gettoverwaltung Litzmannstadt" 1940–1944.* Hamburg 2009.

Klein, Peter: "Die Rolle der Vernichtungslager Kulmhof (Chelmno), Belzec (Belzec) und Auschwitz-Birkenau in den frühen Deportationsvorbereitungen," in: Dahlmann, Dittmar & Hirschfeld, Gerhard (Hg.): *Lager, Zwangsarbeit, Vertreibung und Deportation. Dimensionen der Massenverbrechen in der Sowjetunion und in Deutschland 1933 bis 1945.* Essen 1999, S. 459–81.

Klemperer, Victor: *"Ich will Zeugnis ablegen bis zum letzten." Tagebücher 1933–1945.* Hrsg. von Walter Nowojski. Bd. 1 und 2, 11., neu durchges. Aufl. Berlin 1999.

Klemperer, Victor: *Warum soll man nicht auf bessere Zeiten Hoffen. Ein Leben in Briefen.* Berlin 2017.

Kogon, Eugen: *Der SS-Staat. Das System der deutschen Konzentrationslager.* München 1974.

Köhler, Ingo: "Die 'Arisierung' jüdischer Privatbanken," in: Ziegler, Dieter: *Die Dresdner Bank und die deutschen Juden.* München 2006.

Köhler, Jochen: *Klettern in der Großstadt. Geschichten vom Überleben zwischen 1933–1945.* Berlin 1981.

Koonz, Claudia: "Courage and Choice among German-Jewish Women and Men," in: Paucker, Arnold et al. (Hg.): *Die Juden im nationalsozialistischen Deutschland 1933–1943.* Tübingen 1986, S. 283–94.

Kosmala, Beate: "Zwischen Ahnen und Wissen. Die Flucht vor der Deportation (1941–1945)," in: Kundrus, Birthe & Meyer, Beate (Hg.): *Die Deportation der Juden aus Deutschland. Pläne—Praxis—Reaktionen.* Göttingen 2004, S. 135–59.

Kosmala, Beate & Schoppmann, Claudia (Hg.): *Solidarität und Hilfe für Juden während der NS Zeit.* Bd. 5 *Überleben im Untergrund 1941–1945.* Berlin 2002.

Kreutzmüller, Christoph: *Ausverkauf. Die Vernichtung der jüdischen Gerwerbetätigkeit in Berlin 1930–1945.* Berlin 2012.

Kreutzmuller, Christoph & Zatlin, Jonathan (eds.): *Dispossession. Plundering German Jewry 1933–1953.* Michigan 2020.

Krogmann, Carl Vincent: *Es ging um Deutschlands Zukunft 1932–1939. Erlebtes täglich diktiert von dem früheren Regierenden Bürgermeister von Hamburg.* Leoni am Starnberger See 1976.

Krojanker, Gustav: *Rise and Decline of the German Jewry.* Tel Aviv 1937 (Hebr.).

Kulka, Otto Dov (Hg.): *Deutsches Judentum unter dem Nationalsozialismus.* Tübingen 1997.

Kulka, Otto Dov: *German Jews in the Era of the "Final Solution": Essays.* Berlin 2020.

Kulka, Otto Dov & Jäckel, Eberhard (eds.): *The Jews in the Secret Nazi Reports on Popular Opinion in Germany, 1933–1945.* New Haven, CT, 2010.

Kuwalek, Robert: "Das kurze Leben 'im Osten.' Jüdische Deutsche im Distrikt Lublin aus polnisch-jüdischer Sicht," in: Kundrus, Birthe & Meyer, Beate (Hg.): *Die Deportation der Juden aus Deutschland. Plän—Praxis—Reaktionen.* Göttingen 2004, S. 112–34.

Kwiet, Konrad U.: "Forced Labour of German Jews in Nazi Germany," *LBYB* (1991) S. 389–410.

Kwiet, Konrad U.: "'Nach dem Pogrom' Stufen der Ausgrenzung," in: Benz, Wolfgang (Hg.): *Die Juden in Deutschland 1933–1945. Leben unter nationalsozialistischer Herrschaft.* München 1988, S. 545–659.

Kwiet, Konrad U.: "The Ultimate Refuge—Suicide in the Jewish Community under the Nazis," *LBYB* (1984) pp. 135–67.

Kwiet, Konrad U. & Eschwege, Helmut: *Selbstbehauptung und Widerstand. Deutsche Juden im Kampf um Existenz und Menschenwürde 1933–1945.* Hamburg 1984.

Lang, Hans Joachim: *Die Namen der Nummern. Wie es gelang, die 86 Opfer eines NS-Verbrechens zu identifizieren.* Hamburg 2004.

Lavsky, Hagit: *The Creation of the German-Jewish Diaspora: Interwar German-Jewish Immigration to Palestine, the USA, and England.* Berlin 2018.

Lazowik, Yaacov: *Hitler's Bureaucrats: The Nazi Security Police and the Banality of Evil.* Jerusalem 2001 (Hebr.).

Leighton-Langer, Peter: *The King's Own Loyal Enemy Aliens: German and Austrian Refugees in Britain's Armed Forces, 1939–1945.* London 2006.

Limberg, Margarete & Rübsaat, Hubert (eds.): *Germans No More: Accounts of Jewish Everyday Life, 1933–1938.* New York 2006.

Lippmann, Leo: *Zur Geschichte der deutsch-israelitischen Gemeinde in Hanburg in der Zeit vom Herbst 1935 bis zum Ende 1942*. Hamburg 1993.

Loewenberg, Peter: "The Kristallnacht as a Public Degradation in Ritual," *LBYB* 32 (1987) pp. 308–23.

Lohalm, Uwe: *Die Nationalsozialistische Judenverfolgung 1933–1945*. Hamburg 1999.

Lohalm, Uwe: *Fürsorge und Verfolgung. Öffentliche Wohlfahrtsverwaltung und nationalsozialistische Judenpolitik in Hamburg 1933 bis 1942*. Hamburg 1998.

Löhken, Wilfried et al. (Hg.): *Juden im Widerstand. Drei Gruppen zwischen Überlebenskampf und politische Aktion in Berlin 1939–1945*. Berlin 1993.

Longerich, Peter: "*Davon haben wir nichts gewußt!*" *Die Deutschen und die Judenverfolgung 1933–1945*. München 2006.

Longerich, Peter: *Politik der Vernichtung. Eine Gesamtdarstellung der nationalsozialistischen Judenverfolgung*. München, Zürich 1998.

Longerich, Peter & Pohl, Dieter (Hg.): *Die Ermordung der europäischen Juden. Eine umfassende Dokumentation des Holocaust 1941–1945*. München 1989.

Loose, Ingo: "'Kollektivgeschöpfe.' Die Berliner Juden im Ghetto Litzmannstadt 1941–4," *Einsicht. Bulletin des Fritz Bauer Instituts* 1 (2009).

Lorenz, Ina: "Das Leben der Hamburger Juden im Zeichen der 'Endlösung,'" in: Herzig, Arno & Lorenz, Ina (Hg.): *Verdrängung und Vernichtung der Juden unter dem Nationalsozialismus*. Hamburg 1992, pp. 207–47.

Lösener, Bernhard: "Das Reichsministerium des Inneren und die Judengesetzgebung," *VfZ* (1961) S. 262–313.

Löw, Andrea: *Juden im Ghetto Litzmannstadt. Lebensbedingungen, Selbstwahrnehmung, Verhalten*. Göttingen 2006.

Löw, Konrad: *Das Volk ist ein Trost. Deutsche und Juden 1933–1945 im Urteil der jüdischen Zeitzeugen*. München 2006.

Lowenstein, Steven L.: *Frankfurt on the Hudson: The German Jewish Community of Washington Heights, 1933–1983; Its Structure and Culture*. Detroit 1988.

Löwenthal, Gerhard: *Ich bin geblieben. Erinnerungen*. München 1987.

Lowenthal, Marvin: *The Jews of Germany: A Story of Sixteen Centuries*. Philadelphia 1936.

Ludwig, Johannes: *Boykott, Enteignung, Mord*. München 1992.

Lutjens, Richard N.: *Submerged on the Surface: The Not So Hidden Jews of Nazi Berlin, 1941–1945*. New York 2019.

Maier, Dieter: *Arbeitseinsatz und Deportation. Die Mitwirkung der Arbeitsverwaltung bei der nationalsozialistischen Judenverfolung in den Jahren 1938–1945*. Berlin 1994.

Maierhof, Gudrun et al. (Hg.): *Aus Kindern wurden Briefe. Die Rettung jüdischer Kinder aus Nazi Deutschland*. Berlin 2004.

Makarova, Elena et al. (ed.): *University over the Abyss: The Story behind 520 Lecturers and 2,430 Lectures in KZ Theresienstadt, 1942–1944*. Jerusalem 2000.

Manoschek, Walter (Hg.): *"Es gibt nur eines für das Judentum: Vernichtung!" Das Judenbild in deutschen Soldatenbriefen 1939–1944*. Hamburg 1995.

Margaliot, Abraham & Cochavi, Yehoyakim: *History of the Holocaust: Germany*. Jerusalem 1998 (Hebr.).

Margolick, David: *Max Schmeling und Joe Louis—Kampf der Giganten—Kampf der Systeme*. München 2005.

Marr, Wilhelm: *Der Sieg des Judentums über das Germanentum*. 10. unveränd. Aufl. Berlin 1879.

Marx, Leopold: "Otto Hirsch. Ein Lebensbild," *Leo Baeck Bulletin* 23 (1963) S. 295–312.

Matthäus, Jürgen & Bajohr, Frank: *Alfred Rosenberg. Die Tagebücher von 1934 bis 1944*. Frankfurt a.M. 2015.

Matthäus, Jürgen et al. (Hg.): *Ausbildungsziel Judenmord? "Weltanschauliche Erziehung" von SS, Polizei und Waffen-SS im Rahmen der "Endlösung."* Frankfurt a.M. 2003.

Matthäus, Jürgen & Mallmann, Klaus-Michael (Hg.): *Deutsche Juden, Völkermord*. Darmstadt 2006.

Mauch, Christof & Salmons, Joseph (eds.): *German-Jewish Identities in America*. Madison 2003.

Meinl, Susanne & Hindemith, Bettina (Hg.): *Legalisierter Raub. Der Fiskus und die Ausplünderung der Juden in Hessen 1933–1945*. Spangenberg 2002.

Melhuish, Kathleen J.: "The German/Jewish Emigration and the Historian's Craft," in: Kwiet, Konrad (Hg.): *From the Emancipation to the Holocaust*. Lexington 1987, pp. 155–65.

Merritt, Anna J. & Merritt, Richard L. (Hg.): *Public Opinion in Occupied Germany: The OMGUS Surveys, 1945–1949*. Urbana, IL, 1970.

Meyer, Beate (Hg.): *Deutsche Jüdinnen und Juden in Ghettos und Lagern (1941–1945)*. Berlin 2017.

Meyer, Beate: "Handlungsspielräume regionaler jüdischer Repräsentanten (1941–1945). Die Reichsvereinigung der Juden in Deutschland und Deportation," in: Kundrus, Birthe & Meyer, Beate (Hg.): *Die Deportation der Juden aus Deutschland. Pläne—Praxis—Reaktionen*. Göttingen 2004, S. 63–85.

Meyer, Beate: *"Jüdische Mischlinge" Rassenpolitik und Verfolgungserfahrung 1933–1945*. Hamburg 1999.

Meyer, Beate: *Tödliche Gratwanderung. Die Reichsvereinigung der Juden in Deutschland zwischen Hoffnung, Zwang, Selbstbehauptung und Verstrickung (1939–1945)*. Göttingen 2011.

Meyer, Beate & Simon, Hermann: *Juden in Berlin 1933–1945*. Berlin 2000.

Meyer, Michael A. (Hg.): *Deutsch-jüdische Geschichte in der Neuzeit*. Bd. 4. München 1997.

Meyer zu Uptrup, Wolfram: *Der Kampf gegen die "jüdische Weltverschwörung." Propaganda und Antisemitismus der Nationalsozialisten 1919–1945*. Berlin 2003.

Milton, Sybil: "The Expulsion of the Polish Jews from Germany October 1938 to July 1939—A Documentation," *LBYB* (1984) pp. 169–99.

Miron, Guy: "The Politics of Catastrophe Races on I Wait: Waiting Time in the World of German Jews under Nazi Rule," *Yad Vashem Studies* 43/1 (2015) pp. 45–76.

Moeller, Felix: *Der Filmminister. Goebbels und der Film im Dritten Reich.* Berlin 1998.

Möller, Horst: *Exodus der Kultur. Schriftsteller, Wissenschaftler und Künstler in der Emigration nach 1933.* München 1984.

Mommsen, Hans: *Auschwitz 17. Juli 1942. Der Weg zur europäischen "Endlösung der Judenfrage."* München 2002.

Mommsen, Hans: "Hitler's Reichstag Speech of 30 January 1939," *History and Memory* 9/1–2 (1997) pp. 147–61.

Morsch, G. & Perz, B. (Hg.): *Neue Studien zu nationalsozialistischen Massentötungen durch Gas.* Berlin 2011.

Mosse, George L.: *Der nationalsozialistische Alltag.* Königstein 1978.

Mosse, George L.: *German Jews beyond Judaism.* Bloomington and Cincinnati 1985.

Müller, Arnd: *Geschichte der Juden in Nürnberg 1146–1945.* Nürnberg 1968.

Müller, Bernhard: *Alltag im Zivilisationsbruch. Das Ausnahme-Unrecht gegen die jüdische Bevölkerung in Deutschland 1933–1945.* München 2003.

Müller-Hill, Benno: *Murderous Science: Elimination by Scientific Selection of Jews, Gypsies, and Others in Germany, 1933–1945.* New York 1988.

Münch, Ingo von (Hg.): *Gesetze des NS-Staates. Dokumente eines Unrechtsystems.* Paderborn 1994.

Mußgung, Dorothee: *Die reichsfluchtsteuer 1931–1953.* Berlin 1992.

Nicosia, Francis & Scrase, David (eds.): *Jewish Life in Nazi Germany: Dilemmas and Responses.* New York 2010.

Niederland, Doron: *The German Jews—Emigrants or Refugees? Emigration Patterns between the Two World Wars.* Jerusalem 1996 (Hebr.).

Nietzel, Benno: "Die Vernichtung der wirtschaftlichen Existenz der deutschen Juden 1933–1945. Ein Literatur- und Forschungsbericht," *Archiv für Sozialgeschichte* (2009) S. 561–613.

Niewyk, Donald L.: "Solving the 'Jewish Problem'—Continuity and Change in German Antisemitism, 1871–1945," *LBYB* (1990) pp. 335–70.

Noakes, Jeremy: "The Development of Nazi Policy towards German-Jewish Mischlinge, 1933–1945," *LBYB* 34 (1989) pp. 291–354.

Noelzen, Benno: "The Nazi Party and Its Violence against the Jews, 1933–1939," *Yad Vashem Studies* 31 (2003) pp. 245–86.

Nolte, Ernst: *Der Europäische Bürgerkrieg 1917–1945. Nationalsozialismus und Bolschewismus.* Frankfurt a.M. 1989.

Nordmann, Ingeborg & Pilling, Iris (Hg.): *Hannah Arendt und Kurt Blumenfeld: "... in keinem Besitz verwurzelt." Die Korrespondenz.* Hamburg 1995.

Offermanns, Ernst: *Die deutschen Juden und der Spielfilm der NS-Zeit*. Frankfurt a.M. 2005.

Ophir, Baruch & Wiesemann, Frank (Hg.): *Die jüdischen Gemeinden in Bayern 1918–1945: Geschichte und Zerestörung*. München 1979.

Osterloh, Jörg: *"Ausschaltung der Juden und des jüdischen Geistes" Nationalsozialistische Kulturpolitik 1920–1945*. Frankfurt 2020.

Padover, Saul K.: *Lügendetektor. Vernehmungen im besiegten Deutschland 1944/45*. Frankfurt a.M. 1999.

Pätzold, Kurt (Hg.): *Verfolgung, Vertreibung, Vernichtung. Dokumente des faschistischen Antisemitismus 1933–1942*. Leipzig 1983.

Paucker, Arnold: "Resistance of German and Austrian Jews to the Nazi Regime, 1933–1945," *LBYB* 40 (1995) pp. 3–20.

Paucker, Arnold et al. (Hg.): *Die Juden im nationalsozialistischen Deutschland 1933–1943; Jews in Nazi Germany 1933–1943*. Tübingen 1986. Schriftenreihe wissenschaftlicher Abhandlungen des Leo-Baeck-Instituts, Band 45.

Peck, Abraham J. (ed.): *The German-Jewish Legacy in America 1938–1988: From Bildung to the Bill of Rights*. Detroit 1989.

Pehle, Walter (Hg.): *Der Judenpogrom 1938. Von der "Reichskristallnacht" zum Völkermord*. Frankfurt a.M. 1990.

Pellner, Lara et al. (Hg.): *Theresienstadt - Filmfragmente und Zeitzeugenberichte*. Wiesbaden 2021.

Peukert, Detlev: *Volksgenossen und Gemeinschaftsfremde: Anpassung, Ausmerze und Aufbegehren unter dem Nationalsozialismus*. Köln 1982.

Picker, Henry: *Hitlers Tischgespräche im Führerhauptquartier 1941–1942*. Stuttgart 1963.

Piper, Ernst: *Alfred Rosenberg. Hitlers Chefideologe*. München 2005.

Pleticha, Heinrich (Hg.): *Das Bild der Juden in der Volks- und Jugendliteratur vom 18. Jahrhundert bis 1945*. Würzburg 1985.

Pohl, Dieter: *Holocaust*. Freiburg 2000.

Pötzl, Norbert F.: *Casablanca 1943. Das geheime Treffen, der Film und die Wende des Krieges*. München, 2017.

Porat, Dina: "The Legend of the Struggle of the Jews from the Third Reich in the Ninth Fort Near Kovno, 1941–1942," *Tel Aviver Jahrbuch für deutsche Geschichte* 20 (1991) S. 363–92.

Potter, Hilary: *Remembering Rosenstrasse: History, Memory and Identity in Contemporary Germany*. Bern 2018.

Przyrembel, Alexandra: *Rassenschande. Reinheitsmythos und Vernichtungslegitimation im Nationalsozialismus*. Göttingen 2003.

Quack, Sibylle: *Zuflucht Amerika. Zur Sozialgeschichte der Emigration deutsch-jüdischer Frauen in die USA 1933–1945*. Bonn 1995.

Rabinovici, Doron: *Instanzen der Ohnmacht, Wien 1938–1945*. Frankfurt 2000.

Raim, Edith: *Justiz zwischen Diktatur und Demokratie. Ahndung von NS-Verbrechen in Westdeutschland 1945–9*. München 2013.

Raleigh, John M.: *Behind the Nazi Front*. London 1941.

Reichmann, Hans: *Deutscher Bürger und verfolgter Jude. Novemberpogrom und KZ Sachsenhausen 1937 bis 1939*. München 1998.

Richarz, Monika (ed.): *Jewish Life in Germany: Memoirs from Three Centuries*. Bloomington 1991.

Richarz, Monika (ed.): *Jüdisches Leben in Deutschland*, vol. 3: *Selbstzeugnisse zur Sozialgeschichte 1918–1945*. Stuttgart 1982.

Riemer, Jehuda: *Fritz Perez Naphtali: Sozialdemokrat und Zionist*. Gerlingen 1991.

Rigg, Brian Mark: *Hitler's Jewish Soldiers: The Untold Story of Nazi Racial Laws and Men of Jewish Descent in the German Military*. Kansas 2002.

Röcher, Ruth: *Die jüdische Schule im nationalsozialistischen Deutschland 1933–1942*. Frankfurt a.M. 1992.

Roseman, Mark: *Barbarians from Our "Kulturkreis": German Jewish Perceptions of Nazi Perpetrators*. Jerusalem 2016.

Roseman, Mark: *A Past in Hiding: Memory and Survival in Nazi Germany*. New York 2002.

Rosenberg, Alfred: *Die Judenfrage als Weltproblem*. München 1941.

Rosenstrauch, Hazel (Hg.): *Aus Nachbarn wurden Juden. Ausgrenzung und Selbstbehauptung 1933–1942*. Berlin 1988.

Rosenthal, Hans: *Zwei Leben in Deutschland*. Bergisch Gladbach 1980.

Rosh, Lea & Jäckel, Eberhard: *"Der Tod ist ein Meister aus Deutschland."* München 1993.

Rubenstein, William D.: *The Myth of Rescue*. London 1997.

Rudolph, Katrin: *Hilfe beim Sprung ins Nichts. Franz Kaufmann und die Rettung von Juden und "nichtarischen" Christen*. Berlin 2005.

Rupnow, Dirk: *"'Arisierung' jüdischer Geschichte. Zur nationalsozialistischen 'Judenforschung,'" Leipziger Beiträge zur jüdischen Geschichte und Kultur* 2 (2004) S. 349–67.

Rupnow, Dirk: *"Judenforschung" im "Dritten Reich": Wissenschaft zwischen Politik, Propaganda und Ideologie*. Baden-Baden 2011.

Rürup, Reinhard: "Jewish History in Berlin: Berlin in Jewish History," *LBYB* (2000) pp. 37–50.

Safrian, Hans: *Eichmann und seine Gehilfen*. Frankfurt a.M. 1995.

Safrian, Hans & Witek, Hans: *Und keiner war dabei. Dokumente des alltäglichen Antisemitismus in Wien 1938*. Wien 2008.

Saidel, Rochelle G.: *The Jewish Women of Ravensbruck Concentration Camp*. Madison 2004.

Samter, Hermann: *To Be a Jew in Berlin: The Letters of Hermann Samter, 1939–1943*. Jerusalem 2012.

Sauer, Paul: *Dokumente über die Verfolgung der jüdischen Bürger in Baden Württemberg durch das nationalsozialistische Regime 1933–1945*. Stuttgart 1966.

Sauer, Paul: "Otto Hirsch—Direktor der Reichsvertretung," *LBYB* (1987) S. 341–68.

Schaber, Will (Hg.): *Aufbau Reconstruction. Dokumente einer Kultur im Exil.* Köln 1972.

Scharnberg, Harriet: *Die "Judenfrage" im Bild. Der Antisemitismus im nationalsozialistischen Fotoreportagen.* Hamburg 2018.

Scheffler, Wolfgang: *Judenverfolgung im Dritten Reich.* Berlin 1964.

Scheffler, Wolfgang & Schulle, Diana. *Buch der Erinnerung.* München 2003.

Schleunes, Karl A.: *The Twisted Road to Auschwitz: Nazi Policy towards German Jews 1930–1939.* Urbana, IL, 1970.

Schmid, Monika S.: "'I Always Thought I Was a German, It Was Hitler Who Taught Me I Was a Jew.' National-Socialist Persecution, Identity and the German Language," in: Mauch, Christof & Salmons, Joseph (Hg.): *German-Jewish Identities in America.* Madison 2003, pp. 133–53.

Schoor, Kerstin: *Vom literarischen Zentrum zum literarischen Ghetto. Deutsch-jüdische literarische Kultur in Berlin zwischen 1933–1945.* Göttingen 2010.

Schrafstetter, Susanna: *Flucht und Versteck. Untergetauchte Juden in München.* Göttingen 2015.

Schrafstetter, Susanna & Steinweis, Alan (eds.): *The Germans and the Holocaust: Popular Responses.* New York 2016.

Schreiber, Carsten: "Generalstab des Holocaust oder akademischer Elfenbeinturm? Die Gegnerforschung des Sicherheitsdienstes der SS," *Jahrbuch des Simon Dubnow Instituts* 5 (2006) S. 327–52.

Schüler-Springorum, Stefanie: "Fear and Misery in the Third Reich: From the Files of the Collective Guardianship Office of the Berlin Jewish Community," *Yad Vashem Studies* 27 (1999) pp. 61–104.

Schulte, Jan Erik: *Zwangsarbeit und Vernichtung: Das Wirtschaftsimperium der SS.* Paderborn 2001.

Schwerenz, Jitzchak & Wolff, Edith: "Jüdische Jugend im Untergrund. Eine zionistische Gruppe in Deutschland während des zweiten Weltkrieges," *Leo Baeck Bulletin* (1969) S. 1–100.

Segev, Tom: *The Seventh Million: The Israelis and the Holocaust.* New York 1993.

Seligmann, Avraham: "An Illegal Way of Life in Nazi Germany," *LBYB* (1992) pp. 327–61.

Sheffi, Na'ama: *German in Hebrew: Translations from German into Hebrew in Jewish Palestine.* Jerusalem 1998 (Hebr.).

Shirer, William L.: *Berlin Diary, 1934–1941.* New York 1941.

Silver, Daniel: *Überleben in der Hölle. Das Berliner jüdische Krankenhaus im Dritten Reich.* Berlin 2006.

Simon, Ernst: *Aufbau im Untergang. Jüdische Erwachsenenbildung im Nationalsozialistischen Deutschland als geistiger Widerstand.* Tübingen 1959.

Simon, Hermann: "Die Berliner Juden unter dem Nationalsozialismus," in: Herzig, Arno & Lorenz, Ina (Hg.): *Verdrängung und Vernichtung der Juden unter dem Nationalsozialismus.* Hamburg 1992, S. 249–66.

Smith, Helmut Walser: *The Continuities of German History: Nation, Religion and Race*. Cambridge 2008 (German: *Fluchtpunkt 1941*. Stuttgart 2010).

Smith, Howard K.: *Last Train from Berlin: An Eye-Witness Account of Germany at War*. London 1942.

Sodeikat, Ernst: "Die Verfolgung und der Widerstand der Juden in der Freien Stadt Danzig von 1933 bis 1945," *Bulletin des Leo Baeck Instituts* Nr. 30, 1965, 107–49.

Sparr, Thomas: *Grunewald im Orient. Das deutsch-jüdische Jerusalem*. Berlin 2018.

Stargardt, Nicholas: *The German War: A Nation under Arms, 1939–1945*. New York 2015.

Starke, Käthe: *Der Führere schenkt den Juden eine Stadt*. Berlin 1975.

Steiner, Frantisek: *Fußball unterm gelben Stern, Die Liga im Ghetto Theresienstadt 1943–44*. Paderborn 2017.

Steinert, Marlis G.: *Hitlers Krieg und die Deutschen*. Düsseldorf, Wien 1970.

Steinweis, Alan E.: "Hans Hinkel and German Jewry 1933–1941," *Leo Baeck Yearbook* (1993) pp. 209–19.

Steinweis, Alan E.: *Studying the Jew. Scholarly Antisemitism in Nazi Germany*. Cambridge, MA 2006.

Stengel, Katharina (Hg.): *Vor der Vernichtung. Die staatliche Enteignung der Juden im Nationalsozialismus*. Frankfurt a.M. 2007.

Stoddard, Theodore Lothrop: *Into the Darkness: Nazi Germany Today*. Newport Beach, CA, 2000. Facsimile reprint of the original 1940 edition.

Stoltzfus, Nathan: *Widerstand des Herzens. Der Aufstand der Berliner Frauen in der Rosenstraße 1943*. München, Wien 1999.

Strauss, Herbert: *In the Eye of the Storm: Growing Up Jewish in Germany, 1918–1943*. New York 1999.

Strauss, Herbert: "Jewish Emigration from Germany," *LBYB* (1980) pp. 313–61; 1981, pp. 343–409.

Strauss, Herbert & Röder, Werner (ed.): *International Bibliographical Dictionary of Central European Émigrés*. München 1980–1983.

Strnad, Maximilian: *Zwischenstation 'Judensiedlung'. Verfolgung und Deportation der jüdischen Münchner 1941–1945*. München 2011.

Süllwold, Fritz: *Deutsche Normalbürger 1933–1945. Erfahrungen, Einstellungen, Reaktionen. Eine geschichtspsychologische Untersuchung*. München 2002.

Tausendfreund, Doris: *Erzwungener Verrat. Die Verfolgung "illegal" lebender Juden in den Jahren 1943–1945 in Berlin und Wien durch den jüdischen Fahndungsdienst*. Berlin 2000.

Tausk, Walter: *Breslauer Tagebuch 1933–1940*. Berlin 1975.

Techner, Gerhard: *Die Deportation der badischen und saarpfälzischen Juden am 22. Oktober 1940*. Frankfurt 2002.

Tenenbaum, Joseph: *Race and Reich: The Story of an Epoch*. New York 1956.

Tent, James F.: *Im Schatten des Holocaust. Schicksale deutsch-jüdischer "Mischlinge" im Dritten Reich*. Köln, Weimar, Wien 2007.

Terezin Initiative Institute (Hg.): *Theresienstädter Studien und Dokumente*. Prague 1994–2006.

Thalmann, Rita: "Jüdische Frauen nach dem Pogrom 1938," in: Paucker, Arnold et al. (Hg.): *Die Juden im Nationalsozialistischen Deutschland 1933–1945*. Tübingen 1986, S. 295–302.

Theilhaber, Felix: *Der Untergang der deutschen Juden*. Berlin 1911.

Thoma, Matthias: *"Wir waren die Juddebube." Eintracht Frankfurt in der NS-Zeit*. Göttingen 2007.

Timm, Angelika (Hg.): *Die Fünfte Alijah. Zur Einwanderung deutschsprachiger Juden nach Palästina 1932–1939*. Berlin 1995.

Toury, Jacob: "From Forced Emigration to Expulsion—The Jewish Exodus over the Non-Slavic Borders of the Reich as a Prelude to the 'Final Solution,'" *Yad Vashem Studies* 17 (1986) pp. 51–92.

Tramer, Hans (Hg.): *In zwei Welten*. Tel Aviv 1962.

Trepp, Leo: *Das Vermächtnis der deutschen Juden*. Beer Sheva 2000.

Trunk, Yehiel Yeshaia: *Judenrat: The Jewish Councils in Eastern Europe under Nazi Occupation*. New York 1972.

Unger, Manfred: "Die Juden in Leipzig unter der Herrschaft des Nationalsozialismus," in: Herzig, Arno & Lorenz, Ina (Hg.): *Verdrängung und Vernichtung der Juden unter dem Nationalsozialismus*. Hamburg 1992, S. 267–89.

Unger, Manfred & Lang, Hubert (Hg.): *Juden in Leipzig. Eine Dokumentation zur Ausstellung anläßlich des 50. Jahrtages der faschistischen Pogromnacht*. Leipzig 1988.

Urwand, Ben: *The Collaboration: Hollywood's Pact with Hitler*. Cambridge 2013.

Volkov, Shulamit: "German Émigré Historians in Israel," in: Daum, Andreas W., Lehmann, Hartmut & Sheehan, James J. (eds.): *The Second Generation: Émigrés from Nazi Germany as Historians*. New York 2015.

Volkov, Shulamit: *Germans, Jews, and Antisemitism*. New York 2006.

Walk, Joseph (Hg.): *Das Sonderrecht für die Juden im NS-Staat*. Heidelberg 1996.

Wamser, Ursula & Weinke, Wilfried (Hg.): *Eine verschwundene Welt. Jüdisches Leben am Grindel*. Springe 2006, pp. 298–347.

Wassermann, Henry et al. (Hg.): *Bibliographie des Schrifttums in Deutschland 1933–1941*. München 1989.

Wassermann, Henry & Walk, Joseph (eds.): *Pinkas hakehilot—Germany*, vol. B: Wuertemberg, Baden etc. 1986, vol. C: Hessen, Frankfurt etc. (Hebr.).

Weiss, Yfaat: *Deutsche und polnische Juden vor dem Holocaust 1933–1940*. München 2000.

Weltsch, Robert (Hg.): *Deutsches Judentum. Aufstieg und Krise*. Stuttgart 1963.

Wiesemann, Falk: "Judenverfolgung und nichtjüdische Bevölkerung 1933–1944," in: Broszat, Martin et al. (Hg.): *Bayern in der NS Zeit*. München 1977, pp. 427–86.

Wildt, Michael: *Volksgemeinschaft als Selbstermächtigung. Gewalt gegen Juden 1919–1939*. Hamburg 2007.

Willems, Susanne: *Der entsiedelte Jude. Albert Speers Wohnungsmarktpolitik für den Berliner Hauptstadtbau.* Berlin 2000.

Wippermann, Wolfgang: *Die Berliner Gruppe Baum und der jüdische Widerstand.* Berlin 1981.

Wojak, Irmtrud & Hayes, Peter (Hg.): *"Arisierung" im Nationalsozialismus. Volksgemeinschaft, Raub und Gedächtnis.* Frankfurt a.M. 2000.

Wolf, Gerhard: *Ideologie und Herrschaftsrationalität. Nationalsozialistische Germanisierungspolitik in Westpolen.* Hamburg 2012.

Wollenberg, Jörg (Hg.): *"Niemand war dabei, und keiner hat's gewußt" Die deutsche Öffentlichkeit und die Judenverfolgung 1933–1945.* München 1989.

Wrochen, Wolf von (Hg.): *Nationalsozialistische Täterschaften.* Berlin 2016.

Wünschmann, Kim: *Before Auschwitz: Jewish Prisoners in the Prewar Concentration Camps.* Cambridge, MA 2015.

Wyden, Peter: *Stella.* Göttingen 1993.

Yablonka, Hannah: *The State of Israel vs. Adolf Eichmann.* New York 2004.

Yahil, Leni: "Some Remarks about Hitler's Impact on the Nazis' Jewish Policy," *Yad Vashem Studies* 23 (1993) pp. 281–94.

Zariz, Ruth: *Flight before the Holocaust: Jewish Emigration from Germany, 1938–1941.* Tel Aviv 1990 (Hebr.).

Ziegler, Dieter: *Die Dresdner Bank und die deutschen Juden.* München 2006.

Zimmermann, Moshe: "'Die aussichtslose Republik.' Zukunftsperspektiven deutscher Juden vor 1933," in: Idem: *Deutsch-jüdische Vergangenheit: Der Judenhaß als Herausforderung.* Paderborn 2005, pp. 238–57.

Zimmermann, Moshe: *Die deutschen Juden 1914–1945.* München 1997.

Zimmermann, Moshe: "Mohammed als Vorbote der NS-Judenpolitik?," *Tel Aviver Jahrbuch für deutsche Geschichte* 33 (2005) S. 290–305.

Zimmermann, Moshe & Hotam, Yotam (Hg.): *Zweierlei Heimat. Die Jeckes zwischen Mitteleuropa und Nahost.* Frankfurt 2005.

FILMOGRAPHY

Harlan, Veit (director), *Jud Süss* 1940.

Hippler, Fritz (director), *Der Ewige Jude* 1940.

Link, Caroline (director), *Nirgendwo in Afrika* 2001.

Mätzig, Kurt (director), *Ehe im Schatten* 1947.

Räfle, Claus (director), *Die Unsichtbaren* 2017.

Verhoeven, Michael (director), *Menschliches Versagen* 2008.

INDEX

Ubiquitous names and terms—antisemitism, Gestapo, Hitler, SS, RSHA—were left out of the index.

Fabrikaktion (factories operation), 83, 106, 138, 144, 147, 173, 175

Feuchtwanger, Leon, 189

films: *Casablanca*, 187; *Crossfire*, 190; *Der Ewige Jude*, 170, 189; *Die Drei von der Tankstelle*, 129; *Die Feuerzangenbowle*, 129; *Die Rothschilds*, 171; *Ehe im Schatten*, 141; *Gentleman's Agreement*, 190; *The Great Dictator*, 6; *Jud Süß*, 171; *Kolberg*, 171; *Leinen aus Irland*, 171; *Nirgendwo in Afrika*, 187; *Robert und Bertram*, 170; *Theresienstadt: A Documentary Film from the Jewish Settlement Area*, 96, 129

Final Solution, 2, 29, 35, 42, 55–58, 82, 91, 93, 96–102, 105, 112, 122, 127, 137, 142, 165, 166, 198, 208, 209, 213

Finkelscherer, Bruno, 211

Flannery, Harry, 62, 63

Flatow, Alfred, 131

Flatow, Gustav, 131

forced labor, 81, 82

Frank, Anne, 149

Frank, Edgar, 124

Frank, Hans, 57, 61, 86

Frank, James, 189

Frank, Margot, 149

Frank, Walter, 143

Franke, Joachim, 101

Franz, Günther, 143

Freier, Recha, 24, 51, 53, 64

Freud, Sigmund, 189

Freund, Elisabeth, 164, 165, 174

Frick, Wilhelm, 14, 18, 25, 30

Friedländer, Saul, 2

Fritzsche, Peter, 167

Frommermann, Harry, 10

Fuchs, Gottfried, 10, 189

Funk, Walter, 14

Fürst, Paula, 25, 32, 95

gas chambers, 65, 87, 119, 139, 213

Gay, Peter (Peter Fröhlich), 6, 7, 209

Geitel & Co. (factory), 77

Gelner, Gustav, 168

Geltungsjude ("considered Jew"), 90, 103, 106, 142

Gerron, Kurt, 128–30

ghetto: Kaunas (Kowno), 88, 90, 113, 121, 122, 150; Litzmannstadt (Łódź), 63, 68, 85–87, 90, 112–24, 136, 164, 165; Lublin, 52, 57, 58, 62, 78, 88, 112, 113, 118–20, 165; Minsk, 86–90, 95, 96, 100, 112, 121, 123, 124; Riga, 74, 80, 86, 88–90, 96, 112, 120–23, 161; Theresienstadt, 89–91, 94–96, 98, 125–31, 134, 144, 149, 162; Warsaw, 104, 112, 118, 120, 121, 123, 165

Gilbert, Felix, 189

Giordano, Ralph, 149, 157

Gitai-Weinraub, Munio, 189

Globke, Hans, 97

Globocnik, Odilo, 119

Glücks, Richard, 125

Goebbels, Joseph, 14–19, 25–28, 35, 42, 45, 59, 61, 63, 67, 72, 73, 75, 80, 82, 83, 101, 102, 106, 134, 141, 155, 158, 160, 163, 164, 170–80, 191, 201, 202, 208

Goebbels, Magda, 15

Goerdeler, Carl Friedrich, 176

Goethe, Johann Wolfgang, 195

Goldhagen, Daniel J., 176, 179

Goldmann, Nahum, 54

Göring, Hermann, 13–19, 21, 25, 45, 57, 79, 99, 105, 141, 159

Gottschalk, Joachim, 141

Grab, Walter, 189

Gradnauer, Georg, 130

Grau, Wilhelm, 29, 61, 142, 143

Greifer ("scout"), 147, 148

Greiser, Arthur, 67, 85–87, 114, 119

Gronemann, Sami, 193, 195

Groß, Walter, 105

Grüber, Heinrich, 76

Grünbaum (family), 98

Gruner, Wolf, 4, 51, 157, 167, 168, 211

Grynzpan, Herschel, 17, 18, 22, 208

Gürtner, Franz, 14

Gwatkin, Ashton, 37

Habe, Hans, 150

Haber, Fritz, 164

hachschara, 50, 51, 53

Hagana, 199

Hanfling, M. 193

Harlan, Veit, 172

MOSHE ZIMMERMANN (PhD) is Richard M. Koebner Professor Emeritus for German History at the Hebrew University, Jerusalem. He is the author of *Wilhelm Marr: The Patriarch of Antisemitism*.